PROSECUTION PRINCIPLES

A CLINICAL HANDBOOK

Second Edition

■ ■ ■

George R. Dekle, Sr.
Emeritus Legal Skills Professor
Fredric G. Levin College of Law
University of Florida

Retired Assistant State Attorney
Third Judicial Circuit of Florida
(1975–2005)

WEST ACADEMIC

860 Blue Gentian Road, Suite 350
Eagan, MN 55121
1-877-888-1330

Published in the United States of America

ISBN: 979-8-31770-066-9

To the memory of my parents: Donald James Dekle, a Colonel in the Florida Department of Corrections and a combat veteran of World War II, who taught me to love the law; and Anne Coleman Dekle, a career educator and eleventh-hour typist—from barely legible manuscripts—of most of my term papers, who taught me to love learning.

PREFACE

When I began teaching the prosecution clinic at the University of Florida, I could not find a textbook on prosecution. I found a bountiful supply of trial advocacy materials and criminal defense manuals, but nothing aimed at the student of prosecution. Either there is a great unmet need for such a book or there is no need at all for one. Preferring to believe that there is a need, I undertook to fill it. Many worthy individuals (including a lot of lawyers working in prosecutors' offices) have difficulty understanding that a prosecutor is more than a plaintiff's attorney working for the government. This book seeks to define the role of the prosecutor and to set forth how to perform that role. It begins with the presupposition that the prosecutor works as a minister of justice committed to achieving equitable, truth-based dispositions of criminal complaints by lawful, ethical means. It goes on from that point to describe how the prosecutor should strive to get the right result for the right reason.

This book consists of equal parts practical advice, advocacy theory, and a philosophy of prosecution. Most of the practical examples are real, but with the exception of a few easily recognizable cases, the names and identifying details have been changed. Although court procedures differ markedly from jurisdiction to jurisdiction, there are universal constants to the practice of criminal trial advocacy that were as true in the days of Cicero and Quintilian as they are today. We will speak directly to those universal constants, but will attempt to speak generally enough to cover all procedural variants. Finally, we will seek to present a philosophy of prosecution which sees the American prosecutor as occupying a unique and somewhat paradoxical office in our justice system—an impartial advocate who seeks, not a favorable verdict, but a just one.

We will discuss the various models for criminal prosecution and look at the multiple roles of the American prosecutor. Then we will begin at the intake stage and work through the charging decision to the archiving of the case file. We will work in a roughly chronological order but will take a few subjects out of sequence. Voir dire will come after direct and cross-examination because we want to know how to ask questions before we discuss the topic of questioning jurors. Three chapters are of especial importance—Chapter 4 on the charging decision, Chapter 7 on devising case theory, and Chapter 15 on opening statement. These three subject have a powerful synergy which plays a major role in the success or failure of a criminal prosecution.

This book's insistence on getting the right result for the right reason is not an ivory-tower exposition of the way things ought to be. It is a real-world practical assessment of the way things must be. Everything you do as a prosecutor must rest on the bedrock of truth. In any system of laws there will always be those who manipulate and circumvent the system, but those who do so must always be in the minority—and they must not be among the ranks of the prosecutors.

GEORGE R. (BOB) DEKLE, SR.
LEGAL SKILLS PROFESSOR
FREDRIC G. LEVIN COLLEGE OF LAW
UNIVERSITY OF FLORIDA
GAINESVILLE, FLORIDA

April 27, 2007

PREFACE TO THE SECOND EDITION

> Among all judicial offices, it seems to me the most arduous is that of the prosecuting attorney. As prosecutor he must be as partisan as a lawyer, and as guardian of the law he must be impartial as a judge. A lawyer without passion, a judge without impartiality—these are the paradoxes which the prosecuting attorney must resolve.—Piero Calamandrei[1]

As a young prosecutor I used to tell people that I was a police officer with a license to practice law. I was only partially correct. It took some time for me to realize that in addition to the advocacy role of the trial lawyer and the law enforcement role of the police officer, I had a role as a sort of judge, deciding whom to prosecute, what to prosecute them for, and what remedies to seek. The law enforcement role meant that I had to be diligent in rooting out crime and enforcing the law. The trial advocacy role meant that I had to be a partisan, urging the court to make the desired findings and adopt the desired remedies. The quasi-judicial role required that I be impartial. How can one be the impartial judge of a case that one has labored hard to make? How can one advocate strenuously for a result and at the same time be an impartial judge of the law and facts?

Eventually I learned how to perform the delicate balancing act required of my position as a prosecutor. This book is an attempt to help fledgling prosecutors learn how to balance the competing responsibilities of each of these three roles, and to help them learn the mechanics of competent, ethical prosecution.

GEORGE R. (BOB) DEKLE, SR.
EMERITUS LEGAL SKILLS PROFESSOR
FREDRIC G. LEVIN COLLEGE OF LAW
UNIVERSITY OF FLORIDA

May 21, 2025

---

1 *Eulogy of Judges*, Tr. John Clark Adams and C. Abbott Phillips Jr., Princeton, New Jersey: Princeton University Press, 1942. P.28.

ACKNOWLEDGMENTS

Robert M. Pirsig, in ***Zen and the Art of Motorcycle Maintenance***, lamented that he hadn't had a new idea in years.[1] Few people ever have a new idea because, after several thousand years of human existence, most ideas have already been had. Even the seemingly new ideas turn out to be old ideas that have been forgotten. Trial lawyers know this almost instinctively and remain constantly on the alert to learn, adopt, and adapt the ideas of others—be it a turn of a phrase or a particular way of organizing papers in a file. All of this serves as a long way of saying that none of the ideas in this book have any claim to originality or newness. They have come to the author through thirty-two years of watching, talking with, swapping "war stories" with, reading books by, contesting trials with, and learning from trial lawyers.

It would be impossible to name every person who contributed ideas to this book, and the naming of some will certainly overlook others. Nevertheless, the attempt must be made. Many fellow prosecutors and trial lawyers rendered great help and encouragement: James M. Dedman, Director of Training at the National District Attorneys Association, National Advocacy Center at the University of South Carolina, who first exposed me to the world of prosecutor education some twenty years ago and gave me the opportunity to teach with and learn from some of the finest prosecutors throughout the nation; Ronald H. Clark, Professor of Law at Seattle University School of Law, and former Chief Deputy of the King's County, Washington, District Attorney's Office, who has also given me great guidance and encouragement in prosecutor education over the years; Jennifer Zedalis, Legal Skills Professor, Fredric G. Levin College of Law, without whose help and encouragement this book would never have been written; Angela Corey, Assistant State Attorney, Seventh Judicial Circuit, St. Augustine, Florida; Bill Cervone, State Attorney, Eighth Judicial Circuit, Gainesville, Florida; Chris White, Assistant State Attorney, Eighteenth Judicial Circuit, Sanford, Florida; David Phelps, Chief Assistant State Attorney, Third Judicial Circuit, Perry, Florida; Dennis McGrane, Chief Deputy County Attorney, Yavapai County Attorney's Office, Prescott, Arizona; Gregory McMahon, Assistant United States Attorney, Middle District of Florida, Gainesville, Florida; H. Morley Swingle, Prosecuting Attorney, Cape Girardeau County, Missouri; Janet C. Protasiewicz, Assistant District Attorney, Milwaukee County District Attorney's Office, Milwaukee, Wisconsin; Jerry M. Blair, State Attorney, Third Judicial Circuit, Live Oak, Florida; Jimmy Hunt, Private Practice, Lake City, Florida; Jonathan Ibarra, Senior Trial Attorney, District

[1] Bantam Books, New York, New York, 1981, p. 33.

Attorney's Office, Second Judicial District, Bernalillo County, New Mexico; Kirsten LaCroix, Deputy County Attorney, Missoula, Montana; Lawrence Cunningham, Assistant District Attorney, Bronx County District Attorney's Office, New York; Len Register, Assistant United States Attorney, Northern District of Florida, Pensacola, Florida; M. Blair Payne, Private Practice, Lake City, Florida; Margaret Fent, Assistant Solicitor, Fifth Circuit Solicitor's Office, Columbia, South Carolina; Mark Hessinger, Supervising Deputy County Attorney, Yuma County Attorney's Office, Yuma, Arizona; Martin Brannan, LaPaz County Attorney, Parker, Arizona; Sonia Leerkamp, Hamilton County Prosecutor, Noblesville, Indiana; Teresa Drake, Assistant State Attorney, Eighth Judicial Circuit, Gainesville, Florida; Tina Seifert, Assistant State Attorney, Third Judicial Circuit, Lake City, Florida; Todd Hingson, Assistant State Attorney, Third Judicial Circuit, Lake City, Florida; John Hogenmueller, Executive Director, Florida Prosecuting Attorneys Association, Tallahassee, Florida. I must also acknowledge my mother-in-law, Laverne Dicks, who patiently proofread the manuscript of this work. Finally, I would like to thank my prosecution clinic students in the Spring, Summer, and Fall semesters of 2006 for their enthusiasm, for their use as guinea pigs in the trial runs of previous drafts of this work, and for the hard questions they asked, which sent me scurrying back to the computer to rewrite many paragraphs of this book.

The only really creative thing a trial lawyer does is to take information from other people and restate it as memorably and persuasively as possible. This I have attempted to do. You will judge how well I have succeeded.

Acknowledgments to the Second Edition

In Ecclesiastes the Preacher lamented that "there is no new thing under the sun,"[1] but he was unduly pessimistic. The second edition of this book is a testament to the Preacher's observation. There is nothing new in it other than a reorganization of forensic lore going back at least 2,000 years. Two men who have worked at reorganizing and systematizing the lore of trial advocacy are my good friends Ronald H. Clark, Distinguished Practitioner in Residence at the Seattle School of Law, and James M. Dedman III, Retired Director of Training at the National District Attorneys Association, National Advocacy Center at the University of South Carolina. Both men began their legal careers as prosecutors, and their later work in legal education helped to formulate the theory of prosecutorial advocacy which I try to teach in this book.

It would unduly lengthen these acknowledgements to rename everyone whom I mentioned in the acknowledgements to the first edition. Suffice it to say that their contributions helped to serve as the bedrock for this second edition.

Having been out of active practice for over a decade, I felt it necessary to be updated on the latest developments in prosecution. This update came in the form of a familiarization given me by John Durett, State Attorney for the Third Judicial Circuit, and Assistant State Attorney Sean Crisafulli, a former student of mine in the Prosecution Clinic at the University of Florida. They caught me up on the newest developments in technology which have come about in the time I have been out of the active practice of law, and they also reassured me that the basics of prosecution have not changed radically since the time when Cicero argued in the Roman law courts.

All of these people contributed to the making of this second edition, and anything which is good about it I owe to them. Any mistakes or inaccuracies are attributable solely to me. In closing I want to restate the conclusion of the acknowledgements to the first edition: "The only really creative thing a trial lawyer does is to take information from other people and restate it as memorably and persuasively as possible. This I have attempted to do. You will judge how well I have succeeded."

[1] Ecclesiastes 1:9 (KJV).

SUMMARY OF CONTENTS

TABLE OF CONTENTS

TABLE OF CASES

TABLE OF ILLUSTRATIONS

PROSECUTION PRINCIPLES

A CLINICAL HANDBOOK

Second Edition

CHAPTER 1

THE ROLE OF THE PROSECUTOR

■ ■ ■

The very nature of a [criminal] trial [is] a search for truth.—*Nix v. Whiteside*[1]

[A] special role [is] played by the American prosecutor in the search for truth in criminal trials.—*Floyd v. State*[2]

"What is truth?" said jesting Pilate, and would not stay for an answer.—Francis Bacon[3]

A. CRIMINAL JUSTICE SYSTEMS

1. RIGHT, WRONG, AND REDRESS

When one person feels wronged by another, he wants redress. The offending party has harmed him, and he wants the offender to suffer the consequences of wrongdoing. The most satisfying forms of redress are retribution and restitution. It often gives the victim pleasure to see the offender suffer for his crime, and almost all victims want the offender to make them whole. Before the promulgation of laws, revenge was the most utilitarian method of achieving redress. Self-help redress achieved by deception or coercion comes in the form of revenge. Francis Bacon wrote that "Revenge is a kind of wild justice that, the more man's nature runs to, the more the law ought to weed it out."[4] Because unregulated vengeance often inflicts punishment far in excess of the wrong suffered, a more equitable method of achieving redress is necessary. Because the wrongdoer is oftentimes too strong or too wily to succumb to self-help methods of achieving redress, a more certain method of achieving redress is necessary.

Almost 4,000 years ago, the Babylonian king, Hammurabi, set up a legal method of providing for the measured administration of both restitution and retribution by setting up neutral courts to hear controversies. The offended party complained to a neutral court which adjudicated the complaint. Each side attempted to persuade the court of the justness of their cause; the court decided who was right and forced the

1 475 U.S. 157, 166, 106 S.Ct. 988, 994 (1986).

2 902 So.2d 775, 780 (Fla. 2005).

3 "Of Truth," Essays, <https://www.gutenberg.org/ebooks/56463>.

4 "Of Revenge," Essays, <https://www.gutenberg.org/ebooks/56463>.

other to atone.[5] At least theoretically, excessive punishment was eliminated, more certain punishment was insured, and redress was adjudicated only by the ethical application of coercion based on ethical persuasion. This is the bedrock of any civilized justice system.

2. TRUTH AND JUSTICE

We ultimately seek justice, but we must base that justice upon truth. Thus, every criminal trial asks Pilate's question. "What is truth?" Beginning with the Code of Hammurabi, civilized Western societies have sought the truth through an adversarial system of presenting conflicting claims through the testimony of witnesses. A complainant makes an accusation, the defendant denies the accusation, and an allegedly impartial judge or jury decides the truth of the matter.[6] Two of the three parties in a criminal trial should already know (or think they know) the truth. Only the fact finder begins the trial in total ignorance. Whereas the fact finder's immediate goal is to find the truth, the other two parties' immediate goal is to persuade the fact finder to return a favorable verdict. Because truth is the bedrock of any civilized justice system, and because the adversarial parties might be motivated to give the court something less than the truth in order to obtain a favorable verdict, Hammurabi ordained severe penalties for both false swearing and subornation of perjury.[7]

3. PRIVATE PROSECUTION

The prosecutors in the first courts were private citizens, and private prosecution has been the preferred method of achieving redress throughout most of Western history. A private citizen would become aware of a crime, file a criminal complaint, and go to court and prosecute it. People filed criminal complaints because they were either the victims of crimes, or were motivated by altruism, or had axes to grind. Enforcement of the criminal law was therefore a hit-or-miss proposition, with criminals going unprosecuted because of fear or apathy and with the innocent being prosecuted because of envy or malice. The consequences of malicious prosecution were dire. The course of the Peloponnesian War may have been altered by the private prosecution of Alcibiades, the talented Athenian general who was recalled from the invasion of Syracuse to answer charges of impiety. The invasion foundered, and with it, the hopes of Athenian victory in the wider war. Philosophy suffered a terrible blow with the private prosecution of Socrates on charges of atheism and corrupting the morals of the Athenian youth.

---

5 Code of Hammurabi § 9, <https://www.gutenberg.org/ebooks/17150>.

6 Id. at §§ 9–13.

7 Id. at §§ 3, 4.

4. PUBLIC PROSECUTION: THE INQUISITORIAL SYSTEM

One solution for the problem of malicious private prosecution is to levy severe penalties against those who prosecute unfounded criminal charges, and many ancient penal systems did just that.[8] This measure deals handily with the problem of malicious prosecution but aggravates the problem of prosecutorial apathy. Who would bring a charge, knowing that an acquittal would result in punishment of the prosecutor? Beginning in the Middle Ages, the problem of prosecutorial apathy was solved by a new way of adjudicating criminal cases—the inquisition. If the government could not depend on private prosecutors to bring cases, the government could both become prosecutor and judge. When a single entity performs the role of both prosecutor and judge, problems arise. Having decided that a person is worthy of prosecution, it is then difficult to fairly adjudicate whether the person is actually guilty. The trial of Sir Thomas More on charges of treason was an inquisition, as was the trial of Galileo. At More's arraignment, after the reading of the indictment, the Lord Chancellor's first words were "You see now how grievously you have offended his Majesty?"[9] These are hardly the words expected of an impartial judge. More was beheaded for refusing to take an oath that the king was superior to the Pope. Galileo escaped severe punishment by agreeing to heed the warning of Cardinal Bellarmine (who conducted the inquisition) not to hold, teach, or defend Copernican theory. Clearly, the judge should not also be the prosecutor.

Modern European judicial systems have modified the pure inquisitorial system to vest prosecutorial and adjudicative powers in different offices. Some have even gone so far as to create a third office, the investigating magistrate, to serve as a buffer between prosecution and adjudication. Depending upon the jurisdiction, the investigating magistrate, who acts as an inquisitor, must approve various prosecutorial measures, up to and including the filing of formal criminal charges.[10] After criminal charges are brought, the system becomes more adversarial in nature. Book Nine of *The Brothers Karamazov* demonstrates how the pre-indictment phase of an inquisitorial prosecution might be conducted, with both a prosecutor and an "investigating lawyer" (i.e., investigating magistrate) interviewing witnesses independently but in concert. The investigating magistrate investigates to actively adjudicate whether formal charges should be filed, while the prosecutor investigates to build a

---

[8] Id. at § 11.

[9] Linder, Douglas, "Thomas More Trial," Famous Trials. 2007. The University of Missouri-Kansas City School of Law. 19 March 2007. <https://famous-trials.com/thomasmore/986-home>.

[10] van Koppen, Peter J., & Steven D. Penrod, Eds., Adversarial versus Inquisitorial Justice: Psychological Perspectives on Criminal Justice Systems, Plenum Publishers, New York, New York, 2003, pp. 9–10.

winnable case. When charges are filed, the investigating magistrate then drops out of the case and the prosecutor conducts the prosecution. In Book Twelve of *The Brothers Karamazov*, which describes the trial, the "investigating lawyer" has disappeared and the prosecutor plays an active role almost indistinguishable from the role of the American prosecutor. With an independent government agent deciding whether charges should be filed, the problem of prosecutorial apathy found in the private prosecution system is theoretically eliminated. With the prosecutive and adjudicative duties assigned to different governmental agencies, there is a buffer between prosecution and adjudication.

5. PUBLIC PROSECUTION: THE ADVERSARIAL SYSTEM

Unlike Continental Europe, common law jurisdictions in the English tradition have clung tenaciously to a purely adversarial system. Most common law jurisdictions even today will countenance private prosecutions,[11] and some states continue to allow private prosecution in minor cases.[12] At some point, however, even the common law jurisdictions recognized the wisdom of taking the authority to prosecute from private citizens and vesting it in an officer whose primary interest would be, not winning the prosecution, but establishing truth. The American colonies came to realize the value of a governmental prosecutor much earlier than most common law jurisdictions. Probably the first attorney in America to serve in such a capacity was Adriaen van der Donk, who assumed the office of *schout* in New Netherlands in 1641. The *schout* was a Dutch officer who acted as both a prosecutor and a law enforcement officer. When England annexed New Netherlands and renamed it New York, the office of the *schout* survived the transition, and the Dutch *schout* can be considered the precursor of not only the modern American prosecutor, but also the modern American sheriff.[13] Public prosecutors thus occupy a special role in the American justice system. They are more than advocates for a cause. In *Berger v. United States*,[14] the Supreme Court said:

> The [prosecutor] is the representative not of an ordinary party to a controversy, but of a sovereignty whose obligation to govern

---

[11] See, e.g., Public Prosecution Service of Canada, Federal Prosecution Service Deskbook. Part 5.9 § 1. 2014. Canada Department of Justice, Ottawa, Ontario. 3 May 2020. https://www.ppsc-sppc.gc.ca/eng/pub/fpsd-sfpg/fps-sfp/tpd/index.html; Director of Public Prosecutions of United Kingdom, "Private Prosecution." 2005. Crown Prosecution Service, London, England. 7 May 2007.

[12] State v. Martineau, 148 N.H. 259, 808 A.2d 51 (2002) (Private prosecution exists as a matter of common law, but not for crimes punishable by imprisonment); In re Grand Jury Appearance Request by Loigman, 183 N.J. 133, 139 n.1, 870 A.2d 249, 253 (2005) (Private prosecution in municipal court allowed but not favored); Cronan ex rel. State v. Cronan, 774 A.2d 866 (R.I. 2001) (Private prosecutor could properly bring charges of misdemeanor assault).

[13] Jacoby, Joan E., "The American Prosecutor in Historical Context," The Prosecutor's Deskbook, 3rd Ed., American Prosecutors Research Institute, Alexandria, Virginia, 2001, p. 47.

[14] 295 U.S. 78, 88, 55 S.Ct. 629, 633 (1935).

impartially is as compelling as its obligation to govern at all; and whose interest, therefore, in a criminal prosecution is not that it shall win a case, but that justice shall be done. As such, he is in a peculiar and very definite sense the servant of the law, the twofold aim of which is that guilt shall not escape or innocence suffer. He may prosecute with earnestness and vigor—indeed, he should do so. But, while he may strike hard blows, he is not at liberty to strike foul ones. It is as much his duty to refrain from improper methods calculated to produce a wrongful conviction as it is to use every legitimate means to bring about a just one.

The American prosecutor, although usually an elected public official rather than an appointed public servant, performs duties very similar to those of the European inquisitorial public prosecutor, and in large part performs them in much the same way. The American prosecutor, when performing the job properly, can be thought of as an inquisitorial officer in an adversarial system.

B. THE AMERICAN PROSECUTOR'S TRIPARTITE ROLE

1. LAW ENFORCEMENT OFFICER

As a minister of justice[15] and not just an advocate, the prosecutor wears three hats. In the pre-arrest stage, the prosecutor retains the law enforcement function of the *schout*. In the charging stage the prosecutor performs the judicial function of the inquisitorial system's investigating magistrate, and in the post charging stage he performs the advocacy role of the inquisitorial prosecutor, seeking not just a favorable verdict but a fair one. As a law enforcement officer, the American prosecutor is just as concerned with the detection of crime and the arrest of criminals as the cop on the beat. In America, both court decision[16] and statute[17] recognize the prosecutor's role as a law enforcement officer. In their role as law enforcement officers, prosecutors can become involved in almost all aspects of the investigation of a case, and it is sometimes very easy for them to become too much the law enforcement officer and too little the minister of justice. Because the apprehension and arrest of suspected criminals can

[15] Standard 3–1.2, *Criminal Justice Standards for the Prosecution Function*, 4th ed. American Bar Association (2017) (Hereafter cited as ABA Prosecution Standards); Standard 1.2(a), *Prosecutorial Investigations*, 3rd Ed. American Bar Association (2014) (Hereafter cited as ABA Prosecutorial Investigation Standards); Standard 1–1.1, *National Prosecution Standards*, 4th ed. National District Attorneys Association (2023) (Hereafter cited as National Prosecution Standards).

[16] Krischer v. D'Amato, 674 So.2d 909 (Fla.App.4th DCA 1996); District Attorney for Norfolk Dist. v. Flatley, 419 Mass. 507, 509 n.3, 646 N.E.2d 127, 128 (1995); People v. Jackson, 192 Mich.App. 10, 15, 480 N.W.2d 283, 286 (1991); State v. Vitiello, 377 N.J.Super. 452, 457, 873 A.2d 591, 594 (2005).

[17] Fla.Stat. § 790.001(8)(f)(2024); N.J. Rev. Stat. § 2A:158–5 (2024).

become a highly competitive endeavor, prosecutors engaged in this highly competitive undertaking can easily lose the objectivity necessary to perform their other two functions.

2. JUDGE

While fulfilling the law enforcement role of collecting evidence to present a winnable case, prosecutors simultaneously perform an adjudicatory role. While wearing the law enforcement officer's hat, prosecutors must simultaneously wear the hat of a judge. At the point in the proceedings when prosecutors must decide whether to file charges, whom to file charges against, and what charges to file, the law enforcement hat comes off and they become purely a judge. From the diligent nose-to-the-ground bloodhound, they must shift to the impartial, discerning arbiter of fact. It is a difficult transformation to accomplish. Having worked hard to identify and apprehend a culprit, it is difficult to then say, "I don't have enough evidence. I'll have to let him go. Oh, well, better luck next time." It is far more tempting to say: "The evidence is a little thin, but I think I can stretch it far enough to get a conviction." The worth of prosecutors is measured by how well they can make the shift from police officer to judge.

3. ADVOCATE

Once the filing decision is made, prosecutors put on the third hat—the hat of the advocate. But they never take off the hat of the judge. Consequently, the advocate's hat does not fit as comfortably as the advocate's hat worn by privately retained counsel. The prosecutor's client is neither the victim nor the police. Better put, the prosecutor's client base includes more than the victim and the police. The client base includes all the people of the jurisdiction. "All the people of the jurisdiction" includes the defendant's family—even the defendant himself. Prosecutors are the guardian of the rights of all the people, which means that their job is to get the right result for the right reason. If they get the right result for the wrong reason, they have gotten the wrong result. Once again, the competitive drive impedes the ability to be impartial, and the need to be impartial impedes the ability to advocate. How can the prosecutor perform such a delicate balancing act? The first step is to come as near as humanly possible to discovering the whole truth of a matter. Having determined the truth, the next step is "to keep on the side of what he believes to be truth; and, avoiding all sophistry, to aim only at setting forth that truth as strongly as possible, * * * without any endeavor to gain applause for his own abilities."[18]

---

[18] Whately, Richard, Elements of Rhetoric Comprising an Analysis of the Laws of Moral Evidence and Persuasion with Rules for Argumentative Composition and Elocution, Kessinger Publishing Company, Whitefish, Montana, 1854/2005, p. 167.

The prosecutor's duty to seek a just verdict can be analyzed in this manner: A verdict can reflect courtroom proof but bear no resemblance to real-world truth.

A verdict is valid insofar as it reflects proper courtroom proof.

A verdict is invalid if it (a) does not reflect courtroom proof, or (b) reflects improperly established courtroom proof.

A valid verdict is sound if it reflects (a) proper courtroom proof, AND (b) real-world truth.

A valid verdict is unsound if it (a) reflects proper courtroom proof but not real-world truth, (b) reflects real-world truth but not proper courtroom proof, OR (c) does not reflect real-world truth regardless of the quality of the courtroom proof. Proper courtroom proof is evidence and argument which legitimately persuades the jury.

The advocacy role of the prosecutor therefore is to ensure that a verdict is sound—that it reflects both proper courtroom proof and real-world truth.

C. TRUTH VALUE IN THE ADVERSARIAL SYSTEM

If both parties value the truth, then the adversarial system can work. All relevant evidence is fairly presented, the merits of the evidence are logically debated, and the fact finder renders judgement in conformity with the equities. If one side values victory over truth, then the adversarial system becomes, not a contest between rival interpretations of the truth, but a war between truth and fiction. The nightmare scenario is two con artists trying to deceive the fact finder. Finding the truth in either of the latter two situations can cause premature greying of the fact finder's hair. Do you wonder that Pilate asked, "what is truth?" Bacon interpreted Pilate's question as the question of a jaded cynic who cared little for anything except his own self-advancement. Others have read the question as the honest query of a bemused judge. If the second interpretation is correct, Pilate shares the company of a long line of judges and jurors who have confronted dishonest litigants. If you cannot ensure that both litigants are wedded to the truth, the second best situation is to have at least one litigant wedded to the truth. In a war between truth and fiction, you have at least a 50% chance of finding the truth and achieving a just verdict. The American prosecutor, as a minister of justice and not a plaintiff's attorney, is the one litigant in the adversarial system whose express duty is not to achieve a favorable verdict, but to achieve a truthful one. What is truth? Many advocates posit that there is no truth beyond the authorized pronouncements of a duly constituted fact finder. The term "verdict" comes from the Latin phrase *vere dictum* (truly said). A jury thus purportedly "speaks the truth" when it renders a verdict, but its verdict is really an interpretation of truth which may or may not have truth value.

1. FACT AND FICTION

The prosecutor asserts: "Jack Ripper killed Elizabeth Stride." It is a fact that the prosecutor makes this assertion, but is it a fact that Jack killed Elizabeth? The statement "Jack Ripper killed Elizabeth Stride" may or may not be true, but the English language has no name for an assertion of questionable truth value. The best we can do is call it a "fact." A colloquial attempt to separate assertions of questionable truth value from assertions that are true beyond peradventure is to talk about "facts" and "true facts." The Enlightenment philosopher Wilhelm Leibniz gave "true facts" the label "necessary truth." Facts of debatable truth value he called "contingent truth." We can borrow a convention from logic to make a monosyllabic distinction. Logic uses the terms "if" and "iff." "Iff" means more than "if." "Iff" means "if and only if." We can adopt this convention and give "true facts" (or "necessary truth") the label "ffacts." Mere facts of questionable truth value (or "contingent truth") we will call "facts." Assertions can thus be divided into the trichotomy: ffact, fact, fiction. Few assertions are ffacts. Most are facts, and facts are almost always subject to being falsified and shown to be fiction.

The Austrian philosopher Karl Popper taught that in the world of science, beyond ffacts like the assertion that a triangle has three sides, investigation can never result in knowing a proposition as a ffact.[19] The best we can do is say that a fact has a high degree of truth value. Even if we assign facts a truth value of 99.99% probability, they can be (and often have been) shown to be false. For example, for more than 1,000 years Aristotle's First Law of Motion, "nothing moves unless you push it," was a ffact. This was a logical interpretation of all known data gathered by investigation, and it could not be refuted by any known data—until Galileo devised the concept of inertia, which Newton refined into his First Law of Motion—"Every object in a state of uniform motion tends to remain in that state of motion unless an external force is applied to it." Popper taught that an assertion is not a scientific fact unless it is at least theoretically falsifiable by the discovery of inconsistent facts. If the assertion is not falsifiable, it is not a matter for science but faith.

Where does that leave us? In order to function in life, we seldom require ffacts. We can get by with facts—if we are satisfied the facts have a sufficiently high truth value. It may not be a ffact that the sun will come up tomorrow, but the proposition has sufficiently high truth value that you should set your alarm clock. As in everyday life, so also in the courtroom—we do not need ffacts, we simply need facts with a comfortably high truth value. It may not be a ffact that John Hinckley, Jr., shot President Reagan (it may have been Hinckley's mysterious disappearing twin brother), but

[19] Popper taught that the essence of scientific fact was falsifiability. This idea permeated his philosophy. For a good summary of his ideas, see Popper, Karl, Conjecture and Refutation, Routledge, New York, New York, 2002. ch. 1.

we can attach enough truth value to that fact to have kept Hinckley institutionalized for more than twenty years.

The world of a criminal trial or hearing is an artificial world in which facts must pass several tests before they will be considered—tests of relevancy, materiality, prejudicial nature, constitutionality, and admissibility. Each of these tests is designed to eliminate certain facts from evidence based upon various considerations as to the expediency of allowing the fact finder to consider them. These considerations sometimes have very little to do with the truth value of the facts involved. The verdict is thus based upon an artificial set of facts which may bear little resemblance to the real-world facts of the case.

2. ADVERSARIAL PROSECUTION AND REAL-WORLD TRUTH

Suppose Elizabeth Stride disappears, and Jack Ripper becomes a suspect. The police arrest him without probable cause and interview him without benefit of Miranda warnings. Jack confesses that he dismembered Elizabeth and deposited her body parts in various dumpsters scattered throughout the town. He then leads the officers to all the body parts. The judge rules that the fact of Jack's confession is inadmissible because the officers made an unlawful arrest and failed to read Jack his Miranda rights. The judge further rules that the fact that Jack led the officers to Elizabeth's body parts is also inadmissible as fruit of the poison tree. The jury, being unaware of Jack's confession and unaware that he showed the officers to Elizabeth's body parts, finds Jack not guilty. The verdict bears no resemblance at all to the real-world facts of Jack's case. In the real world we can attach a high degree of truth value to the assertion that Jack killed Elizabeth, but in the courtroom we can attach none.

Although truth in the artificial world of the courtroom may bear little resemblance to real-world truth, you can sometimes have more certainty in a courtroom than you can achieve in real life. Ffacts are few and far between in the real world, but they can be quite common in a courtroom. Whatever the parties agree upon is a ffact—even real-world fiction. Suppose Jack Ripper committed an armed robbery but the parties strike a plea bargain allowing Jack to plead to unarmed robbery. It now becomes a courtroom ffact that Jack was not armed when he committed the robbery.

3. THE ADVOCATE'S ALLEGIANCE TO TRUTH

Some lawyers seriously contend that if someone (usually a criminal defendant) says something is so, no matter how preposterous, it is evidence which can ethically be presented and argued. After all, what is truth? Who can ever know what really happened? Lawyers sometimes obtain suppression of evidence and then go to trial and try to pretend that the suppressed evidence does not exist. E.g., In a DUI case, the defense gets the blood alcohol test results suppressed and then argues to the jury that the police did not test the defendant's blood alcohol level. There are several ways to deal with the artificial facts that are introduced into evidence in a criminal trial.

(1) The artificial facts can be argued as true regardless of what the real-world facts are.

(2) The artificial facts can be argued as true only insofar as they comport with real-world facts, but it is fair game to draw reasonable inferences known to be contrary to real-world facts.

(3) The artificial facts can be argued as true only insofar as they comport with real world facts, and reasonable inferences can be argued only insofar as they comport with real-world facts.

Method (1) is a sure-fire method for getting disbarred. Advocates have a duty to try to make the artificial facts comport with real-world facts. You cannot knowingly offer perjured testimony and argue it as true. The key word is "knowingly." Suppose you have a witness who will give your client an ironclad alibi. You know, but the prosecutor does not, that the witness is lying. Do you call the witness? It goes without saying that you should not call the witness. Suppose you don't know, but have good reason to believe, that the witness is lying? Here is where win-at-all-costs advocates will emulate Pilate. What is truth? The witness said it, who is the lawyer to judge? Isn't that what the jury is for? Setting aside the rhetorical consideration that you will ruin your credibility by arguing implausible facts, a lawyer should weigh the truth value of the facts, and only present those facts to which the lawyer can assign a sufficiently high truth value.[20] "Counsel's duty of loyalty to and advocacy of, the defendant's cause is limited to legitimate, lawful conduct compatible with the very nature of a trial as a search for truth."[21]

Method (2) is more problematical. Take the murder case in which the prosecution presented satisfactory proof that Aaron Johnson shot Matthew Lanatus but came up short in proving that Lanatus was in fact dead. Defense counsel argued that Lanatus was still alive and hiding out in a distant city. For the sake of argument, we will assume that the prosecution's failure to prove fact of death gives rise to a reasonable inference that Lanatus is still alive. Is it proper for a lawyer who knows beyond peradventure that Lanatus is dead to argue to the jury that Lanatus is still alive? Would it be proper to go further and argue that

[20] A lawyer cannot knowingly be a party to a client taking the stand and committing perjury. A knottier problem arises when the client insists on taking the stand to tell an implausible story which the lawyer strongly suspects, but does not know, to be untrue. One of the benefits of being a prosecutor is that you do not have to confront this problem.

[21] Nix v. Whiteside, 475 U.S. 157, 158, 106 S.Ct. 988, 994 (1986).

Lanatus is hiding out in a distant city? Everyone would agree that it would be improper for a prosecutor to argue as true reasonable inferences the prosecutor knew to be false. Isn't sauce for the goose also sauce for the gander? In the case under discussion, the defense acted improperly in arguing that Lanatus was alive and well and living in a distant city.

Method (3) is the proper method for prosecutors, but it is too restrictive for defense attorneys. Prosecutors are not just advocates, they are ministers of justice, and it is their duty to see to it that jury verdicts comport, not only with the artificial facts of the trial, but also with the real-world facts. Any advocate representing a party subject to a burden of proof should be constrained to method (3). Criminal defense attorneys, however, do not have a burden of proof. Their only burden is to point out the reasonable doubts to the fact finder. Returning to the case of Matthew Lanatus, adherence to method (3) would prevent the defense attorney from pointing out reasonable doubt. Although it would be improper for the defense to argue that Lanatus was still alive, the defense should be allowed to argue that the prosecution had not proved that Lanatus was dead and that therefore the reasonable inference that Lanatus was still alive gave rise to a reasonable doubt as to Aaron Johnson's guilt. Thus, in the criminal justice arena, we must add a fourth method open to defense attorneys, but not prosecutors:

> (4) The artificial facts can be argued as true only insofar as they comport with real world facts, but reasonable inferences contrary to real-world facts can be argued, not as facts, but as reasonable doubts arising from the evidence or lack of evidence.

D. PROSECUTORIAL IMMUNITY

Because the public prosecutor should be less inclined than private prosecutors to press fiction as a basis for achieving a favorable verdict, there should be less need for deterrence with the threat of punishment for malicious prosecution. The law has recognized this lesser need to deter the public prosecutor from ill-advised prosecutions and has given the American prosecutor protection in carrying out the duty to prosecute. The degree of protection the law affords varies depending upon which hat prosecutors wear. When acting as a law enforcement officer, they have the qualified good faith immunity from suit of the law enforcement officer. Thus, when attending to those parts of the job that are not forensic in nature, they are immune from suit only insofar as they act reasonably and from pure motives. When prosecutors perform their judicial function, however, they have the same absolute immunity that judges enjoy. *Imbler v. Pachtman*[22] recognized this immunity, finding that it was of ancient vintage. *Pachtman* said that the first American case to address the question of prosecutorial

[22] 424 U.S. 409, 96 S.Ct. 984 (1976).

immunity was *Griffith v. Slinkard*.[23] The complaint charged that a local prosecutor without probable cause added the plaintiff's name to a grand jury true bill after the grand jurors had refused to indict him, with the result that the plaintiff was arrested and forced to appear in court repeatedly before the charge finally was nolle prossed.[24] Despite allegations of malice, the Supreme Court of Indiana dismissed the action on the ground that the prosecutor had absolute immunity from civil suit. Absolute immunity is a much better thing to have than qualified good faith immunity. The one completely bars suit while the other is an affirmative defense that must be proven. *Pachtman* observed, however, that prosecutors were not immune to bar disciplinary proceedings for misconduct, nor were they immune to criminal prosecution.

PRACTICAL EXERCISE

Sometimes the line between absolute and qualified immunity can be indistinct. Try to determine where the line between qualified immunity and absolute immunity should be drawn in the following factual scenarios:

A. Officer Javert comes to you and recites a factual scenario to you. You advise Officer Javert that he has probable cause to arrest Jay Gatsby, and since it is a felony, he does not need a warrant. Officer Javert goes out and arrests Jay Gatsby without a warrant.

B. Officer Javert comes to you for help drafting a complaint affidavit seeking an arrest warrant. You review the facts and decide that probable cause exists. You advise Officer Javert that, since the charge is a felony, he does not need a warrant. You go with Officer Javert as he makes a warrantless arrest.

C. Officer Javert comes to you for help drafting a complaint affidavit seeking an arrest warrant. You review the facts and decide that probable cause exists. You draft the complaint affidavit and a warrant. You send Officer Javert to the on-call judge, who issues the warrant. You remain in your office while Officer Javert makes a warranted arrest of Jay Gatsby.

D. Officer Javert comes to you for help drafting a complaint affidavit seeking an arrest warrant. You review the facts and decide that probable cause exists. You draft a complaint affidavit and have Officer Javert swear to it. You then draft an information, sign it, and swear to it. You file the information, the clerk issues a capias, and you sit in your office as Officer Javert serves the capias on Jay Gatsby.

---

[23] 146 Ind. 117, 44 N.E. 1001 (1896).

[24] A "nolle prosequi" is an instrument filed in court by the prosecutor stating that the prosecutor has abandoned the prosecution.

E. Officer Javert comes to you for help drafting a complaint affidavit seeking an arrest warrant. You review the facts and decide that probable cause exists. You tell Officer Javert he must draft his own complaint affidavit, and if he does so, you will be glad to assist him. Officer Javert drafts his own complaint affidavit, which you review and find to state probable cause. You have Officer Javert swear to the complaint affidavit. You then draft, sign, and swear to an information, which is filed with the clerk of courts. A capias is issued, and you are sitting in your office when Officer Javert serves the capias on Jay Gatsby.

Imagine now, in each of these scenarios, that you discover Officer Javert has lied to you; there is no probable cause; Jay Gatsby is innocent. In which of the above situations do you have qualified immunity? In which do you have absolute immunity? Is the safest course of action the one always to be preferred? Now imagine further that Jay Gatsby sues you personally for 1.75 million dollars for false arrest. How do you like your chances in a lawsuit in each of the above scenarios? What factors indicate good faith? What factors indicate bad faith? Can a prosecutor's office completely abdicate its law enforcement role? Should it do so?

CHAPTER 2

RELATIONS WITH LAW ENFORCEMENT AGENCIES

■ ■ ■

The prosecutor should maintain respectful yet independent judgment when interacting with law enforcement personnel.—Standard 3–3.2, ABA Prosecution Standards

As a prosecutor the first thing you should do on a crime scene is put your hands in your pockets. The second thing you should do is keep them there.—Anonymous

A. INTERACTION WITH LAW ENFORCEMENT AGENCIES

In the role of law enforcement officer, the prosecutor must interact with other law enforcement agencies, but not as a simple fellow officer. While fulfilling your law enforcement role, you must simultaneously act as a judge and an advocate. Each separate role you perform causes a different type of friction between you and your fellow law enforcement officers. Turf issues arise when you act as a law enforcement officer. Officers frequently resent and feel frustrated by the actions you will take as a judge or an advocate. You may, in your role as a judge, decline to file that case the officer worked so hard to make. You may, in your role as an advocate, be compelled to take a stance that the officer finds repugnant.

1. THREE MODELS

There are three models for such prosecutor-police relations. The police can work for the prosecutor, the prosecutor can work for the police, or the police and prosecutor can work together as independent but allied agencies. In some inquisitorial systems the police work under the direct supervision of the prosecutor, who has the power to direct the police on conducting investigations and collecting evidence, and the police must comply.[1] In England until 1986 the prosecutor worked for the police.[2] The police

[1] Opinion No.10 (2015) of the Consultative Council of European Prosecutors to the Committee of Ministers of the Council of Europe on the role of prosecutors in criminal investigations. 20 November, 2015. <rm.coe.int/1680747720>.

[2] McDonald, Sir Ken, QC, Director of Public Prosecutions, "Building a Modern Prosecution Authority. 2006. <https://www.crimeandjustice.org.uk/building-modern-prosecution-authority>.

department which investigated the crime and made the arrest was also the agency which hired the prosecutor and oversaw the prosecution. It was finally recognized that the investigating agency could not be relied upon to make a fair decision whether to prosecute. In 1985, Parliament adopted the third model by creating the Crown Prosecution Service, an independent prosecution agency.[3] Canada has a similar independent prosecution agency in the Federal Prosecution Service,[4] and the United States has locally elected, independent prosecutors who exercise largely unreviewable prosecutorial discretion.[5] Just how the United States arrived at a system of locally elected public prosecutors is a matter of debate, but the American system is unique in common law jurisdictions.

2. WHO IS IN CHARGE?

In most counties of the United States the sheriff is the chief law enforcement officer. Or is it the elected prosecutor? It might depend on which one you asked, or on the laws of a particular jurisdiction.[6] There once was a prosecutor who joked that he was the highest law enforcement officer in the county because his office was on the fourth floor of the courthouse, and the sheriff's was on the first. Nationwide, the sheriff and the district attorney head separate agencies with different but complementary missions, each needing the help of the other, and each wary that the other might usurp their prerogatives. Of course, the sheriff's office is not the only law enforcement agency in a jurisdiction. To a greater or lesser degree, the same problems exist between the prosecutor's office and each law enforcement agency with which the office deals. The problems tend to be most acute with sheriffs, who, like prosecutors, are elected public officials.

3. FRICTION POINTS

Meanwhile, down in the trenches, the uniformed officers and assistant prosecutors experience their problems, too. Both the officer and the prosecutor have difficulty fully appreciating the roles played, and the difficulties faced by their counterparts. From the vantage point of the assistant prosecutor, you see officers bringing you flawed, under-investigated cases and expecting you to perform miracles. From the officers' vantage point, you are seen as the one who sits in an air-conditioned office sipping coffee and casually dismissing those cases that

---

[3] *Id.*

[4] Federal Prosecution Service Deskbook, 2000. <https://www.ppsc-sppc.gc.ca/eng/pub/fpsd-sfpg/fps-sfp/fpd/index.html>.

[5] Ashe v. Swenson, 397 U.S. 436, 452, 90 S.Ct. 1189, 1198 (1970); People v. Jackson, 153 Mich.App. 38, 44, 394 N.W.2d 480, 483 (1986); Johnson v. State, 611 P.2d 1137, 1141 (Okl.Cr. 1980); State v. Ramirez, 83 Wis.2d 150, 155, 265 N.W.2d 274, 276 (1978).

[6] See, e.g., State v. Vitiello, 377 N.J.Super. 452, 873 A.2d 591 (2005) (County prosecutor is the chief law enforcement officer of the county); Boyd v. Robeson County, 169 N.C.App. 460, 621 S.E.2d 1 (2005) (Sheriff is the chief law enforcement officer of the county).

they literally risked life and limb to make. Officers do not know the nuances of the law, and prosecutors do not know the realities of the street. Communication can go a long way toward solving these problems.

When officers complete a report at the end of a shift, they are likely fatigued, emotionally drained, and overburdened by other duties. Not having seven years of college and not having a law degree, they do not always know what facts must be included in an affidavit to state probable cause or to sustain a prosecution. Not being finalists for the Pulitzer Prize in literature, they are not going to write as clear and cogent a report as you would like. Not having read the latest cases from the Supreme Court, they may have done something which endangers the admissibility of crucial evidence. Upon reviewing the file, you can make a snide remark about dumb, donut-eating flatfeet and dismiss the case while pouring another cup of coffee, or you can lean forward, pick up the telephone, and call the officer to discuss the case. You might even make arrangements for a face-to-face discussion of the file. Between you and the officer, you just might find a way to salvage the case. In the pre-file stage, it might even be helpful if you got out of your chair, left the office, and went out and did some field work with the officer. You would be abandoning absolute immunity for mere qualified immunity, but the case might just be salvaged in the process.

4. COMMUNICATION

Courts and legislatures have begun to decide that victims ought to have rights, and there are provisions galore for notification of victims of every critical stage of a prosecution. What about investigating officers? They may not have any lawful ownership of the case, but they certainly feel some moral ownership of and obligation to it. Keeping them aware of the progress of the case and discussing proposed dispositions of the case with them will go miles toward maintaining good relations. Officers who feel shut out from the prosecution, will assume the attitude "I arrested him, now you convict him." If you give them an interest in the prosecution, their attitude will be "What can I do to help us win our case?" When the case is over, win, lose, or draw, the officers' superiors should be made aware of the good work they did on the case. And you should be the one to make their superiors aware. With minimal effort you will not only improve the quality of your prosecutions and improve interagency cooperation, you will make real, permanent friendships.

The filing stage and the plea bargaining stage are not the only stages in which you can involve the law enforcement officer. Trial preparation and trial strategy are other areas in which both the officer and prosecutor can benefit from collaboration. If you have not already done so, go to the scene of the crime with the officers. Have them explain the scene to you. Involve them in photographing and diagraming. Enlist their aid in marshaling the witnesses and evidence. Talk trial strategy with them. The more you involve the officers, the more ownership of the case that you give them, the better your cases will become—not just the ones you are currently handling, but the ones that they will bring you in the future.

B. THE INVESTIGATIVE FUNCTION

Many European legal systems expect their prosecutors to confine themselves to the office and the courtroom. Many American prosecutors, in seeking to minimize civil liability, voluntarily confine themselves to the office and the courtroom. Many other prosecutors stand ready and willing to leave their offices and involve themselves in aspects of the criminal process traditionally thought of as the realm of the law enforcement officer. Sometimes you are well-received in these areas, sometimes you are most unwelcome. Well-received or not, you have a right and a duty to investigate. Although the prosecutor traditionally depends upon law enforcement officers to perform the investigative tasks necessary to the prosecution of criminal cases, the prosecutor has a both the authority and duty to investigate.[7] You typically fulfill the investigative role by acting as a police legal advisor,[8] becoming involved in the approval of arrest and search warrants,[9] issuing investigative subpoenas,[10] and advising grand jury investigations.[11] Some prosecutors' offices even have in-house investigators[12] on staff who are sworn law enforcement officers and can perform all law enforcement functions.[13]

1. POLICE ADVISOR

Prosecutors most often become involved in the investigative function when the police request assistance. Since the police have far greater manpower than the prosecutor, the assistance rarely involves hands-on investigative activity. More often, the requests seek advice and counsel. Although law enforcement officers are well-informed on the mechanical and personal safety techniques for making arrests and collecting evidence, they are less well-informed of the legal strictures upon such procedures and almost always totally ignorant of the most recent appellate pronouncements on the nuances of the exclusionary rules. They are certainly not as well-equipped as prosecutors to evaluate the probative merit of the available evidence or to make charging decisions. A young prosecutor was once awakened from a sound sleep at 2:00am by a call from an officer seeking advice. The officer explained his situation and concluded

---

7 ABA Prosecution Standard 3–3.1; National Prosecution Standard 3–1.1.

8 National Prosecution Standard 2–5.6.

9 ABA Prosecutorial Investigation Standard. 2.8; National Prosecution Standard 3–2.1.

10 ABA Prosecutorial Investigation Standard. 2.7.

11 ABA Prosecutorial Investigation Standard. 2.9.

12 National Prosecution Standard 3–2.3.

13 See e.g. Fla.Stat. § 27.255.

by saying "so I arrested him." The prosecutor asked, "What did you arrest him for?" The officer replied, "That's why I called you. What did I arrest him for? I know he's done something illegal, but I just can't figure out what it is." The prosecutor was able to supply the correct charge and return to his interrupted sleep. As a prosecutor, you will be asked to make certain that evidence is collected so as to ensure its admissibility at trial and to evaluate the available evidence to help determine whether an arrest is advisable. You will receive calls for advice both during and after office hours; you will be asked to meet and confer with groups of officers both during and after office hours; you will be consulted during the preparation phase of major law enforcement efforts such as drug sweeps, undercover stings, and the like; and you will often be called to the scene of major crimes—most notably the scenes of homicides.

2. ON THE CRIME SCENE

When called to the scene of a homicide or other major crime, you must always remember several salient points, the first being that you are not in charge. The chief investigating officer or case agent has charge of the crime scene, and you are there as a guest who might be called upon to render valuable assistance. Frequently there are turf squabbles on scenes, as agencies with overlapping jurisdictions sort out which agency will take primary responsibility for the scene. In such situations you can and should act as a mediator and peacemaker. In no case should you enter the fray as a combatant. You will be working with both agencies again on other cases, and you want to maintain cordial relations with all parties if possible.

The next thing to remember is that you provide another set of eyes and ears on the scene, but you should not provide another set of hands. Your objective in being there is not simply to monitor the lawful collection of evidence, but also to prepare yourself to go to court and try the case. You cannot try the case if you have made yourself a witness by becoming actively involved in the collection of evidence, nor do you want those unidentified fingerprints found all over the crime scene to finally be identified as yours.

As you survey the scene, you will see it from a different perspective than that of the law enforcement officer. You will be looking at the scene and thinking about presenting evidence from that scene to a jury. The officers will simply be thinking about collecting, preserving, and documenting the evidence. Evidence can be efficiently collected, preserved, and documented, but not persuasive when presented at trial. You should make suggestions that will help to ensure that the evidence is not only admissible, but persuasive. Note the word "suggestions" in the last sentence. You do not make demands. You make suggestions. At the risk of redundancy, you are not in charge of the scene. The urgency of your suggestions may vary with the importance attached to the suggestion. You might want to be more insistent that the officers obtain a warrant before kicking in the door of the defendant's home than you would when suggesting that they photograph the defendant's home from a certain perspective.

Criminals do not confine their activity to between the hours of eight and five Monday through Friday. Larger prosecutors' offices throughout the nation establish on-call rotations in which prosecutors are expected to be available twenty-four hours a day, seven days a week, 365 days a year. Smaller prosecutors' offices may not have on-call rotations, but assistant prosecutors are expected to be available at all hours of the night or day to answer questions, render advice, and go to crime scenes. If you practice in a jurisdiction where prosecutors are expected to appear on crime scenes, there are a few things that you might want to keep in the trunk of your car. You might want to stock your trunk with maps of the jurisdiction; arrest and search warrant forms; a statute book; a telephone directory; a list of telephone numbers for judges, law enforcement agencies, and fellow prosecutors; gloves; boots; coveralls; a reflective vest; a flashlight; and an umbrella. You might also do well to stock some plastic baggies, brown paper bags, and evidence tape. You won't need these items, but you just might find yourself on a scene with officers who do not have these necessary evidence collection accessories. You might also want to have a toolbox, a first aid kit, a laptop, and a portable printer.

3. INTERDEPENDENCE AND INDEPENDENCE

How you behave and interact with law enforcement on a scene has much to do with whether or not you will be invited to come to the next scene. Jealous, short-sighted agencies will neglect to call you if they begin to suspect that you are "horning in" on their sacred turf. The worst way in the world for you to learn of a major crime in your jurisdiction is to read about it in the paper the morning after it happens. It is not much better to have the police agency call you after they have cleared the scene and made an arrest. The best time is immediately, while the officers are still on the scene. You must work at maintaining good relations with your law enforcement agencies in order to ensure that you hear about these crimes at the best time. Take care, however, to maintain your independence from law enforcement. Too close a relationship with an officer can cloud your judgement. It can be too easy to slip into the role of advocate for the police instead of advocate for the people. This danger should not prevent you from working as closely as possible with law enforcement. It should, however, keep you on your guard as you deal with them.

C. ZEALOUS ENFORCEMENT

Most law enforcement officers, like most human beings, are basically good people. Because law enforcement officers are recruited from the ranks of human beings there will inevitably be a minority of officers who will exhibit one or more of the Seven Deadly Sins. Since you, as a prosecutor, are a minister of justice and not an attorney for miscreant officers, you must develop a strategy for dealing with these occasional incidents of misbehavior. The ways that an officer can fall short of the highest standards of excellence are numberless, but excessive zeal in the performance of their duties is one way. A common subtype of the overzealous officer is the serial resisting arrest victim. Some officers can retire after a long career and never make a case against anyone for resisting arrest. Other officers cannot get through a shift without making such a case. Serial resisting arrest victims fall into three main types: those who lack the interpersonal skills necessary to obtain suspect compliance, those who verbally bait suspects, and those who are so thin-skinned that they overreact to suspect noncompliance. Seldom should you encounter an officer who purposely set out to falsely convict a suspect of resisting arrest. Sometimes an officer will have unintentionally mishandled a situation, and you are burdened with a case where the defendant is technically guilty of the crime, but victim precipitation issues make a conviction unlikely. Quick-witted officers who always have a quip on the tip of their tongues frequently let fly with those quips at the most inopportune times, resulting in black eyes, bruises, and a questionable case against a defendant who, again, is technically guilty but was goaded into acting out. Finally, there are officers who are so quick to take offense that they will arrest at the drop of a hat for the most inconsequential misbehavior. A certain degree of noncompliance comes with the officer's territory, and the officer should have sufficient judgement to decline to arrest at all in *de minimis* situations.

These types of cases are relatively easy to spot, and when one of them comes across your desk, you must handle it appropriately. Rubber stamping the officer's decision can sometimes be appropriate, but more often you must make the unpleasant decisions to dismiss the charges, to file reduced charges, or to accept reduced pleas. Such decisions are rarely popular with officers, but you must make them and stand by them firmly but diplomatically. The officer, as a victim, deserves and has a right to an explanation of your rationale for your charging decision or your plea decision, and he has a right to lobby you to change your decision before you finalize it. Unpleasant as it may be, a face-to-face explanation is preferable to sending the officer a letter. Lawyer-bashing is a favorite pastime of law enforcement officers, and lawyers often give officers good reason to engage in the sport. Holding face-to-face meetings at which you patiently listen to the officer's complaints and tactfully explain the reason for your decision will not render you immune to being lawyer-bashed, but over the long run it will earn the respect, if not the love, of most reasonable law enforcement officers.

1. TRUTH VALUE AND TRUST

The highly competitive nature of ferreting out crime presents a huge temptation to fudge the facts to make a case. You should never tolerate such activity. Alan Dershowitz long ago pronounced thirteen sardonic "rules" of the criminal justice system, and two of them are relevant to this discussion. "Rule 4: Almost all police lie about whether they violated the constitution in order to convict guilty defendants." The good news about Dershowitz's aphorism is his recognition of the fact that almost nobody lies to convict innocent defendants. More good news about the aphorism is that almost all statements about the faults of "almost all" of any group of people are almost always wrong. The bad news about the aphorism is that if you substitute "some" for "almost all" in the statement, it is true. It is small comfort that an officer is not lying about the guilt of the accused, but simply how the evidence of that guilt was gathered. Remember, the right result for the wrong reason is the wrong result. No conviction should rest on material misstatements of fact, regardless of whether those misstatements are on the substantive issue of guilt or on the procedural issue of how that guilt is proven.

The law enforcement role tempts prosecutors as well as police, and prosecutors also face temptation from their other role as an advocate. In recognition of this dual temptation, Dershowitz pronounces another rule. "Rule 6: Many prosecutors implicitly encourage police to lie about whether they violated the Constitution in order to convict defendants." Again, there is solace in Dershowitz's recognition that few prosecutors suborn perjury. And again, the aphorism is vulnerable to the conventional wisdom that as a general rule, general rules are generally wrong. But again the bad news about this aphorism is that if you substitute "many" with "some," it is true. If you engage in this type of activity, you have forsworn your oath as a minister of justice, and you are not truly a prosecutor. You are merely an ethically challenged plaintiff's attorney working in a prosecutor's office. At the risk of redundancy, your objective is not a favorable verdict, but a just one.

Prosecutors rarely encourage lying by police officers, either implicitly or explicitly, but sometimes they take Pilate's attitude toward the truth. As discussed in Chapter 1, some advocates accept favorable testimony at face value regardless of its suspect truth value. Some of those "gullible" advocates are prosecutors. You should not depend on testimony unless you assign it a high degree of truth value. A just verdict can only be obtained if it is based on truth. Notwithstanding the ethical considerations, there are good and sufficient practical reasons for rejecting testimony of questionable truth value. If an officer's testimony causes you to suspect its veracity, it will cause others to have the same suspicions. When an officer crawls out onto the limb of improbability to make evidence admissible, the defense is likely to saw it off. You do not want to be out on that limb with the officer when it comes crashing to the ground. At the very least, indiscriminate proffering of implausible testimony will get you an unsavory reputation among the members of the bench and bar.

2. POSTURAL ECHO

Officers who lie to make evidence admissible are relatively easy to identify. Once they are identified, how do you deal with them? As to the specific case at hand, is the evidence admissible based on the true facts? Oftentimes the officer wastes a lie through ignorance of the laws of search and seizure. If the true facts support admissibility and you can prove them, then you can still go forward with your case. In dealing with the lying officer, a good maneuver is to demonstrate to him how easily he can be crushed on cross-examination. In such a case he will likely thank you for dropping the charges or declining to present the illegally seized evidence. Should you prosecute the officer for perjury? Perjury is one of the most difficult crimes to prove, and seldom will you be able to file a winnable case in such situations. Implausibility, lack of verisimilitude, and conflict with other witnesses may be reason to suspect perjury, but they are not proof of perjury beyond a reasonable doubt. When officers learn that they are dealing with an office which is not going to tolerate shenanigans and not going to be gulled, it has a beneficial effect on the future veracity of most of them. When you deal with law enforcement officers, you can control the dynamic of that relationship by demonstrating courtesy, competence, and rectitude. There is a psychological phenomenon known as "postural echo." Postural echo occurs when one party to a transaction begins, almost subconsciously, to echo the behavior of the other party to the transaction. If you model courtesy, competence, and rectitude, the officers with whom you deal will echo that model. There is wisdom in the saying "A soft answer turns away wrath."[14] By adhering to principle, by courteously insisting that those with whom you deal do the same, by modeling good behavior, you will build rewarding professional relationships among the officers with whom you must work.

PRACTICAL EXERCISES

How should you handle each of the following situations?

1. Officer Javert brings an application for search warrant to you seeking to search Edward Hyde's home for cannabis. The warrant alleges that Officer Javert knows there are drugs in Hyde's home because he has received a report from "a confidential informant known to this officer to be trustworthy because of reliable information of this type provided by said informant in the past." You decide that the affidavit for search warrant states probable cause and draft a search warrant. Officer Javert serves the warrant, and five pounds of cannabis

---

[14] Proverbs 15:1 (NRSV).

are found on the premises. You later discover that the confidential informant had never been used by Officer Javert or any other law enforcement officer before. You confront Officer Javert. He readily admits what he did, but he says, "I thought you had to say that in an application for search warrant."

2. Officer Javert comes to you for help in drafting an application for search warrant seeking to search Edward Hyde's home for cannabis. He tells you that he knows Hyde has cannabis in his home because Javert supervised the informant as the informant made a tape-recorded controlled purchase of cannabis inside Hyde's residence. Javert produces the tape recording of the transaction, you listen to the tape, and you hear Hyde tell the informant "Come back any time. I always keep four or five pounds here at the house." Officer Javert does not want to put this information in the application for search warrant because it might "burn" his informant.

3. Officer Javert brings an application for search warrant to you seeking to search Edward Hyde's home for cannabis. The unsigned application alleges that Officer Javert knows there are drugs in Hyde's home because he has received a report from "a confidential informant known to this officer to be trustworthy because of reliable information of this type provided by said informant in the past." You question Officer Javert on the specifics of the information given in the past by the informant, and

A. Officer Javert refuses to give you any information at all about the confidential informant, citing confidentiality concerns.

B. Officer Javert admits to you that the confidential informant has never been used before, but he knows the information is reliable because he supervised the informant as the informant made a tape-recorded controlled purchase of cannabis inside Hyde's residence. Javert produces the tape recording of the transaction, you listen to the tape, and you hear Hyde tell the informant "Come back any time. I always keep four or five pounds here at the house." Officer Javert did not want to put this information in the application for search warrant because it might "burn" his informant.

CHAPTER 3

RELATIONS WITH THE DEFENSE BAR

■ ■ ■

Do as adversaries do in law,
Strive mightily, but eat and drink as friends.
William Shakespeare, *The Taming of the Shrew*,
Act I Scene 2, lines 257–258

Had I but said, I would have kept my word,
But when I swear, it is irrevocable.
William Shakespeare, *King Henry VI, Part 2*,
Act III Scene 2, lines 304–305

A. GAME THEORY

Game theory is a field of economics and mathematics which analyzes conflict in terms of gains and losses among opposing parties. Its precepts apply as readily to a game of tic-tac-toe as they do to thermonuclear war. The trial of a criminal case falls somewhere between those two extremes and is susceptible to game theory analysis.[1] Game theory recognizes different types of games, which can be exemplified by the games of tic-tac-toe and thermonuclear war. Tic-tac-toe is a two-player, zero-sum game, while thermonuclear war is a multi-player non-zero sum game. In a zero-sum game one side wins and another loses, or the game is drawn. In a non-zero-sum game both sides can win, both sides can lose, and sometimes victory can be defined as escaping with minimal loss. Western civilization did itself a disservice when it named the adversary system. On the "adversary" model, we think of a criminal trial as a contest, a zero-sum game in which, for one side to win, the other must be defeated. If we define winning as making the other side lose, we often have an unrealistic concept of what is at stake, and we wind up losing ourselves. Too often we forget the judge's customary admonition to the jury that "the lawyers are not on trial."[2] Too often lawyers treat the trial of a criminal case as a two-player zero-sum game between the prosecutor and the defense attorney. If you think of the criminal trial on this model, you are headed for disaster.

---

1 See, e.g., Baird, Douglas G., Robert H. Gertner, and Randal C. Picker, Game Theory and the Law, Harvard University Press, Cambridge, Massachusetts, 1994.

2 Florida Standard Jury Instructions in Criminal Cases, § 3.10. <https://www.floridabar.org/rules/florida-standard-jury-instructions/criminal-jury-instructions-home/criminal-jury-instructions/sji-criminal-chapter-3/>.

Opposing counsel becomes, not just an adversary, but an enemy. A great deal of unpleasantry occurs in the courtroom because the lawyers are fighting each other as enemies in a zero-sum game rather than trying their respective cases as two of many players in the non-zero-sum game of criminal justice.

When you go beyond thinking of opposing counsel as colleagues presenting contrasting views in a civilized debate and begin thinking of them as enemies, then the next step is to think of them as evil. From thinking of your enemies as evil, the next step is to tend to read evil motives into every action they take. Having cast your adversary in the role of an evil enemy fighting you with evil acts, you have only a short step to begin to think that you must "fight fire with fire," and follow, not the Golden Rule of civility, but the Iron Rule of retaliation. You might even conclude that you should engage in preemptive retaliation. After all, didn't Machiavelli teach that the end justifies the means?

The mere fact that you disagree with someone does not mean that the other person is your enemy. Even if your adversary is your enemy that does not mean that your adversary is evil. You must not fall into the trap of buying into an adversarial "adversary" system. We should rename our justice system. Call it the "dialectical system" rather than the "adversarial system." On a dialectical model, differences would be discussed, positions mooted, and an informed decision reached by way of civilized debate. On an adversarial model, sophistry, polemics, and demagoguery reign supreme.

Richard Whately, a prominent Nineteenth Century rhetorician, penned one of the most damning indictments of our "adversarial" system when he wrote the following words:

> I should * * * counsel him who wishes to produce a permanent effect (for I am not now adverting to the case of a barrister) to keep on the side of what he believes to be truth; and, avoiding all sophistry, to aim only at setting forth that truth as strongly as possible, * * * without any endeavor to gain applause for his own abilities.[3]

Whately's statement is ironic because, although it perfectly describes what a lawyer should do, he does not expect lawyers to even attempt it. Ambrose Bierce, a near contemporary of Whately, defined "liar" as "a lawyer with a roving commission."[4] This view of lawyers and lawyering considerably predates the Nineteenth Century, and survives to this day. Sadly, many

---

[3] Elements of Rhetoric Comprising an Analysis of the Laws of Moral Evidence and Persuasion with Rules for Argumentative Composition and Elocution, Kessinger Publishing Co., Whitefish, Montana, 1854/2005, p. 167.

[4] Bierce, Ambrose, The Devil's Dictionary, Dover Publications, Mineola, New York, 1911/1993. p. 71.

lawyers seemingly do everything in their power to confirm it. You, as a prosecutor, must pursue convictions based upon truth, sound reasoning, and fair dealing.

You must reverse Machiavelli's dictum. Rather than believing that the end justifies the means, you must act as though you believe that the means can ennoble (or debase) the end. You must not sacrifice your integrity on the altar of victory. You must banish the idea that your adversaries are evil enemies who must be defeated at all costs and rather look upon them as colleagues in a civilized dialectical discourse. Through the collision of the thesis of your case theory with the antithesis of your adversary's case theory, you collaborate in working out the synthesis of the jury verdict.

B. CAESAR'S WIFE

You have just begun when you commit yourself to presenting your case with honesty and integrity. You must behave outside the courtroom with the same rigid allegiance to truthfulness. A wise old attorney once said that a prosecutor must be like Caesar's wife, above suspicion. You must mean what you say and say what you mean. When you tell opposing counsel something, you must live up to what you say.[5] Do not make promises you cannot keep. Do not mislead opposing counsel as to your intentions or your evidence. If the bench and the bar cannot trust you, you might as well find another line of work. "Who steals my purse steals trash * * *. But he that filches from me my good name robs me of that which not enriches him and makes me poor indeed."[6] To have one steal your reputation for verity is unfortunate, but if you yourself are the thief, it is a tragedy. If you are to maintain your word as your bond, you must be circumspect; choose your words wisely when making representations to opposing counsel. Deliberation must precede vocalization lest you find yourself in the predicament that Herod the Tetrarch faced with Herodias' daughter.[7] Once you have given your word, you cannot withdraw it simply because it has become inconvenient.

You can be a paragon of moral rectitude but still fall short of the mark of being a good prosecutor. To character you must add courtesy. You must be courteous to those members of the defense bar with whom you deal, as well as with all other court functionaries, witnesses, victims, and even defendants. You must return telephone calls, you must keep your promises, you must not needlessly hector the opposition, you must observe the formal rules of etiquette. Cicero stood at the pinnacle of the Roman criminal defense bar, but his penchant for acid-tongue repartee at the expense of his adversaries eventually led to his ruin. Cicero's contemporary and sometime

---

[5] National Prosecution Standard 1–2.1b.

[6] Shakespeare, William, Othello, Act 3, Scene 3, Lines 158–162.

[7] Matthew 14:3–11.

ally, Cato the Younger, was renowned as a man of uncompromising ethics, but he was despised as ill-tempered and pugnacious. Some interpret courtesy as a sign of weakness, but in truth truculence more often serves as a mask for inability.

The foregoing standards are far easier to attain in jurisdictions with smaller bars, where lawyers daily deal with the same opposing counsel year after year. Misbehavior is more readily observable in a small bar, and lawyers can ruin their reputations in short order. Whereas scoundrels can go unnoticed for a longer time in a crowd, they are immediately discovered in a small group. If you are in a large bar and are dealing with a lawyer you will hardly ever face again, the temptation for sharp dealing increases. You might be able to put one over on an unwary opponent who may never be able to repay the favor. There is less impetus to be polite to someone you may never see again. Although legendary feuds can erupt between lawyers who face each other daily, most lawyers thrown in close contact for extended periods will try to deal with one another fairly and courteously. Fair, courteous dealing is easier in small jurisdictions, but it is just as important in larger ones. In a larger bar it may take longer to develop the reputation for courtesy, square dealing, and straight shooting, but this makes striving to maintain such a reputation all the more desirable.

1. COURTESY, PROBITY, VERITY

Most lawyers, if confronted with courtesy, probity, and verity, will respond in kind. It is important to remember, however, that although standards of courtesy are the same for prosecution and defense, standards of fairness are not. The defendant has certain constitutional rights which preclude the defense attorney from divulging information which the prosecutor could be disbarred for withholding. Not only are defense attorneys precluded from full disclosure, they also have a discretionary privilege of withholding certain types of information which prosecutors must disclose. Many would argue that standards of verity differ between prosecutors and defense attorneys, but this is not an argument which should command assent. Although some may take a relativist approach to truth, the burden of striving for absolute truth should be shared equally by all. The Fifth Amendment gives the defendant a privilege of non-disclosure, not a license to dissemble.

Although you may feel betrayed, misled, or otherwise mistreated by defense counsel's legitimate exercise of the privilege of nondisclosure, you have no right to do so. You must factor this variable into the equation of prosecutor-defense relations and respond accordingly. If you cannot abide being held to a higher standard of disclosure than your adversary, you have a simple solution—find another job.

You will meet opposing counsel who studiously adhere to the highest standards of courtesy, probity, and verity. You will also encounter opposing counsel who adhere to their own slightly skewed interpretation of those standards. There will be others who live up to the standards on most occasions but will lapse into offending against them when constrained by dire circumstance. Then there will be a small minority of lawyers who only consult the standards to make sure that they are violating them. You will also run into the full spectrum of degrees of compliance with the canons of courtesy. Do not confuse discourtesy with dishonesty. Some of the most disagreeable attorneys you will ever meet will be the most punctilious in dealing fairly and truthfully, while some of the most affable will turn out to be the least trustworthy.

2. TRUST AND TRUSTWORTHINESS

In dealing with opposing counsel, a good rule of thumb is: "Always get it in writing." A close corollary of this rule is Sam Goldwyn's apocryphal comment, "An oral promise isn't worth the paper it's written on." If defense counsel is going to waive something or stipulate to something, get it in writing. If you reach an oral understanding with opposing counsel about an issue, go back to the office and send opposing counsel a memo reciting your understanding. Consider copying the judge with the memo.[8] If opposing counsel leaves a representation on voicemail—save the voicemail. Document, document, document. If you cannot get it confirmed in writing, be able to go forward in case the promise is repudiated. For example, if you have only defense counsel's oral representation to not to hold you to a strict chain of custody on an item, you may feel secure offering the item into evidence without a complete chain, but you should still be able to prove up the chain in the event that, contrary to expectations, defense counsel interposes a chain of custody objection.

After years of dealing with Laura Litigator, you may decide that Litigator is the type who unfailingly hews to the highest standards, and you will feel comfortable relaxing your vigilance. In such a case, you are likely to discover to your chagrin that she is really the type who only abandons the standards in dire straits, and you have never had her in dire straits until this one time when you let your guard down. One common manifestation of this phenomenon occurs with private counsel who do court appointed cases. Court appointed attorneys oftentimes are paragons of virtue—until they get a paying client. Not only can paying clients sometimes relax counsel's adherence to high standards, serious charges can have the same effect. An attorney who is straight as an arrow in a DUI might become crooked as a corkscrew in a murder case. Regardless of how

[8] It goes without saying that if you copy the judge with the memo, you must immediately make opposing counsel aware of that fact. Otherwise you will have engaged in impermissible ex parte communication with the judge.

poorly your opponent adheres to acceptable standards of courtesy, probity, and verity, you must never waver in your devotion to those standards.

C. DEALING WITH DIFFICULT ATTORNEYS

Just as you will encounter unfailingly courteous blackguards, you will meet bullies, curmudgeons, and other highly disagreeable sorts among the ranks of those whose integrity cannot be questioned. In dealing with the bully, you must never for a moment be cowed or back down out of fear. Because human beings sometimes have difficulty discerning assertiveness from aggressiveness, in dealing with the legal bully you may find it difficult to stand your ground and politely assert your position without lapsing into aggressiveness. You must nevertheless undertake to accomplish that feat. It would be impossible to catalog the myriads of ways in which one human being can hector and otherwise torment another human being, but it is plausible to assert that at some point in legal history, each one of those ways has been practiced by one lawyer upon another. You begin learning countermeasures to such tactics in kindergarten, and the good ones are just as applicable in the courtroom as they are on the sandlot. One apocryphal story from North Florida lore illustrates a sandlot method unsuitable to the courtroom. A young court clerk had been elevated to the position much against the wishes of a local prosecutor, and the prosecutor took great pleasure in verbally harassing and embarrassing the clerk at every opportunity. Court retainers debated whether it was stoicism or cowardice that prevented the clerk from retaliating, but he endured his persecution like a martyr. This situation continued for several months with the presiding judge taking no steps to intervene on the clerk's behalf. One morning the clerk was late for court, and as he scurried into the crowded courtroom, the prosecutor launched into a tirade, berating the clerk for his inefficiency. The stream of invective continued as the clerk got within arm's reach of the prosecutor and ended abruptly when a roundhouse blow flattened the prosecutor. The clerk then took his assigned place in the courtroom and the judge, who had watched the entire proceeding from his vantage point on the bench, pronounced his finding of fact: "I didn't see a thing." The prosecutor climbed back to his feet, the judge called court to order, and the business of the day was concluded without further incident.

1. DEALING WITH THE TRUE BELIEVER

There are three species of disagreeable attorney which merit special consideration. The first we will call the true believer. True believers can be prosecutors or defense attorneys. True believing prosecutors look upon themselves as avenging angels, all defendants as minions of Satan, and all defense attorneys as shysters. Each case becomes a crusade against the forces of evil, and doing justice is equated with achieving vengeance. Defense attorney versions of the true believer never represented a guilty client, never confronted an ethical prosecutor, never cross-examined a truthful witness, and feel duty bound to communicate their displeasure over these "facts" at every available opportunity to every available audience. With both versions of true believer, there are no legal issues, there are only personal issues. The most toxic form of true believer is the lawyer who feels that occupation of the moral high ground gives a license to engage in unethical behavior to advance the "greater good" of winning at all costs. At both trial and in pretrial the true believer does not make legal arguments so much as personal attacks, and those attacks can have a devastating effect if they are not properly handled.

2. ANSWERING AD HOMINEM ATTACKS

Let us first analyze these attacks in nonjury settings. It goes without saying that the first line of defense against a personal attack is to be innocent of the accusation. The second step is somewhat more difficult. Follow the first half of Everett Dirksen's Third Rule of Politics: "Don't get mad; get even,"[9] but ignore the second. Do not fall prey to emotion, but do not seek revenge. If you do so, you will wind up fighting opposing counsel rather than trying your case, a maneuver which is more often fatal to prosecutions than to criminal defenses. The natural reaction to a personal attack is the *tu quoque*[10] defense, a logical fallacy in which the defender counterattacks by fastening the same criticism upon the attacker. Such a defense is emotionally satisfying, but it is fatal to your case. Guilty parties responding to an attack with a *tu quoque* defense seek to divert attention from their guilt by means of the counterattack, and they can have spectacular success in confusing the issues by such a maneuver. At least in the legal setting, an innocent party responding with a *tu quoque* defense is playing into the enemy's hands. The following example is illustrative of the point.

> Q: Now, Officer Friendly, what did my client's wife tell you during the interview about my client's exemplary military record?
>
> BY THE PROSECUTION: Objection. Hearsay.
>
> BY THE DEFENSE: Your honor, the prosecutor is intentionally and dishonorably trying to circumvent my client's constitutional right to offer a defense by seeking to withhold vital defense evidence from the finder of fact!
>
> BY THE PROSECUTION: Your honor, it is the defense attorney who is being sleazy here. He's completely ignoring the rules of

---

9 The full text of Dirksen's Rules is as follows: "(1) Get elected. (2) Get reelected. (3) Don't get mad, get even."

10 Literally, "you, too." It is a sophisticated equivalent of the schoolyard retort, "Oh, yeah? Well same to you but more of it!"

evidence and scurrilously trying to subvert justice by putting inflammatory and inadmissible evidence before the finder of fact.

BY THE COURT: Gentlemen, the court's patience with this sniping and backbiting is wearing thin. I'll not tolerate any more of this behavior. Mr. Witness, answer the question.

A: She told me he won the Bronze Star and a Purple Heart.

In the foregoing example, the prosecutor, by playing into defense counsel's hands, managed to get the hearsay issue gobbled up by the animosity issue. If you can keep your eye on the objective, you can master the third step: "Do not answer fools according to their folly, or you will be a fool yourself."[11] You want to argue issues, not personalities. Let us replay the foregoing example.

Q: Now, Officer Friendly, what did my client's wife tell you during the interview about my client's exemplary military record?

BY THE PROSECUTION: Objection. Hearsay.

BY THE DEFENSE: Your honor, the prosecutor is intentionally and dishonorably trying to circumvent my client's constitutional right to offer a defense by seeking to withhold vital defense evidence from the finder of fact!

BY THE PROSECUTION: Your honor, I'll be glad to withdraw my objection if defense counsel can show me a proper exception to the hearsay rule which allows such testimony.

BY THE COURT: Can you make the court aware of such an exception?

BY THE DEFENSE: [Further irrelevant comments reflecting adversely upon the prosecutor's human worth but not answering the court's question].

BY THE COURT: Sustained.

Step three works well in the nonjury setting because the judge is rarely impressed by such unsubstantiated fulminations, and it can also work well in most jury settings. Replay both versions of the foregoing hypothetical as speaking objections before a jury. What would the jury, consisting of rookie fact finders, think of the first exchange? Might it begin to suspect the bona fides of the prosecutor? It could certainly have no doubts about his self-control. Now consider their reaction to the second. They should be favorably impressed by the prosecutor's refusal to play *tu quoque*. In most cases before a jury, you can answer such attacks by demonstrating a fair-minded determination to keep to the real issues. Occasionally a personal attack requires more. Sometimes a disdainful or slightly amused or irritated air

---

[11] Proverbs 26:4 (NRSV).

toward the slur will be enough, but sometimes you must show emotion. It might be helpful to look at this exchange from an old prosecution of a father whose two-year-old daughter had died of peritonitis after he kicked her in the stomach. The defense offered a theory, concocted of equal parts fantasy and fiction, that the prosecution had been undertaken to protect the local hospital from a malpractice suit. Defense counsel expounded at length on this theory in final argument and capped the argument off by claiming that the defendant was being prosecuted because of his ethnicity. This statement provoked a thunderous objection from the prosecutor, which succinctly stated the legal grounds for the objection but nonverbally communicated fury at such an unfounded accusation of racism. If the personal attack is so flagrant that the jury will expect an emotional reaction, you will weaken your case if you do not deliver one. Here is where self-control is of paramount importance. You will be angry, but you must not behave angrily. You must display an appropriate level of outrage without falling prey to an inappropriate level of rage. It is difficult, but doable.

3. DEALING WITH THE OBSTRUCTIONIST

The second species of disagreeable attorney we will study is the obstructionist. This sort of attorney lives and dies by a simple motto, "If you're for it, I'm against it." Obstructionists confuse advocating their client's cause with obstructing your efforts. Never quite realizing that the two objectives are not necessarily complementary, they automatically oppose anything you try to do on general principles. Occasionally opposing counsel will suggest a course of action that is actually beneficial to the other side or that, while not benefitting the other side directly, will enhance judicial efficiency. Obstructionist defense attorneys will never completely disabuse themselves of the notion that if the prosecutor asks for it, it must be bad for their client. The result is that the trial is slowed, and you jump through hoops that really don't need to be jumped through. If both the prosecutor and the defense attorney are obstructionists they can take a one-day trial and stretch it out to a week.

Occasionally obstructionist tactics will produce a minor victory, but equally as often (if not more often) they redound to the detriment of the client. Obstructionist prosecutors are far more likely to shoot themselves in the foot than obstructionist defense attorneys. If, through obstructionism, you can prevent inept opposing counsel from presenting relevant, admissible evidence, you may achieve an immediate victory, but it will come at a cost. For prosecutors who achieve such victories, there is a hereafter which comes in the form of post-conviction attack on the competence of defense counsel. You can also suffer more immediate punishment for obstructionism. If the jury ever decides that you are taking advantage of an inept attorney to prevent them from hearing relevant evidence, they will unhesitatingly vote not guilty.

4. DEALING WITH THE CIRCUMVENTER

The third species of aggravating attorney is the one who perfectly exemplifies Ambrose Bierce's definition of a lawyer—one skilled in the circumvention of the law.[12] We will therefore call this type the circumventer. Around the peripheries of almost every case you will find facts that are less than complimentary to one side or the other. Elsewhere in the fact pattern will be bits of information that the laws of evidence justly hold inadmissible. Circumventers deem it their solemn duty to place this information before the jury by fair means or foul, and many circumventers take more pleasure in accomplishing the task by foul means than fair. They will engineer awkward situations in which they can insinuate the information into the jury's knowledge base, relying on the old saw that an instruction to disregard only serves to further imprint the information in the jury's memory banks. You will find a trial with a circumventer to be a tedious affair, during which you must exercise constant vigilance to forestall the circumventer's shenanigans. The best way to deal with a circumventer is to identify all the stink bombs pretrial and file a motion in limine to prevent the "oops" moments the circumventer would otherwise inevitably engineer. Of course, an order in limine will never serve as a 100% effective prophylaxis against such tactics, but it should lighten your burden. It is of utmost importance that you control your emotions when the circumventer finally succeeds in setting off such a forensic stink bomb. Your reaction could further amplify the damage—or it could stop the bleeding. The best attitude to adopt is that of the purist who is irritated that the circumventer has pulled a shenanigan, and not that of the advocate who is mortified because harmful information has been shared with the jury. The first attitude stanches the flow of blood, the second opens another, and possibly deeper, wound.

The circumventer can sometimes achieve a victory at trial, but such victories can come at a high cost. Although the state cannot appeal an acquittal, defense circumventers do long range damage to their credibility and to the playing field upon which their future clients must contest their cases. Nobody likes to be victimized by sharp tactics, and attorneys have long memories. Today's victim likely will become tomorrow's potential benefactor. Circumventers oftentimes get cold receptions when they come before former victims seeking a concession. In addition to this long-range damage, prosecution circumventers can inflict both immediate and short-range damage to their cause. That slick trick of putting inadmissible evidence before the jury might not seem so clever when the judge declares

[12] Bierce, Ambrose, The Devil's Dictionary, Dover Publications, Mineola, New York, 1911/1993. p. 61.

a mistrial, or worse yet, when the appellate court rules that the judge should have declared a mistrial. Even if the defense attorney does not object to such tactics, the case might succumb to a claim of fundamental error on appeal[13] or a claim of ineffective assistance of counsel on post-conviction attack.[14] Make sure the conviction is obtained right the first time and you will not be faced with the task, possibly years later, of having to obtain it a second time.

5. DEALING WITH THE BUNGLER

There is one additional species of attorney to discuss—an attorney whose attributes are not so much disagreeable as distressing. This attorney is the bungler. A license to practice law entitles anyone who feels up to the task to walk into court and try a case before a jury—entitles but not enables. People who know nothing of the law sometimes hire lawyers who know nothing of advocacy. In civil court, where an attorney's first allegiance is the client, it may be great fun to steamroll a bungler, but this form of entertainment has no place in criminal court. You, as a representative of all the people (including the defendant), have a higher duty than simply winning one for the Gipper. Regardless of how guilty defendants may be, if they wind up convicted because their attorney is incompetent they have been unjustly convicted. It is your duty to see to it that the defendant is not only convicted but convicted justly. What can you do? Certainly the prosecution does not and should not have veto power over the defendant's choice of counsel, but the prosecution does have the power to take steps to mitigate and even prevent the adverse effects of defense counsel's incompetence. This can mean explaining the significance of evidence to an obtuse counsel. It can mean refraining from an objection when opposing counsel seeks to introduce admissible evidence by an inadmissible procedure. It can mean suggesting motions and arguments to opposing counsel. It can mean doing any number of creative things to see to it that when the jury says "guilty," it is because the defendant is guilty, not because he has incompetent counsel. If moral and ethical considerations do not move you to such actions, then consider the post-conviction consequences of taking advantage of the bungler.

PRACTICAL EXERCISE

You are in trial with Lawrence Litigator, a true believer who is also an obstructionist and a circumventer. Every motion opposing counsel has filed and every objection he has made, he has managed to work in an attack on your

---

[13] Sochor v. Florida, 504 U.S. 527, 547, 112 S.Ct. 2114, 2127 (1992) (Stevens, J., concurring in part & dissenting in part); Prewitt v. State, 761 N.E.2d 862 (Ind.App. 2002); Blue v. State, 41 S.W.3d 129 (Tex.Crim.App. 2000).

[14] Every U.S. jurisdiction has a procedure whereby a defendant can collaterally attack convictions obtained by unconstitutional means. See, e.g., Ariz. R.Crim.P. 32; Fla.R.Crim.P. 3.850; Hawaii R.Penal Proc. 40.

integrity. He has opposed every suggestion you have made to expedite the trial, and he has repeatedly attempted to place inadmissible evidence before the jury. You are tired, frustrated, and angry, but so far you have been able to keep your temper in check. You rest, and Litigator announces as his first witness the name of a deputy sheriff you know to be out of state on vacation. Litigator demands that you tell him where the deputy is, and you advise him that the witness is on vacation in Hawaii. Litigator demands to know why you released the deputy from subpoena. You reply that you did not subpoena him and remind Litigator that you advised him weeks ago you would not be calling the officer. There is no record of this communication, and Litigator tells the judge that you never said any such thing. Litigator demands that you be held in contempt for failure to subpoena a witness whom you disclosed in discovery, and he further demands that the case be dismissed because of prosecutorial misconduct. Failing dismissal, he wants a mistrial. He shows the judge a page from the deputy's deposition which contains testimony he claims to be exculpatory. You look at the testimony and determine that it would be marginally relevant, but not especially helpful, to the defendant's claim of self-defense. How do you respond?

CHAPTER 4

THE CHARGING DECISION

■ ■ ■

The first two questions a prosecutor should ask: "Can we charge? Should we charge?"—Teresa Drake[1]

The third question the prosecutor should ask is: What should we charge?—Anonymous

A. PROVABILITY, PROPRIETY, PRUDENCE

Any criminal prosecution begins with someone believing that a wrong has been done and that somebody should be punished for it. Many times, when prosecutors ask complainants how they know that a potential defendant is worthy of punishment, the complainants will reply "I just know he's guilty." That may be sufficient to give rise to a desire for revenge, but not to achieve justice in a court of law. The charging decision is arguably the most distinctive and the most difficult aspect of the prosecutor's role. In making the decision, the prosecutor makes a three-stage evaluation:

(1) Provability: Does sufficient evidence exist to warrant the filing of charges?

(2) Propriety: Notwithstanding the existence of sufficient evidence to warrant charging, is the public interest served by the filing of charges?

(3) Prudence: Given the propriety of filing charges, which charges (among those supported by the evidence) should be filed in this particular case?

B. THE PROVABILITY EVALUATION

In seeking a provable charge, you ask three preliminary questions: (1) Has a crime been committed? (Criminality). (2) Did the defendant commit it? (Culpability). (3) Can we prove it? (Convictability). In order to be able to answer these questions, you must be knowledgeable in three areas—the substantive law, the available evidence, and the procedural law. The substantive law establishes criminality. The evidence establishes

[1] Emeritus Senior Legal Skills Professor, Levin College of Law; formerly Domestic Violence Division Chief, State Attorney's Office, Gainesville, Florida.

culpability. The procedural law establishes convictability. Of the three questions, criminality is usually the easiest issue to resolve. Culpability can be somewhat more difficult, and convictability oftentimes can present a conundrum. You resolve criminality by reference to the substantive law. Did an act contravene the law? If so, you have answered the first question in the affirmative. You resolve the question of culpability by reference to the available evidence. What facts tell you the defendant committed the crime? You decide the third question, convictability, by reference to the procedural law. What percentage of the available evidence will the exclusionary and procedural rules allow you to present to the jury? What is a jury likely to decide based upon only the evidence that is presented? Having knowledge of inadmissible evidence of guilt can make this third assessment very difficult.

1. A HYPOTHETICAL PROVABILITY EVALUATION

Suppose you know that Violet Smith dies when her car collides with a car driven by Jack Woodley. Should Jack be charged with Violet's death? You do not know unless you know two things: the substantive law of homicide and the evidence available to prove that Jack broke that law. In most jurisdictions it is against the law to drive with a blood alcohol level above 0.08 and thereby cause the death of another human being. Suppose Jack is above 0.08. Should he be charged? You need more facts. Suppose Violet ran a stop sign and T-boned Jack. He did not cause the accident and under most DUI manslaughter statutes should not be charged. Suppose Jack T-boned Violet and the evidence shows that Jack was DUI. Let us revisit the three questions:

(1) Criminality: Has a crime been committed? Yes.

(2) Culpability: Did Jack Woodley commit it? Yes.

(3) Convictability: Can you prove it? Maybe.

You have determined that Jack Woodley is guilty of DUI manslaughter, but there is still the possibility that you should not charge him. Even if he is guilty, you must be reasonably certain you can convict him before you charge him. Can you prove it? Here you must have a firm grasp of the procedural law, especially that part of the procedural law which governs the submission of evidence before a jury.

When Officer Baynes arrived, he saw Violet's car T-boned by Jack's and Violet dead under the steering wheel. Officer Baynes saw that Jack's car was empty, and Jack was sitting under a tree near the crash. Otto Onlywitness, an elderly gentleman with a bad heart, reported that he saw Jack T-bone Violet, stagger out of the car, and sit under the tree. Officer Baynes immediately arrested Jack and Jack refused to make a statement. When the EMT's arrived to transport Jack to the hospital, Officer Baynes had them draw Jack's blood for submission to the crime lab. Jack's blood alcohol level was 0.28. While the EMT's were loading Jack for transport to the hospital, Otto Onlywitness had a massive heart attack and died on the scene.

You do not need a law degree to know that a jury will never hear Otto's statement that Jack was driving. It is hearsay, and the procedural law of evidence says it is inadmissible. When you subtract the inadmissible evidence from all the known evidence, all you have is Jack sitting drunk on the side of the road near a fatal car crash. Without more, you have no legal proof that Jack was driving. The answer to question three under the state of available evidence, "You cannot prove it."

Suppose that you know Jack has hired Millicent Malpractice as his lawyer. Millicent, who slept through Evidence class in law school, never heard of the hearsay rule. You have a 99% certainty that Millicent will fail to object to the proffer of Otto's hearsay statement and that you can convict Jack at trial. Suppose Jack hires Peter Pleabargain, who never goes to trial and always gets his clients to plead guilty. Suppose you know you will appear before Judge Hardcase, who never dismisses a charge, never suppresses evidence, and never enters a directed verdict. Should you file charges in any of these eventualities? This is not Renaissance Italy and you are not Niccolo Machiavelli. The end does not justify the means. The prosecutor's job is not to get convictions but to do justice. What should you do, then? If you work in an office where the elected prosecutor has abdicated his law enforcement role for fear of being sued, your inquiry is over—you close the case with a no file decision and go on to the next. If you work in an office where the elected prosecutor performs all three facets of the job, then you roll up your sleeves and actively help law enforcement find additional evidence upon which to base a charge. Only after all avenues for discovery of evidence have been explored with no success do you finally decide that you cannot file charges.

2. THE EVIDENTIAL STAGE

In England, the Crown Prosecution Service calls the provability evaluation the "Evidential Stage,"[2] and requires something more than a bare bones legally provable case before charges can be filed. Crown prosecutors must be satisfied that there is enough admissible evidence to provide a "realistic prospect of conviction."[3] A realistic prospect of conviction is a heavier burden than mere probable cause, but is less than proof beyond a reasonable doubt.[4] Evidence sufficient to provide a reasonable prospect of conviction must pass the dual tests of both

---

[2] The Code for Crown Prosecutors, Crown Prosecution Service, 2018, ¶ 4.6. (Hereafter cited as Crown Code).

[3] Id.

[4] Id. ¶ 4.7.

reliability[5] and admissibility.[6] Although the *Code for Crown Prosecutors* does not specifically address the issue of the persuasiveness of the evidence, this concern is addressed by the criteria set forth by the *Code* for assessing reliability.[7]

3. THE SUFFICIENCY OF THE EVIDENCE TEST

Canada's *Public Prosecution Service Deskbook* calls the provability evaluation the "Reasonable Prospect of Conviction Standard."[8] This test asks how strong the case is likely to be when presented at trial. It assumes that the fact finder will act impartially and according to law.[9] The *Deskbook* requires more than a prima facie case. There must be a "reasonable prospect of conviction."[10] This doesn't mean that the finder of fact will find the defendant guilty upon the production of sufficient evidence. It presumes that the case will be tried before "an impartial trier of fact acting in accordance with the law."[11] Sometimes this presumption is in error. Frequently, due to public sentiment, a conviction will be nearly impossible. Other times the mood of the community will be so hostile to the defendant that a conviction is almost assured on the presentation of any evidence whatsoever. We shall discuss these matters when we get to the Propriety Evaluation.

The *Deskbook* requires that the "Reasonable Prospect of Conviction Standard" be applied not only during the charging phase of the prosecution, but also throughout the course of the entire prosecution. It is particularly important for Crown counsel to reconsider the criteria when new and credible information comes to light, including from the accused."[12] This is an excellent requirement. During the pendency of the prosecution, you should review the charging decision and then review it again. The initial charging decision is seldom made in the light of total knowledge. As the case progresses, new and additional information comes to light which can completely change your assessment of the case. It is entirely proper, in light of this new information, to drop or change the charges, or to modify the objective of the prosecution.

---

5 Id. ¶ ¶ 4.8.

6 Id. ¶ 5.4a

7 Paragraphs 5.4e and 5.4f of the Code speak to various issues affecting credibility of the evidence.

8 *Public Prosecution Service of Canada Deskbook*, Director of Prosecutions, 2023, ¶ 4.1. <https://www.ppsc-sppc.gc.ca/eng/pub/fpsd-sfpg/fps-sfp/tpd/p2/ch03.html>. (Hereafter cited as PPSC Deskbook).

9 Federal Prosecution Service Deskbook ¶ 15.3.1; Commonwealth Prosecution Policy ¶ 2.5.

10 PPSC Deskbook ¶ 4.1

11 Id.

12 *Id.* ¶ 4.

Another significant factor that the *Deskbook* warns against is "tunnel-vision."[13] This is a common problem. Upon your evaluation of the evidence presented at intake, you decide that Dirk Dastardly is definitely guilty. You embrace this belief so completely that when confronted with contrary evidence, you immediately dismiss it without investigation. The philosopher Saul Kripke called this the dogmatism paradox. He maintained that if we know the Earth revolves around the Sun, we may be justified in rejecting out of hand any evidence to the contrary, but we are being irrational.[14] Where we run into problems with Kripkean Dogmatism, is where we believe a defendant guilty and further believe *ipso facto* that evidence negating guilt is automatically false. This is not only irrational, it is fatal to the proper administration of justice. The fact of a defendant's guilt is never as firmly established as the fact that the Earth revolves around the Sun. If we are doing our job properly, we will consider all evidence, the good, the bad, and the ugly.

The American Bar Association recognizes the provability evaluation by stating that a charge should not be made unless it is grounded on both probable cause and admissible evidence sufficient to support a conviction.[15] The National District Attorneys' Association Standards on screening simply state that the prosecutor file charges "which he or she reasonably believes can be substantiated by admissible evidence."[16]

The provability evaluation should be an exercise in weighing the truth value of the evidence, the believability of the evidence, and the admissibility of the evidence. No hard and fast rules have been set for resolving these issues, but there are a number of common sense factors that you would do well to consult before deciding to file charges: Is the evidence admissible? Is there any reason to question the reliability of admissions by the defendant? Do any witnesses have motives to embellish their testimony? Is there any reason to question a witness's powers of observation or recall? Do any witnesses have a motive to lie? Does any witnesses have "baggage" in the form of collateral matters (e.g., scores of previous felony convictions) which will seriously damage their credibility? Will the witness make a "good" witness; in other words, will the witness impress the jury favorably or unfavorably? Can the witness withstand cross-examination? Does the witness have a physical or mental disability which will affect his credibility? Is there too much conflict in the testimony? Is there too little conflict in the testimony? Can you procure the attendance of all necessary witnesses? If you have child witnesses, will they be able to testify? How reliable is the evidence of identity? With multiple defendants,

---

13 PPSC Deskbook ¶ 2.

14 K Lajevardi, Kripke and the Dogmatism Paradox, philpapers.org, 2016. <https://philpapers.org/archive/LAJKAT.pdf>.

15 ABA Prosecution Standard 3–4.3(a).

16 National Prosecution Standard 4–2.2.

can you really prove the case against each and every one of them at either a consolidated or severed trial?

C. THE PROPRIETY EVALUATION

When prosecutors start asking questions about the believability of truthful evidence as a consideration, they have begun to leave off asking questions about provability and begun to ask questions about the propriety of filing charges. What if the evidence of guilt is both truthful and believable, but there is a high probability bordering on certainty that a jury is not going to convict the defendant? We have here completely left the realm of provability and entered the realm of propriety. Is it proper to charge a defendant with a crime knowing that the jury is likely to ignore good evidence and find the defendant not guilty? There is another question which might be asked as a consideration of propriety. Are there any situations where you should decline to file charges, notwithstanding the guilt of the accused and the near certainty of conviction by a jury? In the provability evaluation, the prosecutor merely looks to the evidence to determine the sufficiency of the evidence to demonstrate criminality, culpability, and convictability. The propriety evaluation does not ask questions of sufficiency, but of weight. You still consider factors of criminality, culpability, and convictability, not as to their existence, but as to their weight. In the propriety evaluation, you add a fourth C—consequence. What are the consequences of filing charges? To the victim? To the defendant? To society as a whole? The *Code for Crown Prosecutors*, calls this evaluation the "Public Interest Stage" of the charging decision: "The public interest must be considered in each case where there is enough evidence to provide a realistic prospect of conviction."[17] "In every case where there is sufficient evidence to justify a prosecution or to offer an out-of-court disposal, prosecutors must go on to consider whether a prosecution is required in the public interest."[18]

1. FACTORS WHICH SHOULD BE CONSIDERED

The *Code for Crown Prosecutors* lists a variety of factors which prosecutors should consider when making the propriety evaluation. These factors include:

a. The seriousness of the offense. ¶ 4.14(a). If I shove you while we are standing in line at the movie theater, but I inflict no injury upon you, I have technically committed a battery. This sort of *de minimis* infraction of the law would probably be better left unprosecuted.

---

[17] Crown Code ¶ 5.7.

[18] Crown Code ¶ 4.9.

b. The suspect's level of culpability. ¶ 4.14(b). How involved was the suspect in the crime charged? To what extent was the offense premeditated or planned? How did the suspect benefit from the offense? What is the prior criminal record of the suspect? Is the suspect likely to reoffend?

c. What is the effect of the offense upon the victim? ¶ 4.14(c). Did the suspect violate a position of trust? Was the victim particularly vulnerable? Will a prosecution have an adverse effect on the victim? What are the wishes of the victim as relates to prosecution?

d. What is the suspect's age and maturity level? ¶ 4.14(d).

e. What is the impact to the community? ¶ 4.14(e).

f. Is prosecution an appropriate response? ¶ 4.14(f). Is this a matter which could be disposed of by diversion? Does the cost of prosecution outweigh any benefit which might accrue from conviction?

g. Do sources of information need to be protected? ¶ 4.14(g). If the only evidence of guilt comes from a confidential informant whose identity should be protected, then no prosecution might be the appropriate decision.

ABA Prosecution Standard 3–4.4 gives a list of sixteen factors to be considered in the propriety evaluation:

a. The strength of the case. 3–4.4(i).

b. The prosecutor's doubt that the accused is in fact guilty. 3–4.4(ii).

c. The extent or absence of harm caused by the offense. 3–4.4(iii).

d. The impact of prosecution or non-prosecution on the public welfare. 3–4.4(iv).

e. The background and characteristics of the offender, including any voluntary restitution or efforts at rehabilitation. 3–4.4(v).

f. Whether the authorized or likely punishment or collateral consequences are disproportionate in relation to the particular offense or the offender. 3–4.4(vi).

g. The views and motives of the victim or complainant. 3–4.4(vii).

h. Any improper conduct by law enforcement. 3–4.4(viii).

i. Unwarranted disparate treatment of similarly situated persons. 3–4.4(ix).

j. Potential collateral impact on third parties, including witnesses or victims. 3–4.4(x).

k. Cooperation of the offender in the apprehension or conviction of others. 3–4.4(xi).

l. The possible influence of any cultural, ethnic, socioeconomic or other improper biases. 3–4.4(xii).

m. Changes in law or policy. 3–4.4(xiii).

n. The fair and efficient distribution of limited prosecutorial resources. 3–4.4(xiv).

o. The likelihood of prosecution by another jurisdiction. 3–4.4(xv).

p. Whether the public's interests in the matter might be appropriately vindicated by available civil, regulatory, administrative, or private remedies. 3–4.4(xv).

Finally, National Prosecution Standard 4–1.3 lists these considerations:

a. Doubt about the accused's guilt. 4–1.3a.

b. Insufficiency of admissible evidence to support conviction. 4–1.3b.

c. The negative impact of a prosecution on a victim. 4–1.3c.

d. The availability of adequate civil remedies. 4–1.3d.

e. The availability of suitable diversion and rehabilitative programs. 4–1.3e.

f. Provisions for restitution. 4–1.3f.

g. Likelihood of prosecution by another criminal justice authority. 4–1.3g.

h. Whether non-prosecution would assist in achieving other legitimate goals, such as the investigation or prosecution of more serious offenses. 4–1.3h.

i. The charging decisions made for similarly situated defendants. 4–1.3i.

j. The attitude and mental status of the accused. 4–1.3j.

k. Undue hardship that would be caused to the accused by the prosecution. 4–1.3k.

l. A history of non-enforcement of the applicable law. 4–1.3*l*.

m. Failure of law enforcement to perform necessary duties or investigations. 4–1.3m.

n. The expressed desire of an accused to release potential civil claims against victims, witnesses, law enforcement agencies and their personnel, or the prosecutor and his personnel, where such desire is expressed after having the opportunity to obtain advice of counsel and is knowing and voluntary. 4–1.3n.

o. Whether the alleged crime represents a substantial departure from the accused's history of living a law-abiding life. 4–1.3*o*.

p. Whether the accused has already suffered substantial loss in connection with the alleged crime. 4–1.3p.

q. Whether the size of the loss or the extent of the harm caused by the alleged crime is too small to warrant a criminal sanction. 4–1.3q.

In the Propriety Evaluation, common sense serves you far better than the common law.

2. FACTORS WHICH SHOULD NOT BE CONSIDERED

In making the prosecution decision, the race, religion, national or ethnic origin, gender, or sexual orientation of the defendant, victim, or witnesses should have no bearing.[19] Nor should the political associations, activities, or beliefs of the defendant, victim, or witnesses play any part in the decision. Personal feelings about the defendant or victim should play no part in the charging decision,[20] nor in any other aspect of the prosecution. In smaller communities, where prosecutors know a large segment of the community, and where certain individuals become regulars in court, there is a real danger that personal feelings might cloud the judgement. In larger jurisdictions where the prosecutor is less likely to know the defendants or victims, there is still a small segment of the population with which he can become very familiar—the defense bar. Prosecutors may have personal feelings toward, animosities against, and axes to grind with various members of the defense bar, but they cannot allow these personal feelings to color their judgement when handling cases against those lawyers. Nor should they allow their judgement to be swayed by considerations of possible political advantage or disadvantage,[21] or any other considerations of the effect of the decision upon their personal or professional circumstances.[22]

---

[19] ABA Prosecution Standard 3–1.6(a); National Prosecution Standard 4.1–4a.

[20] ABA Prosecution Standard 3–4.4(b)(i).

[21] National Prosecution Standard 4.1–4b.

[22] National Prosecution Standard 4.1–4c.

Your conviction rate is not a factor to consider when making the charging decision.[23] Vince Lombardi is reputed to have said that "Winning isn't everything. It's the only thing." Many people subscribe to Lombardi's dictum to the extent that they take great pains to win. Winning can be achieved by diligent preparation and flawless execution. It can also be achieved by careful selection of opponents. Although you should file only cases with a reasonable prospect of conviction, you can pad your won/lost percentage by filing only the very best of cases and dismissing cases with even the smallest prospect of acquittal. If a crime has been committed; if the defendant has committed it; if you can prove it; you should not decline to file it because the proof is less than ideal or because there is a prospect of acquittal due to jury apathy. Nobody likes to lose, but fear of losing should not deter you from filing charges or going to trial. To those prosecutors who say, "I have never lost a case," must come the reply, "You have not tried enough cases." At any time in any office there are cases which have an uncomfortably high possibility of acquittal but which should be filed and tried. The worth of a prosecutor is not measured by his ability to win ironclad cases—anyone can win such a case. The worth of a prosecutor is measured by his ability to recognize the marginal cases which should nonetheless be filed, and then to win those marginal cases. In order to display an ability to win marginal cases, you must try marginal cases. If you make a habit of trying marginal cases, you will lose. Inexperienced or incapable prosecutors will file a marginal case because they lack the judgement to recognize it as a marginal case. Good prosecutors will file a marginal case because they have the judgement to determine which marginal cases should nevertheless be filed and which marginal cases should not. Depending upon the interplay of the factors we have previously discussed, you should tolerate a lesser probability of conviction in certain types of cases and require a higher probability of conviction in others—and you should never let fear of losing cause you to dismiss a case worthy of prosecution.

3. ALTERNATIVES TO PROSECUTION

In weighing all of the foregoing factors, you are not simply deciding the issue of whether to charge. These factors also help you determine what to charge and also what remedies to seek. The mere fact that an action by the defendant violates the letter of the law does not mean that it would be within the spirit of the law to prosecute him to the fullest extent possible, nor does it mean that you should seek the most severe remedy available. Justice might well be served by prosecuting a defendant who committed a felony in misdemeanor court. Or it could be served by measures short of prosecution. Modern court systems have all sorts of pretrial diversion programs, pretrial intervention programs, and deferred prosecution

[23] National Prosecution Standard 4–1.4a.

programs. You should use them but should vigilantly guard against the tendency to want to use deferred prosecution programs as dumping grounds for bad cases. You should never say to yourself, "I'll probably lose this case at trial, so I'll see if I can get the defendant to agree to pretrial diversion." This takes the teeth out of pretrial diversion programs. Defendants in pretrial programs often violate the programs' terms. These violations often occur months after the commencement of the program. When that bad case that you put into the program several months ago comes back to you for prosecution on a violation, it has not improved, it has gotten worse; but now it is imperative that you prosecute that bad case. If you make a habit of dismissing diversion cases when the defendant violates, word will get around among the defendants that an offer of diversion is an admission that you think your case is a loser.

D. THE PRUDENCE EVALUATION

The final issue the prosecutor confronts is the prudence evaluation. What charges should you file? Because almost any criminal transaction will offend against a spectrum of laws, you will therefore have several charges to choose from. The NDAA Standards prescribe that the prosecutor should file only those charges which adequately encompass the defendant's offense and are consistent with the interests of justice.[24] The ABA Standards say that the prosecutor should not file charges greater in number or degree than are necessary to fairly reflect the gravity of the offense.[25] Both sets of standards require that the charging decision must be supported by a reasonable belief that the charges can be substantiated at trial by admissible evidence.[26] The *Code for Crown Prosecutors* strictly forbids the filing of extra charges for use as bargaining chips in plea negotiations.[27]

1. OBJECTIVES OF THE PRUDENCE EVALUATION

In deciding which charges to file, you should aim at filing charges which reflect the seriousness and extent of the offense, give the court adequate powers to sentence and impose appropriate sanctions, and enable you to present the case clearly and simply.[28] The ideal charge or charges will adequately address the wrong committed by the defendant, significantly enhance the strength of the state's case, provide for an appropriate punishment of the defendant, and result in restitution to all victims.[29] In other words, the charge should adequately address the

[24] National Prosecution Standard 4–2.2.

[25] ABA Prosecution Function Standard 3–4.4(d).

[26] NDAA National Prosecution Standard 43.3; ABA Prosecution Function Standard 3–3.9(f).

[27] Crown Code ¶ 6.3.

[28] Crown Code ¶ 6.1

[29] Rev.Code Wash. § 13.40.077(3)(a).

criminality, allow an appropriate consequence for the culpability, and insure maximum convictability. You should not charge higher crimes than are called for by the circumstances of the case, nor should you file more charges than are called for by the circumstances of the case.[30]

Another prudence consideration involves the sufficiency of the available information. One old prosecutor described the charging decision as: "Making life-changing decisions on the basis of insufficient evidence." Although charging decisions are usually made upon incomplete information, you should try to make sure that you have enough of the story to feel comfortable in filing.

Ideally, before filing you should have been provided with interviews of the material witnesses, the results of laboratory tests, and a statement from the accused. In the early days of cannabis enforcement, charges were sometimes made when the substance involved was oregano or some other plant matter. You would want to avoid such embarrassment. Because laboratory reports are notoriously slow in coming, you will often file cases when the results are pending. In one small rural jurisdiction, the police were notorious for arresting without bothering to speak to the accused. The local prosecutor's office solved the problem by declaring that they would not file charges without either a statement from the accused or a good explanation why no statement was taken.

2. A HYPOTHETICAL PRUDENCE EVALUATION

Bart Barfly and Nevin Numbskull are playing a game of pool at the Inferno Club when they get into an argument over whether Barfly made a proper shot. Barfly announces that he is going to kill Numbskull and proceeds to break a pool cue over Numbskull's head. Numbskull shakes his head while Barfly arms himself with another pool cue, and as Barfly raises the cue to deliver another blow, Numbskull knocks Barfly out cold with a right cross. Both require medical attention. Dr. Shotz puts a butterfly bandage on Numbskull's head and sets Barfly's broken jaw. Few prosecutors would consider charging Numbskull, who arguably acted in self-defense. There are a number of possible charges that could be brought against Barfly. Barfly announced an intent to kill and proceeded to carry out that intent by striking Numbskull to the head with a deadly weapon. When that first assault failed, he took steps to make a second attempt but was prevented by Numbskull's pugilistic virtuosity. You could charge attempted murder. Or you could ignore the evidence of threat and charge Barfly with aggravated battery. A third option is to charge Barfly with the misdemeanor offense of simple battery. Which of these three charges is the best charge to file? In most jurisdictions, attempted murder is a felony

[30] Rev.Code Wash. § 13.40.077(3)(b).

which carries a draconian penalty; aggravated battery is a felony with a lesser penalty; and battery is a misdemeanor.

In deciding what charge to file, you consider a number of issues. You look at convictability considerations to try to decide what charge you can prove, what charge you can prove most easily, and what you can hope to accomplish with each possible charge. You look at consequence considerations to determine what you should aim to accomplish with the charging decision. You must also look at case theory considerations, which we will discuss more fully in the chapter on case theory. In brief, you must look at your case theory, the likely defense theory, and the issues that arise from the tension between the two competing case theories. You must craft a charge that is most compatible with your case theory and most likely to defeat the defense theory.

Let us return the Barfly case. Attempted murder gives you the maximum flexibility as to sentence, but quite possibly not maximum convictability. Premeditation is a complex concept, and jury instructions defining premeditation are confusing even to lawyers. On so heavy and so complex a charge, it is possible that a jury may throw up its hands in total confusion and find the defendant not guilty. If Barfly had broken several pool cues over Numbskull's head, and Numbskull had lain near death in the hospital for days, the charge would be easier to sustain, but Numbskull simply shook his head and knocked Barfly out.

Aggravated battery gives less flexibility as to sentencing, but is the flexibility enough? If Barfly is a first-time offender, and Numbskull's only medical expense is a butterfly bandage and an aspirin, you need less flexibility than the charge gives you. If Barfly has a long history of crimes of violence or Numbskull has significant medical expenses, then the lengthy sentence achievable with an aggravated battery charge might be advisable. Aggravated battery, being simply a battery with a deadly weapon, is a much more convictable charge than attempted murder. The jury's biggest hangup would probably be determining whether a pool cue is a deadly weapon. A typical jury instruction defines "deadly weapon" in the following manner:

> A "deadly weapon" is any object * * * that will likely cause death or great bodily harm if used in the ordinary and usual manner contemplated by its design and construction.[31]

Given this definition, the defense can mount a cogent argument that the pool cue was not a deadly weapon because the way it was used produced neither death nor great bodily harm. If the jury buys this argument, then you will wind up with a battery conviction. The jury will be more inclined to buy the argument because of the "street justice" which has already been

[31] Florida Standard Jury Instructions in Criminal Cases § 10.5.

meted out to Barfly. Remember, at the conclusion of the confrontation, Barfly was unconscious and Numbskull was victorious. Should you then charge simple battery, apparently the most convictable charge? Or should you file aggravated battery with the caveat that you will be willing to accept a battery plea? Barfly should be more willing to plead to battery if confronted with the possibility of an aggravated battery conviction than if facing only the possibility of a battery conviction. Is this a proper factor to consider in filing charges? Would it be acceptable to simply file the misdemeanor battery charge and threaten to refile the charge as aggravated battery if Barfly refused to plead to battery? In *United States v. Goodwin*,[32] a prosecutor made good on such a threat to file felony charges, and the Supreme Court held that absent evidence of malice or vindictiveness, the action was a proper exercise of prosecutorial discretion. Is such a threat *per se* malicious? Suppose, due to caseload, the prosecutor's office instituted a policy of following the "Hundred Stitch Rule" (If the victim is sewed up with fewer than 100 stitches, file misdemeanor charges), but the office also adopted the policy that if the act could be shown to be a felony and the defendant wanted a jury trial, the case would be refiled in felony court so that the defendant could have a jury trial on felony charges. Many prosecutors' offices have such a policy. If the crime is a felony but not really a serious felony, they will file a misdemeanor charge because misdemeanor charges make their way through the system much more expeditiously than felony charges. If, however, the defendant wants to make the handling of the case as much work as if it had originally been filed in felony court, then the reasoning goes that the increased work deserves the increased potential reward of a felony conviction. Thus, the various considerations of convictability and consequence help to determine the appropriate charge.

Although the three evaluations (provability, propriety, and prudence) have been dealt with sequentially, they are normally conducted concurrently. Indeed, sometimes it is difficult to categorize a specific rationale for your decision as to whether it is a consideration of provability, propriety, or prudence. Whatever the rationale for your charging decision, you should record it. Recording these considerations makes it easier to explain decisions when they are the subject of inquiry. It also makes it easier to reconstruct what you were thinking when, several months later, you pick up the file again and ask yourself "Why in the world did I file that charge?"

E. THE GRAND JURY

The decision to prosecute may not always be a unilateral decision made by the prosecutor. Sometimes charges must be approved by a grand

[32] 457 U.S. 368, 102 S.Ct. 2485 (1982).

jury. Sometimes it is prudent to consult the grand jury even though it is not necessary. The roots of the grand jury go as far back as 997 when Ethelred the Unready, a Saxon king of England, decreed: "Let twelve elder freemen, and the foreman with them, retire and swear upon the holy book which is given into their hands that they will not accuse any innocent person, nor screen any criminal."[33] Thus was born the accusatorial body which would evolve into our modern grand jury. Ethelred's charge to the "twelve elder freemen" was very similar to the oath that a modern grand jury takes, swearing that it "shall not make a presentment against a person because of envy, hatred, or malice, and * * * shall not fail to make a presentment against a person because of love, fear, or reward."[34] In 1166 the Norman King Henry II established the Assize of Clarendon, which provided for an accusatory body of twelve men to make sworn complaints of criminal activity.[35] This proto-grand jury appeared before itinerant judges appointed by the king. In a secret meeting, the judges would present the jurors with a list of crimes. The judges would then go down the list crime by crime asking whether or not the jurors knew of any man in their jurisdiction who had committed the crime. The jurors were not precluded from making accusations because they might have been witnesses to the crime, and the judges could question the jurors to determine whether the charges were well-founded.[36] The grand jury remained a tool of the King until 1681, when the London grand jury considered the complaint of King Charles II against the Earl of Shaftesbury and one Stephen Colledge, political enemies of the King. Charles wanted public proceedings before the grand jury, but the grand jury insisted on meeting in a secret session. The king wanted a quick indictment, but the grand jury refused to indict either man.[37] This twofold defiance of the king's will (meeting in secret and refusing to indict) established the tradition of grand jury secrecy, and won for the grand jury its fame as a "shield of justice * * * because it is protection of the innocent against unjust prosecution."[38]

Writing in the late 1760's the English jurist William Blackstone described the operation of the grand jury in this fashion:

> As many as appear upon this panel, are sworn upon the grand jury, to the amount of twelve at the least, and not more than twenty three; that twelve may be a majority. Which number, as

---

[33] Bennett v. Kalamazoo Circuit Judge, 183 Mich. 200, 206, 150 N.W. 141, 144 (1914).

[34] Fla.Stat. § 905.10.

[35] Assize of Clarendon, The Avalon Project. 2007. Yale Law School. <https://avalon.law.yale.edu/medieval/assizecl.asp>.

[36] Petition of McNair, 324 Pa. 48, 56 n. 1, 187 A. 498, 502 n. 1 (1936).

[37] United States v. Navarro-Vargas, 408 F.3d 1184, 1190–1191 (9th Cir. en banc, 2005).

[38] The Supreme Court Committee on Standard Jury Instructions, Florida Grand Jury Handbook <https://miamisao.com/wp-content/uploads/2020/12/Florida-Grand-Jury-Handbook.pdf>.

> well as the constitution itself, we find exactly described, so early as the laws of king Ethelred. * * *[39]
>
> The grand juries are previously instructed in the articles of their enquiry, by a charge from the judge who presides upon the bench. They then withdraw, to sit and receive indictments, which are preferred to them in the name of the king * * *; and they are only to hear evidence on behalf of the prosecution: for the finding of an indictment is only in the nature of an enquiry or accusation, which is afterwards to be tried and determined; and the grand jury are only to enquire upon their oaths, whether there be sufficient cause to call upon the party to answer it. A grand jury however ought to be thoroughly persuaded of the truth of an indictment, so far as their evidence goes; and not to rest satisfied merely with remote probabilities: a doctrine, that might be applied to very oppressive purposes.* * *[40]
>
> When the grand jury have heard the evidence, if they think it a groundless accusation * * *, they assert in English, more absolutely, "not a true bill;" and then the party is discharged without farther answer. But a fresh bill may afterwards be preferred to a subsequent grand jury. If they are satisfied of the truth of the accusation, they then endorse upon it, "a true bill[.]" * * * The indictment is then said to be found, and the party stands indicted. But, to find a bill, there must at least twelve of the jury agree.[41]

Not much has changed in the past 240 years. Grand juries usually number between 15 and 23.[42] They meet in secret to consider charging certain types of crimes, and they are assisted in their investigations by the prosecuting attorney for the jurisdiction in which they sit. A vote of at least twelve is required to find an indictment, and a no true bill is not a bar to further prosecution. The prosecutor may present the case to a subsequent grand jury, or if he works in a state which allows prosecution by information, he may file an information charging the defendant with a crime. The Constitution requires the government to prosecute by grand jury indictment on all felony charges, but due process does not require the states to employ a grand jury. Indeed, the Supreme Court long ago held that in state court a prosecution for capital murder need not be by indictment if it were prosecuted "by information after examination and commitment by a magistrate, certifying to the probable guilt of the defendant, with the right

[39] 4 Blackstone's Commentaries on the Laws of England, *299, The Avalon Project. 2007. Yale Law School. <https://avalon.law.yale.edu/18th_century/blackstone_bk4ch23.asp>.

[40] Id. at *300.

[41] Id. at *301.

[42] E.g. Ga.Code § 15–12–61(a) (16–23 members); Mass.Gen.Laws 277 § 2 (23 members).

on his part to the aid of counsel, and to the cross-examination of the witnesses produced for the prosecution * * *."[43]

The grand jury is selected for a limited term, usually six to eighteen months, depending upon the jurisdiction.[44] It sits in secret, with its express purpose being to determine whether probable cause exists for the prosecution of individuals whose cases are referred to them. Some jurisdictions prosecute all felony cases by grand jury indictment.[45] Others require only the most serious of crimes to be prosecuted by grand jury indictment.[46] The local prosecutor acts as advisor to the grand jury,[47] but the grand jury is independent of the prosecutor and may investigate matters on its own initiative.[48] It may even investigate the prosecutor, and grand juries have done so on more than one occasion.[49] Although the grand jury has historically been a local institution, within the last several years some states have created grand juries with statewide jurisdiction.[50]

1. PROCEEDINGS BEFORE THE GRAND JURY

A typical grand jury proceeding begins with the summoning of a venire of potential jurors, from which the judge will draw at random the specified number of persons required to make up the grand jury.[51] The grand jury is then sworn and given preliminary instructions by the judge. The officers of the grand jury typically include a foreperson, a vice foreperson, and a clerk. The foreperson may be appointed by the judge or the judge may defer to the grand jury to elect their own foreperson. After being sworn and instructed, the grand jury retires to secret session, where the prosecutor presents to them whatever cases he deems appropriate. The cases are presented in the form of live testimony by witnesses and the display of properly authenticated tangible evidence, photographs, and recordings. After all evidence is submitted, the prosecutor instructs the grand jury on the law applicable to the specific case, and retires from the grand jury room to allow the grand jury to deliberate upon the matter in secret. When the grand jury has arrived at a conclusion, they summon the prosecutor back into the grand jury room, and the proper documents, either indictments or no true bills, are signed. At the conclusion of the session, the grand jury

[43] Hurtado v. California, 110 U.S. 516, 538, 4 S.Ct. 111, 122 (1884).

[44] Hawaii Rev.Stat. § 612–16(e) (one year); La.Code Crim.P. Art. 414.B. (four months to a year); Rule 6(g), Fed. R.Crim.P. (eighteen months).

[45] E.g. Del.Const. Art. 1 § 8; Virginia Code 1950, § 19.2–217.

[46] E.g. Fla.Const. Art. 1 § 15(a) (capital felonies); La.Const. Art. I § 15 (capital or life felonies).

[47] E.g. E.g. Idaho Code 19–1111 (2023).

[48] E.g. Idaho Code § 19–1108 (2023).

[49] Bennett v. Kalamazoo Circuit Judge, 183 Mich. 200, 150 N.W. 141 (1914); Ex parte Jones County Grand Jury, 705 So.2d 1308 (Miss. 1997).

[50] E.g. West's Fla.Stat.Ann. § 905.34 (2024); Wyoming Stat.1977, § 7–5–302 (2024).

[51] This description is based upon the author's personal experience in conducting numerous grand jury proceedings over a period of years from 1975 until 2005.

reconvenes in open court and presents their findings to the judge. If the defendant is in custody, the indictment is published and the grand jury is excused to be reconvened at the call of the court. If the defendant is not in custody, the indictment is sealed and a capias is issued for his arrest. The indictment remains sealed until the defendant is taken into custody. As a rule, only the elected prosecutor or his assistants, the court reporter, and the witness may appear before the grand jury while it is in secret session. Some jurisdictions provide that witnesses may be represented by counsel before the grand jury, but counsel is there only as an advisor and may not interfere with the proceedings.[52] Witnesses have historically been required to keep their testimony secret,[53] but some jurisdictions allow for varying degrees of disclosure of grand jury testimony.[54]

Normally the grand jury is satisfied to confine itself to the consideration of cases presented by the prosecutor, but sometimes the grand jury takes it upon itself to investigate other matters. More infrequently, the grand jury engages in activity of questionable wisdom. There once was an instance where a governor suspended a public official for misconduct despite the fact that the grand jury had refused to go forward with charges by filing a "no true bill of indictment" The grand jurors issued a subpoena commanding the governor to appear before them to explain his actions. He declined. When a grand jury engages in this type of activity, it is referred to as a "runaway grand jury,"[55] and such a grand jury can be a real headache for prosecutors who must deal with them.

Initially the grand jurors will be somewhat wary of the prosecutor appearing before them and will tend to question and test the evidence closely. As the prosecutor gains the grand jurors' trust, they will become more comfortable with him, asking fewer questions of the witnesses and being less critical of the evidence presented. Because grand jury proceedings are informal, and hearsay evidence is admissible,[56] it is easy for the prosecutor to make a sloppy presentation. This tendency must be guarded against vigilantly. Although the rules of evidence may be relaxed,

---

[52] E.g. West's Fla.Stat.Ann. § 905.17(2)(2024); Neb. Rev.Stat. § 29–1411(2); Wisconsin Stat. Ann. 968.45(1)(2023).

[53] E.g. Alabama Code 1975, § 12–16–216(2023); West's Ann.Ind. Code § 35–34–2–4(i)(2024).

[54] E.g. Alaska R.Crim.P. 6(*l*)(1999) (No obligation of secrecy imposed upon witnesses); Miss.Code 1972, § 13–7–25 (Defendant has right to transcript of recorded grand jury testimony); N.H. State Sup.Ct.R. 52(6) (Testimony may be disclosed on a showing of "particularized need"); North Dakota Century Code 29–10.1–30 subd. 4(Witnesses may not disclose their testimony until indictment filed and accused in custody); Rhode Island Gen. Laws 1956, § 12–11.1–5.1 (Witnesses free to disclose their testimony); West's Rev.Code Wash.Ann. § 10.27.090(5) (Testimony may be disclosed to the witness upon proper application, and to the defendant upon a showing of good cause to prevent injustice).

[55] Tyler v. Polsky, 57 A.D.2d 422, 424, 395 N.Y.S.2d 21, 23 (Sup.Ct.App. Div. 1977).

[56] E.g. Ala.R.Evid. 1101(b)(2); La.Code Evid. Art 1101C(6)(2023)(Rules of evidence not applicable to grand jury proceedings);Oregon Rev.Stat. 132.320(3)(2023) (some forms of hearsay but not others); State v. O'Daniel, 62 Hawaii 518, 523 n.3, 616 P.2d 1383, 1388 (1980) (hearsay admissible, but discouraged).

they are not completely abrogated. As the grand jurors begin to trust the prosecutor, they may ask factual questions of him rather than of the witnesses. This must be discouraged. The grand jurors also may sometimes try to deliberate while the prosecutor is instructing them on the law and may even try to enlist the prosecutor into the deliberation process. This also must be discouraged. The indictment should be a product of the grand jury's independent deliberation.

2. THE INQUISITORIAL NATURE OF THE GRAND JURY

A grand jury is an inquisitorial proceeding, not an adversarial proceeding. The prosecutor should be as satisfied by a no bill as by an indictment. Before the filing of formal charges, there is nothing to advocate for or against. There is only a decision to be made—should the defendant stand trial? At this stage of the proceeding, you are a judge, not an advocate. You as a guardian of the public trust should carefully weigh and evaluate this decision. A no file decision is not a loss. The duty to decline to file improper charges weighs every bit as heavy as the duty to file proper charges. Even in jurisdictions where only first-degree murder cases must be prosecuted by indictment, it is desirable to have all homicide cases reviewed by a grand jury. We have not far to look to find the wisdom of this policy. Twenty-three citizens picked at random off the street usually have better judgement about whether homicide charges should be filed than do prosecutors. If a grand jury does not want to indict, the prosecutor is wasting time by going ahead and informing against the defendant. Such cases seldom result in a conviction at trial. Some may wonder why a grand jury has better judgement than a prosecutor whether charges should be filed. The persuasiveness of a case is ultimately decided, not by lawyers, but by juries. A grand jury is a jury. A prosecutor is not. A grand jury will react to a case much as a petit jury will.

Critics of the grand jury system frequently chant the mantra that a good prosecutor can talk a grand jury into indicting a ham sandwich. A prosecutor who would do such a thing is dumber than a ham sandwich. After the ham sandwich is indicted, it must be convicted. Getting the indictment is just the beginning. It leads inevitably to courtroom confrontation in which the ham sandwich is defended by a lawyer. No one, not even a prosecutor, enjoys being embarrassed in public. Anyone with enough brainpower to get through law school should realize that indicting a ham sandwich will inevitably lead to a very public humiliation. A grand jury no billing a case behind closed doors should be preferable to getting embarrassed in open court with the TV cameras rolling and the newspaper reporters taking copious notes. If defendants are going to go free, they should go free at the earliest possible moment. In the best-case scenario, they are never arrested. Second best, the case is no billed by the grand jury or no filed by the prosecutor. Worst case, they are acquitted after a protracted, highly publicized jury trial, their defense costs are taxed to the county, the arresting officer is sued for false arrest, the complaining witness is sued for malicious prosecution, and the prosecutor receives universal criticism for being an incompetent as a prelude to being voted out of office. Is a good prosecutor going to ask a grand jury to indict a ham sandwich? Not a good one. A good prosecutor facilitates the grand jury's traditional role as a shield for the innocent. A good prosecutor gives the grand jury every scrap of available evidence which tends to negate the guilt of the accused.[57] A good prosecutor tells a grand jury when the evidence does not warrant an indictment and recommends to them that they not indict.[58] The wisdom of this position is strongly supported by the fiasco of the Duke LaCross Team case, in which District Attorney Michael Nifong, while campaigning for re-election, indicted three "ham sandwiches" who happened to be innocent members of the Duke LaCross team on a charge of rape. He followed this up by withholding exculpatory evidence from defense counsel, and he was eventually jailed for contempt, disbarred, sued by the wronged players, and bankrupted.[59]

3. PRESENTING A CASE TO THE GRAND JURY

What follows is a suggested procedure for presenting a homicide case to a grand jury so as to have it perform as a shield for the innocent, and as a shield for the prosecutor by no billing unwinnable cases. Draft indictments for the highest crime chargeable, every lesser included offense, and a no true bill. Invite defendants to testify.[60] Invite defense counsel to supply you with witnesses who can present the defense side to the grand jury. Present the case fairly and impartially. After every witness, invite the members of the grand jury to ask the witness questions. Listen to the questions the grand jurors ask. They will be asking the same questions that the petit jury will want you to ask. Problems that they perceive in the case are problems that a petit jury will perceive in the case. If they indict, then go out and find the evidence to resolve those issues that concerned them.

Ask the grand jury to hold you to a higher standard than probable cause. Suggest that they should not indict unless they feel strongly that a petit jury will convict. Suggest that if they do indict, they should indict for the highest crime for which they have probable cause. Present any witnesses the defense gives you. Present them fairly. Allow defendants to testify if they are willing to do so. Examine them fairly. Do not cross-examine defendants. Of course, ask questions, just save cross-examination

[57] ABA Prosecution Standard 3–4.6(e); National Prosecution Standard 4–8.2a.

[58] ABA Prosecution Standard 3–4.6(a); National Prosecution Standard 4–8.1d.

[59] See Parrish, R.B. *The Duke Lacrosse Case: A Documentary History and Analysis of the Modern Scottsboro* (BookSurge Publishing 2009).

[60] In some jurisdictions witnesses are given immunity for their testimony before the grand jury. If this is the case, be sure to get a signed waiver of immunity.

for trial. Remember Professor Wigmore's old saw about cross-examination being the "greatest legal engine ever invented for discovering the truth?"[61] It is not. It is a tool of persuasion—persuading the fact finder to arrive at your predetermined conclusion. Before the filing of charges, you have no predetermined conclusion. That's what the grand jury is for, to make the determination. If the defendant is eventually going to talk her way out of trouble, she ought to be allowed to do so at the earliest possible moment. First walk the defendant through her story, taking notes and evaluating, looking for internal inconsistencies, inconsistencies with her prior statements, and inconsistencies with the testimony of others. When you have gone completely through her story, go back and confront her with the inconsistencies, but do not be confrontational. Make the points politely, according the defendant respect and dignity, and offer her every opportunity to reconcile the inconsistencies. Explore all the ramifications of the defendant's testimony. If she seems to have omitted something helpful to her defense, bring it out. At the end of your questioning, invite the defendant to make any further statements she wishes to make, and open the floor to the grand jury for them to ask any questions they wish. If, after this, there is an indictment, you can be sure that the transcript of the defendant's testimony before the grand jury will provide a wealth of impeaching material.

Ask the grand jury if there is any other witness they would like to hear. If law enforcement has conducted a thorough investigation and you have made an evenhanded, thorough presentation, they will be satisfied with what you have shown them, but if they want to hear from someone else, procure that witness's attendance and hear her testimony. When all the witnesses are heard, instruct the grand jury on the law and answer their questions as fairly as possible, being careful not to help them deliberate. Hide nothing from them. If they ask about inadmissible matters, tell them if they insist upon hearing about those matters, they certainly may, but the petit jury is not going to hear them, and those matters should not influence their decision to indict or not indict. Discourage them from hearing the evidence, but if they insist, give it to them. The ABA Standards forbid the making of "impermissible" arguments to the grand jury.[62] No argument is proper before a grand jury. Argument is a persuasive tool designed to gain a petit jury's assent to a predetermined conclusion. Before the grand jury you have predetermined nothing. You are trying to predetermine the conclusion you will argue to the petit jury. Share your insights and analysis with the grand jury, but do not argue to them. When all is said and done, leave them with all proposed indictment forms and the no bill, instructing

---

[61] United States v. Salerno, 505 U.S. 317, 328, 112 S.Ct. 2503, 2510 (1992); Perry v. Leake, 488 U.S. 272, 283 n.7, 109 S.Ct. 594, 601 (1989); California v. Green, 399 U.S. 149, 158, 90 S.Ct. 1930, 1935 (1970).

[62] ABA Prosecution Standard 3–4.5(c).

them to have the foreperson sign the form they deem appropriate. Retire from the grand jury to await their decision.

This method is not going to get that ham sandwich indicted, but the ham sandwich was going to get acquitted before the petit jury anyway. This method results in more no bills than when the prosecutor browbeats the grand jury into indicting, but it results in more convictions when an indictment is returned. On balance, grand juries will do a far, far better job of deciding who should be charged than any prosecutor can. Prosecutors from large metropolitan offices contend that the crush of cases prevents the presentation of all homicides to the grand jury. That may well be so, but it is unfortunate. In a jurisdiction where the case load allows for it, the grand jury should consider all homicide cases.

PRACTICAL EXERCISE

You have just been transferred into the special prosecution unit upon the retirement of a senior attorney. Sarah Reed comes to you seeking the prosecution of her daughter-in-law, Grace Poole Fairfax, for murdering her son Edward Fairfax. This is a case that has been reviewed by your predecessor, who has determined that insufficient evidence exists to warrant filing charges. Sarah insists that the case be reconsidered, and you agree to look into it. You determine that Grace fatally stabbed Edward at home during an argument. Grace says that she was standing at the sink slicing meat when Edward walked up behind her, grabbed her, and spun her around to face him. They lost their balance and as they fell, he was impaled on her butcher knife. You have neither eyewitnesses nor other crime scene evidence to refute her story. You also learn that after your predecessor declined to prosecute, Sarah sued Grace in a wrongful death action and achieved a judgment against Grace for $3,000.00. During your investigation you learn the following facts previously unknown to your predecessor: (1) Before the killing Grace had told several persons that she wanted to stab Edward. (2) A few months before Edward's death Sarah attempted to stab him but failed when he barricaded himself in the bathroom. Not being able to stab Edward, Grace repeatedly stabbed the bathroom door. You have photos of the "stab wounds" to the bathroom door. Should you file or decline to file charges? Should you present the case to the grand jury? If so, what should be your objective before the grand jury?

CHAPTER 5

PLEA BARGAINING

■ ■ ■

To fight and conquer in all your battles is not supreme excellence; supreme excellence consists in breaking the enemy's resistance without fighting.—Sun Tzu[1]

Come to terms quickly with your accuser while you are on the way to court with him, or your accuser may hand you over to the judge, and the judge to the guard, and you will be thrown into prison.—*Matthew* 5:25 (NRSV)

A. GAME THEORY REVISITED

1. WINNERS AND LOSERS

As we saw in Chapter 3, a criminal trial has all the trappings of a two-player zero-sum game. You have the prosecution and the defense as the parties and you have verdicts of guilty as charged (prosecution wins/defense loses) or not guilty (defense wins/prosecution loses) as the results. Appearances can be deceptive. A criminal case is in actuality a non-zero-sum multi-player game. The players include but are not limited to the defendant, the victim, the lawyers, the witnesses, and the investigating officers. For example, the infamous Scopes Monkey Trial could be analyzed as a simple criminal prosecution, or as a duel between the greatest orator[2] and the greatest defense attorney[3] of the age, or as a contest between Darwinism and Creationism, or as a war between freedom of speech and censorship. The concept of victory was also skewed in that contest. The defense so eagerly sought a guilty verdict (they wanted an appellate decision validating Darwinism) that they asked the jury to find Scopes guilty. Scopes' conviction got reversed on appeal, to the defense's bitter disappointment. The Tennessee Supreme Court sidestepped the issue of Darwinism, reversed the case on a technicality, and counseled the prosecution not to retry the case.[4] The city fathers of Dayton, who set up the trial in hopes of some favorable publicity, saw the national press

---

1 Sun Tzu on the Art of War: The Oldest Military Treatise in the World, trans. Lionel Giles. <https://www.gutenberg.org/ebooks/66706>.

2 William Jennngs Bryant.

3 Clarence Darrow.

4 Scopes v. State, 154 Tenn. 105, 289 S.W. 363, 367 (1927).

portray their city as a laughingstock village of hayseeds. Clarence Darrow's mean-spirited conduct during the trial so alienated observers, that many analysts give the trial credit for the subsequent wave of anti-evolution laws that swept the country. The McCarthy-era morality play, *Inherit the Wind,* rewrites history as a victory for Darwinism, but the Scopes Trial in reality was a multi-player game with no winners.

Consider the typical jury trial. For innocent defendants, even a not guilty verdict is a loss. Although they have "won," they have undergone arrest and (at least minimal) incarceration, spent money on premiums paid to bail bondsmen, spent more money hiring a lawyer, withstood the inevitable public censure and suspicion, undergone the roller coaster ride of emotion during the protracted litigation, and will ever after suffer a stain on their reputation. For the innocent defendant, "not guilty" is a smaller loss than "guilty as charged," but it is a loss nonetheless. For a guilty defendant, even a guilty verdict and a prison sentence can be a win. More than one guilty defendant facing a draconian sentence has celebrated when convicted of a lesser crime and sentenced to the maximum for a minor felony.

2. VICTORY CONDITIONS

In a non-zero-sum game the players can define their own victory conditions. Take the crime of first-degree murder. An obviously guilty defendant can define victory as a verdict of manslaughter, or even murder in the second degree. The prosecution could be satisfied with a verdict of murder in the second degree or even manslaughter. If the prosecution has defined victory as a verdict of murder in the first degree and the defense has defined victory as "not guilty," then a verdict of manslaughter is a loss for both. If both sides have defined victory as a second-degree murder verdict, then this is where plea bargaining comes into play. Why should either side risk a loss by going to trial? What complicates things is the fact that criminal trials are not two-player games. We need not consider how many players there may be on the defense side of the courtroom, but those on the prosecution side should be consulted before any plea bargain is accepted. At a minimum, the homicide victim's family members should be consulted, and the prosecutor who wishes to maintain good relations with law enforcement will include the investigating agency as a player worthy of input into the plea bargaining process.

B. MAKING PLEA OFFERS

The next chapter will suggest making plea offers with the initial discovery disclosure. In the mid-twentieth century, prosecutors scoffed at the idea that they should make a plea offer at any time. They felt that the prosecution had stated its position by filing formal charges, that it was a sign of weakness to make a plea offer, and that it was incumbent upon the defense to come forward with the olive branch of a plea offer. Somehow, by the early 1980's, this had changed, and prosecutors were regularly making plea offers to the defense. Whether plea offers by the prosecution are advisable or inadvisable, laudable or blameworthy, they are a fact of life in the modern courtroom. Since prosecutors are expected, even encouraged, to make plea offers, they should make them in the right way.

1. CONSULTATION

Before making a plea offer, consult with the concerned parties. As early as possible, preferably in the intake stage, you should determine the attitudes of the victim or victim's family and of law enforcement. Many prosecutors' offices do this by mailing the victim a victim impact statement to be filled out listing, among other things, the monetary damages to the victim and the victim's wishes as regards sentencing. Ideally, you should call in the victim or victim's family for a face-to-face discussion of what they can expect from the criminal prosecution and a candid talk about what they want to achieve from the criminal prosecution. Although victims are not parties to the litigation and their wishes are not controlling, it is both good public relations and good sense to consult. Of course, minor crimes do not warrant an all-out effort to keep the victim informed, but the more serious the crime, the more effort should be put into the consultation process.

2. INVITING PLEA OFFERS

In cases which are highly charged with emotion, such as homicides and child sex abuse cases, it is incumbent upon you to consult early with the victim's family and make them aware of what is in store for them. Initially they may not feel inclined to discuss plea bargaining so soon after the trauma of their loss. In that case, make them aware of the probability of a defense plea offer in the future and tell them that they will be informed when one is made. In these cases, it would be better to be old-fashioned and not make a plea offer but to extend the defense an invitation to make an offer. Courts tend to consider plea bargains according to contract law,[5] and black letter contract law defines a contract as an offer and an acceptance. If you make only an invitation to offer, then you are not contractually bound to accept the resulting plea offer by the defense. If you make an offer, the defense accepts, and then after consulting with the victim's family you back out of the plea agreement, the court may not specifically enforce the contract, but you will have begun building a reputation as someone whose word is not to be trusted. If you extend an invitation to the defendant to make a plea offer rather than making an offer yourself, you can avoid the

[5] E.g. State v. Garvin, 242 Conn. 296, 314, 699 A.2d 921, 929 (1997) ("The validity of plea bargains depends on contract principles"); State v. Fairman, 945 So.2d 783, 785 (La.App. 5th Cir. 2006) ("Criminal plea agreements are analogous to contracts in that they are formed by the consent of the parties established through offer and acceptance"); State v. Bembenek, 296 Wis.2d 422, 724 N.W.2d 685 (App.2006).

perception that your word is not your bond. Such an invitation could be extended in a form similar to the following.

> This is a serious case, and I am not going to make a firm plea offer to you. I couldn't make an offer without getting the consent of the victim's family, and I don't want to traumatize them by talking to them about a possible plea on the off chance that your client will accept a plea offer. I will, however, tell you that if you give me a written offer of plea which includes the following terms, I will speak to the victim's family and recommend it to them. [State terms]. If the family agrees, we will then accept the plea. If you want to make some other written plea offer, feel free to do so and I will take it to the family. Depending on what they say, we may or may not accept the lesser plea or may make a counter-offer.

3. VICTIM INPUT

Do not be afraid to put this language in writing in the form of a letter to be sent to defense counsel. If a plea offer is forthcoming, then you can take it to the victim's family, and will not be vulnerable to a charge of duplicity if the plea is rejected. In talking to the family, a face-to-face conference is not absolutely essential, but it is certainly advisable. Such a conference should follow a set format. Give them a history of the litigation to the point of the conference. Tell them the projected course of the litigation through trial and appeal. Give them a realistic assessment of the strengths and weaknesses of the case. Then communicate the plea offer to them in the language similar to the following.

> You remember when we first met, I told you that there was a possibility that the defense might make a plea offer. They have done so. It is my duty to tell you about the plea offer. Before I tell you what the defense is offering, you need to understand that we can answer the plea offer in one of three ways. (1) 'Yes.' (2) 'No.' (3) 'No, but . . .' If we say 'Yes,' that settles it. We take the plea on the terms offered. If we say 'No,' that settles it. We're going to trial unless the defense makes another offer which is acceptable. If we say 'No, but . . .,' we are giving them a counter-offer. We outline what we want in a plea and then they can either accept it or reject it. There might be several rounds of back and forth haggling, or we might just give them an ultimatum. If we give them an ultimatum and they come back with a counter-offer, I'll still be duty bound to talk to you about it, but we won't have to accept it. Now, in the final analysis, whether to accept the plea is my decision, not yours, but I am going to give great weight to your wishes, and if I can, I'm going to take a plea that you are happy with. Do you have any questions about what I have said so far? No questions? Okay, the offer is [give them the offer].

Depending on how you assess the plea offer, you can strongly recommend it be accepted, strongly recommend it be rejected, recommend a counter-offer, or withhold recommendation. If you feel the plea offer is a good one, your goal is to get the family's blessing. If you are ambivalent, your goal is to get the family's guidance. If you do not like the plea offer, your goal is simply full disclosure to the family and possibly getting their blessings for a counter-offer to convey to the defendant. If you do not like the plea offer, but the family is strongly in favor of it, then maybe you should reassess your position. If you feel the plea is a good one and the family disagrees, then you should not strong-arm them into agreeing to the plea, but you can certainly solicit their understanding for your decision to take the plea. If they cannot be happy about the plea, then your next objective is to have them only moderately dissatisfied. If the plea is a good one and they are unreasonable, then you must prepare them for the unpleasantry of your taking the plea against their wishes.

C. THE PLEA COLLOQUY

If the plea is accepted, schedule the plea as soon as possible. Defendants are prone to vacillate, and when a plea has been agreed upon, it should be finalized sooner rather than later. Unlike the prosecutor, the defendant has no reputation for square dealing to uphold and can renege on the plea at any time up until the judge formally accepts it. Prepare or gather all the necessary paperwork (sentencing score sheets, certified copies of previous sentences, jail credit certificates, etc.) and have it ready to produce when it is called for. There are as many different plea colloquies as there are judges. Each judge is different, but some formats are better than others. If at all possible, you should be the one who announces the plea offer. Your statement of the offer will be more likely to be in an acceptable format, and the victim's family will be more accepting of it if you state it. Also there is less potential for defense counsel (who can never completely get out of defense mode) to say something self-serving to the defendant which may put the agreement on the rocks. The judge will make an inquiry into the knowingness and voluntariness of the plea, and you must make sure that the judge covers all the bases and asks all the necessary questions. If the judge does not, then you must, by gentle reminder, or by asking the questions yourself, make sure that everything necessary is put on record. Common questions include the defendant's educational level, mental health history, understanding of the crime charged and the penalties, whether the defendant has been coerced into pleading, whether the defendant is satisfied with her attorney, and also the defendant's understanding of certain collateral effects of the plea. Some collateral effects which might be inquired into include the possibility of deportation if the defendant is an alien, and if the crime is a sex crime the possibility of being committed as a sexually violent predator at some future date. Finally the judge will inquire into the factual basis for the plea. Because the law frowns on people being punished for things that they did not do, as a part of every plea the judge makes an inquiry to determine whether the defendant is actually guilty. The inquiry is not as rigorous as a full-blown trial, but the judge must find satisfactory evidence of guilt.

1. WRITTEN PLEA OFFERS

Pleas of guilty are almost always accompanied by written offers of plea executed by the defendant. (See Appendix 5-A for the plea form approved the Seventh Judicial Circuit of Florida).[6] If there is a plea bargain, the parties usually set forth the terms of the bargain within the four corners of the offer of plea. The defendant signs the plea attesting to her understanding of and agreement to the terms of the plea. The prosecutor and the defense attorney sign the form attesting to their concurrence, and the judge signs signifying her acceptance. These written pleas can be quite detailed and lengthy, and court personnel sometimes skimp on the oral colloquy because they feel that everything has been placed in writing in the plea form. No matter how detailed a piece of paper may be, it will not save an inadequate oral inquiry by the judge. Always prompt the judge to make an adequate inquiry, and do not be timid about volunteering questions yourself if the need arises.

Set forth below, you will find the text of a standard sort of plea offer form used in many courts throughout the United States. Typed and double-spaced on 8 ½″ by 11″ paper, some plea forms cover nine or more pages. With copies to the defendant, defense attorney, prosecutor, probation officer, and other interested parties, that kills a lot of trees in a year's time. No matter how many pages a plea form may cover, length will not make up for an inadequate oral colloquy.

IN THE CIRCUIT COURT, SEVENTH JUDICIAL CIRCUIT IN AND FOR ST. JOHNS COUNTY, FLORIDA

CASE NO:__________

STATE OF FLORIDA

Versus

OFFER OF PLEA

____

Defendant

[6] <https://circuit7.org/wp-content/uploads/Plea-form.pdf>. (2025).

1. I, [NAME], Defendant, withdraw my previously entered plea(s) of Not Guilty, and enter plea(s) of:

( ) Guilty ( ) Nolo Contendere to [CHARGE], a ____ degree felony/misdemeanor

( ) Guilty ( ) Nolo Contendere to [CHARGE], a ____ degree felony/misdemeanor

( ) Guilty ( ) Nolo Contendere to [CHARGE], a ____ degree felony/misdemeanor

2. I understand that I have the right to plead Not Guilty or persist in that plea if it has already been made. I also understand that if the Court accepts my plea(s) I give up my right to a trial with the assistance of a lawyer, and at that trial, I would have the following rights: (1) to have a jury determine whether I am guilty or not guilty, or to have a judge make such a determination in a non-jury hearing; (2) to see and hear witnesses testify and to have my lawyer question them for me; (3) to subpoena and present witnesses in my defense to a jury or judge; (4) to testify or remain silent; and (5) to require the prosecutor to prove my guilt by admissible evidence beyond a reasonable doubt before I can be found guilty. I also understand that by pleading Guilty or Nolo Contendere, the judge may ask me questions about the offense(s) to which I have pleaded, and if I answer those questions under oath, on the record, and in the presence of counsel, the answers may later be used against me in a prosecution for perjury. I further understand that without express reservation of the right to appeal I give up my right to appeal all matters except court rulings issued after this plea is entered, an illegal sentence, or the court's authority (jurisdiction) to hear my case, and I agree to pay all costs and attorneys' fees of any appeal which I attempt to pursue on any other subject. My lawyer has explained to me what an appeal is, and I understand that changing my mind about entering this plea, after it is accepted, will not require the court to let me withdraw it, nor will it make the court's sentence illegal or deprive the court of authority to sentence me.

3. I understand that a plea of "Not Guilty" denies that I committed the crime charged and a plea of "Guilty" admits I committed the crime charged. A "Best Interest Guilty" plea or a plea of "Nolo Contendere" mean I do not contest the state's evidence against me. By entering the above plea(s) I am voluntarily submitting myself to the court's sentencing authority. I understand that if the court accepts my plea(s), the sentence(s) imposed will be based on my plea(s). I agree that a factual basis for the court to accept my plea(s) is contained in documents in the court file, including the complaint affidavit(s). I understand that if I am not a citizen of the United States, I will be deported. I understand that the court may impose monetary penalties/assessments to include fines, court costs, restitution (if applicable) and/or other fees.

4. I have read the Information or Indictment in this case, and I understand the charges to which I am pleading. My lawyer has explained to me: the maximum and minimum penalty(ies) for the charges against me, including enhanced sentencing laws for which the state has given my lawyer notice; the essential elements of the crime(s) I am charged with; and all defenses I might have. I understand that if I am on parole or probation in any other case, this plea can cause that parole or probation to be revoked, and I can receive a separate sentence up to the maximum allowed by law for that (those) case(s).

5. I understand that if I receive a sentence of probation in this case, I may be required to serve time in the county jail as a condition of probation. Additionally, I understand that if I violate that probation, I can be sentenced to the maximum allowed by law.

6. No one has promised me anything to get me to enter this (these) plea(s), except as stated herein. If entering an open plea: I understand that I am pleading open to the Court. My lawyer and the judge have not promised me that I will receive a specific sentence. I also understand that the judge is not required to follow any state or defense recommendation regarding sentencing. If entering a conditional plea: I understand that I am entering a plea based upon an agreement between the State and myself. My lawyer has not promised me anything more than what has been agreed upon in this conditional plea agreement. If the judge accepts the terms of the agreement, I understand that I will be sentenced in accordance with the agreement.

a. I am entering a(n): ( ) Open Plea: ( ) Conditional Plea:

b. The state recommends the following sentence: [INSERT RECOMMENDATION].

7. No one has pressured, coerced, or forced me to enter this (these) plea(s). I am entering this (these) plea(s) because I am guilty of the crimes charged or I believe it is in my best interest to do so. I am doing this voluntarily and of my own free will.

8. I understand that my sentence will be imposed under the Sentencing Guidelines that apply to my case, unless I qualify for enhanced penalties under Chapter 775, Florida Statutes, or other statutes. If no enhanced sentence is requested or applies, I understand that the court can impose a sentence exceeding the guideline range only by stating clear and convincing reasons under the guidelines law. If the court imposes a sentence exceeding the guidelines range, I will have the right to withdraw my plea(s) or appeal the sentence, unless enhanced penalties apply and are lawfully imposed. No representations or promises have been made to me regarding "gain time," "good time," "early release," or prison credit toward my sentence, which I understand the court and my lawyer cannot affect. Only the Department of Corrections can calculate a release date.

9. I understand that if I am pleading to a sexually violent or sexually motivated offense, or if I have previously been convicted of such an offense, my plea may subject me to involuntary civil commitment under the Involuntary Civil Commitment of Sexually Violent Predators Act. My lawyer has explained the aspects of civil commitment to me and the mandatory, statutory conditions of sex-offender probation, including the requirement to wear a GPS monitor at all times.

10. I understand and have discussed with my lawyer that if I am entering a plea of Guilty or Nolo Contendere to an offense for which automatic, mandatory driver's license suspension or revocation is required by law to be imposed, by the court or by a separate agency, the plea will provide the basis for the suspension or revocation of my driver's license/privilege.

11. My lawyer has reviewed the nature of the evidence with me and I am not aware of any physical evidence containing DNA that could exonerate me.

12. I understand and agree that if the judge permits me to remain at liberty pending sentencing, I must notify my lawyer, my bondsman and/or pretrial services officer (if any), and the Clerk of Court of any change of my address. I also understand that if a Pre-Sentence Investigation (PSI) is ordered and I fail to appear for an appointment with the Department of Corrections for the PSI interview, the court can revoke my release and place me in jail until the PSI is completed or until sentencing.

13. I understand that if I willfully fail to appear for sentencing, any conditions of a "conditional plea" will no longer be binding upon the judge, and that I may be sentenced to any lawful sentence that could be imposed without the conditions.

14. I can read, write, speak and understand the English language or have had an interpreter read this document to me in my native language with my lawyer present. I have _______ years, or equivalent, of education (example: high school or GED = 12 years). I am not under the influence of any drug, medicine or alcohol at the time I sign this plea form. I am not suffering from any mental problems at this time that affect my understanding of this document, other than as explained to the judge on the record in open court, or as reflected in the court file.

15. I have read and understand every printed or handwritten word in this plea form and have discussed it with my lawyer. I am fully satisfied with the services of my lawyer and have had ample opportunity to discuss this case and my plea(s) with my lawyer. I have told my lawyer everything I know about my case. No one, including my lawyer, has made any promises or representations to me which modify or contradict this plea document, other than what I have told the judge in open court.

SIGNED, or acknowledged, in open court in St. Johns County, Florida on [DATE].

S/DEFENDANT

CERTIFICATE OF DEFENDANT'S ATTORNEY

I hereby certify that as counsel for Defendant, I have discussed this case with my client and explained the rights, defenses and evidence relating to it with him/her. I have discussed this written plea form with my client and have answered all of his/her questions regarding it. In my professional opinion, as an officer of the court, Defendant understands everything in this plea form, his/her rights, and the consequences of this (these) plea(s). His/her plea is being made freely, voluntarily and knowingly. I have made no promises or representations to my client which modify or contradict this plea document.

S/COUNSEL FOR DEFENDANT

CERTIFICATE OF ASSISTANT STATE ATTORNEY

I confirm that the recommendations set forth in this plea form are the recommendations of the Office of the State Attorney.

The State has complied with the Victim Rights statute, if applicable.

S/ASSISTANT STATE ATTORNEY

ORDER ACCEPTING PLEA

The foregoing plea document was received and accepted in open court. Defendant signed, or acknowledged signing, this document while under oath and subject to the penalties of perjury. The court finds the plea to be freely and voluntarily entered and that a factual basis exists in the record for the court to accept it. By accepting this (these) plea(s), the court is not required to follow any state or defense recommendation stated herein, unless a "Conditional Plea" is fully described in paragraph 6, above.

Accepted by the court.

S/CIRCUIT JUDGE

2. THE FACTUAL BASIS

The judge can consult one of three sources for a factual basis. The judge can ask the defendant to "Tell me what it is that you did that makes you guilty of the crime you have just pled guilty to." This is the most problematic source. Many defendants are so caught up in self-justification that they cannot bring themselves to admit the facts necessary to prove the crime. The defense attorney is a second source of factual basis, but this is also problematic. Defense attorneys tend to revert to defense mode, and although they might state sufficient facts to sustain the plea, they might do it in such a way as to enrage the victim's family. If the judge is predisposed to ask the defendant or defense attorney for the factual basis, seek an opportune lull in the action to volunteer it before the judge can ask someone else. Even when you state the factual basis there is potential for misadventure. You might state the factual basis in such a way as to enrage the defendant and cause him to withdraw the plea or cause the defense attorney to quibble over details. The best way to state factual basis is to make a vague recitation covering the elements of the crime and refer the judge the arrest affidavit and other documents in the court file for more particulars. This advice, of course, presupposes that those documents do state a factual basis.

D. EVALUATING AND STRUCTURING THE PLEA BARGAIN

1. TYPES OF PLEA BARGAINS

There are three basic types of plea bargaining. You can charge bargain, count bargain, or sentence bargain. In count bargaining, you agree to drop a certain number of counts in return for a plea of guilty or nolo contendere to a certain number of counts. In charge bargaining, you agree to a plea to a lesser degree or lesser included offense of the crime charged. In sentence bargaining, the defendant pleads guilty as charged, but the prosecution agrees to recommend a specific sentence to the court. One young prosecutor encountered difficulty with sentence bargaining because defense attorneys felt free to recommend lesser sentences than the agreed-upon sentence, and judges sometimes imposed the lesser sentence. He solved this problem by rewriting plea offers to state that recommended sentences were recommended by both sides. to state that recommended sentences were recommended by both sides. You can craft a plea which displays characteristics of all three forms, as when a defendant charged with first degree murder, and grand theft agrees to plead guilty to second-degree murder and the prosecutor agrees to drop the grand theft charge and recommend a twenty-year sentence. There are things to be said both for and against each form of plea bargaining, and each form of plea bargaining can be done well—or poorly. One immediate consideration of plea bargaining is public perception. Many pleas, vulnerable to attack, have had their shortcomings ballyhooed in the media. You should be ever vigilant to try to craft a plea which is reasonably safe from public opprobrium. We say reasonably safe rather than immune because there is nothing that one person does that cannot be criticized by another.

2. PERCEPTION AND REALITY

Many of the things which lead to public distaste for plea bargaining are more matters of perception than reality, and they can be easily avoided. Taking a plea in a murder case without at least consulting with the victim's family can result in adverse public perception if the victim's family disapproves of the plea and takes their grievance to the press. Speaking with them ahead of time tends to defuse this possibility. Even if they disagree with the plea, they will be less inclined to complain to the media; and even if they complain to the media, they cannot complain that they were "out of the loop" in the decision-making process. Taking a plea to one count and dropping 99 counts may not be giving away the farm, but it certainly looks like it. In count bargaining, it is preferable to take a plea to a majority of counts for cosmetic reasons if for nothing else. Secretaries also tend to get a little testy when their prosecutors drop 99 counts of that 100-count information they typed. They justly feel that their time, energy, and effort have been wasted. A plea to petit theft on a charge of armed robbery might "do justice," but it is going to make you look rather foolish, as is agreeing to a county jail sentence on a plea to second-degree murder.

Prosecutors often put themselves in such public perception fiascos by grossly overcharging in the intake stage. By overcharging, we do not mean charging crimes or counts that are not supported by the evidence. Prosecutors seldom overcharge in this fashion—and when they do, it is inadvertent, not intentional. The more common type of overcharging comes when the prosecutor charges every conceivable crime supported by the evidence. The mere fact that a crime is provable doesn't mean that charging it is prudent. Charge crimes just high enough to address the wrongdoing; file the smallest number of counts necessary to address the wrongdoing; err on the side of undercharging rather than overcharging. The higher the charge, the greater the expectation for disposition.

3. FACTORS TO CONSIDER

There are many factors which drive the plea bargaining decision, but case quality is arguably the most significant. In the filing stage, you filed a charge which you hoped would adequately remedy the wrong by giving you a sufficiently broad enough range of sanctions to satisfy considerations of retribution, restitution, and even rehabilitation. When you approach the plea bargaining process, you seek a remedy which is achievable and which meets both your needs and desires. Achievability trumps need and desire. You may desire or need a certain outcome, but if it is not achievable, you are not going to get it. Case quality governs achievability. The better the case quality, the more likely the defendant is to accept your terms without the hazard of a jury trial. A high-quality case is not a license to achieve a draconian remedy far in excess of the needs of justice.

Other factors affecting achievability are the jury pool and the judge. If you practice in a district made up of multiple smaller jurisdictions (such as several counties in a circuit), you will soon learn that each small jurisdiction has its own personality. A sure winner of a case in one county might be a sure loser in another. More often a strong case in one county might be an iffy case in another. The personality of the jurisdiction must be consulted in determining the achievability of a certain end. There may be little sense in holding out for a plea as charged in a county which has a history of never convicting as charged. The personality of the judge must also be consulted. All judges will have their own idiosyncracies, and sometimes a judge will enter a much lower sentence than the defendant would have agreed to as a condition of a plea bargain. Suppose you have a defendant charged with second-degree murder who is willing to plead guilty as charged for a twenty year sentence. If you refuse the plea, the jury finds the defendant guilty of manslaughter, and the judge sentences the defendant to ten years, you have not won. You have lost. You could have gotten twice the sentence for a fraction of the effort. If you realized at the outset that the jury pool had a history of consistently returning lesser verdicts and the judge had a history of passing out light sentences, you have not only lost, you have been suicidal.

There are occasions, however, when it is preferable to turn down an achievable-but-undesirable plea bargained remedy and run a great risk of loss. If you have a guilty-as-sin murderer, a marginal case, and an unreasonably lenient plea offer from the defense, it is preferable to take the risk of acquittal at trial than to take the plea. You might consider taking the plea offer if the victim's family were strongly in favor of it, but otherwise you should try the case. You might lose, but you might win. If you lose, you have in truth lost very little, because all you could have achieved by pleading the case was a woefully inadequate remedy. If you achieve a conviction, you have won much.

In deciding upon what offer to make or whether to accept the offer made, you must consult many factors. Reconsider all the factors discussed in the chapter on the charging decision, aiming to find a resolution which adequately addresses the triad of concerns about criminality, culpability, and consequence. Does the sentence fit the magnitude of the act for which the defendant is being prosecuted? Does it reflect an appropriate response to the defendant's degree of culpability for that act? Does it, insofar as possible, repair the damage resulting from the act? If the proffered plea satisfactorily addresses all these considerations, then you should strongly consider accepting it. Throughout this process, remember that you spell prosecutor with a P–R–O . . ., not a P–E–R. . . .

PRACTICAL EXERCISES

1. Henry Dobbs goes to James Kelly to buy crack cocaine. Henry buys a dime rock and drives off without paying for it. After smoking the rock, Henry goes back looking for Kelly to buy some more. Henry runs into Tom Blake, who is out on bail on drug sale charges, and Blake tells Henry to avoid Kelly because Kelly has said he will kill Dobbs for cheating him. Dobbs finds Kelly and drives up to him to make another purchase. Kelly pulls a pistol, fires one shot, and

shoots Dobbs dead. The grand jury indicts Kelly for first degree murder. Although Kelly has a lengthy record for drug abuse, he has no prior history of violence. Kelly's lawyer comes to you and makes a plea offer of second-degree murder, which is punishable by life in prison without parole. Dobbs's family opposes the plea. Should you take the plea? What other factors would you want to consider before making a decision? What if Blake is currently unavailable as a witness, but you have hopes of finding him before trial?

2. Romeo McSwain is on probation for statutory rape on Sarah Sweetheart, who loves him very much and wants to marry him when she comes of age. Six months before Sarah becomes old enough to marry without consent, Romeo violates the no contact provision of his probationary sentence and impregnates her, he is jailed to face charges of probation violation, and you file felony charges of statutory rape. Romeo's lawyer comes to you asking whether a plea bargain can be arranged which will keep McSwain out of prison and allow him to marry Sweetheart as soon as it is legally permissible. Should you take such a plea? If so, how should it be structured?

3. Georgia Red Orman periodically beats up her husband, Carl Orman. Orman has shot her on two occasions trying to stop her from hurting him. While Georgia Red is still recuperating from the latest gunshot wound inflicted by her husband, she gets drunk and begins to beat her husband with her metal crutch. Carl pulls a gun and shoots her, inflicting a minor flesh wound. She takes the gun away from him and shoots him dead. Georgia Red hides the gun and first claims that an intruder shot Carl. She later changes her story, admitting she shot him, but claims self-defense. Carl's good friend, Hugh Stuart, was present when the incident occurred but fled the scene before the police arrived. Stuart finally comes forward and tells what he saw. He says that Georgia Red attacked Carl, that Carl defended himself with the pistol, that Georgia Red disarmed Carl and shot him dead. Stuart is a huge, muscular five-time convicted felon with a speech impediment and a heavily scarred face. The grand jury indicts her for first degree murder. Georgia Red's attorney offers you a plea to second degree murder with an agreed-upon twenty year sentence. Orman's family, which wants the death penalty, vehemently opposes such a disposition. What factors favor accepting the offer? What factors favor declining it? How should you respond to the offer?

4. Frederick Hunter has been arrested in possession of a half kilo of cocaine and is charged with drug trafficking. You have a good case. Hunter's lawyer offers to enter into a substantial assistance agreement which will entail Hunter making twenty controlled purchases of crack cocaine from street level dealers (and testifying against them in court) in return for a three-year probationary period. The drug task force is enthusiastic about the deal and strongly urges you to take the plea. How should you respond? Would it make any difference if your case had marginal prosecutive merit? Should you respond differently if Hunter offered to make a controlled purchase from his supplier?

5. Suppose the defendant in Problem 4 was Tom Blake (from Problem 1) instead of Frederick Hunter. Suppose further that Blake now refuses to testify at James Kelly's murder trial unless you agree to place him on probation. How should you respond? Would this situation cause you to reevaluate your decision in Problem 1?

CHAPTER 6

CASE MANAGEMENT FROM IN BASKET TO ARCHIVE

■ ■ ■

When you're up to your neck in alligators, it is sometimes hard to remember that your primary objective was to drain the swamp.—Anonymous

Nothing moves unless you push it.—Aristotle's First Law of Motion

A. TWELVE STRATEGIES FOR EFFECTIVE CASE MANAGEMENT

While a particular lawsuit can take years to work its way through the criminal justice system, with each passing day of each of those years, countless new cases come to the DA's office for prosecution. On any given day in any given prosecutor's office, there will be a backlog of intake or a log-jammed docket with many cases languishing while others go through the office like Sherman through Georgia. If you are a typical prosecutor, you will have too many cases and too little time to devote to each case. Faced with such a prospect, you can begin to cut corners, procrastinate, sell cases short, and otherwise do a slipshod job of managing the caseload. Or you can become more efficient. We will follow a case file from intake to archive in hopes of demonstrating an efficient method for handling a monster caseload.

1. THE FIRST STRATEGY: PUSH YOUR CASES TOWARD DISPOSITION

Remember, although Newton's Laws of Motion have superseded Aristotle's, Aristotle's First Law of Motion applies to your caseload. "Nothing moves unless you push it." Defendants may have a right to a speedy trial, but nine times out of ten they do not really want one. If they can put the case off long enough, memories will fade, evidence will get lost, witnesses will move out of the jurisdiction or die, and everyone involved will become generally less enthusiastic about getting the case concluded. It is up to you to push the case through the process. Thus, Aristotle's First Law of Motion becomes the first strategy. "Push your cases toward disposition." Oftentimes you will be the only person pushing until a witness dies or a time limit expires. Then the defense will begin to clamor for that speedy trial they formerly were so studiously trying to avoid.

2. THE SECOND STRATEGY: WHEN YOU TAKE A FILE OUT OF THE IN BASKET, DO NOT PUT IT BACK

During its lifetime, a case file will materialize in your in basket many times before it finally makes its way to the archives. The second strategy is: "When you take a file out of your in basket, do not put it back." Too many times, a prosecutor will pull a file out of the in basket, look it over, develop a headache, say "I'll work on this later," and will put it back in the in basket. You have pulled it out of the in basket. Now do something with it and put it in the out basket. When you get to the office and sit behind your desk, you will seek a stack of case files in the in basket. Take them out and sort them into three categories. Category A is the cases that can be disposed of immediately. Category B is the cases that need work before filing. Category C is the cases that do not need immediate attention. This third category should be very small. Dispose of the Category A cases and put them in the out basket. Now go to Category B. Make the necessary arrangements to get the work done and put the cases in a tickler so that they will reappear in your in basket for review in a set period of time. When they reappear, they belong in Category A. Do something with them. Put the Category C cases in the tickler and when they reappear, they no longer belong in Category C. Do something with them.

3. THE THIRD STRATEGY: MAKE CHARGING DECISIONS WHICH ARE PROMPT, PROPER, AND PRUDENT

When a charging decision is difficult to make, it is easy to put off. Prosecutors have been known to procrastinate on making charging decisions until the speedy trial deadline has expired. Some have even put off the decision until the statute of limitations has run. Do not drag your feet on making a charging decision. Cases are not like wine. They do not get better with age. When you first look at a file, you must ask yourself a series of questions: Has a crime been committed? (Criminality). Did the defendant commit it? (Culpability). Can we prove it? (Convictability). Many times you cannot answer the questions on the basis of the information provided. You must therefore take action out and get that information by calling in witnesses to interview, calling in the investigating officer for a debriefing, writing the investigating officer requesting additional information, or doing whatever else is necessary to answer the three questions and answer them in a timely fashion. If a case cannot or should not be filed, do not procrastinate on making and communicating the decision. Postponing the unpleasantry usually magnifies it. Be able to say "no" to complainants and investigating officers firmly but politely.

4. THE FOURTH STRATEGY: SET AN ACHIEVABLE OBJECTIVE FOR THE PROSECUTION

The facts will only support a certain range of charges. The charges will only support a certain range of remedies. Be certain that the charge you file will be both provable and will support the necessary range of remedies. If a penurious defendant has done $100,000.00 worth of damage, then charging him with a misdemeanor does not provide for a sufficient probationary period to corkscrew the necessary funds out of him. If you think a defendant deserves 50 years in prison, but the highest crime you can charge carries a penalty of only 15 years, you must satisfy yourself with the lesser charge. A defendant might have done something that really makes you angry. You might want to punish him severely. If the law does not provide for as severe a punishment as you want, you must settle for what the law allows. You may feel warm and fuzzy when you overcharge in such a case, but there will be a hereafter to that decision. At the end of the prosecution you will be standing in court with egg on your face—or worse.

5. THE FIFTH STRATEGY: ASSUME THAT EVERY CASE YOU FILE WILL GO TO TRIAL BEFORE A JURY

You should consider your signature on an information as a certification that "I am willing to try this case before a jury." Those cases that are filed in hopes of concluding a quick, painless plea bargain are the ones which will cause you the most headaches. When you file a case in hopes of working it out, rest assured that it will not get worked out. Do not file bad cases. They will devour your time like a black hole pulling in a star, and there will come a time when you will confront the dilemma of dismissing the case or embarrassing yourself and your office before a jury. Neither alternative is desirable. The more bad cases you file and the more bad cases you dismiss at the eleventh hour, the more defense counsel will come to believe that you are a barking dog who does not bite. You do not do much better, and you probably do worse, if you file numerous bad cases and then waste much time, energy and effort by taking them to trial. Achieving the occasional not guilty verdict in a hotly contested case will not damage your credibility with defense counsel, but regularly getting laughed out of court as the result of ill-conceived filing decisions will. When you file a good case, do not assume that the defendant will agree with your assessment and plead guilty. You are courting disaster if you put off necessary case preparation tasks in the expectation that the defendant will plead guilty. When the guilty plea does not come, you will be scrambling at the last minute to marshal your evidence for trial. To insure peace, you must prepare for war—and your opponent must be aware that you are ready for war.

6. THE SIXTH STRATEGY: IF YOU WORK SMART, YOU WON'T HAVE TO WORK NEARLY AS HARD

Once you have decided to file, and have settled upon the desired charge, you are not yet ready to drop the file into the out basket. There are at least six things you can do to make your life easier down the road.

(1) Go ahead and draft your initial discovery worksheet. Put the worksheet in the file. When the defense discovery demand comes in, the secretary will pick up the file, get the worksheet, type the discovery, and put it on your desk for review. You can review it to make sure nothing additional has come in since you first looked at the file, sign the discovery, and put it in the out basket. If you do not go ahead and do the discovery at the filing stage, here is what will happen: weeks or months later, when your memory of the case is fuzzy, the discovery demand will come in and your secretary will pull the file and put it in your in basket. You will do the discovery and give it back to the secretary. The secretary will then type the discovery and give it back to you. You will sign the discovery and give it back to the secretary. The file will go through your hands twice as many times. Or you could be slipshod and tell your secretary to do the discovery with your only contribution to the process being to sign the disclosure without even proofreading it. If you do this, you have missed a golden opportunity to review the file, insure that your evidence is in order, and repair any shortcomings in the case. If you delegate the chore of doing discovery to your secretary, you will suffer embarrassment in court because of sloppy discovery—and the fault will be yours, not your secretary's.

(2) Calculate, as best you can, a provisional sentencing guidelines or punishment code score sheet. This will give you a better idea of the range of punishments and will be at your fingertips when the defense attorney calls to discuss plea bargains. It should not be set in stone because rap sheets are notoriously unreliable. It will, however, give you a handle on the potential sentence pending the receipt of a presentence investigation with a more complete and accurate history.

(3) Go ahead and decide upon a plea offer, discuss it with whoever you have to discuss it with (victim, investigating officer, supervisor), get whatever advance permission you need to get, reduce the plea offer to writing, and send it to the defense attorney at your earliest convenience. Who knows, the defendant may just plead. An efficient way to handle the plea offer is to send it (and the provisional sentencing score sheet) to the defense attorney when you send out the initial discovery answer. Place a deadline

for acceptance on the offer. Then adhere to the deadline. A plea taken after the expiration of a deadline should be more severe than the expired plea offer. Defendants who have no incentive to plead early will not plead early. If the plea offer is going to be the same on the morning of jury selection as it was at arraignment, the defendant might as well wait to the last minute to plead. A witness might die. Evidence might get lost. Anything might happen. The defendant can roll the dice and see if something turns up and plead on the morning of trial without penalty if nothing turns up. If you are one of those prosecutors who gets sweaty palms and cold feet and actually makes a better plea offer on the morning of trial than you did at arraignment, then the defendant is a fool to plead early. Unless the case falls apart, successive plea offers should be more severe rather than less severe—and each plea offer should have a deadline for acceptance.

(4) Review the case file, decide what additional evidence and witnesses you will need to prove the case and achieve the objective, make a "to do" list for getting that information, and then go out and get it. There will always be something else you will need before you can go to trial, whether it is a witness to value in a grand theft case, the address of an essential witness, the restitution amount, certified copies of convictions, or any of a myriad of other things. You may think that these things can be put off until after plea bargaining breaks down and the case gets set for trial. If you wait, you can be sure of six things. First, plea bargaining will be more likely to break down because the defense will know that you are not really prepared for trial. Second, you will be scampering around at the last minute gathering this information in panic mode. Third, the defense attorney will complain loudly about belated discovery when you make an eleventh-hour disclosure of information that you should have ferreted out weeks or months previously. Fourth, the judge will be unhappy when the defense attorney complains, and the displeasure will not be aimed at the defense attorney. Fifth, the judge may manifest displeasure by suppressing the belatedly disclosed evidence and the jury may never hear it. Sixth, you may just lose the case because of your slothfulness.

(5) Establish the statutory and rule-imposed deadlines and make sure you do not miss them. Many jurisdictions have promulgated numerous deadlines to insure that the case moves through the system with celerity. There may be time limits for the first appearance of the defendant before a committing magistrate, for the finding of probable cause, for the filing of formal charges, for the filing of other types of pleadings, and for disposition of the

case by trial. The defense may not be interested in insuring that the deadlines are met but will be extremely interested in complaining when they are missed. Establish these deadlines and make sure they are easily found in the case file—either written on the outside of the file folder or behind a prominent tab inside the file. Many offices will have preprinted file fronts which give you a place for making those notations, but they can be jotted down just as easily on a blank file front. Write highly important dates, like the speedy trial deadline, in bold red on the file front. Annotate just as prominently any waiver that the defendant enters as to any deadline.[1]

(6) Organize the file in the same format as every other file you have. If your office does not have a prescribed organization format for files, and many do not, devise your own and stick to it. Make sure every file you have is in the same format. It makes finding things in the file so much easier. Every time you put the file back in the out basket, take a few seconds and tidy it up, making sure it is in the correct format. Few things will engender more frustration than trying to make sense of a jumbled, disorganized file.

7. THE SEVENTH STRATEGY: EVERY TIME YOU PUT DOWN A CASE FILE, IT SHOULD BE CLOSER TO BEING READY FOR TRIAL THAN WHEN YOU PICKED IT UP

When a case file appears in your basket, it does not necessarily need a filing decision. A discovery demand may have come in. Additional reports may have been received. Something may have happened which needs to be addressed. Address the issues and put the case file in the out basket. Take time to review the case file again. You may have overlooked something the last time you handled the file.

8. THE EIGHTH STRATEGY: BE PREPARED

Unless there are bond motions or other similar matters, the next time you will see the file it will come to you in a bucket or banker's box with scores of additional files set on an arraignment docket. Which brings us to the eighth strategy: "Be prepared." Take the docket and go through the files to make sure discovery has been done, the plea offer made, and the files readied for the cattle call of arraignment day. One efficient way of handling the mass of cases is to take the copy of the docket and annotate it with essential information for plea bargaining or other pretrial matters that might arise. Check on the jail status and jail credit for each defendant on

---

1 Some information, such as "victim won't cooperate," should be written inside the file rather than on the file front.

the docket. Recently bonded defendants sometimes do not receive proper notice that their appearance in court is required, and in most jurisdictions the defendant will be entitled to credit on the ultimate sentence for any time served in jail pending trial. If jail credit information is not at your fingertips, it can cause either delays in sentencing or post-conviction motions to correct sentences. It is far better to resolve jail credit issues at sentencing than to try to reconstruct jail credit months and even years after the fact. As you call the cases at arraignment, make annotations either on the docket or the case file of what happened in court. Be specific. There may come a time in the future when you will desperately want to remember what happened at the hearing. The less you note down, the greater the likelihood of your needing to remember. Also note down on a "to do" list any new tasks that need to be done in light of what happened in court. When you return to the office, give the files with their dispositions to your secretary and immediately begin with your "to do" list. You will carry the file to court several more times before you dispose of it—for docket days, pretrial conferences, motion days, and the like. Each time you take a batch of files to court, no matter what the court appearance is called, redo all the tasks set out in this paragraph.

Knowing your cases is only one aspect of being prepared. Knowing the applicable law is another. If you do not know the applicable law, you need to know how to find it quickly. All sorts of unexpected issues arise during a day in court, and you cannot possibly have briefed every conceivable thing that might happen. You need to keep up with the recent case law, and you need to be able to find and cite it quickly. Although many courtrooms have internet access ports for ready access to Westlaw, many do not. If you keep a small notebook of case squibs on frequently encountered issues, and keep it updated, you will always have a resource to reach for when the unexpected occurs. You do not need law review style case notes; a simple sentence or two describing the holding will be enough. If you have a laptop computer, keeping the case squibs on disk makes them ready at hand and easily searchable. Failing that, a conventional three ring notebook containing squibs alphabetized by subject matter will do almost as well. As a rookie prosecutor, you will not immediately command your judge's respect. Lacking respect, you will need those squibs in that notebook to add weight to your arguments. As the judge gets to know you, and as your hair greys, you will find less and less need to give legal citations for every sentence you utter. Until the time comes that you have the judge's respect, the squib notebook will be almost essential. Even after that time comes, the notebook will be helpful.

9. THE NINTH STRATEGY: KEEP PEOPLE INFORMED

When you decide to decline prosecution on a case, inform the concerned parties and diplomatically tell them why. Patiently listen to their complaint. Consider any additional information they may have. Change your decision if it should be changed in light of any new information but never change it simply because somebody is angry. Make sure when plea bargaining to keep the victim, the investigating agency, and your immediate supervisor informed as to what is going on. As you craft a resolution to the case, you will want to do it in such a way as to have everyone as happy as possible, or failing that, at least have everyone reconciled to the disposition. The victim and law enforcement do not make the decision what plea to take. The final decision on plea bargaining rests with the prosecutor's office. The only person it is absolutely essential to satisfy is your boss, but it certainly makes life easier if victims and law enforcement agree to the plea. Remember that a criminal prosecution is not a zero-sum game in which one side must win and the other must lose. Sometimes the best way for both sides to lose is to go to trial. Sometimes the best way for both sides to win is to strike a plea bargain.

Keeping people informed means keeping yourself informed. If all you do is sit in your office and wait on law enforcement to bring you information on your cases, you are not informed. You must take proactive steps to inform yourself about your cases. When a batch of cases gets set for trial, immediately gather up the files and take them with you to the criminal investigation department and to the evidence vault. Review the original law enforcement files on each case to make sure that you have all the pertinent documents and reports. Do not be surprised when you discover that there is a great deal of information in the file that law enforcement thought you would not need. Go to the evidence vault and examine the evidence. Do not take it for granted that law enforcement will be able to immediately lay hands on all items of evidence. They will not. This preliminary trip saves lots of headaches as you near trial. There is nothing more nerve wracking than to be in jury selection at the same time that the evidence custodian is frantically searching the evidence vault for your essential exhibit. Do not expect law enforcement to bring the evidence to court without being prompted. Prompt them. If you have not already done so (and you should have already done so), get copies of all photographs, make sure that everything that should be sent to the crime lab has been sent to the crime lab, watch all videotapes, listen to all tape recordings. Do not rely on reading a transcript of the tape recording. Transcripts can be disappointingly inaccurate. Call the crime lab and speak to the analysts who worked on your exhibits. Do not assume that the written report records all that the analyst can say about the exhibit. Make sure of the whereabouts of all your witnesses. Make sure they are all subpoenaed. Make sure all subpoenas are served. Bring your witnesses in and prepare them to testify. Make sure that what they can say is what has been written in the reports. If they cannot or will not testify in conformity to your expectation, take appropriate remedial action. Appropriate remedial action does not include subornation of perjury or browbeating witnesses into saying what the report says. Prepare a trial brief. Then go try your case, or (more likely) plead it out. Because you have prepared for war, the defense will sue for peace.

10. THE TENTH STRATEGY: GET TO THE COURTROOM EARLY

Get there at least half an hour early. Forty-five minutes early is better. An hour early is best. You will learn many useful things being the first person in the courtroom and watching the interactions between the defendants and attorneys as they straggle in. As Yogi Berra once said, "You can observe a lot just by watching." This admonition is especially important when you are going to trial. On the morning of trial, get to the courthouse at least one-half hour early, preferably an hour early. Meet with your witnesses. You should have subpoenaed them to appear that half hour to one hour early. Having your witnesses there ahead of time gives you time for last-minute trial prep, time to make sure that all your witnesses are present, and time to cellphone those who have overslept and roust them out of their beds. Once again, watching the interaction among the prospective jurors as the courtroom fills up will tell you volumes about who should and should not serve as jurors.

11. THE ELEVENTH STRATEGY: DELIVER THE GOODS AT TRIAL

Willingness to go to trial earns the respect of your peers. Too many "trial lawyers" are really "plea lawyers." If you get a reputation as a "plea lawyer," you will get less satisfactory pleas than you will when your opponent knows you will go to trial. Being willing to go to trial is only half of delivering the goods. The other half is making a professional, persuasive presentation. Everything you say in trial should be concise, candid, and courteous, and everything you do in trial should be purposeful, powerful, and principled. You do not merely proffer in the evidence, prove up all the elements, and pray the jury has good sense. You discover the most persuasive interpretation of your facts, devise the most persuasive presentation of those facts, and deliver that presentation in the most professional manner possible.

When you go to sentencing, be prepared to provide the judge with all the necessary information. Have all the documentation you will need: certified copies of convictions, presentence investigation reports, restitution amounts, jail credit numbers, guideline or sentencing code score sheets, letters from victims. Be able to produce any of these things or all these things at the moment the judge mentions them. As the judge pronounces the sentence, make careful notes of it in the case file. Then make sure the written judgement is really what the judge said. If the judge places the defendant on probation, note every special condition and make sure that every special condition is put into the written order of probation. If the judge makes any special admonition to the defendant, note down that admonition so that you can remind the judge of it when the defendant reappears before her on violation of probation.

12. THE TWELFTH STRATEGY: STOW YOUR TOOLS WHEN YOU FINISH THE JOB

"When you return to the office after sentencing, you must sit down and tidy up the file before it gets sent to archives. Especially if the case went to trial, the file will have become disarrayed in the hubbub of getting it to disposition. If there is a hereafter on the case, it will be nice to go back to the file and actually be able to find things and figure out what happened. Rest assured, the heavier the sentence, the more likely there is to be a hereafter in the form of a post-conviction collateral attack.

B. PRETRIAL PUBLICITY

One aspect of case management presents special problems—pretrial publicity. Most cases get filed, litigated, and tried under the radar screen of public notoriety, but when the occasional case comes along that garners intense media attention, you must negotiate numerous pitfalls in order to obtain a sound conviction. Although many worthy people believe that the First Amendment's guarantee of freedom of the press seriously interferes with the defendant's Sixth Amendment right to a fair trial, recent statistical studies suggest that publicity appears to have a negligible effect on trial conviction rates.[2] Nevertheless, the conventional wisdom teaches that prosecutors build their careers on high conviction rates, and they achieve their high conviction rates by manipulating the press through leaks. As the conventional wisdom goes, by dribbling out inflammatory tidbits, these evil manipulators create a hostile environment for the trial and insure that the jury panels which are ultimately called to hear the case will be infected with preconceived notions of the defendant's guilt. This conventional wisdom is exemplified by such movies as *Absence of Malice,* in which a gnomish, overly ambitious prosecutor ruined the hero's life with a cleverly leaked piece of misinformation. Pitted against such devious prosecutors, so the conventional wisdom goes, are hapless defense attorneys not nearly so experienced in or able at the game of infecting juries with pretrial publicity. The reality is somewhat different. Few prosecutors confront more than one or two highly publicized cases in their careers, and most go their entire careers without confronting a media circus. When such cases come along, most prosecutors will have no experience with such things and no idea how to handle them. If they ultimately perpetrate a media *faux pas,* they will more often have victimized themselves than those

[2] See Bruschke, Jon, and William Earl Loges, Free Press vs. Fair Trial: Examining Publicity's Role in Trial Outcomes, Lawrence Earlbaum Associates, Inc., Mahwah, NJ 2004.

they accuse. Pretrial publicity is anathema to the prosecution's efforts to convict. If you have made a circumspect, judicious charging decision, you have no need to prejudice a jury panel against the defendant. If you have made a good charging decision, fair-minded people of good intelligence who have no previous knowledge of the case are going to agree with you when they hear the evidence. Fair-minded people of good intelligence who have been bombarded by pretrial publicity touting the defendant's guilt are not likely to agree with your charging decision because they are not likely to survive the voir dire examination. The more pervasive the publicity, the larger the percentage of fair-minded, intelligent prospective jurors who will be challenged for cause because of their too-great "knowledge" from the media reports. In a case suffering from pervasive publicity, almost all fair-minded people of good intelligence will have become so saturated with publicity that they will be challenged off the jury for cause. This results in selecting juries from a group of people who, as Mark Twain once said, "don't know anything and can't read." Pervasive pretrial publicity shrinks the pool of good jurors but does nothing to shrink the pool of potential jurors who "don't know anything and can't read." The smaller the pool of good jurors and the correspondingly larger the pool of ignorant illiterates, the less likely you are to get a good jury. The less likely you are to get a good jury, the less likely you are to get a good verdict. If the defendant is guilty and the evidence is overwhelming, a good verdict is the last thing the defendant wants. Fortunately, in most cases there is a simple solution—change of venue. Changes of venue cause all sorts of logistical problems and inconveniences, with the attorneys having to go to distant cities and live out of suitcases during the trial, and witnesses having to be brought in and housed in hotels, but they increase the pool of fair-minded jurors of good intelligence who can survive a challenge for cause.

1. NOTORIETY AS AN INTOXICANT

Media hype results in other ill effects besides difficulty in selecting juries. Everyone likes to be recognized, and the more recognition the better. We tend, however, to behave much differently when we know people are watching than we do when we are in relative obscurity. In most situations this tendency keeps us from embarrassment. In some it causes us embarrassment. When before a relatively small audience of people we know, we tend to behave more admirably than we sometimes do when nobody is watching. But the larger and the more anonymous the audience, the more likely we are to engage in unseemly behavior. This accounts for the popularity of "reality" shows. Point a camera at people and tell them that millions of strangers are watching, and they will engage in unreal behavior. Consequently, the greater the media attention that is focused on a case, the more surreal the case becomes, with lawyers on both sides and even the judges engaging in ill-conceived behavior.

As the media has grown more powerful, and as some lawyers have become more skillful in manipulating said media, the problems confronting the prosecutor have mushroomed. Fortunately, most criminal trials occur under the radar screen of even the local media. The litigants perform in virtually empty courtrooms populated, if at all, by small numbers of spectators who are vitally interested in the outcome of the case. When cases do attract the attention of the media, it is usually only a notice in the paper. Sometimes it is a brief mention on the local TV station, but whatever it is, it tends to infect the process. The efficiency with which a case is handled varies in inverse proportion to the amount of attention it receives in the media. The occasional case which garners nationwide attention becomes not so much a criminal trial as a Franz Kafka novel.

2. GUIDELINES FOR MEDIA COMMENT

Many elected prosecutors make life easy for their assistants by appointing press information officers and forbidding other employees to comment to the press. If you work in such an office, you have a simple solution when the press thrusts a microphone in your face—refer them to the press information officer. In other offices, assistants are allowed to speak to the press, and disaster can result. Most assistants, not being well schooled in dealing with the press, do not know what may and may not be said and frequently wind up saying things far better left unsaid. You never know when you are going to become involved in a case that draws media attention, and if you wait until it happens to become familiar with the pitfalls of media relations you are quite likely to encounter problems. You must become familiar with the ABA and NDAA guidelines for media comment and also with any relevant bar disciplinary rules in your jurisdiction. Being forearmed with this knowledge, you are far less likely to stick your foot in your mouth when a reporter sticks a microphone in your face. Reporters are not going to be satisfied if you simply say "no comment," and they have ways of punishing you if you completely refuse to talk to them. There is an old saying that you should try to stay on the good side of someone who buys ink by the barrel. If you must speak to them, then you need to be able to say something which is both innocuous and nontoxic.

You are forbidden to say anything that you know or reasonably should know will be published in the news media and will "have a substantial likelihood of materially prejudicing the defense.[3] It allows you to say:

(1). The identity, residence, occupation and family status of the accused.[4]

---

[3] Rule 3.6(a), ABA Rules of Professional Conduct.

[4] Rule 3.6(b)(7)(i), ABA Rules of Professional Conduct; National Prosecution Standard 2–14.3a.

(2). Information necessary to aid in the arrest of an accused who is at large.[5]

(3). The fact, time, and place of arrest.[6]

(4). The identity of investigating and arresting officers and agencies and the lengthy of the investigation.[7]

(5). The crime charged and, except where prohibited by law, the identities of the persons involved.[8]

(6). Information contained in a public record.[9]

(7). The fact that an investigation is under way.[10]

(8). The scheduling or result of any stage of the prosecution.[11]

(9). A request for assistance in obtaining evidence.[12]

(10). A warning of danger concerning an unarrested accused.[13]

(11). You may respond to adverse publicity in order to protect the prosecution's legitimate official interests. Such responses should be strictly limited to only what is necessary to mitigate the adverse publicity.[14]

You may also disclose information which is a matter of public record,[15] but care should be taken with regard to such disclosures. The public records may contain information which you should not give out yourself. In such a situation, you should not be giving out the information, even though it is a matter of public record. You cannot prevent reporters from finding the information if they exercise enough diligence in seeking it, but you should not yourself be the source. You should not even direct reporters to the information in the public records. Suppose a reporter asks you to confirm whether or not the defendant is a serial rapist, and you say, "That is a matter upon which I may not comment, but if you look at document thirty-seven filed in case number 1234 in the clerk's office, you will find the information you want." You can be sure that the next day's headlines will

---

5 Rule 3.6(b)(7)(ii), ABA Rules of Professional Conduct.

6 Rule 3.6(b)(7)(iii), ABA Rules of Professional Conduct; National Prosecution Standard 2–14.3e.

7 Rule 3.6(b)(7)(iv), ABA Rules of Professional Conduct; National Prosecution Standard 2–14.3d.

8 Rule 3.6(b)(1), ABA Rules of Professional Conduct; National Prosecution Standard 2–14.3b.

9 Rule 3.6(b)(2), ABA Rules of Professional Conduct; National Prosecution Standard 2–14.3f.

10 Rule 3.6(b)(3), ABA Rules of Professional Conduct.

11 Rule 3.6(b)(4), ABA Rules of Professional Conduct.

12 Rule 3.6(b)(5), ABA Rules of Professional Conduct.

13 Rule 3.6(b)(6), ABA Rules of Professional Conduct.

14 ABA Prosecution Standard 3–1.10(f).

15 ABA Fair Trial and Public Disclosure Standard 8–4.1(b).

read something to the effect "Assistant Prosecutor Confirms Defendant Serial Rapist." You will probably have a fair chance of winning the bar complaint or contempt citation filed against you, but why put yourself in such a position in the first place?

You should be able to make reasonable and fair response to comments made by opposing counsel or others,[16] but here again you should exercise circumspection. A reporter may make a remark to the effect that "opposing counsel has said that you arrested his client for purely political motives and that he will trounce you when the case comes to trial, what do you have to say to that?" The first impulse when confronted with such a comment is to lash out at opposing counsel, to speak about his lack of professionalism in making such a remark, and to outline just exactly how guilty his client is. Do not do it. In the first place, opposing counsel may not have said any such thing. The reporter may have grossly misinterpreted what was said, or she may be making it up in order to bait you into saying something you will regret. Remember your days in public school when your so-called friends would run back and forth between you and your enemy carrying tales about the slanders you had allegedly uttered against each other? All your "friends" wanted was a fight, and all the reporters want is a juicy quote. It would be far better if you made a remark to the effect that you would be sorely disappointed if opposing counsel made such a comment and that you look forward to resolving the relevant issues in the courtroom.

In addition to remaining silent about the existence and contents of a confession,[17] you should refrain from: commenting on the prior criminal record of the defendant;[18] voicing any opinion on the character of the defendant;[19] expressing any personal opinion on the guilt or innocence of the defendant;[20] commenting on the fact that the defendant refused to make a statement;[21] disclosing the performance of any examinations or tests, the defendant's refusal to submit to such tests,[22] or the nature of any physical evidence;[23] the identity or expected testimony of any potential witnesses;[24] the possibility of a guilty plea or other disposition of the case;[25] or the nature of any inadmissible evidence.[26]

---

16 ABA Prosecution Standard 3–1.10(f).

17 ABA Fair Trial and Public Disclosure Standard 8–2.2(a)(iv).

18 ABA Fair Trial and Public Disclosure Standard 8–2.2(a)(i).

19 ABA Fair Trial and Public Disclosure Standard 8–2.2(a)(ii).

20 ABA Fair Trial and Public Disclosure Standard 8–2.2(a)(iii).

21 ABA Fair Trial and Public Disclosure Standard 8–2.2(a)(iv).

22 ABA Fair Trial and Public Disclosure Standard 8–2.2(a)(v).

23 Id.; ABA Fair Trial and Public Disclosure Standard 8–2.2(a)(vi).

24 ABA Fair Trial and Public Disclosure Standard 8–2.2(a)(vii).

25 ABA Fair Trial and Public Disclosure Standard 8–2.2(a)(viii).

26 ABA Fair Trial and Public Disclosure Standard 8–2.2(a)(ix).

"How," you may ask, "do all those lawyers on all those news programs get away with saying so many things that are so much in conflict with the rules?" It is one of life's mysteries. The only reply one can make to that question is, "The fact that another breaks the rules with impunity does not give you a license to break them." When Francis Bacon took bribes to influence his judicial decisions, almost all other judges were taking bribes. When, for political reasons, he got arrested for taking bribes, he did not say "everyone else is doing it," he went to prison without complaint. He is to be praised for taking his punishment without protesting that others were getting away with the same thing. He would have deserved more praise if he had not taken bribes. Observe the rules about media comment regardless of what others do.

"If I can say so little, and if reporters will likely punish me for saying 'no comment,' what can I do?" Give them what they are looking for, but give it to them in nontoxic form. Radio and TV reporters are looking for sound bites and print reporters are looking for pithy quotes to put into sidebars. Work out a repertoire of bland sound bites which are suitable for all occasions: "The jury is the final arbiter of fact." "We are prepared to present our case before a jury." "We intend to try this case in the courtroom and not in the newsroom." "The judge has made her ruling, and we intend to honor it to the letter." "We understand the defense position, and at the appropriate time and place, we will present our contrasting views." "We will leave no stone unturned in seeing to it that the defendant receives a fair trial." Quotations from the Bible and from Shakespeare can work quite well, especially if they are ambiguous. Work hard to keep from making an unguarded remark which will give the media an embarrassing sound bite.

PRACTICAL EXERCISE

On Monday you return to the office from vacation and find that your in basket contains a huge stack of paperwork. You sort through the basket and find that you have:

1. A motion to suppress the defendant's confession in the capital murder case set for trial two months hence. A quick review of the motion leads you to believe that it is a boilerplate pleading.

2. A lengthy intake report on a complex embezzlement case. No arrest has yet been made.

3. Four intake reports on felony arrests. A quick glance through the reports tells you that two cases have all the information necessary and can be filed on without further inquiry, but two require further inquiry. You notice that one of the incomplete reports concerns an arrest made five months previously.

4. A pretrial conference docket listing sixty of your cases. Pretrials are set for this coming Thursday. Your secretary has put

the case files in three banker's boxes and set them on the floor beside your desk. You have had no communication with any of the defense attorneys involved in the cases.

5. A felony intake file from the tickler. Two weeks of the three-week time limit for filing formal charges have expired, but you feel you do not have adequate information to make a charging decision because Officer Baynes still has not answered the questions you sent him.

6. A message to call the victim in a sexual battery case. She says the defendant is stalking her, has keyed her car, and has left threatening messages on her answer machine.

Formulate a "batting order" for addressing these matters. Describe the measures you would take in dealing with each issue.

CHAPTER 7

ESTABLISHING CASE THEORY

▪ ▪ ▪

[A case theory should be] lucid, brief, and * * * deserving of belief.—Quintilian, 4.2.31[1]

When I went to the Bar as a very young man (said I to myself said I)
I'll work on a new and original plan (said I to myself said I) * * *
I'll never throw dust in a juryman's eye's (said I to myself said I)
Or hoodwink a judge who is not overwise (said I to myself said I).
The Lord Chancellor's Song from *Iolanthe* by Gilbert & Sullivan

A. RHETORICAL CONSIDERATIONS

1. THE DEPARTMENTS OF RHETORIC

For more than 2,000 years rhetoricians have divided their field into three departments: judicial, deliberative, and ceremonial.[2] Ceremonial rhetoric, such as a sermon or eulogy, looks to the present and seeks to praise or blame. Deliberative rhetoric, such as a speech in Congress, looks to the future and seeks to encourage or discourage future conduct. Judicial rhetoric looks to the past and seeks to censure or exonerate. The prosecutor seeks censure by making accusation and the defendant seeks exoneration by defending against that accusation. A criminal trial therefore concerns itself with the history of a transaction. The two sides present competing histories of an incident in hopes that they can persuade the fact finder to accept their version of history and render a favorable verdict. The more compelling the evidence, the more tolerance the fact finder will have for a sloppy presentation, but a poor enough presentation can ruin even the most compelling evidence. The presentation must aim toward a clearly defined, attainable objective. "Guilty as charged" may be a clearly defined objective, but is it attainable? If you have made a wise charging decision, it ought to be. You simply must craft a compelling presentation of your history.

---

[1] *Quintilian's Institutes of Oratory: or, Education of an Orator*, trans. John Selby Watson, London: Henry G. Bohn, 1856. p. 279.

[2] Aristotle, Rhetoric, 1356b.

2. BREVITY, CLARITY, VERITY

Prosecutors recount histories, but they also build. They build a case that they hope will survive the slings and arrows of outrageous litigation. The edifice of their case rests upon a cornerstone, and that cornerstone is the case theory. A case theory is a simple statement of the case that entitles your side to win. Ancient rhetoricians wrote that the ideal case theory had three attributes: brevity, clarity, and plausibility.[3] They went on to say that it was especially important that the case theory have plausibility if it was false.[4] "If you're going to tell a lie, make it a good one," is not a motto which advocates, especially prosecutors, should embrace. We might better name the third attribute verity, which we will define as the quality of being both truthful and believable. The wise builder builds upon bedrock, and there is no firmer bedrock for your cornerstone than the bedrock of truth.

3. THE IDEAL CASE THEORY

The ideal case theory consists of one or two sentences using words of one or two syllables. Think Ernest Hemingway, not James Joyce. Once you settle on a compelling case theory, that theory can be fleshed out into an introduction for the opening statement. When an opening statement begins with a compelling statement of the case theory, you have made a good beginning toward a guilty verdict. Some example case theories follow.

> (1) Frank Leonard shot Rebecca MacGregor in the back, and he shot her in the back, and he shot her in the back, and he shot her in the back, and he shot her in the back, and he shot her in the back, and he shot her in the back, and he shot her in the back.
>
> (2) Three people went into a locked, empty house; two of them died in that house; and the third came out alive. That third person, Sebastian Moran, today stands trial for the murder of the other two.
>
> (3) On July 3, 2000, at Newgate Prison, as Inmate Elvis Gard lay bleeding and near death, Tony Brisbie Chad Jackal tied a cord tight around Gard's neck. Then they sat back, lit up cigarettes, and watched Gard die.
>
> (4) Grace Fairfax talked about killing her husband Edward Fairfax. She talked about using a knife. Then one night she tried to kill him. She used a knife. A few months later, she killed him. She used a knife.

---

[3] 2 Cicero, De Inventione, 1.20.28, Trans. H.M. Hubbell, Harvard University Press, Cambridge, Massachusetts, 1949. p. 57.

[4] 1 [Cicero], Rhetorica ad Herennium, 1.9.16, Trans. Harry Caplan, Harvard University Press, Cambridge, 1954. p.29.

(5) Robert Joiner on April 15, 1995, went and got his shotgun. He loaded the shotgun. He stepped onto the porch of his single wide trailer, raised that shotgun to his shoulder, and shot and killed his good friend, Rodney Howard. And what did he kill him over? A $40.00 bag of pot.

(6) This case is as easy as A. B. C. A: Dan Higgins was arrested in Hazel Carroll's house. B: He had Hazel's belongings in his pocket. C: He confessed to the burglary.

(7) Branko, the drug sniffing dog, smelled methamphetamine on Clyde Huston; Officer Friendly pulled the methamphetamine out of Huston's pocket; and Huston admitted the methamphetamine was his.

Each of these case theories truthfully stated the facts so as to logically show the defendants' guilt. Each also tried to appeal to more than simple reason. Each case theory aimed to make the jury not only believe the defendant's guilt, but also to feel that it had no alternative but to find him guilty. The fact that the actors of situation (3) sat back and lit up cigarettes didn't contribute to the victim's death, but it did have logical relevance to the element of premeditation. It also appealed quite strongly to the emotion of pity for the victim. The fact that the victim in situation (5) was the defendant's good friend did not make the victim any deader, but it did make a strong appeal to the defendant's character as a bad person.

4. THE RHETORICAL TRINITY

If the jury does not believe your case theory, you lose. If the jury is not moved by the case theory, you lose. It may seem paradoxical that even if the jury believes your case theory, you still can lose, but it is a fact of life. Jurors realize that a verdict of guilty hurts the defendant, and most people do not enjoy hurting others. A winning case theory makes the jury want to hurt the defendant or at least makes the jury feel that it would not be a bad thing if the defendant got hurt because of his crime. How do you accomplish this? You take your direction from a 2,000 year old book, *Rhetoric*, written by a relatively intelligent gentleman by the name of Aristotle.

Aristotle taught that we are persuaded by appeals to one of three things: ethos, logos, and pathos—the rhetorical trinity.[5] Ethos is the character of the messenger. Logos is the logic of the message. Pathos is the emotion stirred by the message. When we see a celebrity hawking a product in a commercial, we see the classic appeal to ethos. The fact that Shari Starlet uses Acme Deodorant tells us nothing about the utility of the product. The advertiser expects us to buy the product because we are

[5] Aristotle, Rhetoric. 1356a.

smitten with Shari's character. Appeal to ethos. Imagine a commercial which has some star walking the streets of a third world country surrounded by dirty, hungry children. Is the commercial designed to demonstrate the efficacy of the charity involved? Or is it designed to make us so emotionally aroused that we will send our dollars to the charity? Appeal to pathos. Aristotle taught that the only proper appeal was the appeal to logos. He believed pathos and ethos to be false guides, and likelier to mislead than to show the way to a correct decision.

> It is not right to pervert the judge by moving him to anger or envy or pity—one might as well warp a carpenter's rule before using it. Again, a litigant has clearly nothing to do but to show that the alleged fact is so or is not so, that it has or has not happened.[6]

Ethos and pathos have ever after suffered as the ugly ducklings of the rhetorical trinity. Study the case law. Appellate courts most often reverse convictions in situations where the prosecutor has gone overboard in an attempt to appeal to ethos or pathos.

This appellate disfavor toward ethos and pathos creates a real problem for prosecutors. Considerations of ethos and pathos are why we have a judicial system. Society feels angry about crime (a consideration of pathos) and thinks criminals are bad people who merit punishment (a consideration of ethos). Prosecutors, however, must strictly confine themselves to appeals to logos. You cannot appeal to ethos and pathos, but juries are reluctant to convict unless they are angry about the crime and think the defendant is a bad person. You break the horns of this dilemma by structuring strictly factual, logical appeals which incidentally resonate with ethos and pathos. Although you cannot make an argument so extremely logical that it inflames the passions of the jury, you can easily go overboard in appeals to ethos and pathos. A prosecutor seeking to prove up a grave robbery once introduced a videotape of the deceased's body lying in a pasture some 30 miles from the grave site. This videotape quite logically proved that the body had been removed from the grave. Unfortunately, it also quite graphically depicted decomposed body parts which buzzards and other scavengers had scattered over a half-acre of pasture. The conviction was quite rightly reversed for excessive prosecutorial appeal to pathos.[7] On retrial, instead of the videotape, the prosecutor introduced a photograph of the interior of the empty casket sitting at the bottom of the grave. This also constituted unassailable logical proof that the body had been removed from the grave, but not such an overblown appeal to pathos as to even rate a mention in the appellate opinion affirming the second conviction.[8]

---

[6] Aristotle, Rhetoric. 1354a.

[7] Pottgen v. State, 589 So.2d 390 (Fla.App.1st DCA 1991).

[8] Pottgen v. State, 616 So.2d 1125 (Fla.App.1st DCA 1993).

5. COUNTERFEIT APPEALS TO THE RHETORICAL TRINITY

As you seek to persuade, you must not only guard against excessive appeals to the rhetorical trinity, you must also guard against counterfeit appeals. Each member of the rhetorical trinity has an evil twin, and you must be ever vigilant not to appeal to them. The consequences of making such appeals can range from censure to laughter. Such appeals might occasionally result in success, but at what cost? It is not enough to achieve victory; you must do more; you must deserve it. Ethos, or appeal to character has genus, or appeal to identity as its counterfeit. Logos has sophism, or fallacy, and pathos has bathos, or false emotion as its counterfeit. The most patently blameworthy of the counterfeit appeals is the appeal to genus. The mere fact that someone belongs to a recognizable group (professional, ethnic, or otherwise) says nothing about the issue of the person's human worth. Poor does not mean lazy. Rural does not mean ruffian. Educated does not mean intelligent. We could multiply the stereotypes *ad infinitum*, and they would tell us very little about the character of the person under consideration. The surest way to get a mistrial or a reversal is to appeal to genus. Typical appeals to genus include race, religion, national origin, sexual orientation, political party, and in some situations can even include what sports team you support. Even understated appeals to genus merit censure and should be avoided.

Sophism is defined by Webster as "an argument apparently correct in form, but actually invalid; especially: such an argument used to deceive." Some attorneys work on a strategy of trying to select the most unintelligent jury possible and then deceiving them with sophism and overblown or counterfeit appeals to ethos and pathos. You do not need to be a logician to counter such tactics, but you do need to have a firm grasp of informal logic and critical thinking skills. You must make absolutely certain you do not fall into fallacious argument, and you must be ever vigilant to identify and expose the fallacious arguments of your adversaries. An unchallenged fallacious argument might be accepted, but once you point out that the emperor has no clothes, the faulty reasoning usually becomes painfully (and often embarrassingly) obvious.

We need to expand our definition of sophism to include not only logical fallacy, but rhetorical fallacy as well. Rhetorical fallacy occurs when you do one of two things: when you argue "facts" not in evidence, and when you knowingly draw reasonable but untrue inferences from the facts in evidence. When a prosecutor's case is hamstrung by either the Constitutional exclusionary rules, the Byzantine rules of evidence, or logistical inability to prove up favorable facts, the temptation is great to go ahead and mention those facts anyway. Arguing unproven facts is blameworthy, but the offender can plead mitigation because she has at least argued facts. Sometimes, when the provable facts suggest a conclusion that the attorney knows to be false, attorneys will go ahead and argue the false conclusion as proven. Remember the Matthew Lanatus murder case[9] in which the prosecution fumbled its proof that the victim was in fact dead. Due to a malfunctioning camera in the medical examiner's office and a shabby chain of custody on the victim's body, the prosecution failed to prove the body that was autopsied was the victim's body. The defense attorney argued to the jury that the victim had actually left town and was living and working in a far distant city. Aside from the fact that the argument drew snickers from the jury and may actually have helped to convict the defendant, it was not proper. The defense attorney knew full well that the victim was dead. To argue otherwise was improper. The proper arguments at the defense attorney's disposal have already been discussed and need not be repeated.

The third counterfeit appeal, bathos, most often brings self-executing punishment. Cicero wrote that "Nothing dries quicker than tears."[10] When you (or one of your witnesses) cries crocodile tears, the jury will more often than not pick up on the insincerity. If they discern the insincerity, they will be disposed to punish it with an adverse verdict. A famous case of bathos occurred during the Triangle Shirtwaist Fire trial in New York at the turn of the last century. Scores of young women working in a tenement sweatshop died when a fire broke out on the premises. The owners of the sweatshop had chained the outside doors shut so that the workers could not sneak out for unauthorized breaks. The owners stood trial on charges of unlawful homicide, and a young survivor of the fire testified as the star witness for the prosecution. On direct examination she recounted a pitiful tale of woe describing the horrific deaths of her co-workers, and there was not a dry eye in the jury box when she was turned over for cross-examination. During the course of a lengthy cross-examination, defense counsel Max Steuer realized that the young lady had memorized her testimony. He took her through the testimony several times, demonstrating beyond peradventure that she had definitely memorized it. The jurors, who had been so moved by her direct examination, completely turned against her (and the prosecution) upon the exposure of her careful memorization.[11]

6. THE EVIDENTIARY AND FORENSIC TRINITIES

You persuade by appealing to the rhetorical trinity, but you must appeal from something. The something you appeal from is evidence, and evidence comes in three types—favorable facts, unfavorable facts, and fiction. These three types of evidence make up the evidentiary trinity and

[9] Chapter 1.

[10] 2 Cicero, De Inventione, 1.56.109, Supra at 163.

[11] Wellman, Francis, The Art of Cross-Examination, Kessinger Publishing, Whitefish, Montana, 1910/2005. pp. 50–53.

provide the raw materials of persuasion. You take this raw material and fashion it into a work of persuasion that you present at trial. A criminal trial does not exist in a vacuum. It is part and parcel of the human struggle that began when our ancestors were still rubbing sticks together to make fire and will end in the (hopefully) far distant future. Mankind's history records three things: building, preservation, and destruction. We build, we attempt to preserve what we have built, and others attempt to destroy what we have built. Some building projects have lasted: Stonehenge, the Pantheon in Rome, the Easter Island statues. Others have not fared so well: the Hanging Gardens of Babylon, the Parthenon in Athens, the Colossus of Rhodes. Fate dooms some building projects to a short life: ice sculpture, a nicely mown lawn, a case before a jury. You thus work with the three types of evidence in three ways. You attempt to build your case with favorable facts. You attempt to preserve your case against unfavorable facts. If you are ethical, you attempt to destroy fiction. The threefold endeavors of building, destroying, and preserving make up the forensic trinity.

Fiction actually comes in two types, favorable and unfavorable. When your opponent employs unfavorable fiction against you, you seek to destroy it. What of favorable fiction? There is no place in advocacy for favorable fiction. Even assuming you were 100% sure you could escape criminal liability and professional discipline for subornation of perjury, you should not use it. Sooner or later your duplicity will either be discovered or suspected, and your credibility will be ruined.

As you seek to build your case upon favorable fact, you must remember that nobody ever reported an incident with 100% accuracy. Even a video recording is open to interpretation. Although you can never attain perfect knowledge of exactly what happened, in most cases you can achieve enough certainty to satisfy the reasonable doubt standard. Thus, the prosecution seeks to present a history which can never be "exactly what happened." The defense's counter-history likewise is never "exactly what happened." Ethics dictate that the attorneys craft a history as close to "what really happened" as humanly possible, but exactitude is not humanly possible. If exact histories ever become possible, trial lawyers will be out of a job.

Sometimes the parties agree on the basic facts of the history. Then the battle of is not over which history the jury should accept, but how they should interpret the history presented. Example: A group of teenagers taunted and physically abused a mentally ill alcoholic over a period of two days. The alcoholic died as a result of the abuse. Because they took change out of his pockets and stole his cigarettes, the charge read "first-degree felony murder." The prosecution's thesis: "Four teenagers beat and kicked a homeless Vietnam veteran to death, and as he lay dying the defendant urinated on his head." The defense antithesis: "Although the thirteen-year-old defendant was present when a group of children accidentally killed an alcoholic hobo, he did little to cause the hobo's death, didn't steal anything, and was more or less a spectator." The synthesis: a second-degree murder conviction.

7. THE TYPES OF ISSUES

If perpetrators face an accusation of wrongdoing and cannot run away, they can defend themselves in one of three ways: They can deny doing it. They can claim justification, excuse, or mitigation for doing it. Or they can proudly say, "Yes, I did it. So what?" Ancient rhetoricians recognized these three basic types of factual issues in criminal cases, calling them conjectural, qualitative, and definitional.[12] Conjectural issues ask the question: "Did the defendant do it?" Qualitative issues ask: "Was the defendant justified in doing it?" Definitional issues ask: "Accepting the state's case at face value, does it prove anything at all?" We can call the three types of cases whodunnits (conjectural), whydunnits (qualitative), and what-of-its (definitional). Based upon the nature and quality of the prosecution's evidence, the defense will fall into one or more of these three types of issues.

The defense will make the issue conjectural in one of three instances:

(1) When there are no eyewitnesses; or

(2) When the eyewitnesses have credibility problems; or

(3) When the defendant is too hard-headed to admit the obvious.

The issue will be qualitative when:

(1) You have a sympathetic defendant; or

(2) You have an unlovely victim; or

(3) It is impossible to deny doing it.

The issue will be definitional in any of the following situations:

(1) On motion to dismiss or for summary judgment.

(2) On motion for directed verdict or judgment of acquittal.

(3) When you have a high probability of jury apathy toward the crime charged.

Since jury apathy is not a legally recognized defense, this third use of the what-of-it defense will usually be tacit, with either a denial or justification offered as an excuse rather than a reason for acquittal.

[12] 1 [Cicero], Rhetorica ad Herennium. 1.11.18–15.25, Supra at pp. 33–49.

8. THE POINT TO ADJUDICATE

The broad issue of whodunnit or whydunnit usually resolves itself to some smaller issue of fact whose decision will govern the outcome of the case. In a conjectural case, for instance, the smaller issue of fact could be "Does the sole eyewitness have such poor eyesight that we cannot credit his identification of the defendant?" Ancient rhetoricians called this central fact in issue the point to adjudicate. The key to victory in any criminal case is to identify the point to adjudicate.[13] Once you identify it, you know what you must prove and can marshal your evidence accordingly. If you cannot identify the point to adjudicate, or if you have misidentified it, the defense attorney will be more than happy to point it out to the jury for you. If she can identify it. There is nothing more frustrating than watching two lawyers litigate a case when they have no clue as to the main issue. If you are successful in carrying the point to adjudicate, the defense will sometimes try to redefine the point. You must be ever vigilant for a shift in emphasis. It should mean victory, but if you don't recognize the shift, it could mean you are about to fall flat on your face.

9. THE CANONS OF RHETORIC

The ancients recognized five canons of rhetoric: invention (or discovery), arrangement, delivery, style, and memory.[14] Three of those canons are highly relevant in the modern courtroom. Invention dealt with deciding what to argue; arrangement with marshaling the arguments; and delivery with making the arguments. Style dealt with choice of ornamental words. Style is a very minor consideration. Plain talk well-delivered wins out over bankrupt bombast nine times out of ten. Memory, or recalling what to say, had great relevance in a preliterate society. Today's technology, with written notes, cue cards, teleprompters, and the like, makes memory less important than it once was.

The term invention carries some negative ethical connotations. Invention suggests fabrication, and fabrication is another word for lying. Whatever you do in a courtroom, you cannot lie. Some writers use the alternative title of discovery. Discovery is much more descriptive of the process. To repeat *Ecclesiastes*, "there is nothing new under the sun."[15] All possible arguments have already been made. There are no new arguments to invent. What you are really doing is not inventing new arguments, but discovering which old ones best fit your facts.

---

13 1 [Cicero], Rhetorica ad Herrenium. 1.16.26–17.27, Id. at pp. 55–53.

14 2 Cicero, De Inventione, 1.7.9, Supra at pp 19–20.

15 Ecclesiastes 1:9 (NRSV).

10. TECHNICAL AND NONTECHNICAL PROOFS

Aristotle divided proofs into two categories: technical proofs and nontechnical proofs. His definitions for these two terms were rather complex, but for our purposes, we can simplify them. Technical proofs are arguments. Nontechnical proofs are evidence. He taught that the art of rhetoric applied only to technical proofs.[16] In other words, you persuaded with argument and not with evidence. Evidence was not persuasion, it was the raw material from which you drew your arguments. As great a mind as Aristotle had, he sometimes went astray. This restriction of rhetorical techniques to argument has led to the loss of countless jury trials. Many lawyers spend most of their careers simply proffering the evidence mechanically in the misguided belief that they can "pull it all together" in final argument. If the persuasion has not been pulled together before final argument, it is unlikely to get together in final argument. Quintilian was not nearly as smart as Aristotle, but he was a seasoned trial lawyer. He knew that rhetorical principles not only applied to arguing evidence, they applied to presenting the evidence as well.[17] Whereas many ancient rhetoricians offered advice as to how to argue from testimony, Quintilian stands alone among ancient rhetoricians in offering advice on the argumentative presentation of testimony.[18] We will follow Quintilian's lead and apply the canons of rhetoric not only to arguing the evidence but also to presenting it.

In the best of all possible worlds, once you file a provable, proper, prudent charge, all that remains to be done is to present the evidence to the jury and show them where to sign on the form for the guilty verdict. Alas, a mechanically correct, legally sufficient presentation of the evidence is not always a persuasive presentation. Many prosecutors believe that they can simply proffer in the evidence, prove up all the elements, and presume the jury has good sense. This might work in the best of all possible worlds, but we live in this world, and convictions are somewhat harder to achieve here. The Three C's of charging (criminality, culpability, and convictability) only address logos. Jurors (and everyone else in the world) do not make decisions based solely on cold logic. Ethos and pathos figure greatly in most decisions and in almost all jury verdicts. If the jury does not think the defendant is a bad person, if they are not angry about what the defendant has done, they are unlikely to convict. You must craft a presentation that will not only convince the jury of the defendant's guilt, but stir their emotion to the point that they feel this bad person must be punished, and you must do so without running afoul of the legal restrictions on appeals to ethos and pathos.

---

16 Aristotle, Rhetoric, 1355b.

17 2 Quintilian, The Orator's Education, 5.1.2, Trans. Donald A. Russell, Harvard University Press, Cambridge, Massachusetts, 2001. p. 325.

18 2 Quintilian, The Orator's Education, 5.7.9–34, Id. at pp. 339–353.

B. INVENTION OF CASE THEORY

The building project begins with the case theory, which should resonate with all three members of the rhetorical trinity: ethos, logos, and pathos, and should build on favorable facts, preserve against unfavorable facts, and destroy fiction. The tension between the case theory and the defense counter theory gives you the point to adjudicate. Once you have determined the point to adjudicate, you should give some thought to restating your case theory so as to resolve the point to adjudicate in your favor. If the defense theory can be anticipated early enough, you can carry the point to adjudicate in the charging stage. For example, a fifteen-year old girl accuses a 30-year old man of forcible rape. He counters that she consented. You could file a forcible rape charge with your case theory of nonconsent rape warring against the defense counter theory of consent—or you might file a charge in which lack of consent is not an element. Many jurisdictions have child molesting statutes that specifically say consent is not a defense. Filing a child molesting charge rather than a forcible rape charge resolves the point to adjudicate in the prosecution's favor by making the defense theory a confession of guilt.

Invention involves a three-step process. Like the twelve steps of Alcoholics Anonymous, you may work on more than one step at the same time. As a matter of fact, it is best that you work on all three simultaneously. You assimilate the proof, assess the persuasiveness, and assemble the presentation.

1. ASSIMILATE THE PROOF

You must learn the facts of the case inside out. You must learn the witnesses' testimony. The testimony of a particular witness may or may not conform to the facts of the case, and you had better know where it departs from the facts. Finally, you must learn the witnesses. The character and intelligence of a particular witness are crucial to that witness's believability before the jury. You have to know who the witness is in order to predict how the witness will be received by the jury.

2. ASSESS THE PERSUASIVENESS

Can you see a compelling case theory? Can you support it with convincing proofs? Can it survive counterattack? In order to make these determinations, you should do a pro, con, contra analysis of the case. Make three columns on a page. Label the first column "pro," the second "con," and the third "contra." Your worksheet should look similar to Figure 7-1. In the "pro" column, list every single fact you can think of which resonates favorably for your side. Do not confine yourself to facts logically entitling your side to win. List all facts which resonate favorably with your victim's and witnesses' character and unfavorably with the defendant's character.

For example, if you are prosecuting two co-defendants for battery on a single victim, a "pro" entry might read "two on one." Also list every fact that might make the jury feel sorry for the victim or angry with the defendant. These become the facts upon which you will build your case. In the second ("con") column, list every fact that resonates unfavorably with the victim's or witnesses' character and favorably with the defendant's. For example, if the victim was a homeless alcoholic and the defendant a clean-cut young teenager, those facts would go into the con column. List every fact that might make the jury feel sorry for the defendant or angry with the victim. In the third ("contra") column, next to every unfavorable fact, list a fact or argument which will tend to neutralize or impeach the unfavorable fact. For example, if the eyewitness cannot positively identify the defendant, but merely says he looks like the criminal, you can argue that this fact bolsters the eyewitness's credibility—if he was lying, he would have positively identified the defendant.

It is never too soon to begin working on case theory. If you fill out the case theory worksheet during the charging stage, it can help give you guidance in deciding which charge among the range of available charges would be the most prudent.

Figure 7-1: Case Theory Worksheet

Defendant: Bart Barfly

Pro	Con	Contra
1. Barfly drunk.	**6a.** Numbskull drunk.	**6b.** It <u>was</u> a bar.
2. Argument over pool shot.	**7a.** Numbskull bigger than Barfly.	**7b.** Barfly used a weapon.
3. Barfly threatened to kill Numbskull.	**8a.** Major injury to Barfly.	**8b.** Numbskull just defending himself.
4. Attack was to Numbskull's head.	**9a.** Minor injury to Numbskull.	**9b.** Barfly sure tried for major injury.
5. Used weapon in attack. When weapon broke, re-armed and resumed attack.	**10a.** Numbskull laughed at Barfly.	**10b.** Sticks and stones may break my bones, but words will never hurt me.

Provisional Case Theory

Bart Barfly couldn't sink the 8 ball with his cue stick. When Nevin Numbskull laughed at him, he tried to sink Numbskull with the cue stick. When he broke his cue stick over Numbskull's head, he re-armed and tried again.

Provisional Defense Theory

1. Self defense.
2. Numbskull had it coming for laughing at Barfly.

Provisional Point(s) to Adjudicate

1. Who was the aggressor?
2. Was it self defense?
3. Did Numbskull have it coming?

3. ASSEMBLE THE PRESENTATION

Now that you have assimilated the evidence and assessed its persuasiveness, you begin to assemble your case theory. Compose a case theory which capitalizes on the facts in the *pro* column and neutralizes the facts in the *con* column. The case theory must have three attributes—

brevity, clarity, and verity. It must be brief, clear, and both true and believable. Now look at the *con* column and try to anticipate the defense case theory. When you have decided on the likeliest counter theory, write it down. There should be tension between the prosecution and defense theories. The issue which resolves that tension in favor of one or the other is the point to adjudicate. Write it down. Now look back at your case theory and determine if it should be revised in light of the defense theory and the point to adjudicate. The case theory must maximize the pros and minimize the cons. As you set about to discover your case theory, you must be careful to consider not only the point to adjudicate, but the type of the case as well.

Deciding upon the point to adjudicate tells you much about how to devise your case theory, but you must also decide the type of the case. Ancient rhetoricians divided case types into four categories, which they called honorable, dishonorable, doubtful, and trivial.[19] In an honorable case, all considerations of ethos and pathos are on the side of the prosecution, in a dishonorable case, ethos and pathos are in the defense camp. In a doubtful case, considerations of ethos and pathos are divided between the prosecution side and the defense side. A trivial case has no hint of ethos or pathos anywhere in sight on either side.

When you prosecute an unemployed, beer guzzling, live-in boyfriend for killing a child while mom is away at work, you have an honorable case. When Dad uses his fists to beat Granddad to death because Dad has just discovered Granddad was molesting Junior, you have a dishonorable case. When the defendant shoots an unarmed victim close upon the heels of the victim punching the defendant, you have a doubtful case. Suppose, as in the Triangle Shirtwaist case, the fire safety laws of your jurisdiction required the exterior door of a public building to remain unlocked during regular business hours. If you are prosecuting an obtuse business owner who insists on chaining the outer doors to his sweatshop so as to keep the workers from leaving early, you have a trivial case. It would not be trivial if a fire killed scores of young workers because they could not escape through the locked doors, but you could not argue such a possibility to the jury—you would have made an improperly inflammatory appeal to pathos.

Most cases fall into the doubtful range with the weight of ethos and pathos tending toward one side or another. You need to know where on the continuum from honorable to dishonorable the case falls. You need to know this so that you can devise a case theory which pushes the weight of the case toward honorable. Take the case of the teenagers who killed the Vietnam veteran. Depending on how you look at the case, you can push it toward honorable or dishonorable. Study the competing case theories again.

---

[19] 1 [Cicero], Rhetorica ad Herennium, 1.3.5, Supra at p. 11.

(1) Prosecution theory: "Four teenagers beat and kicked a homeless Vietnam veteran to death, and as he lay dying the defendant urinated on his head."

(2) Defense theory: "Although the thirteen-year-old defendant was present when a group of children accidentally killed an alcoholic hobo, he did little to cause the hobo's death, didn't steal anything, and was more or less a spectator."

The homeless Vietnam veteran was just as truthful a characterization as the alcoholic hobo. An alcoholic hobo, however, has far less ethos than a homeless Vietnam veteran. The fact that the defendant urinated on the victim did not contribute to the victim's death, but it speaks volumes about the defendant's ethos. Thus, as you truthfully state the facts of the case, you can (and must) shift the emphasis so as to move the case toward the honorable side of the scale. The same reasoning applies to trivial cases. If your statement of the case theory can push them toward honorable, so much the better.

4. THE COMPONENTS OF CASE THEORY

Although the National College of District Attorneys has been absorbed by the National District Attorneys Association, it was an excellent school for prosecutors. The NCDA taught that a case theory actually has two components, a legal theory and a factual theory. The legal theory is the crime charged. The factual theory is a simple statement of the facts supporting the legal theory. A factual theory may or may not be persuasive to a jury. You must rework the factual theory in light of all the foregoing considerations and devise a case theory, which will have brevity, clarity, and verity, will resonate with all three prongs of the forensic trinity, will resolve the point to adjudicate in your favor, and will move the case from dishonorable or doubtful toward honorable.

Oftentimes, the defense theory will be inconsistent with the factual theory but still be consistent with the legal theory. If this is the case, you must recognize this fact and take advantage of it. In the instance of the defense theory being compatible with the legal theory, the case theory can be amended to include the defense theory as a theory of guilt, thereby robbing the defendant of his point to adjudicate. For example, the defendant pawns a recently stolen motorcycle. On a charge of dealing in stolen property, he says that he did not know it was stolen, he found it lying on the railroad track next to a hole in the fence behind the dealership. To be guilty of dealing in stolen property, the defendant does not have to know beyond peradventure that the property was stolen, he simply should have known that the property was stolen. If the case is presented to the jury on a case theory that "he stole it and sold it" competing with a defense theory of "he didn't know it was stolen," you might lose. If you change your case theory to "When he sold it, he should have known it was stolen," the defense factual theory (he found it by a hole in the fence behind the dealership) confirms your case theory and you are more likely to win.

Other times, the defense theory is inconsistent with the legal theory of guilt but is consistent with another available legal theory of guilt. In the above motorcycle scenario, if you had charged common law larceny of the motorcycle (caption and asportation of the goods from the custody of the owner), then the defense theory would exculpate the defendant of the crime you charged. He did not steal the property, somebody else did, and he just received it under suspicious circumstances. It would still inculpate him for dealing in stolen property (transferring property when he knew or should have known it was stolen). Instead of going to court and warring over whether the defendant actually stole the motorcycle (and possibly losing), you amend your information to charge dealing in stolen property, change your case theory and the supporting legal theory, and rob the defendant of his point to adjudicate.

More than one defendant has achieved an unmerited acquittal because the jury accepted the defense theory without the prosecution pointing out to them that even under the defense theory, the defendant was still guilty. More than one defendant has achieved an unmerited acquittal because the prosecution did not recognize that the defense theory, although acquitting the defendant of the crime charged, made him guilty of another. You must be ever vigilant to the interplay among legal theory, factual theory, case theory, and defense theory.

PRACTICAL EXERCISE

Treetop celebrates his recent release from prison by attending a party at Harry Outlaw's single wide trailer. During the evening, Treetop bemoans the fact that his wife has taken up living with another man while he has been in prison. Outlaw consoles Treetop by telling him "I'm moving out of town and I'm not taking my old lady. She's going to need someone to take care of her. You can have her." Treetop thanks Harry and purchases a Taurus .22 magnum revolver from Outlaw. The party breaks up, and Treetop goes home.

The next morning, Treetop decides that he will accept Outlaw's offer. He gets into his pickup truck and drives to Harry's single wide, getting there at breakfast time. Outlaw invites him in, and they sit at the kitchen table drinking coffee. Treetop reminds Outlaw of the promise Outlaw made the night before and tells Outlaw that he has come to take Outlaw's old lady home with him. At first Outlaw thinks Treetop is joking, but Treetop persuades Outlaw that he is in earnest. Outlaw is astonished. He tells Treetop "I was drunk last night. That was the whiskey talking. You can't just give away a woman like a hound dog." Outlaw's girlfriend, who witnesses this exchange, decides that she needs to leave the kitchen. She goes into the bedroom and hears, but does not see, the remainder of the transaction.

Treetop argues with Outlaw for a brief period of time, then gets up, goes outside and retrieves his revolver. He walks back into the trailer, announces "By God, nobody goes back on his word to me," and shoots Outlaw in the chest. Outlaw jumps to his feet, runs outside, and falls on his face in the front yard. As Treetop walks back to his pickup, he leans over Outlaw and whispers into his ear "If you live, get your butt out of Camden County and never come back." Outlaw's girlfriend hears the remarks Treetop makes inside the trailer but does not hear the conversation outside the trailer. She calls 911 from the bedroom and hides there until law enforcement arrives. Outlaw receives emergency medical attention, and his life is saved through emergency surgery.

When he is arrested, Treetop has the .22 magnum pistol stuffed down into his waistband with his jacket fully covering it. After being advised of his rights, Treetop says "That sorry skunk Outlaw ain't got the guts to come to court and testify against me. I ain't got nothing else to say until I get my lawyer." Treetop is incarcerated in the local county jail on $250,000.00 bond, where he will remain until the disposition of the charges against him. Treetop's prior record includes two prison terms—the first for grand larceny, and the second for possession of a firearm by a convicted felon. He also has an arrest for four aggravated assaults with a firearm, but the jury convicted him of four misdemeanor counts of improper exhibition of a dangerous weapon. Upon his release from the hospital, Outlaw leaves town giving no forwarding address. The girlfriend is available to testify.

Based upon these facts, what charges (if any) do you file? What will be your case theory as to each of those charges? What sentence will you seek? What sort of plea offer should you make?

CHAPTER 8

MARSHALING THE EVIDENCE

■ ■ ■

I'm a great believer in luck and I find the harder I work, the more I have of it.—Thomas Jefferson

Give me six hours to chop down a tree, and I will spend four of them sharpening my axe.—Abraham Lincoln

A. PREPARATION AND CASE LOAD

Trial preparation should begin the moment you become aware of the case, and it should continue until both sides have rested. You prepare for trial with a three-tiered process of assimilation, assessment, and assembly, but you do not do them sequentially. The tasks exert a synergy on each other as you perform them simultaneously. As you assimilate new facts, you modify your assessment of the case. Modified assessment tends to result in modified assembly of the proof, which in turn impels you to seek new facts to assimilate into the proof. This threefold process continues apace throughout the life of the case and can even continue into the post-conviction stage. Most advocates do not have the luxury of carrying a one-case caseload. Each time you pick up the file, you must go through a relearning process. The less orderly the case file, the less attention you have paid to documenting the stages of assimilation, assessment, and assembly, the more time you will waste and difficulty you will have in the relearning process.

B. PREPARING THE SIMPLE CASE

In a busy prosecutor's office, line prosecutors in the misdemeanor and general felony divisions have caseloads sufficient to crush Atlas. Many prosecutors cope with the crush by cutting corners and doing slipshod work. By the time they graduate to more significant caseloads, they have so habituated themselves to subpar performance that they sometimes do not even realize they do sloppy work. Because of this many civil litigation firms look with a jaundiced eye at the prospect of hiring a former prosecutor. It is a far, far better thing to become adept at handling cases efficiently rather than sloppily. Efficiency does not cut corners so much as take shortcuts. You can minimize the pain of case preparation and maximize your efficiency by the use of form worksheets. We have already seen the case theory worksheet. We will now examine some additional worksheets which should expedite the trial preparation process.

1. THE WITNESS/EVIDENCE WORKSHEET

As early as possible, you will want to begin to marshal your evidence. Before you can marshal your evidence, you must have an idea of what you need to prove and the evidence available to prove it. Fill out the witness/evidence worksheet (Figure 8-1). At the top, enter the competing case theories. Below, list the names of every witness who may conceivably testify at trial and set forth the material facts to which the witness can attest. Also note whether the witness is potentially a prosecution witness, a defense witness, or both. List every piece of tangible evidence and set forth its relevancy, noting whether it is potentially a prosecution or defense exhibit.

Either place the worksheet in the file at the top of one side or tab it prominently. When you return to the file several weeks to a month later you will have handled so many additional cases that you may not recall anything about the case. You must reeducate yourself as to the facts and issues, and the worksheet serves admirably for this purpose. Instead of scouring through the paperwork trying to relearn the facts and issues, you will have a one-page ready reference to jog your memory. As additional paperwork comes in, you can revisit the worksheet, updating it as to evidence and witnesses and revising or editing your case theory. The case theory is a work in progress and must be reviewed in light of new developments.

When you graduate from many simple cases to fewer more complex cases, the witness/evidence worksheet will expand to multiple pages, and it may be helpful to divide it into separate witness and evidence inventories. Section C of this chapter will discuss how this is done.

State versus Michael Edwards (the case set out in Figure 8-1) was a relatively simple case involving few witnesses and a limited number of evidentiary exhibits. Once the prosecutor had prepared this document, she had made a giant stride toward being ready to handle any pretrial matters or even to go to trial. At a glance she could evaluate the prosecutive merit of the case, weigh the advisability of any plea offers made, and quickly marshal the witnesses and evidence for the trial of the case.

Figure 8-1: Witness/Evidence Worksheet

Defendant: Michael Edwards

Prosecution Theory: Two huge boats disappear from the parking lot at Mann's Marine Village & reappear 15 miles away in front of Michaels' hotel room. He says a mysterious disappearing stranger gave them to him.

Defense Theory: A mysterious disappearing stranger gave them to me at a bar to repair for him. He was going to come get them when I was through with them. I can't quite recall his name.

Witness	Testimony Synopsis	Pros	Def
Chuck Green	Owns first boat. Had it in for repairs. Nonconsent to taking. Value.	X	
Evan Johns	Owns second boat. Bought it but hadn't picked it up. Nonconsent to taking. Value.	X	
Marion Mann	Owns Mann's Marine Village. Found boats missing. Value. Venue.	X	
Dudley Preston	Officer on scene who took report.	X	
John Wooten	Deputy who found boats & arrested Defendant.	X	
Watson James	Officer who took defendant's statement.	X	

Evidence – Relevance	Pros	Def
Photo of Green's Boat – Identification	X	
Photo of Johns' Boat – Identification	X	
Photo of Mann's Marine Village – Scene of crime	X	
Photo of Boats in front of Def's hotel room – Possession	X	
Map of area – Distances between locations	X	

2. THE ELEMENTS WORKSHEET

On the elements worksheet (Figure 8-2), set out each and every charge filed against the defendant. For each count, list every element of each crime and the witnesses or proof that you expect to use to establish that element at trial. The earlier you fill out this worksheet the better. If you do it during the charging stage, you just may discover that the charge you were contemplating cannot be proved, or that you need to go out and find an essential witness to prove up a technical element of the charge you want to file.

Figure 8-2: Elements Worksheet

Defendant: Edward Michaels

Count 1: Second Degree Grand Theft
Victim: Chuck Green

Elements	Witness/Proof
Date	Marion Mann
Venue	Marion Mann
Obtain or Use	Marion Mann/John Wooten
Property of Another	Chuck Green
Without Consent	Chuck Green
Intent to Deprive	Circumstances
Value	Chuck Green/Marion Mann

Count 2: Second Degree Grand Theft
Victim: Evan Johns

Elements	Witness/Proof
Date	Marion Mann
Venue	Marion Mann
Obtain or Use	Marion Mann/John Wooten
Property of Another	Evan Johns
Without Consent	Evan Johns
Intent to Deprive	Circumstances
Value	Evan Johns/Marion Mann

3. THE ORDER OF PROOF

You have decided upon your case theory as set forth in the previous chapter (Figure 7-1), you have assimilated the evidence onto your witness/evidence worksheet (Figure 8-1), and you have assessed the necessary proof by deciding upon the elements of the crime and how you are going to establish them on your elements worksheet (Figure 8-2). As you draw closer to trial you are ready to begin assembly of your presentation. First you write your opening statement, making sure that your opening statement rests firmly on the cornerstone of your case theory, and your case theory on the bedrock of truth. After writing your opening statement, order the witnesses and evidence to confirm your opening statement. The order of proof (Figure 8-3) gives you a roadmap for that proof. Fill in the case theory and list the witnesses in the order in which you anticipate calling them. Beside each witness, write the material fact to be proven. As the witnesses are either called or omitted, check them off in the "call/omit" columns. Often witnesses will get called out of the anticipated order. If you put numbers in the "call" column indicating when the witnesses were actually called, at the end of the trial you will have a record of the true order in which you called them. Next fill in the elements. As each element is proven, check it off and indicate which witness or item of evidence proved that particular element. Do not rest your case until you have reviewed the elements checklist and made sure that each and every necessary element has been proven.

Figure 8-3 continues with the Michael Edwards case and demonstrates how the information from the witness/evidence worksheet and the elements worksheet are transferred to the order of proof so as to have the information in a more user-friendly format. It would be possible, though not advisable, to try the case completely off of this one sheet of paper. Notice how the case theory has morphed from a rather prolix theory as stated in the witness/evidence worksheet to a briefer, more forceful statement of the case. In this particular case, there was no defense beyond the defendant's testimony. If, however, the defense had disclosed witnesses and evidence, it would have been advisable to fill out a second order of proof setting forth the defense case as the prosecutor anticipated it. In the elements section of the defense order of proof, the prosecutor could enter the material facts which the defense must prove in order to establish the defense theory.

Figure 8-3: Order of Proof

Defendant: Edward Michaels

Case Theory: Possession of Recently Stolen Property + Silly Explanation = Theft

#	Witness	Material Fact	call	omit
1	Chuck Green	Nonconsent. Value.	1	
2	Evan Johns	Nonconsent. Value.	5	
3	Marion Mann	Venue, Date.	2	
4	Dudley Preston	Took Report.		X
5	John Wooten	Found boats. Made Arrest.	3	
6	Watson James	Def's statement.	4	
#	**Element**	**Witness/Evidence**	**Proved**	
1	Date & venue	Marion Mann	√	
3	Obtain or Use	John Wooten	√	
4	Property of Another	Victims	√	
5	Nonconsent/Value	Evan Johns/Chuck Green	√	
7	Intent to Deprive	Circumstances	√	
#	**Evidence**	**Sponsor**	**ID**	**IN**
1	Photo of Green's Boat	Chuck Green	A	1
2	Photo of Johns' Boat	Evan Johns	D	4
3	Photo of Mann's Marine Village	Marion Mann	B	2
4	Photo of Boats in front hotel	John Wooten	C	3

Under the heading evidence, list the evidentiary exhibits and their sponsors. As the witnesses identify them, check them off in the "ID" column. When you move them into evidence, check them off in the "IN" column. If the court will allow you to pre-number the evidence, give each evidentiary exhibit the number corresponding to the number of the row in which you have entered it. Do not worry if some exhibits fail to be admitted.

There is no law which says that exhibits must be consecutively numbered. In fact, pre-numbering can allow you to be creative with your numbering scheme. You may wish to discriminate which count the particular piece of evidence supports (e.g., 1–I; 2–III; 3–II; etc.) or whether a piece of evidence relates to one or both of two co-defendants (e.g., 1–J; 2–A; 3–B). When the jury retires to deliberate, the numbering system will give them a ready reference for sorting through the evidence. If the court requires that exhibits be identified by letter and marked into evidence by number, then put the letter in the "ID" column and the number in the "IN" column. Do not rest your case until you have reviewed the evidence inventory and determined that everything you need in evidence has actually been placed in evidence. Do not rely solely upon your evidence inventory. Check with the clerk and make sure the clerk has indicated that each exhibit was received in evidence.

4. DIRECT EXAMINATION WORKSHEETS

For each witness you expect to call, fill out a direct examination worksheet (Figure 8-4). Write the witness's name at the top of the page, followed by the material fact that you expect to prove by that witness. Beneath the material fact section come three sections labeled "build," "preserve," and "destroy." Under "build" list every fact to which the witness can testify that will help your case. In the column marked "reference," write down where you can find that fact so as to be able to refresh the witness's recollection should she stray from the anticipated path. Under "preserve," list (again with references) every fact to which the witness can testify that will undermine your case. These facts must be assessed and minimized. If the witness carries too much baggage in the "preserve" column, you might consider calling another witness to prove the material fact. Finally, under the heading "destroy," write down (again with references) any prior inconsistent statements by the witness, any inconsistencies with other witnesses, or any other facts which tend to discredit the witness. If the witness has too much baggage in the "destroy" section, you may want to find another witness to prove your material fact. Finally, outline your direct examination and list the tangible evidence you will be using during your direct examination of the witness. You can then draft a more complete order of testimony for the witness, or you can simply conduct your direct examination from the worksheet. In the chapter on direct examination we will discuss a more thorough method for preparing direct examinations.

Figure 8-4: Direct Examination Worksheet

Witness: **Janet LaFleur**

Material Fact: Determined 2 year old Victim's bruising from blunt trauma as result of child abuse, not due to blood disorder.

Build: Favorable	**Reference**
Bruises on Victim's ears, forehead, neck, & buttocks.	Deposition 42:7-24
Blood tests within normal range. Ruled out blood disorder.	44:1-25
Bruises inconsistent with fall. Most consistent with child abuse.	60:5-15
Preserve: Unfavorable	**Reference**
Mother claimed bruises came from fall.	Deposition 43:14-24
Blood tests showed low iron.	44:1-21
Victim reported to nurse that she fell.	53:7-10
Destroy: Impeachment	**Reference**
First thought it might be von Willebrand's Syndrome.	Deposition 39:1-23

	Outline of Testimony	**Reference**
1	Name, Rank, Serial number.	
2	Qualifications.	
3	Father brings in child.	
4	Findings as above.	
5	Opinion.	

	Evidence	**ID**	**IN**
1	Medical Records.		
2	Photograph of bruising to forehead.		
3	Photograph of bruising to neck.		
4	Photograph of bruising to buttocks.		

5. CROSS-EXAMINATION WORKSHEETS

On the cross-examination worksheet (Figure 8-5), write the witness's name and your case theory at the top of the page. If you can discern a defense theory, write that down underneath your case theory. Use the case theory as the polestar of your cross-examination. Use your cross to confirm your case theory. Failing that, you want to undermine the defense theory. If you can accomplish both objectives on cross-examination, so much the better. Then there are three sections labeled "build," "preserve," and "destroy." Under "build," write down (with references) every fact to which the witness can testify that will help to establish your case theory. Under "preserve," write down every fact within the witness's knowledge which undercuts the defense theory. Finally, in the "destroy" section, write down every fact with which you can impeach the witness. Every fact in every section should have a reference. After filling out the worksheet, assess the witness's testimony. If you have many entries in the "build" and "preserve" sections, you may be able to turn the witness into a stealth prosecution witness. From the cross-examination worksheet you can prepare more elaborate notes for cross-examination, or you can simply conduct your cross-examination from the worksheets. See the chapter on constructive cross-examination for a more complete exposition of how to prepare a cross-examination.

Cross-examination is the area of trial most feared by rookies, and it is the area of trial at which prosecutors on all levels get less practice. Direct examination, handling of exhibits, and jury speeches will become almost second nature after a year or two in the arena, but cross-examination may still be a challenge. The key to cross-examination, as with any other aspect of trial, is careful evaluation and planning. The cross-examination worksheet, working in synergy with the other worksheets for trial preparation, gives you a format and a procedure for making the careful evaluation and preparing the careful plan which is necessary to a successful cross-examination. Even when time is limited, it can give you a quick, efficient format for assimilating the testimony of belatedly disclosed witnesses, assessing how to nullify their probative value, and assembling an effective cross-examination. Given the heavy docket of misdemeanor court, this can be invaluable.

One common feature on the misdemeanor docket is the surprise witness. Given the crush of cases on the public defender's docket, she may not be as prompt in making discovery as you would like or the rules require. Since suppression of such witnesses' testimony is next to impossible, something must be done to deal with them. The cross-examination worksheet can help even in the dire event of your being ambushed by a surprise witness. We will delay discussing how the cross-examination worksheet can be used in such a situation until Section C of Chapter 12, where we will discuss the cross-examination worksheet in greater detail.

Figure 8-5: Cross Examination Worksheet

Witness: Darrel LeBarron

Case Theory: LeBarron came to Victim's house uninvited & would not leave. When Victim tried to make LeBarron leave, Lebarron stabbed him to death.

Defense Theory: Self Defense. [Revealed for the first time in opening statement].

Build: Favorable	**Reference**
1. Admits to having knife.	Opening
2. Admits to arguing with Victim.	Opening
3. Admits to wrestling with Victim.	Opening
4. Admits to stabbing Victim.	Opening
Preserve: Unfavorable	**Reference**
1. Victim attacked Def with a broom.	All witnesses.
2. Victim displayed a knife.	All witnesses.
3. Victim drunk.	All witnesses.
4. Victim cursing.	All witnesses.
Destroy: Impeachment	**Reference**
1. "I never saw a knife at all."	Statement 1:11
2. "I never had a knife in my hand."	Statement 2:23
3. "I don't carry knives."	Statement 2:27
4. "I had no weapons."	Statement 3:33
5. "I didn't even touch a knife tonight."	Statement 6:55
6. "I never once touched the knife."	Statement 6:56

6. THE TRIAL FOLDER

Once you have filled out all the pertinent worksheets, fasten them into a manila folder with the case theory worksheet, the witness/evidence inventory, the elements worksheet, your opening statement, and the order of proof on the left side. Place them into the folder with the case theory worksheet on the bottom and the order of proof on the top. On the right side of the manila folder, fasten your direct and cross-examination worksheets, with the first witness you expect to be called on top and the last witness you expect to be called on the bottom. As you conduct your examinations of the witnesses, you have the folder open before you on the lectern, so that you can refer to the data on the examination worksheet and check off the various boxes on the order of proof as you establish them.

7. SHORTCUTS

You may feel that you have such a huge trial docket you cannot do even these simple steps in trial preparation. If constrained, you can get by if you only fill out your case theory worksheet, your order of proof and your direct examination worksheets. Even the heaviest of dockets should allow time for the performance of those small tasks in preparation for trial. You will have done them in your head. You should be able to jot them down on paper. Be sure that if you cut back to this bare minimum, you have done so because of a crushing caseload and not because of a lack of initiative.

8. THE SKELETON TRIAL BRIEF

There once was a young prosecutor who carried a very heavy docket of drug sale cases made by the local drug task force. The trials came so fast and so furious that he had difficulty fully preparing them until he realized something. They were all pretty much the same case with different actors. He put a skeleton drug sale trial brief on disk and began using it as a template for all his drug sale cases. As cases came up for trial, he simply went to the skeleton brief and modified it. Using the Edit>Find and Replace function on his word processor, he changed the names of his witnesses, and then he fleshed out their order of testimony based on the specific facts of their case. Armed with the skeleton trial brief, he tried cases at a rate double that of other line prosecutors in his office. If you carry a heavy case load of relatively simple cases, you would do well to consider making a skeleton trial brief for each of the most commonly tried crimes on your docket.

9. SIMPLE AND COMPLEX

The foregoing trial preparation protocol is suited to the simplest cases and the heaviest dockets, and it can readily serve to prepare relatively simple cases with relatively few witnesses and evidentiary exhibits. Such cases may be documented by no more than an arrest affidavit, an incident report, a property receipt, and possibly a witness statement or two. The system begins to break down as the case involves more and more witnesses, evidentiary exhibits, and documents. It can accommodate approximately ten witnesses, five or six evidentiary exhibits, and twenty or so pages of reports and statements. At some point near these numbers, the case reaches a critical mass and you must use a more thorough system. If you make a career as a prosecutor, you will graduate to these more important and more complex cases, and you must develop a more thorough system for preparing them.

C. PREPARING THE MORE COMPLEX CASE

A small case might involve two or three witnesses, a tangible object or two, and 5–10 pages of reports and statements. A complex case can have scores of witnesses, hundreds of tangible objects, and thousands of pages of reports and statements. With a small case, you do not have a lot of trouble locating reports and information. With a larger case, keeping track of all the witnesses and evidence can be a major headache. You must devise a system for marshaling the evidence, and the sooner the better. A method suited to small cases will not work for a large case, but a large case method can be scaled back to work on smaller cases. Even in cases that are so small you think you do not need to implement it, you should use the system because it gives you practice, and when the larger cases come around, the system has become second nature to you. The following description is definitely not the only way to organize a case, and it may not fit your work habits. It is, however, a good system, and you can modify it to suit yourself. You should try it "as is" for a few cases before you begin to implement modifications, and as you modify it you should be vigilant to make sure your "improvements" are motivated by a desire for efficiency rather than sloth.

As the paperwork comes in, it should be date stamped in a location that will not obscure information on the papers. After date stamping, collect the documents into binders and paginate them. Pagination can be as simple as taking a heavy pointed felt pin and marking the page number in the lower right hand corner of the page, again taking care not to obscure information. If you can make reduced 8 ½ × 11 copies of oversize documents without rendering them illegible, do so. If your documents are all the same size and shape, it makes working with them much easier. Keep a pristine (except for the addition of date stamp and page number) copy of all documents for discovery purposes and make a working copy of the documents that can be highlighted and otherwise annotated. If you refuse to keep a pristine copy, use only a yellow highlighter to mark your copies. The yellow highlighting will not show up on photocopies made for discovery disclosures.

1. INVENTORY

Make an inventory of the documents as they come in. The best form of inventory is a three-column table on a good word processor like Microsoft Word or Corel Word Perfect. The first column will contain the page number of the first page of the document. Column two will list the author's name with the last name first. Column three has a description of the document. See Figure 8-6(a) for an example document inventory. Save this inventory to disk, so that it can be updated as you receive additional paperwork.[1] You recorded the author's name with the last name first so that you can readily sort the documents. Click on "Tools" on the toolbar and then click on "Sort" in the drop-down menu. Then click on "Sort by: Second Cell in Table Row," and now all documents authored by the same individual are collected together. See Figure 8-6(b). To return the table to numerical order, simply click "Tools" > "Sort" > "Sort by: First Cell in Table Row," and it will immediately return to numerical order. Print out the inventory both numerically and alphabetically.

You may be more comfortable using a spreadsheet than using a word processor table. Whichever you use, you will be making giant strides toward being prepared for trial. The less time you must spend finding documents, the more time you can devote to other aspects of trial preparation and advocacy. The inventory set out in Figure 8-6 is the beginning of a document inventory for State of Florida versus Theodore Robert Bundy. Such an inventory, if completed, would run to several hundred witnesses. When Bundy was tried, the electric typewriter was the latest innovation in mechanized office equipment, and compiling such an inventory would have been extremely time consuming. No such document inventory was used in the actual trial, and document retrieval became a chaotic process. Multiple photocopies of each document were made and they were placed in separate folders for each witness or each topic of consideration. These multiple copies multiplied the space taken up by the paperwork on the case, until the "case file" consumed the space of several four-drawer filing cabinets. As the trial team worked with the "case file," individual file folders became misfiled or, worse yet, lost. Shortly after Bundy's execution, the same trial team had occasion to present a murder case every bit as complex and every bit as expansive, but the computer age had arrived. They were able to make use of the document inventory and the other worksheets described in this section, and trial preparation time and effort was reduced by a factor of ten.

---

[1] You will use it not only as an inventory of the documents, but it will figure prominently in the discovery process as you will see in the next chapter.

Figure 8-6(a): Document Inventory: Numeric Sort

Page	Author	Document
001	Leach, Tom	Request for Assistance
002	Fenwick, Jack	Investigative Report
003	Fenwick, Jack	Investigative Report
004	Fenwick, Jack	Investigative Report
005	Jackson, J.O.	Investigative Report
006	Jackson, J.O.	Investigative Report
007	Jackson, J.O.	Investigative Report
008	Jackson, J.O.	Investigative Report
010	Jackson, J.O.	Investigative Report
011	Jackson, J.O.	Investigative Report

Figure 8-6(b): Document Inventory: Alpha Sort

Page	Author	Document
012	Boatright, Ken	Investigative Report
022	Daugherty, J.L.	Interview Report
026	Daugherty, J.L.	Interview Report
018	Daugherty, J.L.	Interview Report
004	Fenwick, Jack	Investigative Report
003	Fenwick, Jack	Investigative Report
023	Fenwick, Jack	Investigative Report
002	Fenwick, Jack	Investigative Report
016	Gay, Fay D.	Memorandum
011	Jackson, J.O.	Investigative Report

2. INDEX

With the documents paginated and inventoried, you must now inventory and index the witnesses. Read through the working copy of the reports with a yellow highlighter. Highlight each and every appearance of a person's name. As you highlight each new witness's name, add it to a three-column witness inventory. Column one contains the witness's name, column two contains the witness's contact information, and column three will give a very brief synopsis of the witness's testimony. When you complete the inventory, sort it so that the witnesses will be in alphabetical order. See Figure 8-7. Prepare a similar inventory of all tangible objects which will potentially be used as evidence. Include a description of the evidentiary item, an explanation of its relevance, and the names of the witnesses who will identify and authenticate the item at trial.

Once again, you may be more comfortable using a spreadsheet than using a word processor table. Whichever you use, you must make witness and evidence inventories. It is obvious that the witness/evidence inventory of Figure 8-1 is simply not up to the task of documenting all the witnesses and evidence involved in a complex case. Additionally, you will need more information on each witness readily available. You will find use for such an inventory when you start issuing subpoenas for various court proceedings. When that happens, you will begin to get telephone calls from the numerous witnesses in the case. Unless you have total recall, you will not be able to remember the significance of every witness in the case. When a witness calls wanting to know why she has received a subpoena, you can either scratch your head and say "I really don't know. I'll have to research that and get back with you," or you can turn to the witness inventory and scan it to find the witness's entry. You will immediately be able to talk to the witness without having to promise to call them back when you get things figured out. Figure 8-7 depicts a hypothetical inventory for the Bundy case. Once again, no such inventory was actually used for the case, but one was sorely needed. Witness information was kept in a 3 by 5 card catalog, and for some reason cards seemed to disappear from the catalog quite regularly.

A similar working inventory should be made of all tangible evidence. Such an inventory should include information relating to the description of the tangible evidence, its relevance to the case, chain of custody information, and a listing of all control numbers placed on the evidence by all personnel who have handled the evidence. As more fully described in Section C.7, each item of evidence may have been labeled with many different control numbers, and it is essential that you keep track of all of them so that you can identify the various items of evidence when they are referred to by different control numbers in different reports. With all the evidence entered into a table or spread sheet, the task of marshaling the tangible evidence becomes much less onerous.

Figure 8-7: Witness Inventory

Witness	Address	Synopsis
Anderson, C.L.	Lake City Fire Dept., Lake City, FL	Eyewitness to abduction of victim.
Boatright, Kenneth	FHP, Lake City, FL	Led search party for victim.
Duncan, Jack	FDLE Crime Lab, Tallahassee, FL	Processed crime scene.
Edenfield, Clinch	Lake City Jr. High, Lake City, FL	School crossing guard who saw defendant at school.
Farhat, John	Green Acres Sporting Goods, Jacksonville, FL	Sold hunting knife to defendant.
Henderson, Lynn	FDLE Crime Lab, Tallahassee, FL	Fiber analysis, shoe track comparison.
Jackson, J.O.	FDLE, Live Oak, FL	FDLE case agent.
Lipkovic, Dr. Peter	Medical Examiner's Office, Jacksonville, FL	Performed autopsy, determined cause of death.
Pace, Sgt. T.A.	FHP, Lake City, FL	Team leader on search party which found victim's body.
Robinson, Kenneth	FHP, Lake City, FL	Member of search party who discovered victim's body.

Now go back and index each place in every document or report where a witness's name is mentioned. Merely indexing the names to page number will not be discriminating enough. You must approximate the location of the name on the page. You may annotate the location with the letters "TMB," which will denominate top, middle, or bottom of the page. If the pages have discrete paragraphs, you may number the paragraphs. Now you are ready to prepare an index of all references to all witnesses throughout the documents.

Use a two-column table to make your index. Column one gives the witness's name. Column two contains the location of the reference. Once you have read every page, highlighted every witness, and entered every witness's name into the index, sort on the first column to alphabetize the entries and arrange all entries for each witness together. See Figure 8-8. Save the index to disk, and as additional reports and statements come in, annotate them and add them to the index. When indexing the reports, you should also index every mention of the defendant's name, and in a murder case index every mention of the victim's name.

Indexing will be the most tedious and time-consuming aspect of assimilation of the evidence, and it will be the aspect you will most likely want to omit. It is also the worksheet that you are most able to do without. Although helpful, it is certainly not essential. By the time, however, that you graduate to cases which are complex enough to benefit from the making of an index, you will most likely be able to requisition the assistance of a legal intern or extern to perform the task for you. If you are able to get the index done, it will prove invaluable assistance in assessing and assembling the testimony of the various witnesses. When preparing a witness's testimony by use of the index, hidden conflicts in testimony will be revealed, subtle nuances of testimony will become apparent, and additional facts will be uncovered that are not readily apparent from reports and statements authored by the witness.

The witness index will prove most helpful in preparation for cross-examining the defendant. The defendant will quite likely not have made a formal statement to the police but may have made numerous oral statements to various witnesses. The witness index will facilitate your finding these nuggets of information which will prove ever so helpful in constructing a cross-examination of the defendant. Take the example of the Darryl Lee LeBarron cross-examination set forth in Chapter 13.C.6. There the defendant had made numerous oral statements to several different witnesses, none of which had been collected into a single location. Indexing the appearance of the defendant's name in each report and statement will uncover all those various statements and make them readily available for use in cross-examination. Although the witness index itself is almost useless for conducting a witness examination, it does greatly assist in the preparation of the examination by facilitating the preparation of the abstract of testimony, which we will discuss in the next section.

Figure 8-8: Witness Index

Unsorted		Sorted	
Witness	**Ref**	**Witness**	**Ref**
Leach, Freda	1:M	Bailey, Glen	5:T
Fenwick, Jack	2:T	Beach, Col. E.	5:T
Jackson, J.O.	2:T	Beach, Col. E.	6:T
Hooker, Steve	3:T	Bondurant, T.	5:T
Fenwick, Jack	3:T	Fenwick, Jack	2:T
Orr, Richard	4:T	Fenwick, Jack	3:T
Fenwick, Jack	4:T	Fenwick, Jack	4:T
Jackson, J.O.	4:T	Fenwick, Jack	7:M
Beach, Col. E.	5:T	Hooker, Steve	3:T
Bondurant, T.	5:T	Jackson, J.O.	6:T
Philpot, John	5:T	Jackson, J.O.	4:T
Jackson, J.O.	5:T	Jackson, J.O.	5:T
Bailey, Glen	5:T	Jackson, J.O.	2:T
Beach, Col. E.	6:T	Leach, Freda	1:M
Jackson, J.O.	6:T	Love, Jimmy	7:M
Love, Jimmy	7:M	Orr, Richard	4:T
Fenwick, Jack	7:M	Philpot, John	5:T

3. ABSTRACT OF TESTIMONY

As you approach trial, make an abstract of each witness's potential testimony. Go to your inventory and find every document authored by the witness you are abstracting. Read and annotate each document onto a three-column abstract of testimony. Leave Column one blank; you will use it to sort the information. Column two contains every fact from every document that could conceivably have a bearing on the witness' testimony. Column three contains the page and location of each fact. After you have read and annotated the documents authored by the witness, you will go to your witness index and find every other reference to the witness wherever located in the reports and add that information to the abstract. Finally, if the witness has been deposed or given testimony at a preliminary hearing or motion hearing, you will also incorporate the information from the transcript into the abstract. Once you have all facts entered into the abstract, number the first cell of each row in the order in which you think most appropriate, either chronologically or topically. See Figure 8-9(a). Next sort the rows by the numbers in the first cell. You may redo this step several times before you get the facts in the desired order. See Figure 8-9(b). Notice that in Figure 8-9(a) the annotations come from pages 454, 455, and 765 of the collected reports. The annotations are noted down by paragraph in the order in which they appear on the reports as the prosecutor came to them reading through the reports. The prosecutor then went to the left-hand column and entered numbers so as to sort the annotations into a chronological order. After sorting, the annotations were ordered as you see them in Figure 8-9(b). It goes without saying that you do not use the abstract of testimony to conduct your examination of the witness. In Figure 8-9(b) you will notice that the last chronological fact is the witness's failure to identify the defendant from a photospread. You definitely do not want to end your direct examination at this point. We will wait until the chapter on direct examination to discuss how to use the abstract as the resource from which to write your direct examination.

Although the abstract of testimony is primarily a resource for preparing the witness's examination, it does serve a purpose in the actual conducting of the examination. Trials seldom go exactly as planned, and facts which initially seemed irrelevant can assume an unexpected importance to the examination. Because these facts were believed to be unimportant, they will not be included in the examination worksheet. They will, however, be recorded in the witness abstract. These facts will usually assume their importance during the cross-examination of the witness. You will need to find them, and find them quickly and surely. Keep the abstract of testimony close at hand, preferably directly behind the examination worksheet in your trial brief. It can prove essential to finding references to those previously unimportant facts.

Figure 8-9(a): Abstract of Testimony, Unsorted

##	Clinch Edenfield	
01	School crossing guard at LCJH.	454:1
02	Employed at LCJH 4-5 years.	454:1
03	Came on duty 7:25-7:30 on 2/8/78.	454:1
04	Saw van driving east very slow.	454:2
12	Driver looking towards school.	454:4
11	Between 8:15-8:20 saw van again.	454:4
10	Driver looking hard at school on second pass.	454:3
08	Noticed van because driver looking hard at school.	454:2
09	Saw van shortly after 8:00 driving west.	454:3
16	8:45 went off duty. Came back on duty around 2:30 & heard Kim missing.	455:2
19	Recognized Bundy as driver of van.	455:3
18	Later saw Bundy appearing in court on TV.	455:3
13	Driver white male, 30-35, clean shaven.	455:1
14	Nobody else in van besides driver	455:1
15	Almost stopped van to tell driver to move on.	455:1
17	Certain observation made on day Kim disappeared.	455:2
20	Unable to identify Bundy in photospread.	455:3
06	Saw Bundy on US 90 running E & W in front of LCJH.	765:2
05	Saw Bundy three times between 7:30-8:30 on 2/8/78.	765:2
07	Bundy backing up traffic driving so slow.	765:2

Figure 8-9(b): Abstract of Testimony, Sorted

##	Clinch Edenfield	Ref
01	School crossing guard at LCJH.	454:1
02	Employed at LCJH 4-5 years.	454:1
03	Came on duty 7:25-7:30 on 2/8/78.	454:1
04	Saw van driving east very slow.	454:2
05	Saw Bundy three times between 7:30-8:30 on 2/8/78.	765:2
06	Saw Bundy on US 90 running E & W in front of LCJH.	765:2
07	Bundy backing up traffic driving so slow.	765:2
08	Noticed van because driver looking hard at school.	454:2
09	Saw van shortly after 8:00 driving west.	454:3
10	Driver looking hard at school on second pass.	454:3
11	Between 8:15-8:20 saw van again.	454:4
12	Driver looking towards school.	454:4
13	Driver white male, 30-35, clean shaven.	455:1
14	Nobody else in van besides driver	455:1
15	Almost stopped van to tell driver to move on.	455:1
16	8:45 went off duty. Came back on duty around 2:30 & heard Kim missing.	455:2
17	Certain observation made on day Kim disappeared.	455:2
18	Later saw Bundy appearing in court on TV.	455:3
19	Recognized Bundy as driver of van.	455:3
20	Unable to identify Bundy in photospread.	455:3

4. DIGITAL FILES AND OPTICAL CHARACTER RECOGNITION

All the foregoing tasks can be quite tedious when done by hand, but there is a more efficient way to assimilate the information. Many copiers will now copy documents to digital files. If you have access to such a copier and have access to a program such as Adobe Acrobat or Microsoft Document Imaging, you can make your assimilation much more efficient. Copy all documents to digital files. Tagged Image File Format is a good format which can be read by either Adobe Acrobat or Microsoft Document Imaging. Once the files are in this format, they can be rendered readable by the optical character recognition functions found in Adobe Acrobat and Microsoft Document Imaging. Once they are rendered readable, they can be searched with the search function. Click on the search function on the toolbar and type in the witness's name. Hit Enter and the program will take you to every place the witness's name is mentioned. You can completely dispense with the witness index (Figure 8-6) and work directly to the abstract of testimony. Prosecutors' offices are notoriously behind the times when it comes to technology, but this technology comes with most commercially marketed computers, and freeware versions are available on the internet. With a little initiative you can make yourself extremely efficient in handling the paperwork. It is even conceivable that you could leave that cart full of banker's boxes in the office and go to court with every paper from every file on your docket digitally stored on your laptop computer—if you can talk your office manager into getting you a laptop.

5. SHARPENING THE AXE

As you work through the process of assimilating and assessing the case and assembling your presentation, you will find deficiencies in the case which need to be remedied. The "to do" lists discussed in Chapter 4 should be worked diligently, and other "to do" tasks should be pursued. The first thing to do is to make absolutely sure that you have all the information in the possession of the police. This means making a personal trip to the criminal investigations division and personally inspecting the file. There are all sorts of documents that law enforcement generates and collects in connection with a case, and those documents often do not find their way into your hands. Whether by accident or design, the police will have information that you should also have. The only way to ensure that you have it is to go get it.

Do not take it for granted that you are aware of all possible items of tangible evidence, and do not take it for granted that all items of tangible evidence reported as seized are available. In one memorable possession of burglary tools case, on the eve of trial the prosecutor discovered that the investigating officer had released the tools to the defendant. You must also make a trip to the evidence vault. At the evidence vault you will inspect, copy, handle, and otherwise fully familiarize yourself with the evidence, its location, chain of custody, and all aspects of the handling of the evidence. If evidence needs to be tested, make arrangements to test it. If evidence is "at the crime lab" in a distant city, contact the crime lab and make sure the evidence is there. Get a digital camera. Photograph everything from every angle. When you are back at the office after 6:00pm putting the trial brief together, these identification photographs will be invaluable in helping you to understand how to put together your presentation. Copy all evidence logs, evidence receipts, and chain of custody documents. These documents will again be invaluable as you attempt to sort out which officer seized what piece of evidence, who got it, and whether it was sent to the lab. You will notice a rather strange phenomenon relating to control numbers. Good officers, as they seize a piece of evidence, will mark it with some sort of control number. Evidence custodians, as they receive evidence, will mark the evidence with their own control number. When the evidence is sent to the crime lab, the laboratory technicians mark the evidence with their own control numbers. If you have done your homework correctly, you gave the evidence your own control numbers when you inventoried them back at the intake stage. By the time you are ready to go to court, evidence will often have as many as four separate control numbers given by different officers and agencies. Different reports will refer to the same piece of evidence by different control numbers. You need to keep track of all these numbers so that you can identify and connect the specific items of evidence when you read about them in the various police reports, lab reports, property receipts, and evidence inventories. Finally, when you mark it into evidence, it can get as many as two more control numbers ("State's Exhibit for Identification A" and "State's Evidentiary Exhibit 1," for example).

6. MARSHALING THE WITNESSES

In addition to marshaling the evidence, you must also marshal the witnesses. You must maintain a system for keeping track of witnesses—where they are, where they have moved, their telephone numbers and email addresses. If your office has a victim/witness coordinator, you can make use of that resource, but most likely you and your secretary or legal assistant will bear the burden of keeping track of all the witnesses. We will discuss the mechanics of getting your witnesses ready to testify and present their testimony in the chapter on direct examination.

7. THE TRIAL BRIEF

In presenting their case, some prosecutors work from a three-ring notebook, others from a banker's box filled with folders on each aspect of the trial. Some may even work directly from a laptop computer. Whether you work from a notebook, a banker's box, or a laptop, your trial brief should contain at a minimum the following sections:

(1) Charging Document: If you do not know where you are going, you may not realize when you have gotten there. A handy copy of the charging document is essential. It is the polestar of your presentation.

(2) Discovery: A section where you can quickly lay hands on all discovery filed in the case is very useful, especially when the opposition begins to assert that you have failed to disclose some important item.

(3) Legal Issues: Motions, orders, or legal authority for anticipated issues at trial should be placed in the Legal Issues section.

(4) Voir Dire Notes: A copy of the venire, any notes you can scrounge up on the individual jurors, and a list of topics for questioning.

(5) Opening Statement: Once you have completely assimilated and assessed the case, the first step after discovering your case theory is to write the opening statement.

(6) Elements Checklist: Every criminal act is subdivided into elements. The elements are set forth in the standard jury instructions. You want to list each element of each crime, list by each element how you intend to prove the element, and provide a blank to check off when you prove it up during the trial. When you get to the point of resting your case, you turn to the elements checklist and make sure you have proven everything you need to prove.

(7) Order of Proof: A list of witnesses in the order in which you expect to call them. Make copies of the order of witnesses to pass out to the bailiff, clerk, court reporter, judge, and opposing counsel. They will appreciate it, and you will look prepared even if you are not. Some young prosecutors think they are committing a security breach by telling defense counsel the order in which they intend to call their witnesses. It is not a problem. Good defense counsel will anticipate your ordering anyway, and incompetent or inexperienced defense counsel will hold up the trial while they search for their material on each witness. ("Excuse me, your honor, I didn't expect that witness to be called today, and I seem to have left my file on her back at the office. May I have a half hour recess to go and retrieve it?") Giving defense counsel an indication of witness order does not compromise your presentation in any way, and when it comes time for the defense to put on their case, they might even feel constrained to reciprocate.

(8) Evidence Inventory: A list of the exhibits you intend to introduce into evidence. If you want to be very thorough, you can put in a column indicating the witness or witnesses who will sponsor the exhibit. Again, copies for distribution to court personnel will earn all sorts of goodwill.

(9) Order of Testimony: In this section you place the worksheets from which you intend to conduct your direct examination of the prosecution witnesses.

(10) Defense Case: Here you put the worksheets from which you will cross-examine the potential defense witnesses.

(11) Final Argument: Conventional wisdom teaches that the final argument is the first thing you should write. It is not the first thing you should write (the case theory is the first thing, followed by the opening statement), but before the trial ever begins, you ought to have at least a rough draft of the final argument, making sure that it conforms to and confirms the opening statement.

8. ORDERING WITNESSES & TESTIMONY

In ordering witnesses, you must consider the length of the trial, the day-to-day availability of witnesses, and the legal predicates for specific types of evidence. A single example from the Orlando trial of Theodore Robert Bundy will suffice. On Friday of the third week of the trial, the prosecution had two "modules" to present: the fingerprint evidence and a presentation on Bundy's attempt to kidnap a child in Jacksonville. The presentation on the attempted kidnaping was compelling. Two eyewitnesses positively identified Bundy as the man who tried to kidnap a little girl who looked very much like the victim Kimberly Diane Leach. The presentation on fingerprint evidence was long, technical, and soporific, but it could be summed up in one sentence: Despite a diligent search, nobody could find Bundy's fingerprints anywhere. Each presentation would take half a day. The prosecution team put on the attempted kidnaping evidence in the morning. That afternoon they bored the jury to death with the non-evidence on fingerprints. During the lengthy defense cross-examination of the fingerprint expert, which covered each piece of evidence that did not have Bundy's fingerprints on it, the prosecution team noticed distressed looks on some of the jurors' faces. They were beginning to entertain doubts about Bundy's guilt. Because the fingerprint evidence was the last thing heard on Friday, the jury would have all weekend to stew over the weakness before the prosecution could wash away the doubt with further damning evidence. The misstep was not fatal, but it might have sunk a weaker case. The fingerprint evidence should have gone on Friday morning, and the attempted kidnaping Friday afternoon.

Once you have determined the most persuasive order of witnesses, give close attention to the most persuasive order of testimony from each of the witnesses. Do not mechanically do a chronological direct examination. Movies and books oftentimes begin in the middle of the story at an exciting part and then flash back to the chronological beginning. One false step in ordering testimony could prove fatal. Fiber evidence serves as a good example. Fiber evidence is never logically conclusive, but if it is handled correctly, it can be highly persuasive. When the microanalyst explains that each factor (fiber type, chemical composition, color, cross section, diameter, delustrant, *etc.*) must coincide exactly before the fibers can be matched, catalogs the numerous different factors, says they all coincide exactly, and then calls it a match, the jury can be swayed mightily. The first thing you have to do, though, is have the microanalyst say emphatically that a match cannot be conclusive. If the microanalyst emphasizes the nonconclusiveness first and then catalogs all the similarities, the jury will nevertheless be persuaded by the testimony. If the nonconclusiveness is brought up at the tail end of the direct, or worse yet, saved for cross-examination, the testimony will fall flat.

Give great care to the introduction and display of tangible evidence. Do not just mark it into evidence and hand it to the clerk. Think about the most dramatically persuasive way to publish the evidence to the jury. Bullet riddled shirts can be pegged onto an easel, and the firearms examiner can step to the easel with a pointer to elucidate his distance determination for each bullet hole. Waving the bloody shirt can be very effective, but it can also backfire horribly. A young prosecutor, confronting a consent defense in a rape case, thought that the victim's torn panties were an unimpeachable refutation of that defense. If she had consented, how did her panties get torn? Unfortunately, he did not inspect the panties before trial. When he came to the point of introducing the victim's panties into evidence, he removed the panties from their brown packaging and brandished them in front of the jury. They were indeed torn, but there was also an obscenity sewn onto the panties. Jury verdict of not guilty. Had he inspected the panties beforehand, he might have decided to have the witnesses describe the tear in the panties without removing them from the bag, or without proffering them into evidence at all.

PRACTICAL EXERCISE

You have just been handed a misdemeanor file charging Red Brown with battery upon Hugh Glass. The file contains an incident report and four sworn witness statements. The case is set for trial tomorrow. Using the following documents, prepare an abbreviated trial brief consisting of the Witness/Evidence Worksheet, the Elements Worksheet, the Order of Proof, and Direct and Cross-Examination Worksheets.

1. **Incident Report by Officer B. Friendly:** On January 22, 2007, at 2:20am, I was dispatched to Route 13 Box 1313, in the Deep Creek area of Camden County, and I arrived at the residence, consisting of a log cabin set approximately 100 yards off of a dirt road, at 2:45am. Upon arriving at the scene, I made contact with Hugh Glass, w/m, 6′4″, 278 lbs., DOB 5/2/48, who was obviously suffering from a heavy blow to the head with blood oozing from a knot on his right temple. Also present at the scene were Daisy Glass, W/F,

5′2″, 115 lbs., DOB 4/23/50, who had scratch marks on her throat and a black eye, and their 14-month-old granddaughter, Sweetpea Brown. Glass advised that his wife had been attacked by his daughter, Cora Brown, and he had been attacked by Cora's husband, Red Brown. He advised that he had shot Red Brown, who ran into the woods, and that Cora had jumped into her car and driven away at a high rate of speed. I photographed the injuries to Glass and his wife and took Glass's pistol into custody. The pistol was a S & W Model 14 revolver with five .38 cal. semiwadcutter reloads and one expended .38 cal. cartridge casing in the cylinder. I then proceeded to Route 13, Box 1314, a single wide trailer which was the Brown residence. At the Brown residence I spoke to Cora Brown, W/F, 5′6″, 125 lbs., DOB 4/4/80, who smelled of alcohol and was suffering from a severe bruise to her side which I photographed. I spoke to Red Brown, W/M, 6′4″, 260 lbs., DOB 10/18/78, who also smelled of alcohol and had sustained a through and through gunshot wound to his left calf, which I photographed. After assessing the situation, I decided to take sworn written statements from all parties involved in the incident. As a precaution, I advised all parties of their rights and obtained their signatures on rights waiver forms. After taking all four statements, I located a piece of kindling wood in the Glass's front yard. It looked as though it had bloodstains on one end. Hugh Glass advised that the stick was what Brown used to club him. I took the stick into custody. The revolver and the stick were turned over to the Sheriff's Office evidence custodian.

2. **Sworn Statement of Daisy Glass:** I was babysitting for my daughter, Cora Brown, while she supposedly went to the movies with her husband, Red. They didn't get back at the time we agreed on, so I put Sweetpea to bed and went to bed myself. Around 2:00am, I heard a banging on the door, and it was Cora. I went and got Sweetpea and carried her to the door to give to Cora. When I opened the door, I realized that Cora was drunk and on drugs, and I told her that I wasn't going to give Sweetpea to her when she was in that condition. I closed the door and put Sweetpea back in bed. Cora started banging on the door and yelling, and I went outside to try to calm her down. We fussed for a few minutes, and then Cora tackled me and I fell on my back on the ground. Cora got on top of me and started choking me and banging my head against the ground. I started screaming for help, and then I passed out. I was waked up by the sound of a gunshot and when I looked up, I saw my husband holding a pistol, and Red was running down the driveway into the woods across the road. Cora cursed me and got into her car and drove off. My husband had an injury to his head, and I tried to tend to it after I called 911.

3. **Sworn Statement of Hugh Glass:** My wife was babysitting our granddaughter tonight while my daughter and her husband went to the movies. I had worked hard and was tired, so I went to bed early. I am a heavy sleeper, but I was waked up by a commotion going on outside the house around 2:00am. My wife was screaming for help, and my daughter was yelling "I'm going to kill you." I could hear her husband hollering "Choke her, choke her, show that witch who's boss." I got up, pulled on my pants real quick, got my pistol off the nightstand and went outside. I felt like I needed the pistol because

Red is a big, strong man and if he jumped on me, I was afraid I couldn't handle him. Before I left the house, I stuck the pistol into my waistband. When I got outside, I saw my wife on her back on the ground and my daughter on top of her choking her and banging her head on the ground. I saw Red standing by just yelling at Cora to choke Daisy. I hollered at Red to get Cora off Daisy, but he wouldn't do anything. I walked over to Cora and put my foot on her side and pushed her off my wife. About the time I got Cora off my wife, Red had picked up a piece of kindling wood from the wood pile and he hit me upside the head with it. I fell to my hands and knees, and he raised the stick to hit me again. I pulled my pistol and shot him in the leg, and he ran away. Cora got up and started cussing me for shooting her husband, and then she jumped into the car and drove off.

4. **Sworn Statement of Cora Brown:** My husband and I went to the movies tonight and my mother kept my daughter Sweetpea. After the movies, Red and I dropped by the Watering Hole and had a few beers before we went to pick up Sweetpea. When we got to my parents' house, I went and knocked on the door. Mom came to the door cussing me for a dope smoking, beer guzzling hussy, and she told me she was going to file papers to have Sweetpea taken away from me. I started telling her what I thought of her, and she attacked me. We wrestled around for a while, with me having my hands on her throat just trying to keep her off of me, and then we fell to the ground. I got on top and was trying to hold her down to keep her from hurting me, when Dad came out of the house waving a gun. He walked over to me and kicked me hard in the ribs, and I fell off Mom. Then was when Red said, "You can't do that to my wife," and he punched Dad in the nose. Dad fell down and hit his head on the woodpile, and then he cussed and shot Red. Red hollered "You've shot me, you S.O.B.," and Dad said, "I'll shoot you again, and that coke snorting wife of yours too, if you don't get off my property." Red ran into the woods and I jumped in the car and drove away fast. I picked Red up off the side of the road a couple hundred yards away from Mom's house, and we drove home. I was patching Red's gunshot wound up when the police came. I was going to call them, but I wanted to take care of Red first. I think I've got broken ribs where Dad kicked me.

5. **Sworn Statement of Red Brown:** My wife and I went to the movies tonight and my mother-in-law kept my daughter, Sweetpea. After the movies we went to the Dew Drop Inn and had some coffee before going to my in-laws to pick up Sweetpea. When we got to my in-laws' house, my mother-in-law came out raving about how we had stayed out too late. Cora told her to shut up or she'd never see Sweetpea again, and then my mother-in-law slapped Cora. Cora slapped her back, and Daisy tackled Cora to the ground. They were rolling around on the ground when Hugh came out of the house with a pistol in his hand. He kicked Cora off of her mother and then he went over and started to stomp on Cora's head. When he was off balance from raising his foot to stomp, I hit him with a body block and knocked him down. He hit his head against the woodpile, and then he rolled over and cussed me and started shooting at me. He must have shot the gun dry, but he only hit me once in the calf while I was

running away. I ran down the driveway and into the woods, and my wife came and picked me up and we went home. I know you've got it in for me because I've done time in prison for burglary and aggravated battery, but I'm innocent this time.

CHAPTER 9

DISCOVERY

■ ■ ■

Three people can keep a secret if two of them are dead.—Benjamin Franklin, *Poor Richard's Almanac*

Nothing is covered up that will not be uncovered, and nothing secret that will not become known. Therefore whatever you have said in the dark will be heard in the light, and what you have whispered behind closed doors will be proclaimed from the housetops.—*Luke* 12:2–3 (NRSV)

A. CONCEALMENT OF STRENGTHS AND WEAKNESSES

Chess is a perfect information wargame. Each player sees every piece the other side has, and each player sees every move the other side makes. The players can conceal nothing but their strategies from the opponent. Milton Bradley markets a chess-like game called Stratego, which is an incomplete information wargame. The pieces consist of tiles designed to stand on end. One side of the tile has a blank face, the other the rank of the piece. The players array their pieces on the board with the blank side of the tiles facing their opponent. The players have no idea of the disposition of enemy forces and are therefore blind to their opponent's strengths and weaknesses. For the greater part of U.S. history, criminal trials have been litigated more on the Stratego model than on the model of chess. Both sides could easily conceal their weaknesses to prevent the adversary from taking advantage of them and conceal their strengths to achieve maximum effect through surprise.

1. BRADY V. MARYLAND

Trial-by-ambush can be very effective if you are the party with the ace up your sleeve, but many worthy people believe justice suffers from the process. The Supreme Court recognized the inherent unfairness of the trial-by-ambush school of thought when it decided *Brady v. Maryland.*[1] *Brady* didn't quite transform a criminal trial into a chess game, but it did minimize concealment of weaknesses by requiring the prosecution to disclose some of its weaknesses. *Brady* held that if the prosecution had

1 373 U.S. 83, 83 S.Ct. 1194 (1963).

exculpatory evidence, the evidence must be disclosed. If the prosecution had evidence materially impeaching its evidence of guilt, that impeaching evidence must be disclosed. *Brady* defined "have" quite broadly. If any government agent or agency anywhere has knowledge or possession of exculpatory evidence, you must disclose it whether you know about the evidence or not. "We have held that when the State suppresses or fails to disclose material exculpatory evidence, the good or bad faith of the prosecution is irrelevant: a due process violation occurs whenever such evidence is withheld." *Illinois v. Fisher*.[2]

You have no excuse if some officer had a piece of evidence he forgot to report. If a law enforcement officer has it, you "constructively" know about it. *Brady* doesn't specifically impose a burden upon you to seek out exculpatory evidence, but the circumspect prosecutor will work diligently to uncover all evidence in the possession of all law enforcement agencies, not just the evidence the agencies decide to share. This means leaving the office, going to the agency, and inspecting the agency's file; leaving the office, going to the evidence vault, and inspecting the evidence on file; carefully inquiring of all involved officers whether they have knowledge of any additional information; and otherwise doing whatever it takes to uncover all available evidence. Sometimes you have difficulty assessing the information which has come to light. Is it really exculpatory? Should you disclose it, or can it be withheld? If you must ask, you should disclose it. You do not want to run the risk of an appellate court disagreeing with your assessment, invalidating your conviction, and ruining your reputation for fair dealing.

2. LOST OR DESTROYED EVIDENCE

If exculpatory or impeaching evidence has been withheld, then the case must usually be retried. This can cause quite a hardship if the concealment is discovered years after the trial, after memories have faded and witnesses have died or otherwise been scattered to the four winds. If evidence is destroyed rather than merely concealed, you must make a more thorough analysis. This analysis involves asking three questions:[3]

(1) Was the evidence materially exculpatory? If it was, case dismissed. If it was not, go on to question (2).

(2) Was the evidence potentially useful to the defense? If it was not, stop the inquiry—no harm, no foul. If it was potentially useful, go on to question (3).

---

[2] 540 U.S. 544, 547, 124 S.Ct. 1200, 1202 (2004).

[3] Arizona v. Youngblood, 488 U.S. 51, 109 S.Ct. 333 (1988); California v. Trombetta, 467 U.S. 479, 104 S.Ct. 2528 (1984); United States v. Valenzuela-Bernal, 458 U.S. 858, 102 S.Ct. 3440 (1982); United States v. Agurs, 427 U.S. 97, 96 S.Ct. 2392 (1976).

(3) Did the police act in bad faith when they lost or destroyed the evidence? If they did, case dismissed. If the police acted in good faith, no foul has occurred, and the prosecution can continue.

A rather common destruction scenario arises in DUI cases, where many police agencies have a standard policy of destroying intoxilyzer ampules after a certain period of time. Sometimes the DUI trial date will get continued to a date after the date for the routine destruction of the ampules. The defense will then sometimes move to dismiss the case because of the destruction of the ampules on the grounds that the destruction denies the defendant an opportunity to retest and confirm or deny the validity of the state's intoxilizer results. The analysis should run the following course:

(1) Was the evidence materially exculpatory? No. Presumably, a retest would simply confirm the original results. Go on to question (2).

(2) Was the evidence potentially useful to the defense? Yes. Possibly a retest could cast doubt on the original results. Go on to question (3).

(3) Did the police act in bad faith when they lost or destroyed the evidence? No. They did the destruction pursuant to standard operating procedure, not to frustrate the defense. No foul. Proceed to trial.

3. PLEAS OF GUILTY

Brady mandates disclosure to insure a fair trial. What about disclosure to insure a voluntary guilty plea? The Supreme Court in *United States v. Ruiz*[4] held that the Constitution does not mandate disclosure of material impeachment evidence prior to entering a plea agreement with a criminal defendant. Although the fair trial guarantee of the Fifth and Sixth Amendments provide that defendants have the right to receive exculpatory impeachment material from prosecutors, a defendant who pleads guilty waives the right to a fair trial along with various other accompanying constitutional guarantees.

B. THE PROSECUTOR'S DISCOVERY OBLIGATION

Brady deals with concealment of weaknesses. Should anything be done about the concealment of strengths? The American Bar Association and the National District Attorneys Association have promulgated standards setting forth discovery obligations requiring the prosecution to inform the defendant of not only the weaknesses, but also the strengths, of the

---

4 536 U.S. 622, 623, 122 S.Ct. 2450 (2002).

prosecution's case. To a greater or lesser degree, the various states have adopted these standards as discovery requirements.

There are fifty states, each with different rules of criminal discovery. The Federal Rules of Criminal Procedure have a fifty-first set of rules for discovery. The way discovery usually works is that the defense must request discovery, either by filing a demand or notice or making a request. Upon filing the pertinent documents, the prosecution must make enumerated disclosures to the defense. Regardless of whether the defense requests discovery, the prosecution must turn over some types of information, such as exculpatory evidence.[5]

1. TYPICALLY REQUIRED DISCLOSURES

In some jurisdictions the prosecution must make the disclosures automatically, more often the defendant must make a request or demand. Typical disclosures mandated by statute or rule include:

(1) Oral and written statements of the defendant and a codefendant.[6]

(3) Names and addresses of witnesses.[7]

(4) Written statements of witnesses.[8]

(6) The Nature and circumstances of any agreement between the prosecution and any prosecution witnesses.[9] This sort of disclosure is mandated by some rules of discovery, but must it be made automatically and without demand pursuant to *Giglio v. United States*, 405 U.S. 150 (1972), which extended the *Brady* rule to promises made by the prosecution in return for the witness's testimony.

(7) The reports or statements of any experts; including, in some instances, curriculum vitae of the experts.[10]

(8) Tangible evidence pertaining to the case. Depending on the jurisdiction, this can include:

---

[5] Brady v. Maryland, 373 U.S. 83, 83 S.Ct. 1194, 10 L.Ed.2d 215 (1963).

[6] Standard 11–2.1(a)(I), American Bar Association Standards for Criminal Justice: Prosecution Function and Defense Function, 3rd Ed., American Bar Association Criminal Justice Section, Washington DC, 1995; Ca.Pen.Code § 1054.1(b); Fed.R.Crim.P. 16(a)(1)(A), (B); Fla.R.Crim.P. 3.220(b)(1)(C), (D).

[7] ABA Discovery Standard 11–2.1(a)(ii); Alaska R.Crim.P. 16(b)(1)(A)(i);Ca.Pen.Code § 1054.1(a); Fla.R.Crim.P. 3.220(b)(1)(A); N.Y.Crim.P. Law § 245.20(1)(c), (d); Wis.Stat. § 971.23(1)(d).

[8] ABA Discovery Standard 11–2.1(a)(ii); Alaska R.Crim.P. 16(b)(1)(A)(i); Ca.Pen. Code § 1054.1(f); Fla.R.Crim.P. 3.220(b)(1)(B); N.Y.Crim.P. Law § 245.20(1)(e); Wis.Stat. § 971.23(1)(e).

[9] ABA Discovery Standard 11–2.1(a)(iii). Fla.R.Crim.P. 3.220(b)(1)(M).

[10] ABA Discovery Standard 11–2.1(a)(iv);Alaska R.Crim.P. 16(B); Ca.Pen.Code § 1054.1(f); Fed.R.Crim.P. 16(a)(1)(F); Fla.R.Crim.P. 3.220(b)(1)(J); N.Y.Crim.P. Law § 245.20(1)(f).

(a) Evidence to be used at trial.[11]

(b) Evidence seized from the defendant.[12]

(c) Evidence which is material to the preparation of a defense.[13]

(d) Evidence which may be tested for DNA.[14]

(11) The criminal record of the defendant.[15]

(12) The criminal record of all witnesses including codefendants.[16]

(15) Whether evidence was obtained as a result of an electronic surveillance.[17]

(16) Whether evidence was obtained from a search and seizure, and any documents relating thereto.[18]

(17) Whether information was obtained from a confidential informant.[19]

(18) Those portions of the grand jury proceedings containing testimony of the defendant.[20] Some jurisdictions mandate disclosure of all grand jury testimony.[21]

2. DISCLOSURE FORMAT

In a jurisdiction with liberal discovery, the enormous amount of paperwork in a complex case can overwhelm the attorney who is not well organized. Take the example of the prosecution of Theodore Robert Bundy for the murder of Kimberly Diane Leach in Lake City, Florida. Between October 11, 1978, when the prosecution filed its initial answer to the defendant's demand for discovery, and the commencement of trial on January 8, 1980, the prosecution filed no less than seventy supplemental discovery disclosures, approximately one disclosure per week for over a

---

[11] Ca.Pen.Code § 1054.1(c); Fed.R.Crim.P. 16(a)(1)(E); Fla.R.Crim.P. 3.220(b)(1)(F);

[12] Ca.Pen.Code § 1054.1(c);Fed.R.Crim.P. 16(a)(1)(E); Fla.R.Crim.P. 3.220(b)(1)(K); N.Y.Crim.P. Law § 245.20(1)(m).

[13] Ca.Pen.Code § 1054.1(c); Fed.R.Crim.P. 16(a)(1)(E).

[14] Fla.R.Crim.P. 3.220(b)(1)(L).

[15] ABA Discovery Standard 11–2.1(a)(vi); Alaska R.Crim.P. 16(b)(1)(v); Wis.Stat. § 971.23(1)(c).

[16] ABA Discovery Standard 11–2.1(a)(vi)Alaska R.Crim.P. 16(b)(1)(v); Fed.R.Crim.P. 16(a)(1)(D); Wis.Stat. § 971.23(1)(c).

[17] ABA Discovery Standard 11–2.1(c); Alaska R.Crim.P. 16(b)(1)(A)(v); Fla.R.Crim.P. 3.220(b)(1)(H); N.Y.Crim.P. Law § 245.20(1)(g); Wis.Stat. § 971.23(1)(bm).

[18] ABA Discovery Standard 11–2.1(d); Fla. R.Crim.P. 3.220(b)(1)(I); N.Y.Crim.P. Law § 245.20(1)(n).

[19] Alaska R.Crim.P. 16(b)(2)(I); Fla.R.Crim.P. 3.220(b)(1)(G)

[20] Fla.R.Crim.P. 3.220(b)(1)(E); Wis.Stat. § 971.23(1)(a).

[21] N.Y.Crim.P. Law § 245.20(1)(b).

year. If, during the course of a trial with such a volume of discovery, the defense objects to a piece of evidence on the grounds of nondisclosure, the prosecution can have a difficult time searching through the discovery to document the timely disclosure of the evidence. You need a simple, comprehensive method for making and documenting discovery. We will presuppose a jurisdiction with liberal discovery and outline a system for marshaling the disclosures which will not only work for the largest case, it can be adapted to the smallest case. It can also dovetail with the evidence marshaling procedures discussed in Chapter 8.

If you have inventoried your witnesses and documents in conformity with the system described in Chapter 8, your discovery is almost done. Disclosure of the witnesses listed in your witness inventory and the documents listed in your document inventory will satisfy almost all requirements of the most exacting discovery provisions. Draft a discovery disclosure pleading reciting that you have complied with all pertinent discovery requirements. Such a disclosure, with the formal parts omitted, could read as follows:

COMMONWEALTH'S INITIAL DISCOVERY DISCLOSURE

COMES NOW the Commonwealth, by the undersigned Deputy Commonwealth Attorney, and pursuant to Rule BR–549, C.R.Crim.P., and files this Initial Discovery Disclosure. The Commonwealth shows by way of disclosure as follows:

(1) A list of the names and addresses of all persons known to the Commonwealth Attorney to have knowledge of the offense charged, or of any defense thereto is attached hereto and incorporated herein by reference as Exhibit A to this Discovery Disclosure.

(2) An inventory of reports, statements, and other documents required to be disclosed is attached hereto and incorporated herein by reference as Exhibit B to this Discovery Disclosure.

(3) All other matters required to be disclosed are set forth and described within the documents, reports, and statements listed in Exhibit B hereto.

(4) Arrangements may be made to inspect, copy, test, or otherwise examine the reports, statements, and documents set forth in Exhibit B, and the tangible objects described therein, by contacting the undersigned Deputy Commonwealth Attorney.

[Certificate of Service omitted].

EXHIBIT A

Anderson, C.L........Lake City Fire Department, Lake City, FL
Bishop, James ....Lake City Junior High School, Lake City, FL
Boatright, Ken.......Florida Highway Patrol, Lake City, FL
Daugherty, J.L. .....Lake City Police Department, Lake City, FL
Edenfield, Clinch...Lake City Junior High School, Lake City, FL

EXHIBIT B

Pg#	Author	Description
001	Leach, Tom	Request for Assistance
002	Fenwick, Jack	Investigative Report
003	Fenwick, Jack	Investigative Report
004	Fenwick, Jack	Investigative Report
005	Jackson, J.O.	Investigative Report

Exhibit A is a witness inventory which can be copied out of the running witness inventory you are keeping as described in Chapter 8 (Figure 8-7). The column giving the testimony synopsis will, of course, be omitted. Exhibit B is the running document inventory you are keeping as described in Chapter 8 (Figure 8-6). Save these inventories to disk, because you will be adding to them for supplemental discovery disclosures. As additional information is received, you can file a supplemental discovery disclosure with the new information incorporated into it. Boldface the new information so that it can be readily seen. The first supplemental discovery disclosure for the above case might look something like this:

COMMONWEALTH'S FIRST SUPPLEMENTAL DISCOVERY DISCLOSURE

COMES NOW the Commonwealth, by the undersigned Deputy Commonwealth Attorney, and pursuant to Rule BR–549, C.Crim.P., and files this First Supplemental Discovery Disclosure. The Commonwealth shows by way of disclosure as follows:

(1) A list of the names and addresses of all persons known to the prosecutor to have knowledge of the offense charged, or of any defense thereto is attached hereto and incorporated herein by reference as Exhibit A to this Discovery Disclosure. New or amended information is in **boldface.**

(2) An inventory of reports, statements, and other documents required to be disclosed is attached hereto and incorporated herein by reference as Exhibit B to this Discovery Disclosure. New or amended information is in **boldface.**

(3) All other matters required to be disclosed are set forth and described within the documents, reports, and statements listed in Exhibit B hereto.

(4) Arrangements may be made to inspect, copy, test, or otherwise examine the reports, statements, and documents set forth in Exhibit B, and the tangible objects described therein, by contacting the undersigned Deputy Commonwealth Attorney.

[Certificate of Service omitted].

EXHIBIT A

Anderson, C.L.	Lake City Fire Department, Lake City, FL
Bishop, James	Lake City Junior High School, Lake City, FL
Boatright, Ken	Florida Highway Patrol, Lake City, FL
Daugherty, J.L.	Lake City Police Department, Lake City, FL
Edenfield, Clinch ..	Lake City Junior High School, Lake City, FL
Farhat, John	**Green Acres Sporting Goods, Jacksonville, Florida**
Lipkovic, Dr. Peter	**Medical Examiner's Office, Jacksonville, FL**
Love, J.E.	**Florida Highway Patrol, Lake City, FL**

EXHIBIT B

Pg#	**Author ....**	**Description**
001	Leach, Tom	Request for Assistance
002	Fenwick, Jack	Investigative Report
003	Fenwick, Jack	Investigative Report
004	Fenwick, Jack	Investigative Report
005	Jackson, J.O.	Investigative Report
006	**Jackson, J.O. ....**	**Investigative Report**
007	**Jackson, J.O. ....**	**Investigative Report**
008	**Jackson, J.O. ....**	**Investigative Report**

When you file your second supplemental discovery, you will change the type on all old information to regular font, and then you will boldface the new material. When trial time comes, instead of having sixty or seventy discovery documents to search through for information, you will simply be able to look at the last discovery disclosure, which will contain all previously disclosed information.

Some prosecutor's offices copy the reports, statements, and other documents described in Exhibit B and send them out with discovery. Others make the defense come to their office to inspect the documents. Some make the defense pay for copies. Some provide the copies free. If you have the documents reduced to digital format, you could give the defense a CD or email the documents. How you manage the actual delivery of the discovery documents to the defense will be a matter of office policy and agreement with the individual defense attorneys.

3. DISCOVERY VIOLATIONS

The promulgation of a discovery requirement inevitably leads to the question of what should the court do when the prosecution fails to live up to that requirement. Should the case be dismissed if the prosecution fails to make discovery? What if the prosecution discloses, but the disclosure comes after the expiration of the time limits set for the disclosure? Should all such evidence be summarily suppressed to encourage the prosecution to make timely disclosures in the future? Some states opt for a draconian rule of exclusion unless the party can show good cause for failure to comply,[22] but most courts which have addressed these issues have opted for less severe sanctions. The New York Court of Appeals succinctly stated the prevailing view in *People v. Jenkins* when it said:

> Preclusion of evidence is a severe sanction, not to be employed unless any potential prejudice arising from the failure to disclose cannot be cured by a lesser sanction. "The overriding concern must be to eliminate any prejudice to the defendant while protecting the interests of society." [Citation omitted].[23]

In *Richardson v. State*,[24] the Florida Supreme Court set forth reasonable guidelines for sanctioning non-disclosure:

> [I]f, during the course of the proceedings, it is brought to the attention of the trial court that the state has failed to comply with Rule [3].220(e) CrPR, the court's discretion can be properly exercised only after the court has made an adequate inquiry into all of the surrounding circumstances. Without intending to limit the nature or scope of such inquiry, we think it would undoubtedly cover at least such questions as whether the state's violation was inadvertent or wilful, whether the violation was trivial or substantial, and most importantly, what effect, if any, did it have upon the ability of the defendant to properly prepare for trial.[25]

---

[22] Wis.Stat. § 971.23(7m).

[23] People v. Jenkins, 98 N.Y.2d 280, 284, 746 N.Y.S.2d 651, 774 N.E.2d 716, 719 (N.Y.Ct.App. 2002).

[24] 246 So.2d 771 (Fla. 1971).

[25] 246 So.2d at 775.

After finding a substantial violation affecting the party's ability to prepare for trial, the trial court must craft a remedy, with exclusion of the evidence being the last-resort remedy. This sort of reasoning allegedly applies equally to the defense as to the prosecution, but remedies against the prosecution tend to be more severe than those against the defense.

4. SIMILAR FACT EVIDENCE

Many worthy judges look with a jaundiced eye upon evidence of uncharged misconduct by the defendant. The controversy over this area of evidence has given rise to special discovery measures for similar fact evidence even in jurisdictions with very limited discovery. Aristotle's disfavor of appeal to ethos is taken very much to heart when the prosecution seeks to present evidence of the defendant's bad character. Someone charged with a crime should have to answer only for the crime set forth in the charging document. Even though evidence of this type is sometimes highly relevant, courts are justly circumspect in considering it.

There are two basic models for considering similar fact evidence, one a rule of inclusion and the other a rule of exclusion. Section 90.404, Florida Statutes, typifies the rule of inclusion. It provides that evidence of uncharged crimes, wrongs, or acts by the defendant is admissible if relevant to prove any issue unless its sole purpose is to show bad character or propensity to commit crimes. The statute then enumerates a nonexclusive list of relevant issues, such as motive, intent, preparation, plan, knowledge, or absence of mistake or accident. Section 904.04(2), Wis.Stat., and Rule 404(a), Fed.R.Evid., stand as examples of the rule of exclusion. They provide that evidence of the defendant's character is inadmissible except when it is offered to prove such issues as motive, intent, preparation, plan, knowledge, or absence of mistake or accident. At first glance, this distinction might appear more semantic than substantive, but this is not so. Florida at one time worked from a rule of exclusion with enumerated exceptions similar to § 904.04, Wis.Stat., and Rule 404, Fed.R.Evid., but that all changed with *Williams v. State*,[26] which reversed the presumption from one of inadmissibility unless an exception can be shown to one of admissibility unless it is only relevant to show propensity or bad character. In honor of that decision, similar fact evidence in Florida has ever after been called "Williams Rule" evidence.

Common sense tells us that a defendant charged with burglary will have his chances of acquittal greatly diminished if the jury learns that he has committed 150 previous burglaries. Common sense also tells us that if someone is charged with committing a burglary on Christmas Eve by climbing down the chimney in a Santa suit; it is highly relevant to the issue of guilt that he has committed 150 other burglaries on Christmas Eve by

[26] 110 So.2d 654 (Fla. 1959).

climbing down chimneys in a Santa suit. Whether the jurisdiction has a rule of inclusion like Florida's or a rule of exclusion like the Federal rule, the courts must engage in a weighing test of relevance versus prejudice to decide upon the admissibility of such evidence. Such decisions will oftentimes be heavily litigated, and the middle of the trial is not necessarily the ideal time for the court to initially address the issue. Consequently, it promotes judicial economy if these matters can be discovered pretrial so that they may be disposed of prior to jury selection by motion in limine or otherwise.

Back in the days when criminal trials were contested like games of Stratego, courts began to recognize the desirability of apprising the accused of similar fact evidence and litigating its admissibility before the trial. This led to decisional procedures for giving notice of such evidence. In *State v. Spreigl,*[27] the Minnesota Supreme Court held that when the prosecution intends to proffer evidence of uncharged crimes or misconduct, the prosecution must furnish the defense with a written statement of the prior offense describing it with the particularity of an indictment or information.[28] In *Whitty v. State,*[29] the Wisconsin Supreme Court cited *Spreigl* with approval, and ever after that, Wisconsin prosecutors have filed "Whitty notices" or "Whitty motions" as a predicate for introduction of similar fact evidence. When the Federal Rules of Evidence were promulgated, they mandated pretrial notice. Rule 404(b)(3), Fed.R.Evid., provides that the prosecution must provide, in writing, reasonable notice of similar fact evidence, state the purpose of proffering such evidence, and articulating the reason that the evidence is admissible. Many states enacted this discovery language into their analogous rules, but many did not. Section 904.04, Wis.Stat., does not have such a provision because it is unnecessary. The *Whitty* case had already provided for pretrial discovery of similar fact evidence. Other states, such as Washington, did not include the 404(b) discovery provision in their statutes for another reason. The Federal Rules of Criminal Procedure provide for very limited discovery. A state like Washington, on the other hand, provides for broad disclosure of evidence.[30] With broad disclosure, the defense is going to obtain the names of the witnesses to the similar fact evidence and the police reports and statements about the similar fact evidence in normal discovery. In other words, the defense will become aware of the similar fact evidence without the necessity of requiring the prosecution to give specific notice of the

---

[27] 272 Minn. 488, 139 N.W.2d 167 (1965).

[28] This notice requirement was eventually relaxed with the promulgation of Rule 7.02, Minn.R.Crim.P., which provides that the prosecution must file a written notice in which the uncharged misconduct is "described with sufficient particularity to enable the defendant to prepare for trial." The notice must be filed before the omnibus hearing provided for in Rule 11, Minn. R.Crim.P.

[29] 34 Wis.2d 278, 149 N.W.2d 557 (1967).

[30] Wash.Super.Ct.Crim.R. 4.7.

evidence. Florida has extremely liberal discovery, including discovery depositions,[31] but it also has one of the most draconian notice requirements for similar fact evidence. Section 90.404(2)(b), Fla.Stat., provides for an automatic notice requirement. Not less than ten days prior to trial the prosecution must furnish to the defendant a "written statement of the acts or offenses it intends to offer, stating them with the particularity required of an indictment or information." The superfluous nature of this requirement is highlighted by the language of Rule 3.220(b)(1)(A), Fla.R.Crim.P., which provides that "[w]ithin 15 days after service of the [defendant's] Notice of Discovery, the prosecutor shall * * * disclose * * * a list of the names and addresses of all persons known to the prosecutor to have information that may be relevant to * * * any similar fact evidence to be presented at trial under section 90.404(2), Florida Statutes." Thus, Florida prosecutors must disclose the similar fact witnesses fifteen days after demand but can wait until ten days before trial to give written notice of the evidence. The Florida notice requirement, unlike the Federal notice requirement, is not so much a discovery mechanism as it is a procedural booby trap.

We thus have four different approaches to notice requirements: none, on the Washington model; automatic disclosure required by decisional law on the Minnesota and Wisconsin models; statutory disclosure upon request by the defense; and automatic statutory disclosure on the Florida model. Most notice provisions do not require the noticing of certain types of similar fact evidence. Crimes within the *res gestae* of the crime charged and crimes offered to rebut or impeach defense evidence do not normally require notice. Many prosecutors will want to maximize surprise by waiting until the last minute to file their disclosures and taking advantage of all decisional law regarding types of wrongs which do not require notice. Such a course of action is not necessarily the best. A Florida prosecutor waiting until precisely ten days before trial to file the notice can expect to receive a motion for continuance in the return mail. A prosecutor who finds a case that he believes will allow him to ambush the defense with unnoticed similar fact evidence may confront a judge who fails to appreciate the nuances of the case. The best rule for noticing similar fact evidence is: "disclose it early and often." Waiting until the eleventh hour to file a notice will not surprise a competent defense attorney, but it can cause complications. Filing a superfluous similar fact notice disclosing crimes which do not need to be disclosed will not result in suppression of the evidence, but not filing a similar fact notice in reliance on dubious case authority might just result in suppression of the evidence.

---

[31] Fla.R.Crim.P. 3.220.

C. THE DEFENDANT'S DISCOVERY OBLIGATION

Discovery is not a one-way street. The prosecution must make certain disclosures, but almost every jurisdiction imposing a discovery obligation on the prosecution also imposes a reciprocal obligation on the defendant. The defendant's obligation is usually less comprehensive than the prosecution's, owing to the privilege against self-incrimination, but it is there nonetheless. Typical disclosure requirements for the defendant are:

(1) Names and addresses of defense witnesses.[32]

(2) Written statements of defense witnesses.[33]

(3) Reports or statements of defense experts.[34]

(4) Tangible objects, books, papers, documents, etc., which the defense intends to use at trial.[35]

Thus, although it is not a one-way street, discovery is not quite a two-way street where the sides engage in "you show your cards, and I'll show mine." The prosecution's disclosure obligation is almost universally greater than the defendant's. Under the usual scenario, the defense requests automatic, broad ranging discovery, and the prosecution must respond. Upon receipt of the prosecution's automatic discovery disclosures, the defense must respond with a narrower discovery disclosure. As a result, the prosecution side of the courtroom looks more like a Stratego board while the defense side is closer to a chess board.

1. COMPELLED DISCLOSURE BY THE DEFENSE

Beyond automatic disclosures, other provisions allow both sides to demand, request, or petition for additional discovery. The America Bar Association has promulgated discovery standards for compelling evidence directly from the defendant, and several states have adopted these standards to a greater or lesser degree. Arkansas,[36] Florida,[37] Montana,[38] and Utah[39] have all adopted modified forms of ABA Discovery Standard 11–2.4, dealing with disclosures from the defendant's person. Each state rule has the caveat that such disclosures must be made within

[32] ABA Discovery Standard 11–2.2(a)(I); Fla.R.Crim.P. 3.220(d)(1)(A); Wis.Stat. § 971.23(2m)(a).

[33] ABA Discovery Standard 11–2.2(a)(I); Fla.R.Crim.P. 3.220(d)(1)(B)(I); Wis.Stat. § 971.23(2m)(am).

[34] ABA Discovery Standard 11–2.2(a)(ii); Alaska R.Crim.P. 16(c)(4); Ark.R.Crim.P. 18.2 (upon order of court); Fla.R.Crim.P. 3.220(d)(1)(B)(ii); Wis.Stat. § 971.23(2m)(am).

[35] ABA Discovery Standard 11–2.2(a)(iii); NDAA National Prosecution Standard 54.3.c; Fla.R.Crim.P. 3.220(d)(1)(B)(iii); Wis.Stat. § 971.23(2m)(c).

[36] Ark.R.Crim.P. 18.1.

[37] Fla.R.Crim.P. 3.220.

[38] Mont.Code Ann. 46–15–323(1).

[39] Utah R.Crim.P. 16(h).

constitutional limitations. This should be read to mean that seizures of such items as hair standards and blood samples should be supported by a court order finding probable cause upon the basis of a sworn affidavit. An affidavit stating probable cause and a finding of probable cause are the minimal constitutional requirements for a search warrant, and a discovery order for seizure of evidence from the defendant's person is certainly analogous to a search warrant.

2. DNA

Often such seizures as provided for in these rules have already been made long before the filing of formal criminal charges,[40] but oftentimes they are not. With more and more specimens being contributed to DNA databases, "cold case" hits are becoming more and more prevalent. As inmates are received into prison, their DNA is collected and added to the state DNA database, and then compared against DNA collected in old, unsolved cases. The old, unsolved cases then become old, solved cases. While such hits give probable cause for arrest, most DNA databases do not maintain a sufficient chain of custody for evidentiary purposes. For prosecution, you must pull another DNA sample under strict evidentiary conditions, and the discovery rules patterned after ABA Discovery Standard 11–2.4 provide the mechanism for doing just that.

3. PROBABLE CAUSE

While motions for discovery of materials from the defendant's body should state probable cause and should be supported by oath, some disclosures—such as giving handwriting samples or submitting to fingerprinting—can be compelled without stating probable cause. Most rules make no distinction between those disclosures which may be compelled without probable cause and those which require probable cause. The safer course of action is to state probable cause with every motion for discovery, including disclosures which do not require probable cause. You have probable cause, otherwise you wouldn't have a case pending against the defendant. Judges, like all lawyers, are sometimes ignorant of the nuances of the laws of search and seizure and may be predisposed to require probable cause for all such disclosures.

4. DISCLOSURE OF DEFENSES

ABA Discovery Standard 11–2.2 provides for self-executing discovery by the defense, including the disclosure of certain specific defenses. As promulgated into rule, the disclosure of specific defenses sometimes requires a demand of some sort by the prosecution. Rule 3.200,

[40] Such seizures are normally made during the investigative phase of a criminal prosecution by search warrant, search incident to lawful arrest, consent seizure, or some other exception to the warrant requirement.

Fla.R.Crim.P., provides only for disclosure of the alibi defense and then only if the prosecution first gives the defense a statement of particulars as to the date, time, and place of the crime. It is quite a superfluous provision, as Rule 3.220, Fla.R.Crim.P., provides for disclosure of defense witnesses and depositions on demand. If the defense lives up to its discovery obligation, then the alibi witnesses will be disclosed under Rule 3.220, and the prosecution can discover the circumstances of the alibi by deposing or interviewing the defense witnesses. The tradeoff for this disclosure is that the prosecution will have to respond to the notice of alibi with a list of prosecution witnesses who will break the alibi. Rule 18.3, Ark.R.Crim.P., on the other hand, provides that (subject to constitutional limitations) the prosecutor may request to be informed of any defense in advance of trial, as well as the witnesses supporting the defense. Florida would appear to stand on one end of the spectrum of such provisions (limited disclosure to the point of near uselessness) and Arkansas on the other (disclosure limited only by constitutional strictures). To what extent you should avail yourself of such a state rule would depend upon where on the spectrum your state rule fell.

PRACTICAL EXERCISES

1. You are preparing to try a habitual offender on a charge of aggravated burglary. You have turned down a plea offer of ten years in prison, and you hope to be able to persuade the judge to sentence the defendant to life in prison. You call the victim's home to finalize arrangements for his appearance at trial and learn that he has died suddenly and unexpectedly. You hang up the telephone and begin to review the available evidence to see if there is any way you can prove the case without the victim's testimony. A review of the file satisfies you that you cannot make out a prima facie case. As you are looking through the case file, you receive a call from the defense attorney. The defense attorney advises you that she has persuaded the defendant to make a plea offer of guilty as charged in return for your recommendation that he serve twenty years in prison. How do you respond to this plea offer? How do you justify your response? Suppose you have determined that, although the case has been weakened by the death, you are able to make out a prima facie case without the victim's testimony. Does this make a difference as to how you respond? Why or why not?

2. You have decided to take the plea bargain offered by the defendant because you cannot prove your case without the victim. You have also decided to say nothing to the defense attorney about the death of the victim. You arrange to take the plea that very afternoon. As you walk into the courtroom to take the plea, the defense attorney asks, "You are ready to go to trial, aren't you?" What do you do? Why? What if the defense attorney asks, "You can prove the case, can't you?" What if the defense attorney asks, "You haven't lost any evidence or had any witnesses die, have you?" Suppose you believe you can make out a prima facie case without the victim. Would that make any

difference as to how you respond to each of the foregoing questions? Why or why not?

3. The defense attorney has not asked any embarrassing questions, court is in session, the defendant has proffered his plea, and the judge is now in the process of making his inquiry into the circumstances of the plea offer. The judge asks you "Does the victim have any objection to the terms of this plea agreement?" How do you respond? Suppose the judge asks, "Have you spoken to the victim to find out how he feels about this plea?" How do you respond to this question?

4. The plea has been accepted without any question by the judge or the defense attorney, and the defendant has been sentenced to twenty years in prison. A week after the plea and sentencing, the defense attorney calls you on the telephone and tells you she has just heard that the victim is deceased. She asks if you were aware that the victim was dead when you agreed to the plea offer. How do you respond? She tells you that you have engaged in unprofessional conduct by not telling her about the victim's death. How do you answer this accusation? Would your response to her be any different if you had an honest belief that you could prove the case without the victim's testimony?

5. A few weeks after the telephone call from the defense attorney, you receive a letter from the ethics committee of your state bar association advising you that the defendant has filed a formal complaint against you for withholding the information concerning the victim's death and asking for your version of the circumstances of the plea. How do you respond to this letter? Would you respond differently if it were the defense attorney who complained? Why or why not?

CHAPTER 10

INTERVIEWS, INTERROGATIONS, AND DISCOVERY DEPOSITIONS

■ ■ ■

A fool can ask more questions than a wise man can answer.—Anonymous

There's no such thing as a dumb question, but there are a lot of inquisitive idiots.—Anonymous

A. QUESTIONING

1. THE PARTIES TO QUESTIONING

The questioning process involves three parties—the audience, the witness, and the examiner. Each party plays a distinct role. The examiner defines the area of inquiry, and the witness discloses the desired information to the audience. In the prototypical questioning situation one party plays the role of both audience and examiner; but in the courtroom the audience is a distinct, and usually passive, party. Prototypical examiners engage in a process of exploration—they inquire into areas where they are ignorant, discovering new information as they define the direction of their questioning. In the courtroom examiners engage in a process of exposition—they inquire into areas where they are already knowledgeable, disclosing that information to the judge and jury. There are many types of questioning, and they accomplish many different objectives, but the mechanics of all forms of questioning work in the same way.

2. QUESTIONING AND COOPERATION

All questioning requires cooperation. Unless the examiner and the witness agree upon certain things, questioning accomplishes nothing. Suppose that the examiner wants to learn the witness's name. He asks: "Q: What is your name?" This question, as simple as it seems, begins a three-step process of suggestion, agreement, and disclosure which should result in the examiner learning the witness's name. Step one: The examiner suggests to the witness that he has a name. Step two: The witness agrees that he has a name. Step three: The witness discloses his name.

Unless the witness agrees with the examiner's suggestion, the questioning goes nowhere. Questioning therefore works from presupposed, agreed upon fact to the disclosure of a fact or set of facts unknown to the audience until the answer is given.

> Q: Where do you live? [Presupposed fact: The witness lives somewhere].
>
> A: 325 Pine Street, Anytown, USA. [Disclosed, previously unknown fact].

When the examiner asks the witness about his name, the question makes three suggestions to the witness. Suggestion one: The presupposed fact that the witness has a name. Suggestion two: The presumed field of answers which will satisfy the question. Suggestion three: The prescribed format for the answer.

> Q1: Is your name Alvin? [Presupposed fact: the witness has a name. Presumed field of answers: yes or no. Prescribed format for answer: the witness states whether or not his name is Alvin].
>
> Q2: What is your name? [Presupposed fact: the witness has a name. Presumed field of answers: Tom, Dick, Harry, or any other name. Prescribed format for answer: the witness discloses which among the vast field of possible names is the one he goes by].
>
> Q3: How did you come by the name of Alvin? [Presupposed fact: the witness has a name. Presumed field of answers: Any set of circumstances leading to the naming of a person. Prescribed format for answer: the witness describes the circumstances under which he was named].

These examples exhaust the field of possible question and answer formats. Q1 gives the witness an option between two choices—e.g. yes or no, true or false—and can be called a "whether" question. Q2 can be thought of as a fill-in-the blank or multiple choice question and can be characterized as a "which" question. E.g., which of a range of possibilities is the correct answer? Q3 calls for a narrative or explanation and can be thought of as a "what" question. E.g., what does the witness have to say about this subject?

To make headway in the questioning process, the witness must agree with three suggestions made by the examiner. The witness must affirm the facts presupposed by the question, accept the field of answers presumed by the question, and adopt the answer format prescribed by the question. Without cooperation, the discovery process breaks down. Even when the examiner and witness are working hard to cooperate, there can be problems.

3. PRECISION OF TERMS

Language is imprecise. When you hear the term "salamander," you would normally think of a lizard-like amphibian, but a salamander is also a mythical elemental being that supposedly lives in fire. In Florida, a salamander is also a mammal which tunnels in the ground and throws up unsightly piles of dirt onto lawns, golf courses, and pastures. Outside Florida, this sort of salamander is known as a "pocket gopher." In most states, a gopher is a burrowing mammal, but in Florida it is a burrowing tortoise, also known as a "gopher turtle." The words that the examiner uses to define the presuppositions in the question can be ambiguous or equivocal. For questioning to be productive, the examiner, witness, and audience must all agree on the denotation, connotation, and context of the words used to voice the presuppositions contained in the question. In other words, if the examiner wants useful information about salamanders, the question must make it clear to the witness whether the inquiry concerns amphibians, mammals, or mythical beings.

4. RESPONSIVE, CORRECTIVE, AND EVASIVE ANSWERS

Assuming the witness fully understands the question, the witness may give an answer which is responsive, corrective, or evasive. A responsive answer fully affirms the presupposed facts, accepts the presumed field of answers, and adopts the prescribed format for the answer.

Q: What is your name?

A: My name is Alvin.

A corrective answer seeks to repair some defect the witness finds in the examiner's question.

Q: What is your name?

A: I have no name. [Corrects the presupposition that the witness has a name].

Q: Is your name Alvin or Albert?

A: My name is John. [Corrects the presumed field of answers].

Q: Dr. Obfuscate, please answer this question yes or no, does the transmogrifier invariably mutate the organometer, or does the degree of magnoscopy in any way affect the process?

A: That question cannot be answered yes or no. [Corrects the prescribed format for the answer].

Unless the witness gives a corrective answer, the witness tacitly admits each presupposition contained in the question, even if the witness answers the question in the negative.

Q: Have you stopped beating your wife? [Presupposes witness beats his wife].

A: No. [Admits to beating wife now and in the past].

A: Yes. [Admits only to beating wife in the past].

A: No, I never started. [Denies currently beating wife and corrects presupposition that witness ever beat wife].

An evasive answer seeks to appear either responsive or corrective, but actually is nothing of the sort. With evasive answers, the witness seeks to divert the audience's attention from the fact that the answer is not responsive or tries to mask the fact that she has made an uncomfortable admission. Evasion comes in three broad categories, denial, deflection, and disguise, each of which we will discuss in Chapter 12 on constructive cross-examination.

5. FACTUAL AND FICTITIOUS ANSWERS

Responsive answers can be "true facts," contingent facts, or fiction. As said in the first chapter, "true facts" are few and far between, but for the purposes of the courtroom, contingent facts can sometimes have such a high truth value that they can be treated as "true facts." True facts consist of knowledge gained by personal perception. Contingent facts are usually beliefs based upon deduction. Sometimes the deduction can be sound, as in the following example.

Q: Mr. Smith, you testified on direct that my client bit Mr. Jones' ear off, didn't you?

A: Yes, sir.

Q: But you didn't see my client bite Mr. Jones' ear off, did you?

A: No, sir, I didn't.

Q: Please tell the ladies and gentlemen of the jury just how it is that you can testify so certainly that my client bit Mr. Jones' ear off?

A: I saw him spit it out.

On other occasions the deduction is more the product of wishful thinking that cold logic. Fiction is usually the product of mistake, self-deception, or fraud. If you decide a witness is presenting you with fiction, it is important to try to decide what type of fiction you confront. You should deal with a mistaken witness differently from a witness who is engaging in self-deception or outright fraud. Mistakes come from faulty perception or faulty deduction. Self-deception comes from wishful thinking or excessive emotion. You can lead a mistaken witness to the truth much more easily than you can a self-deceptive witness. Mistaken witnesses usually do not have an emotional investment in what they are asserting and can be coaxed away from those assertions. Self-deceptive witnesses very much want what they are saying to be true and can be very stubborn in refusing to admit their error.

Fraudulent fiction comes in three basic types—equivocation, tergiversation, and prevarication. Equivocation takes advantage of words with multiple denotations. There once was a man who dropped his second wife off to picnic in the cemetery while he went to court to answer charges of bigamy. The jury acquitted him when he testified his second wife was "at this moment in the cemetery."

Tergiversation works off literal but misleading truth.

Q: Did you see the defendant ride by your house on the night in question?

A: No. [He was walking].

Prevarication is outright lying.

Q: Which way did he go?

A: He went west. [He really went east].

The equivocator and tergiversator have an accomplice—the examiner. Both equivocation and tergiversation work off ambiguities in the question, either the stated or the presupposed facts. Equivocators and tergiversators will grudgingly give the truth if they can be pinned down by the form of the question. The questioner's task is simply (or not so simply) to ask questions which are tightly worded enough to deny the witness the opportunity to take advantage of ambiguity. The prevaricator is altogether a different problem, which we will discuss in Chapter 13 when we look at the LIE Principle.

B. THREE TYPES OF QUESTIONING

There are many types of questioning aimed at many different objectives, but we need concern ourselves with only three—interview, interrogation, and examination. Interviews and interrogations occur outside the courtroom, usually in anticipation of some court action, and examinations usually occur inside the courtroom in support of a court action. Interviews and interrogations do not necessarily have to be given under oath, but examinations are almost always conducted with the witness under oath. In interviews and interrogations, the examiner is also the audience, and the examiner seeks to discover information from the witness. In an examination the examiner should already know the witness's information, and the objective is to disclose the information to the audience, either judge or jury. An interview presupposes a cooperative witness, while an interrogation presupposes the witness to be uncooperative. An examination presupposes some sort of legal compulsion to answer, usually in the form of a subpoena. In an examination, the witness may or may not be cooperative depending upon the type of examination being conducted. Direct examination presupposes a cooperative witness, while cross-examination presupposes an uncooperative witness. In a courtroom, on direct examination, even with a truly cooperative witness, all the negative dynamics of questioning come into play with additional considerations. Three other parties impinge on the questioning process: the judge, opposing counsel, and the jury. Two of these parties can interfere with the questioning process, and at least one of the parties (opposing counsel) is actively hostile to the questioning process. After the friendly witness has been questioned, opposing counsel may then cross-examine. On cross-examination the witnesses are presumed to be uncooperative. We will consider direct and cross-examination in separate chapters. Let us now turn our attention to interviews and interrogations.

1. THE INTERVIEW

The interview of a friendly witness presents the examiner with a relatively easy job. The witness willingly discloses the necessary information, if only the examiner can ask the right questions. Too often examiners can fall victim to tunnel-vision, focusing too closely on issues too narrowly defined. A good interview technique is to simply say, "I want you to tell me what happened. Just start at the beginning and go to the end, and don't leave anything out in the middle." Listen and take notes for follow-up questions. After the witness has disgorged her information, follow up with specific questions. Do not fear going "outside the crime scene tape," asking questions on any peripheral areas that may be of interest. Do not neglect the witness's background. Establish the precise nature of any relationships among the principles to the incident. You must be very careful with the facts presupposed in your questions. The witness, wanting to cooperate, may accept presuppositions which are untrue, to the detriment of the truth-seeking process. In one long-forgotten murder case a young assistant public defender got each of the witnesses to say on interview that the victim "ran up on" the defendant's knife. He went to trial confident that he could prove the victim committed the functional equivalent of suicide by impaling himself on the defendant's knife. He was bitterly disappointed when none of the witnesses testified to that "fact" at trial. In re-evaluating his performance, the young attorney realized that when he interviewed the witnesses, they simply tried to be helpful by accepting his preconceived notion of what had happened. Had he more carefully tried to keep from telegraphing his preconceptions, he would not have deceived himself. In addition to being careful with the presuppositions of the question, you should also be expansive with the presumed field of answers, using the least restrictive prescribed form for the answer.

2. THE INTERROGATION

Where an interview is an exercise in education, an interrogation is an exercise in extraction. The interrogation of a suspect presents special problems which we will not address, other than to make one observation. Many examiners approach the interrogation of a suspect with the objective of extracting a confession. This is a capital mistake, as the suspect may be innocent. The examiner should approach the suspect interrogation with the same objective as any other form of questioning—to extract the truth. You are more likely to achieve the truth if you do not try to impose your preconceptions about the truth upon the witness. The interrogation presents this conundrum—although the examiner must still be careful with the facts presupposed in the question, lack of cooperation from the witness demands that the examiner narrow the presumed field of answers and adopt a more coercive prescribed form. How can a witness be coerced into telling the truth without imposing the examiner's preconceptions upon the witness?

A certain amount of coerciveness comes simply from your position as a prosecutor, a law enforcement officer, and an officer of the court. The authority inherent in that position exerts a subtle psychological pressure to come forward with the truth. Beyond that, the witness's desire to appear helpful, inherent in any questioning situation, gives a subtle push toward cooperation. Finally, once the witness begins to cooperate by answering questions, the witness's aversion to being thought dishonest exerts pressure.

The witness will appear dishonest in one of three ways—either the testimony will be illogical, internally inconsistent, or incompatible with other evidence. As the witness's testimony becomes illogical, confront the witness with that illogic and ask that it be reconciled. As the witness attempts to reconcile the illogic, she will either give up the truth or become more illogical. The more illogical the witness becomes, the more ridiculous she looks. The more ridiculous she looks, the greater the pressure will be to tell the truth. As the witness begins to try to repair her credibility, she will begin to make statements at variance with what she has already told you. Confront her with these inconsistencies. As she attempts to repair these inconsistencies, she will either become more inconsistent or more truthful. The witness will also become inconsistent with other known facts. As these inconsistencies arise, contradict her with them. Do not let the witness know what you already know unless and until the witness tells you something at variance with what you already know. Not knowing how much you know and not wanting to be gainsaid on other statements, the witness will either come around to telling the truth, or destroy her credibility, or shut down completely and refuse to give further information. Patience is of paramount importance. The less impatient you appear, the less hostile you are as you point out the problems with the witness's testimony, the longer the witness will talk before shutting down completely. If the witness shuts down completely, you may be able to apply more pressure in the form of an investigative subpoena, which we will discuss later in this chapter.

3. QUINTILIAN'S CORKSCREW

Most people try to be truthful most of the time. Rather than lying, many witnesses will simply become incredibly uncooperative in giving forth the information. They will deploy every available evasive technique in their efforts to prevent you from getting the information you want. The ancient Roman rhetorician Quintilian had this to say about corkscrewing the truth out of a reluctant witness:

> With the witness who is going to tell the truth with reluctance, the prime success for the interrogator is to extort from him what he did not want to say. This can only be done by questioning which starts a long way from the point. He will then give answers which he does not think harm the Cause; later on, he will be led from a number of admissions to the point when he cannot deny what he does not want to say.[1]

Beginning with small, innocuous admissions, the examiner builds on those admissions to larger ones. By the time the witness has made all the preliminary admissions, she will have locked herself into making the targeted admissions. We will return to Quintilian's corkscrew in the chapters on direct and cross-examination.

Interviews and interrogations not only inform the examiner of the witness's knowledge, they also inhibit the witness from changing her story. Once a witness has made a statement, she feels an allegiance to what she has said and is reluctant to take back her word unless compelled to do so. Thus, when you interview a witness, you can have some assurance that when she comes to court, she will testify in conformity with what she has already said. This is less true with an interrogation. Since the witness was reluctant to make the statement to begin with, she will be far less motivated to make the same statement at trial. Simply taking the statement can serve to inhibit changes of testimony, but the witness can be even further inhibited from repudiating her statement if you memorialize it in some way.

4. MEMORIALIZING THE INTERVIEW OR INTERROGATION

The examiner can memorialize an interview or interrogation in several ways. He can (and should) take notes of the interview. He can write an

[1] 2 Quintilian, The Orator's Education, 5.7.17, Trans. Donald A. Russell, Harvard University Press, Cambridge, Massachusetts, 2001. p. 343.

interview report. He can tape record the statement, or he can reduce it to writing and have it signed by the witness. Each method has advantages and disadvantages. Interview notes are often hard to read, even by the examiner who wrote them, and they are also the least likely to inhibit the witness from changing her story. An interview report is somewhat better than notes and can be very good if the examiner has literary skill. The interview report, however, has minimal power to inhibit changes in testimony. The witness feels safe in saying "The examiner misunderstood me and wrote it down wrong." A tape-recorded statement leaves no question about what the witness said, but it causes other problems. The examiner does not take notes as carefully because it is all being recorded. When the tape turns out to be inaudible, the whole process will go for naught because of the sketchy notes. If the examiner does the taped interview thoroughly, lots of extraneous information gets recorded for transcription, wasting countless hours of typing, proofreading, and retyping. Some examiners try to solve this problem by doing an interview off tape and then redoing the interview on tape with the extraneous matter omitted. This saves hours of typing, but it presents another problem. In this format the examiner almost always asks highly leading questions. Although the examiner simply wants to expedite the process by helping the witness along, it sounds like the examiner is putting words into the witness's mouth. Wholesale taping of witness statements places and extreme burden on support staff. It may be justified in a first-degree murder case but not in a simple battery. The written witness statement gives the best format for memorializing the witness interview. If you have an intelligent, articulate witness, you may be able to just hand her a sheet of paper and say, "write out a statement." Many witnesses, however, display neither intelligence nor literacy, and their statements can tend to resemble the following signed, written statement once given by two scholarship athletes charged with burglary. "We plead gutly [sic]." With an unintelligent, inarticulate witness, the examiner should write out the statement for the witness, and then have the witness read, correct, and sign it. You should write the statement in the first person and in the language of the witness. You do not put words into the witness' mouth, you record the words that come out of the witness' mouth. Such a statement might read as follows:

<u>Voluntary Statement</u>

> My name is Oceanus McCall, my date of birth is April 1, 1939, I live at 666 Infernal Place, New River, Florida, and my telephone number is 666–0666. Having been fully advised of my rights to remain silent and to have counsel present with me, I hereby freely and voluntarily waive and give up those rights and make the following statement concerning the death of Benny Boyd Cooley:

I have known Benny Boyd Cooley for as long as I can remember. We lived in the same neighborhood when we were kids. We went to school together, and we worked on the railroad together. He was about the best friend I had, but he was selfish. A few years ago Benny got into an accident working on the railroad, and he got a big worker's compensation settlement from them.

On the 2nd day of November 1974, I was drinking beer with Benny at the Rambling Rose Tavern. We were sitting at the table over in the corner. I asked Benny if he remembered hiring me to lie for him in his worker's compensation case against the railroad. He said he did. I told Benny that he got a good settlement from the railroad, but he never paid me the $1,000.00 that he promised. I told him he should share some of his money with his friends, and I asked him to loan me a dollar. Benny told me he would give me a dollar when a hog could see its tail up an acorn tree. When he said that, it made me so mad I pulled out my pistol and shot him dead. I didn't really mean to kill him, but I did mean to hurt him. He had it coming. Benny got a lot of money from the railroad, and he never worked again. There I was, his friend who had helped him get that money, and he hadn't shared any of it with me. If he had really been a good friend, he would have given me some of that money.

This is to certify that I have read the foregoing statement, consisting of one page, and together with any corrections or additions that I have initialed in, it is true and correct.

S/Oceanus McCall

SWORN TO AND SUBSCRIBED before me by Oceanus McCall, who is personally known to me, this 2nd day of November 1974, at the Camden County Jail in New River, Florida.

S/Notary Public

5. THE INVESTIGATIVE SUBPOENA

When the witness is not merely obstinate, but refuses to speak at all, you need greater compulsion than the authority of your office. That compulsion can come in the form of an investigative subpoena. Many state statutes or rules provide that, in the investigation of a case, prosecutors may compel the attendance and testimony of witnesses.[2] The subpoena compels the witness to answer your questions or answer to a higher authority. If she does not answer questions, she may be held in contempt

---

[2] Arkansas Code Annotated § 16–43–212; West's Fla.Stat.Ann. § 27.04; Hawaii Rev.Stat. § 28–2.5; West's Ann. Ind. Code § 33–39–1–4; La.Code Crim.P. Art. 66; Mich.Comp.Laws Ann. § 767A.7.

and imprisoned until she becomes more cooperative.[3] A simple refusal to answer questions no longer being possible, the witness may attempt to ground her refusal on her fifth amendment privilege against self-incrimination. Depending upon the wording of the enabling statute, an investigative subpoena can defeat the privilege against self-incrimination,[4] but it does so at a price. The compulsion carries a grant of immunity with it.[5] Immunity comes in different forms and gets conferred in different ways. Immunity can be transactional—a witness compelled to testify cannot be prosecuted for crimes within the subject matter of the testimony.[6] Immunity can consist of no more than use and derivative use immunity—the witness's testimony cannot be used against her, nor can it be used as an investigative lead to ferret out other evidence against her. The Constitution only requires use and derivative use immunity,[7] but some statutory provisions grant full transactional immunity.[8] The service of the subpoena and the asking of the questions can automatically confer immunity,[9] or the witness may have to invoke the privilege.[10] Some provisions require the prosecutor to apply to the court for a grant of immunity prior to issuing the subpoena.[11]

Whatever the precise mechanism of the statute or rule, a grant of immunity gives the prosecutor a powerful tool for the extraction of information from witnesses, but it also gives the witness a protective shield against the ill effects of surrendering the information. As with any powerful tool, the investigative subpoena should be used with great care. With a self-executing transactional immunity statute, you can unwittingly destroy a prosecution by issuing a subpoena to the wrong person. Even a self-executing use immunity statute can hamstring a prosecution when you injudiciously issue subpoenas. Before issuing an investigative subpoena, you should make certain that your jurisdiction allows such subpoenas, know what type of immunity flows from such subpoenas, know the mechanism for the granting of such immunity, and make certain that you will not jeopardize your case by issuing such a subpoena.

If you find it necessary to subpoena a recalcitrant witness to coerce her testimony, you can be reasonably satisfied that the witness is not going to capitulate and begin volunteering information. Having raised your hammer, you should promptly communicate to the witness that you are

---

3 Kastigar v. United States, 406 U.S. 441, 92 S.Ct. 1653 (1972).

4 Zile v. State, 710 So.2d 729 (Fla. App. 4th DCA 1998).

5 Kastigar v. United States, supra note 3.

6 Gammarano v. Gold, 51 A.D.2d 1012, 381 N.Y.S.2d 298 (N.Y.S.Ct., Appellate Div. 1976).

7 Kastigar v. United States, supra note 3.

8 Gammarano v. Gold, supra note 6 (interpreting New York-McKinney's CPL § 190.40).

9 Fla.Stat.§ 914.04; McKinney's CPL New York § 190.40.

10 Va.Code § 19.2–208; 18 U.S.C. §§ 6002, 6003.

11 Mich. Comp.Laws § 767A.7.

willing to bring it down upon her. You could introduce yourself and the proceedings to the witness in language similar to the following:

> Good morning, Mrs. McCall, my name is Stanley Hopkins, and I am the prosecutor assigned to investigate this matter concerning the shooting death of Benny Boyd Cooley. You have received an investigative subpoena requiring you to appear before me here today to give testimony relating to that shooting. At this time, I am giving you a true copy of an order entered by Judge Solomon requiring you to give testimony before me here today and granting you immunity from prosecution for any testimony you give here today. This order was entered pursuant to § 767A.7, Michigan Compiled Laws, and it means that you cannot refuse to answer my questions on grounds that they may tend to incriminate you. It also means, and I am reading from the statute, that "No testimony or other information compelled under the order, or any information directly or indirectly derived from that testimony or other information, may be used against [you] in any criminal case, except for impeachment purposes, in a prosecution for perjury, or for otherwise failing to comply with the order granting immunity."[12] This means that nothing you say can be used against you in any kind of a criminal prosecution so long as you tell the truth. Do you completely understand the judge's order? I am now going to place you under oath and ask you questions, and I expect your answers to be full, complete, and truthful.

Witnesses under such compulsion have a right to counsel, and a full and complete record should be made of all communications with the witness, either by use of a tape recording or through the services of a court reporter.

C. THE DISCOVERY DEPOSITION

The deposition is a sort of a hybrid between an interview or interrogation and an examination. The deposition takes place outside the courtroom and before the trial, but it is taken under oath in anticipation of trial. There are two basic types of depositions, the discovery deposition and the deposition to perpetuate testimony. The discovery deposition is more like the interview or interrogation and the deposition to perpetuate testimony is more like the examination. The discovery deposition serves much the same purpose as the interview or interrogation, it informs the examiner, inhibits the witness from changing stories, and serves as the premier method for impeaching the witness should she vary her testimony. Only a few states allow discovery depositions in criminal cases, and Vermont pioneered the practice.

---

[12] Mich.Comp.Laws Ann. § 767.7(2).

The discovery deposition does more than turn an interview or interrogation into a sworn criminal proceeding. It adds a fourth party to the process. Remember, questioning involves a witness, an examiner, and an audience. In a deposition the fourth party has a role as audience and co-examiner, but the party can also play the role of adversarial impediment to the flow of information. With a friendly witness and a cooperative attorney on the other side, the deposition is little more than a formalized interview. With an uncooperative witness it is a formalized interrogation, and opposing counsel can become a fly in the ointment by using objections to assist the witness's efforts to stonewall.

1. A BRIEF HISTORY OF THE CRIMINAL DISCOVERY DEPOSITION

In 1957 the Vermont Legislature enacted a law providing that depositions could be taken by the parties "to any action pending in a county court, court of chancery or municipal court * * * for the purpose of discovery or for use as evidence in the action or for both purposes."[13] In February of 1959, a team of enterprising attorneys defending a murder case in Orange County, Vermont, filed notices of taking depositions on behalf of their clients. The attorney general petitioned for a writ of prohibition, and the Supreme Court granted the writ, noting that depositions in criminal cases were unthinkable and that the statute obviously applied only to civil cases.[14] Once the unthinkable has been thought, it soon becomes the doable. In 1961 the Vermont Legislature enacted 13 Vermont Statutes Annotated § 6721, which provided that a respondent in a criminal case could take the deposition of a witness upon motion and notice, and making a showing that the witness's testimony may be material or relevant on the trial or helpful in the preparation of his case. In 1973, the statute was repealed and replaced by Rule 15, Vermont Rules of Criminal Procedure, which made several changes including giving the state the right to take depositions. Rule 15 was amended again in 1982, 1984, 1985, and 1991.[15]

The Florida Supreme Court followed Vermont's lead in 1967, when it promulgated Rule 1.220(f) of the Florida Rules of Criminal Procedure.[16] Initially the rule provided that depositions could only be taken upon motion by the defense and upon a showing that the witness's testimony was material or relevant to the trial, or of assistance in the preparation of a defense. The defense also had to show that the witness had failed to cooperate in giving a voluntary signed, written statement. Upon such a showing the court could order the taking of a discovery deposition, which could only be used to impeach the witness should she testify contrary to the

---

13 Reed v. Allen 121 Vt. 202, 205, 153 A.2d 74, 76 (1959).

14 Id.

15 Vt.R.Crim.P. 15, Reporter's Notes.

16 In re Florida Rules of Criminal Procedure, 196 So.2d 124 (Fla. 1967).

deposition. In 1972, the Florida Supreme Court reworked the rules of criminal procedure, changing the numbering system, and changing the method for taking discovery depositions. Rule 3.220(d), Florida Rules of Criminal Procedure, provided that defense discovery depositions could be taken as a matter of course in all cases, including misdemeanors.[17] After 1972, the deposition rule was amended twice more in 1989[18] and 1996.[19]

Other states have begun to provide for discovery depositions in criminal cases. With the decision of *State v. Peterson*,[20] Iowa became the third state to allow discovery depositions. Arizona Rule of Criminal Procedure 15.3(a)(2) allows discovery depositions upon motion under circumstances very similar to those set out in Florida's old Rule of Criminal Procedure 1.220. The rule allows discovery depositions of witnesses who have not testified at preliminary hearing upon a showing that the witness's testimony is material to the case or necessary to the preparation of the defense and that the witness will not cooperate in granting a personal interview.[21] The defendant has no right to be present at a discovery deposition.[22] Arizona has had a much different experience with depositions than most other jurisdictions. Because Rule 15.3(a)(2) of the Arizona Rules of Criminal Procedure requires a showing of necessity for the deposition and a showing that the witness will not cooperate, the interview is much more common than the deposition. If the defense attorney requests an interview and the witness consents, then no deposition can be taken. Refusals to give an interview occur so rarely that one prosecutor reports having attended only six depositions over an eleven-year period.[23] Prosecutors customarily attend defense interviews,[24] and frequently assist the defense by making arrangements for the interviews. Unsurprisingly, depositions occur more frequently in those counties where the prosecutor does not provide this service to the defense.[25] On occasion prosecutors will ask the case agent or chief investigating officer to attend interviews of relatively unimportant witnesses.[26] Indiana law appears to allow for free use of depositions in criminal cases, even to the point of allowing

---

[17] In re Florida Rules of Criminal Procedure, 272 So.2d 65 (Fla. 1972).

[18] In re Amendment to Florida Rule of Criminal Procedure (Discovery), 3.220, 550 So.2d 1097 (Fla. 1989).

[19] In re Amendment to Florida Rule of Criminal Procedure 3.220(h) and Florida Rule of Juvenile Procedure 8.060(d), 681 So.2d 666 (Fla. 1996).

[20] 219 N.W.2d 665 (Iowa 1974).

[21] Ariz.R.Crim.P. 15.3(a)(2).

[22] Ariz.R.Crim.P. 15.3(e).

[23] McGrane, Dennis, Chief Deputy County Attorney, Yavapai County Attorney's Office, Prescott, Arizona. Correspondence on December 7, 2006.

[24] Hessinger, Mark, Supervising Deputy County Attorney, Yuma County Attorney's Office, Yuma, Arizona. Correspondence on December 6, 2006.

[25] Brannan, Martin, LaPaz County Attorney, Parker, Arizona. Correspondence on December 6, 2006.

[26] Id.

depositions by written interrogatory.[27] Rules 25.12 and 25.23, Missouri Rules of Criminal Procedure, allow defendants to take and use depositions almost as freely as a party in a civil suit, and Rule 25.15 grants a similar right to the state. Rule 25.14 provides that depositions to perpetuate testimony may be taken by either party.

2. SAFEGUARDS FOR CRIMINAL DISCOVERY DEPOSITIONS

It is no coincidence that Florida and Vermont, having had depositions in criminal cases the longest, have the most elaborate safeguards built into their rules. Those safeguards include:

(1) A time limit for taking depositions. Vermont provides that unless the judge specifies otherwise, depositions cannot be taken more than 90 days after arraignment.[28] If vigorously enforced, this would be an excellent provision, because attorneys are forever requesting continuances on grounds that they have not completed depositions.

(2) Exclusion of the Defendant from the deposition. Unless the parties agree or the court orders it, the defendant cannot attend a discovery deposition.[29] This provision serves to limit intimidation of vulnerable witnesses, such as sexual assault victims and child victims.

(3) Vermont allows any party or witness to concurrently record the deposition.[30]

(4) No witness may be deposed more than once regarding a single case.[31]

(5) Limitations are placed on the taking of depositions of certain types of witnesses.[32]

(6) Depositions may not be taken in misdemeanor cases without leave of court.[33]

(7) Deponents are allowed to have counsel and victim's advocates present.[34]

---

[27] Ind.Crim.R. 2.5(F)(4); Ind.Trial R. 30, 31.

[28] Vt.R.Crim.P. 15(a).

[29] Fla.R.Crim.P. 3.220(h)(7); Vt. R.Crim.P. 15(b).

[30] Vt.R.Crim.P. 15(d)(3).

[31] Fla.R.Crim.P. 3.220(h)(1); Vt. R.Crim.P. 15(e)(1), (2).

[32] Fla.R.Crim.P. 3.220(h)(1)(B), (C); Vt.R.Crim.P. 15(e)(3).

[33] Fla.R.Crim.P. 3.220(h)(1)(D); Vt.R.Crim.P. 15(e)(4).

[34] Vt.R.Crim.P. 15(f)(1). Although no specific provision for this exists in the Florida rule, attorneys and victim's advocates routinely attend depositions with witnesses in Florida.

(8) Special measures are to be taken with child victims under the age of 16, including videotaping and taking of the deposition before a judge or special master.[35]

(9) In Florida, depositions are to be taken at the courthouse or some other place designated by the court. Out-of-county deponents must be deposed in a court reporter's office in their county of residence.[36]

(10) The court may enter such other and further protective orders as it deems appropriate.[37]

Each of these measures was promulgated to address specific abuses encountered in the deposition process, and many worthy prosecutors believe that sufficient abuses remain to justify abolishing depositions altogether. Any good tool can be put to ill use. On balance, if lawyers make judicious use of discovery depositions, they can be quite helpful to both prosecution and defense.

3. TAKING CRIMINAL DISCOVERY DEPOSITIONS

"Good lawyers will use depositions to sharpen the issues, expose untenable arguments and efficiently marshal the facts of the case. They 'freeze' the testimony of the witness at a comparatively early point in time to deter the witness from changing the testimony as the trial date approaches."[38] Mediocre lawyers will use depositions to expose their defenses to the prosecuting attorney, educate the prosecutor to the weaknesses of the case, unearth additional evidence and witnesses for the prosecution, and prepare the prosecution witnesses for the rigors of cross-examination at trial. Inquisitive lawyers with affluent clients can spend inordinate amounts of time, energy, and effort conducting marathon depositions. Much of this time, energy, and effort could be more profitably spent in other pretrial activities. Just as the hammer is a tool for driving a nail, the deposition is a tool for discovery of the other side's evidence. Just as the hammer may be misused as a weapon rather than a tool, so may a deposition be misused as a weapon for intimidation or harassment. Infrequently this misuse bears fruit, but more often it has an opposite effect. Witnesses fear giving testimony. They have all watched the television shows and movies in which crafty lawyers brutalize hapless witnesses, and they think that the very same thing will happen to them. They enter the deposition with fear and trembling, but the deposition works a remarkable metamorphosis—they leave the deposition confident

---

[35] Fla.R.Crim.P. 3.220(h)(4); Vt. R.Crim.P. 15(f)(2).

[36] Fla.R.Crim.P. 3.220(h).

[37] Fla.R.Crim.P. 3.220(*l*); Vt. R.Crim.P. 15(f)(3).

[38] Swingle, H. Morley, "Depositions in Criminal Cases in Missouri," 60 Journal of the Missouri Bar 128, 131 (2004).

and prepared to testify. They survive the hectoring of the defense attorney and come to believe that they can survive the rigors of testifying at trial. As often as not, the belief is justified. The more brutal the examination at deposition, the more it prepares them to withstand cross-examination at trial. Lawyers are often surprised when witnesses who were awful at deposition testify like professionals at trial. On the other hand, witnesses who have been lulled into a false sense of security by a kid-gloves deposition will sometimes self-destruct on cross-examination at trial.

Lawyers can get the most profit from a deposition by simply and courteously using the deposition to accomplish what it was designed for—to find out what the witness knows. Depending on how closely the witness is tied to the defendant, the deposition can take on the nature of either an interview or an interrogation. Preferably it will be an interview, and you should attempt an interview before beginning to interrogate the witness.

> Good morning. My name is Stanley Hopkins, and I am prosecuting this case against Harry Hotspur. You probably know Mr. Dee Fender over there, who is representing Mr. Hotspur. This gentleman over here is the court reporter, and he is going to take down every word we say. Have you ever given a deposition before? You haven't? Let me explain a few things before we get started. Your name has been given to me by Mr. Dee Fender, the defense attorney in this case, and he tells me that you are someone who knows some information that would be helpful to Mr. Hotspur in answering the charges of Failure to Do Right which have been filed against him. You have been subpoenaed in to give this deposition so that I can talk to you and find out what it is that you know. You will be sworn to tell the truth, and then I will ask you some questions. I will try to make the questions as simple and fair as I possibly can. If you don't understand a question, please let me know and I'll try to reword it to make myself as clear as possible. Mr. Fender is here to make sure that everything is done right, and he may have some questions for you when I finish. The court reporter will take down every word we say and type it up so that we can have a record of what we did here today. Do you have any questions about what is going to happen? Are you ready to start? Okay. [Witness sworn].
>
> [Preliminary accrediting questioning].
>
> Q: What do you know that may be helpful to Mr. Hotspur in defending the charges against him?

This lead in will establish in short order whether you can interview the witness. If the witness will allow you to interview her, ask questions using the interview techniques discussed above. If the witness is uncooperative, use the interrogation techniques. No matter whether you have a cooperative or uncooperative witness, do not cross-examine her. At best the only thing you will accomplish by cross-examining the witness is that you will prepare her for cross-examination at trial. At worst, you will anger her enough to turn a friendly or neutral witness into a partisan witness. There is no better example of this phenomenon than the transformation of the eyewitnesses in the prosecution of Theodore Robert Bundy for the Chi Omega murders in Tallahassee, Florida. At the outset, the prosecution had several witnesses who gave tentative identifications of Bundy as being in the vicinity of the Chi Omega sorority house on the night of the murders. These witnesses were rigorously questioned at deposition and thoroughly cross-examined at the hearing on the motion to suppress their eyewitness identifications. By the time they testified at trial, they were veteran witnesses. They easily withstood cross-examination, giving persuasive in-court identifications. J. Victor Africano, the attorney defending Bundy for the murder of Kimberly Diane Leach, took this incident to heart. Although the state had a number of shaky eyewitnesses to Leach's kidnaping, Africano did not rigorously depose them and did not move to suppress their in-court identifications. As a result, when they took the witness stand at trial, they had little experience with cross-examination. He effectively used his considerable skills to cross-examine the witnesses at trial, rendering them highly unpersuasive.

Whether the deposition is more akin to an interview or an interrogation, remember that you are not the only audience for the deposition. The judge and jury are potential audiences. If the witness testifies at trial contrary to the deposition, you can use it to impeach the witness by prior inconsistent statement. This means that every important point made by the witness should be memorialized in a form that expedites impeachment. Narrative questions are excellent tools for economizing your time in discovering the witness's knowledge, but they are not ideal vehicles for impeachment. For example, at deposition the witness testifies:

> Q: Tell me everything that happened when Owen Glendower called Harry Hotspur a walrus?
>
> A: Glendower pulled out his knife and opened it with his teeth right after Hotspur hit him with a pool cue. Glendower was cussing like a sailor, waving that knife around, telling poor Mr. Hotspur all about his ancestry. Then Hotspur pulled a gun and Glendower said "You ain't got the guts to shoot me," but he did have the guts. When Glendower got shot, he staggered forward trying to stick Hotspur with his knife and Hotspur shot him again.

You are satisfied with this testimony, so you move on, covering other topics. At trial the witness testifies that a mysterious disappearing stranger shot Glendower as Glendower was making a shot at the pool table, and that Hotspur was unarmed and had taken no aggressive action against Glendower. If you impeach the witness by prior inconsistent statement, you will have to read the entire question and answer into the record, repeating some information that is not helpful to the prosecution. What you should have done at the deposition was to isolate the good facts from the bad. You could have done it by following up on the narrative answer in this manner:

> Q: Did you say that Hotspur hit Glendower with a pool cue?
>
> Q: Which end of the pool cue did Hotspur hit Glendower with?
>
> Q: What part of Glendower's body did Hotspur hit with the pool cue?
>
> Q: Now you said Hotspur pulled a gun?
>
> Q: Where did Hotspur pull the gun from?
>
> Q: What kind of a gun was it that Hotspur pulled?
>
> Q: Can you describe the gun that Hotspur pulled?
>
> Q: How many times did Hotspur shoot Glendower?
>
> Q: Was Hotspur holding the gun with one hand or two when he shot Glendower?

You now have the facts that Hotspur hit Glendower with a pool cue and shot him with a gun isolated into answers that do not contain information detrimental to the prosecution. When the witness testifies that Hotspur did not attack Glendower, you do not have to impeach the witness with the narrative answer containing the detrimental information. You impeach her with the short, unadorned answers given to your specific follow up questions.

It is important to segregate the good information from the bad for another reason. Not only can you impeach more effectively because it is not encumbered by detrimental evidence, the impeachment is substantive evidence. Whereas most prior inconsistent statements are admissible only to call the witness's testimony into question, prior inconsistent statements made in depositions can be proof of the matter asserted in the prior statement.[39] This provision can be of utmost importance to proving your case. You may argue the prior inconsistent statement as true. If the only prior inconsistent statement you have from the Hotspur/Glendower example above is the first statement, then impeaching the witness with that statement will give the defense substantive evidence that Glendower pulled a knife on Hotspur. The discovery deposition can be more than an investigative tool. Under the right circumstances, it can provide essential substantive evidence.

Oftentimes you will confront disclosures of defense witnesses at or near the eve of the trial. Although most reciprocal discovery provisions

---

[39] Hamilton v. State, 937 P.2d 1001 (Okl.Cr. 1997); West's Fla.Stat. Ann. § 90.801(2)(a); Iowa R.Evid. 5.801d.(1)(A); 12 Okl.Stat.Ann. § 2801.B.1.a.

require the defense to disclose within a short period of time after receiving the state's disclosure, many defense attorneys drag their feet in making disclosures. Part of this results from the lawyer's natural tendency to procrastinate, but sometimes the defense has ulterior motives. The less time between disclosure of the witness and trial, the less time you have to prepare for the witness. Sometimes defense attorneys make belated disclosures to forestall thorough investigation of the witness. Sometimes they make belated disclosures to cause the state to move for a continuance. Your automatic reaction to such a belated disclosure will be to want to depose the witness, and you usually have little time between disclosure and trial to get the deposition done. Suppression of the witness's testimony does not present a viable option. Judges are loath to enter such an order against the defense. A judge will never get reversed for allowing a defense witness to testify and will almost certainly get reversed for suppressing the witness. If the suppression stands up on appeal, then the belated disclosure becomes fodder for a post-conviction motion attacking the defense attorney's untimely disclosure as ineffective assistance of counsel. Although the first impulse may be to move to continue to obtain the witness's deposition, it may not be necessary. The closer to the time of trial a witness is disclosed, the weaker the witness is likely to be. Defense counsel are usually proud of strong witnesses for the defense and disclose them early, as a tactic to get you to consider dropping the charges or taking a lesser plea. With a weak witness, they will want to wait until the last minute to protect her by giving you the shortest amount of reaction time possible. If the witness is weak, then it is likely the defense cannot make the reaction time too short for you to deal with the witness. Have one of the investigating officers do an informal interview of the witness as soon as possible in order to get a preliminary assessment. It is likely that such an interview will be all that is necessary. If the interview discloses the witness to be weak, do not move for a continuance. Announce ready for trial. If the interview discloses some problems, try to take an expedited deposition before moving for a continuance. Defense counsel and the judge should be willing to cooperate in getting the deposition done as soon as possible. After the deposition you will probably be ready to go to trial without any delay. If the deposition discloses something that needs follow up investigation and you do not have time between deposition and trial to get it done, then you can move for a continuance.

4. DEFENDING CRIMINAL DISCOVERY DEPOSITIONS

Prosecutors will spend more time attending depositions taken by the defense than they will in deposing witnesses themselves. Many prosecutors consider depositions the bane of their existence and wish that depositions could be abolished. They are time consuming and expensive, at best they inconvenience witnesses and victims, and at worst they needlessly harass and embarrass witnesses. As described above, Vermont and Florida have repeatedly tinkered with the deposition rules in an effort to discourage and minimize abuse, but you could make a strong case for the proposition that minimal progress has been made toward limiting the taking of depositions to witnesses who actually should be deposed. Many witnesses, such as records custodians, have little knowledge of the case and really do not need to be deposed. Although many rules of criminal procedure provide for prosecutors to disclose witnesses in different categories, many prosecutors are afraid to list witnesses in categories that make depositions difficult or impossible for fear of being accused of a discovery violation. Defense attorneys, especially those defending high-stakes, high-profile cases, tend to take depositions wholesale in order to escape an accusation of ineffective assistance of counsel, because the cases in which defense counsel have been attacked as having given ineffective assistance of counsel for not taking depositions are legion.[40] When Florida's deposition rule was amended in 1996, there was a recommendation that the committee note to the new rule include a comment that failure to take depositions was not *per se* ineffective assistance of counsel.[41] Even when they take depositions, defense attorneys are not immune to criticism. They have been attacked for not asking certain questions at deposition,[42] not reading the transcripts of depositions,[43] not giving the defendant a copy of the depositions,[44] relying on depositions taken by others rather than personally taking depositions,[45] and not performing specific impeachments by prior inconsistent statement from depositions.[46] Usually, the reviewing courts find that such failures and omissions do not constitute ineffective assistance of counsel. Regardless of this fact, however, many defense counsel take unnecessary depositions and ask unnecessary questions at deposition to minimize their

---

[40] See, e.g., Slusher v. State, 823 N.E.2d 1219 (Ind.App. 2005)(Remanding case for evidentiary hearing on whether failure to take depositions constituted ineffective assistance of counsel); In re LaBounty, 177 Vt. 635, 869 A.2d 120 (2005)(Affirming lower court's finding after evidentiary hearing that it was not ineffective assistance to fail to depose the victim in a child sex assault case); Yarbrough v. State, 871 So.2d 1026 (Fla. App.1st DCA 2004)(Failure to interview or depose state's witnesses held to be ineffective assistance of counsel); Brown v. State, 846 So.2d 1114 (Fla. 2003)(Failure to depose a specific witness not ineffective assistance under the circumstances); State v. Broseman, 947 S.W.2d 520 (Mo.App. W.D. 1997)(Failure to depose the doctor performing the autopsy was not ineffective assistance of counsel where defense counsel had the doctor's written report and cause of death was not an issue); White v. State, 939 S.W.2d 887 (Mo. 1997)(Failure to depose witnesses not per se ineffective assistance of counsel); Bernay v. State, 989 P.2d 998 (Okl.Ct.Crim.App. 1999)(Failure to obtain the deposition of an incarcerated witness not per se ineffective assistance of counsel); Carlson v. State, 720 N.W.2d 192 (Iowa App. 2006)(Rejected claim of ineffective assistance for failure to take depositions because defendant pleaded guilty).

[41] In re Amendment to Florida Rule of Criminal Procedure 3.220(h), 668 So.2d 951, 952–953 (Fla. 1995).

[42] Jones v. State, 895 So.2d 1228 (Fla.App.3d DCA 2005)(Concurring opinion)(Defense counsel criticized for not pursuing a certain line of questioning at deposition).

[43] Lanier v. State, 709 So.2d 112 (Fla.App.3d DCA 1998).

[44] Gainer v. State, 671 So.2d 240 (Fla.App.1st DCA 1996); Shaw v. State, 125 S.W.3d 918 (Mo.App. W.D. 2004).

[45] White v. State, 939 S.W.2d 887 (Mo. 1997).

[46] Medeiros v. State, 866 So.2d 778 (Fla.App. 4th DCA 2004).

vulnerability to censure. In this regard, we would do well to remember that "[d]epositions, while valuable, can be a two-edged sword and they are not an absolute requirement of trial preparation."[47]

Although most prosecutors dislike attending defense discovery depositions, they can learn quite a lot about their cases at depositions. Police officers' reports sometimes omit essential information and follow up investigative interviews by prosecutors frequently fail to discover it. The defense attorney, armed with her client's story, comes at the case from an entirely different perspective. She has formulated the beginnings of a factual defense and begun to map out legal attacks on the evidence, and she is searching for evidence which will support her defense and validate her legal attacks. Sometimes the factual defense consists of no more than a shotgun attack on every aspect of the case, but sometimes it is a specific case theory. Early discernment of the defense case theory can give you essential guidance in developing and refining the prosecution case theory. Identification of the defense theories of attack on the prosecution evidence gives you invaluable insight into how to prepare for the anticipated motions in limine and motions to suppress. Defense counsel oftentimes tries to draft motions to suppress as vaguely as possible to ambush ill-prepared and unsuspecting prosecutors with the legal theory at the evidentiary hearing. If you can ferret out the defense theory of inadmissibility at deposition, you can have your homework done before the motion is filed, or at least before it is heard. Gaping holes in the prosecution case can be uncovered at deposition, and the discovery of new prosecution witnesses and evidence at defense depositions occurs almost daily.

Because discovery depositions are usually admissible only for impeachment purposes, prosecutors oftentimes do not ask questions at the deposition and merely take notes on what the witnesses say. The rationale for not asking questions is that the prosecutor, who is usually dealing with a friendly witness, can clear up any questionable matters with the witness off the record after the deposition. You have limited need to ask questions at a deposition, but in some situations you must follow up with the witness to clarify ambiguous testimony and to fulfill your discovery obligation. If, for example, a defense attorney asks a question based upon an erroneous preconception which the witness does not correct with her answer, you must clarify the ambiguity with follow up questions. If you have learned some highly important fact within the witness's knowledge which is not included in the reports, and the defense attorney doesn't ferret it out with her questioning, you should follow up with questioning designed to reveal the fact. If there is a possibility that the deposition might be used for some other purpose than impeachment, you might want to flesh out omissions in the defense attorney's questioning. For example, expert witnesses are often

---

[47] Brown v. State, 695 N.W.2d 44 (Iowa App. 2004), citing Kellogg v. State, 288 N.W.2d 561, 563–564 (Iowa 1980).

given copies of discovery depositions to use as a basis for helping to form their opinions. This frequently happens with insanity defenses. In such a situation, if the defense attorney deposes the witnesses and fully covers all the facts within the witness's knowledge which could indicate insanity, you had better follow up and bring out all the facts that tend to indicate sanity. On other occasions defense attorneys may want to have the judge rule on their motion to suppress without taking live testimony, but by simply reading the depositions. If you have questioned the witnesses at deposition and fully elucidated the grounds for admissibility, it can promote judicial economy to stipulate to this use of the depositions.

At deposition you should take copious notes of the witness's testimony, preferably on a laptop computer. When the deposition is transcribed, you can then go back to the notes of the deposition and annotate each note with the page and line from the deposition which supports the note. Work this annotated abstract of the deposition into the abstract of testimony described in Chapter 8 on marshaling the evidence, and you will be ready to develop your order of testimony for the direct examination of the witness at trial. The notes also serve another purpose. As you discern weaknesses in the case, make notes of those weaknesses. As new evidence and new witnesses are disclosed, notes should be made about these things also. At the conclusion of the deposition, you should have a "to do" list setting forth all the supplementary investigation needed to shore up the weaknesses and run down the new evidence and witnesses.

PRACTICAL EXERCISE

You believe that Sam Mischanko witnessed a shooting that occurred at a bar, but when the police questioned him shortly after the shooting, he would only say "I don't know nothing about nothing." Mischanko has since refused to make any statements whatsoever to the police. Since the initial interview, investigators have uncovered a credit card receipt on Mischanko's Visa account which shows that he made a purchase at the bar fifteen minutes before the shooting occurred. Handwriting analysis confirms the signature on the credit card receipt matches Mischanko's signatures on various booking records and fingerprint cards from the county jail. Videotape removed from a surveillance camera located in the parking lot of the bar shows the figures of two males rushing from the bar shortly after the shooting. The males, whose features are too indistinct for recognition, are depicted getting into a car and speeding from the parking lot. The automobile they drove from the lot is a 1966 Mustang convertible with a dent in the passenger's door and "gangster" white sidewall tires. Mischanko owns a 1966 Mustang convertible with a dent in the passenger's door and "gangster" white sidewall tires. Bertram Mooney has given a statement that he came into the bar about thirty minutes before the shooting, and only the bartender was in the bar. He said that he bought a beer and began to play a videogame located on the wall farthest from the door. Standing with his back to the barroom, he became so engrossed in the game that he noticed nothing about his surroundings until he heard a voice sounding very much like Mischanko's shouting, "No, Duke, don't shoot him!" Mooney then heard a salvo of gunfire and turned to see two figures running from the barroom. Mooney says the two figures looked like Duke Morgan and Mischanko, but he can't be sure. The only other person in the bar at the time was the bartender, who died from multiple gunshot wounds. You have determined from rumors and the reports of confidential informants that Mischanko and Duke Morgan came into the bar together to collect a drug debt, and that Duke Morgan shot and killed the bartender when he refused to pay. You have subpoenaed Mischanko to appear before you on an investigative subpoena. This subpoena automatically confers use and derivative use immunity. Devise a series of questions designed to compel Mischanko to admit being at the bar. Using Quintilian's corkscrew and the interrogation techniques described in this chapter, lead Mischanko from small admissions to larger and larger admissions until he must admit being at the bar. Once you get him to admit being at the bar, compel him to describe what he saw and heard at the bar.

CHAPTER 11

DIRECT EXAMINATION

■ ■ ■

> One who produces a voluntary witness may well know what he is going to say; he therefore appears to have an easier task in questioning him. But even this part requires acumen and watchfulness; care must be taken that the witness is not frightened, inconsistent, or unwise. Witnesses are confused, and are drawn into traps by the advocates on the other side; they do more damage by being caught like this than they would have done good by a firm and fearless performance. They must therefore be carefully rehearsed at home and tested by various questions of the kind that the other side may raise.—Quintilian[1]

A. PREPARATION, PREPARATION, AND PRESENTATION

Any successful forensic presentation consists of three parts: preparation, preparation, and presentation. Prepare yourself, prepare your evidence, and present your case. In preparing yourself as an advocate, you must assimilate the evidence by learning the facts of the case, learning the witnesses' testimony, and learning the witnesses. Two witnesses giving identical testimony may have to be presented differently because of their personalities and abilities. Once you have assimilated all the evidence, you must assess it. Can you see a compelling case theory? Can you support it with convincing facts? Can it survive counterattack? After assimilation and assessment, you move to assembly. Develop a compelling statement of your case theory, design your opening statement around that case theory, and deploy your proof to confirm the opening statement. One might ask what all this has to do with direct examination. It has everything to do with direct examination, because the examination of one witness is a microcosm of the whole trial.

The three parts of performing a successful forensic presentation are the three parts of performing a successful direct examination. Preparation, preparation, and presentation make up the essential elements of a successful direct examination, and only one of them occurs in the presence of the jury: preparation by the examiner to take the testimony; preparation

[1] 2 Quintilian, The Orator's Education, 5.7.10–11, Trans. Donald A. Russell, Harvard University Press, Cambridge, Massachusetts, 2001. p. 341.

of the witness to give the testimony; presentation of the testimony to the audience.

Perform the three steps of preparation with each witness you present. Assimilate and absorb the witness's testimony. Do you know the facts of the case? Do you know the witness's testimony? Do you know the witness? Assess each witness. How can the witness help build your case? What potential testimony must you preserve your case against? Can opposing counsel destroy the witness? Then assemble your direct examination so that it moves you ever closer to achieving your objective of a favorable verdict. How can you best present the witness's testimony in the most compelling fashion? How can you best prevent or minimize damage to the witness? How can the testimony best persuade the jury to find for your side? To answer these questions, you need a worksheet that exemplifies each tier of preparation.

> (1) Assimilation: An annotated abstract of testimony outlining the witness's knowledge of the case.
>
> (2) Assessment: A direct examination worksheet outlining the good and the bad of the witness's testimony and what you hope to accomplish with the witness.
>
> (3) Assembly: An order of testimony setting out the facts you want to cover. The order of testimony should include notations as to the evidentiary exhibits you expect to show the witness and annotations to the statements, depositions, and reports supporting your expectation for the witness's testimony.

Your preparation to examine the witness starts with the abstract of testimony. You review everything you can get your hands on about the witness: his statements, statements of others which mention him, evidentiary exhibits that involve him. You make copious notes of every material fact within the witness's knowledge. As indicated in Chapter 8, the abstract of testimony should note down in chronological order each material fact (favorable and unfavorable) to which the witness can testify. Index those notes to the statements and evidentiary exhibits. Depositions, with their page and line numbers, prove the easiest to index. Index the other documents as described in Chapter 8. You must be able to find these facts at a moment's notice in the heat of battle, and the references provide invaluable help in doing this.

1. THE ABSTRACT OF TESTIMONY

Before computers, the advocate had to put his annotations on 3x5 note cards. He would then shuffle and reshuffle the note cards until he got them in chronological or topical order. Once he got them in order, he would copy the notes in order onto a legal pad with the references highlighted. He consumed an incredible amount of time, but he learned the witness's testimony inside out. The 3x5 card has gone the way of the dinosaur. The computer makes the abstract much easier to compile. Chapter 8 describes one way, but not the only way, to use a computer to compile a witness abstract. If you do not like it, devise another way—but compile the abstract if at all possible. The abstract serves primarily as the source from which you draw up your direct examination worksheet and order of testimony, but it serves another important purpose as well. During a witness's testimony, previously indexed facts may assume an unexpected importance. Those facts may not be noted on the order of testimony or direct examination worksheet, but they should be in the abstract of testimony. The abstract of testimony lets you find them quickly and confidently.

2. THE DIRECT EXAMINATION WORKSHEET

Next you go to the direct examination worksheet. The direct examination worksheet helps you to analyze the witness's potential testimony and map out the framework of your direct examination. The direct examination worksheet should have five sections:

(1) Witness name.

(2) Material facts: Specifically, how you expect to advance your case theory with the witness's testimony.

(3) Build (favorable facts): What the witness can say that will help. That part of the witness's testimony you will use to build your case.

(4) Preserve (unfavorable facts): What the witness can say that will hurt. What you must preserve against in the witness's testimony.

(5) Destroy (inconsistencies): Any anticipated problem with the witness's testimony. What the defense might use to undermine or destroy your case.

Section (2) lists the material fact or facts that you are calling the witness to prove. For example, value of the property stolen is an element of the crime of grand theft. If you are calling a jeweler to opine as to the value of stolen jewelry, then "value" goes into the material facts section. If you can think of nothing to put in the material facts section, perhaps you should not call the witness. Many prosecutors subscribe to the George Mallory school of direct examination. When asked why he wanted to climb Mount Everest, Mallory replied "Because it's there." This is the reason that many witnesses get called at trial, "because they're there." The mere fact that someone witnessed an event does not give you a good reason to call that person. You should have a specific reason for calling every witness who takes the stand. Remember, Mallory died on Mount Everest, and many prosecutors have destroyed their cases by calling witnesses for no better reason than "because they were there." Then you have a section for each aspect of the forensic trinity. Under each heading you list the appropriate facts, supporting each notation with documentary or evidentiary references drawn from your chronological abstract of testimony. These facts become the tactical objectives for examination of the witness. Next you do some brainstorming about how best to accomplish these objectives. If the witness has too much baggage in the preserve and destroy sections, try to find a witness who can accomplish the same objectives without the baggage. After you have mapped out your strategy, move on to the order of testimony. See Figure 11–1 for an example direct examination worksheet. In Chapter 8.B., where we were discussing preparation of the simple case, we included a section on the direct examination worksheet for an outline of the witness's testimony. With the more complex case, this section should be omitted. You will need much more than the bottom third of an 8.5×11″ sheet of paper to outline the testimony of a witness in a complex case.

Prosecutors are frequently blind to considerations of anything but logos. Because they tend to be logical individuals, they only consider logos. As you fill out your examination worksheet, do not forget ethos and pathos. A criminal trial often is a war between prosecution logos and defense ethos and pathos. If you do not tailor your logical appeal to also address considerations of ethos and pathos, your case may very well be crushed by the defense appeal. Be careful, however, to firmly join such appeals to your logical appeal. The worksheet in Figure 11–1 shows how. The mother of the victim was planning to take her daughter to the store to buy a ball gown on the very afternoon of the kidnaping and murder. The daughter had been elected first runner up to the queen of the Valentine Day ball and was very excited about the shopping trip. These facts make a strong appeal to pathos, that a young girl should die on such a day. Missing the ball is a small deprivation compared to the loss of life, but it makes the crime more immediate for the jury. The facts are included on the worksheet and later in the order of testimony as a basis for a very logical argument. "Ladies and gentlemen, we know that the victim had to have been forcibly abducted because no young girl is going to run away from home on the very day she was supposed to buy a ball gown."

Figure 11-1: Direct Examination Worksheet

Witness: Freda Leach

Case Theory: Theodore Robert Bundy took a van from the FSU Media Center. He took that van to Lake City, where he took Kimberly Diane Leach away from the campus of Lake City Junior High School. Then Theodore Robert Bundy took her life.

Defense Theory: Shotgun reasonable doubt theory. She may have run away from school and gotten killed by someone else.

Material Fact(s): 1. Circumstances of Abduction.
2. Identity of body from description of clothing.
3. No motive to run away.

Build: Favorable Facts	Reference
1. Description of Kim's clothing to match clothing found at scene. (Establishes identity).	496:T
2. Happy home life. (Negates runaway theory).	492:1
3. First runner up to Valentine Queen. (Negates runaway theory).	493:3
4. To buy Valentine Ball gown on afternoon of abduction. (Negates runaway theory).	493:3

Preserve: Unfavorable Facts	Reference
Sore throat (Could explain loss of tissue in throat area & impeach ME's testimony). Completely healed.	492:3-493:1

Destroy: Unfavorable & Impeachment	Reference
None	

3. THE ORDER OF TESTIMONY

Using the abstract of testimony and the direct examination worksheet as your reference points, write out your order of testimony. You do not absolutely have to annotate the direct examination worksheet, but you must annotate the order of testimony. The order of testimony forms the ready reference from which you prepare your witness and conduct your direct examination. Some lawyers write out the direct examination question by question. Some simply outline the topics they want to cover. Those who prefer the latter method do so because the former can stifle spontaneity. Either method will get the job done. Experiment with both methods and use the one you find most comfortable. If you use the topical method for direct examination, you can cut and paste the topics to the order of testimony directly from the abstract of testimony. Figure 11–2 depicts an example of a topical order of testimony. In Figure 11–2, the prosecutor simply cut and pasted the desired facts and references from columns two and three of the abstract of testimony. He left column one blank so that he could check off each point as he covered it on direct examination during the witness's testimony.

By the time you graduate to more complex cases, the trial folder discussed in Chapter 8.B.6 will not be able to accommodate your trial brief. You will have to move to a more comprehensive method of putting together your trial brief. Most prosecutors will opt to use either a three-ring binder or a banker's box full of individual witness folders. If you use the banker's box method, you will place copies of every statement or report authored by the witness on one side of the folder and your witness worksheets on the other. You should place the abstract of testimony on the bottom, then the direct examination worksheet, and finally place the order of testimony on top. You will thus have everything you need for the examination of the witness gathered into one place, and document retrieval will be greatly expedited. The drawback to this method is the ease with which witness folders get misfiled and lost. Your neatly organized banker's box will become disarrayed as you work out of it during the trial preparation and trial phases, and it will be quite frustrating when you reach for a witness folder which is not there.

When working out of a three-ring binder, you will have individual tabs for each witness with the witness worksheets placed behind each tab in the same order as in the witness folder. The supporting documents will still be in the banker's box, but you will not have nearly as much occasion to go to the box as you would with the witness worksheets in folders. Put index tabs in the binder marked for each of the eleven sections of the trial brief discussed in Chapter 8.C.7. Place your notes and worksheets behind the appropriate tab. In the order of testimony and defense case sections you should place consecutively numbered tabs for the paperwork on each distinct witness. Only once in a great while will a case outgrow one three ring binder, but sometimes you will be constrained to use multiple large capacity binders.

Figure 11-2: Order of Testimony

##	Freda Leach	Ref
	Preliminary accrediting information.	
	Took kids to school as usual on 2/8/78.	
	Picked up as usual in pm.	493:3
	Going to buy dress for Kim that afternoon.	493:3
	Kim 1st runner up for Queen of Valentine Ball.	493:3
	Did not buy dress on 2/8/78 because of rain.	493:3
	Decided to buy dress afternoon of 2/9/78.	493:3
	Took Kim to school next morning.	494:4
	Describe clothing: 1. Blue jersey # 83 with Kim on back; 2. White turtleneck blouse; 3. Brown vinyl jacket with fur collar; 4. Blue jeans; 5. Blue denim reversible purse.	496:T
	Went home and laid down. Not feeling well.	494:4
	Around 2:30pm got call from school. Kim missing.	495:2
	Went to school and looked for Kim. No luck.	495:2
	Went home & called Kim's friends. No luck.	495:2
	6:00pm called Lake City Police Department.	495:2
	Gave photo of Kim to police. Identify photo.	496:T
	Called Florida Highway Patrol & WDSR radio.	495:2
	From that day to this, haven't seen Kim again.	
	Gave nobody permission to take Kim from school.	

B. WITNESS PREPARATION

If you have not already done so, make out an order of proof and an evidence inventory, and you are ready to go to trial, right? No, not quite yet. You have only prepared yourself to conduct the examination. You have not yet prepared the witness. To ensure maximum persuasiveness, you must not only prepare yourself, you must prepare the witnesses. Witnesses can be incredibly obtuse. The most lucid question can evoke blank stares. The most direct questions can elicit the most non-responsive answers. The antidote? Witness preparation. If you and the witness have gone over the testimony before trial and the witness understands where you are coming from, she will understand the questions much better and give more responsive answers. In preparing the witness to testify, you must establish three expectations. You must make it clear to the witness what you expect from her. You must make it clear with the witness what she can expect from you. And finally, you must make it clear with the witness what she can expect from opposing counsel on cross-examination. You would do well to cover even the most seemingly obvious points with your witness, as one young prosecutor learned in a drug trafficking case when he decided to ad lib a question he had not covered with his college-educated expert witness from the state crime lab.

> Q: Now, two tons of cocaine, does that weigh more or less than 28 grams?
>
> A: I don't know.

The annotations on your witness worksheets first come into play during the witness preparation phase. As you go over the witness's testimony with her, she may stray from what you expect. With the annotations, you can retrieve the documents supporting your expectations and discuss her variance from your expectation. She may have forgotten what she said earlier, or she may have misspoken earlier, or her earlier statement may have been misreported. Whatever the reason, you must discover it and rectify the discrepancy between your expectations and what the witness now says. This does not mean that you instruct the witness "Testify like I tell you!" You work with the witness to determine the true facts, and then you present the correct evidence. You also use the annotations to go over problem areas with the witness and prepare the witness to undergo the rigors of cross-examination on those unhelpful points that crop up in all witness' testimony.

You must not only prepare the witness for what you expect to ask her and make certain of how she is going to answer, you should prepare her as to how to answer. Let us listen to a typical witness preparation session:

> Mrs. Witness, I want you to understand that there are three rules for testifying:
>
> (1) Sit up straight.
>
> (2) Speak up loud.
>
> (3) Tell the truth.

Rule number three is the most important rule. Even if you can't follow any other rule, you must tell the truth.

Do you chew gum? If you chew gum, there's a fourth rule: Don't chew gum.

Just because you're telling the truth, that doesn't mean they're going to believe you. You must tell the truth well. I want to talk to you a little about how to tell the truth well. To tell the truth well, you have to do a number of things:

(1) Listen to the question.

(2) Understand the question.

(3) Answer the question.

(4) Answer only the question.

(5) Do not say what you think happened.

(6) Do not say what you wish had happened.

(7) Do not say what you heard about what happened.

(8) Say what you know happened.

(9) If you are asked what time it is, do not tell us how to build a clock.

(10) If you are asked what time it is, do not give us a weather report.

You can't give a good answer unless you've heard the question. You can't give a good answer unless you understand the question. You can't give a good answer if it's not the answer to the question you were asked. Make sure to listen and understand before you answer.

Most important of all, answer the question you were asked. Do not answer the question you wish you had been asked. Do not answer the question you think you should have been asked. Answer the question you were asked. You don't have to explain your answer. The truth doesn't need help. Just answer the question and don't volunteer explanations.

Now I want to go over the information that I expect to ask you about on direct examination.

[At this point you can either do a complete dress rehearsal of the direct examination or simply overview the topics you expect to cover with the witness. With inexperienced witnesses, do a dress rehearsal. With experienced witnesses, you may be able to use the topical overview. During either the dress rehearsal or the overview, discrepancies may crop up between what you expect the witness to say and what the witness says. This is where the annotations come into play. As discrepancies crop up, go to the reference which supports your expectation, show it to the witness, and iron out any problems in the testimony. When doing this you must remember, if what the witness says now is less agreeable than what the witness said before, you find out which is the correct version, and that is the version you present. You never browbeat a witness into changing her testimony to conform to your expectations. If the new version significantly changes the playing field and you practice in a state with wide-open discovery, you had probably better notify the defense attorney of the new development.

Now, let's talk about cross-examination. Most people are afraid of cross-examination. They've watched TV and they think they know all about it. There's one thing that you should remember about cross-examination. Cross-examination is nothing more than words. Remember what you learned in kindergarten? "Sticks and stones may break my bones, but words will never hurt me." I've been a lawyer for X years, and I've never lost a witness on the witness stand. As long as you're telling the truth, there is nothing that can be said that will hurt you. You may get your feelings hurt, but that is all.

It's not your job to worry about whether the truth helps or hurts. You just tell the truth and let me worry about whether it helps or hurts. Do not exaggerate the good information. Do not minimize the bad information. If you gild the lily, you will destroy your credibility. If you explain things that don't need explaining, you will destroy your credibility. If you are rude, belligerent, or sarcastic you will destroy your credibility.

Sometimes a lawyer will try to slip something into a question hoping to trip you up. For example: 'Have you stopped beating your husband?' Whether you say yes or no, you will have admitted to beating your husband at some time. When you're asked a question like that, it's okay to add in a brief explanation: Q: Have you stopped beating your husband? A: No, I never started.'

Whenever a lawyer slips facts like that into a question and you answer the question without denying the facts, you are admitting them. Don't let a lawyer trick you into admitting facts like that if they're not true. Deny what is untrue about the question, but admit what is true about it. For example: Q: You got the box from the kitchen, didn't you? A: I got the box, but I got it from the bedroom.'

> Sometimes you'll say something on the witness stand that isn't quite what you said before. When that happens, lawyers will remind you of what you said before. It's called impeachment by prior inconsistent statement. Usually, the inconsistencies are minor or explainable. In most cases, the impeachment gets its value, not from the inconsistency, but from the way the witness reacts to the inconsistency. If you're hit with a prior inconsistent statement, don't lose your cool. If you made it, admit it. There's usually a good explanation for a prior inconsistent statement. If you can explain it, you have a right to explain it, but don't say too much when you're explaining it. Too much explanation looks like an excuse.
>
> I've gone over your statements, and I've found some inconsistencies. I want to go over each of those inconsistencies with you so you can be ready for them when the lawyer asks you about them on cross-examination.
>
> [Go over the inconsistencies with the witness and get the witness's explanation for them. Sometimes, it is profitable to have another attorney in your office do a dress rehearsal cross-examination of the witness. A witness undergoing cross for the first time is not going to be as credible as a witness who has already undergone it.]
>
> Finally, and I can't emphasize this enough: I don't want you to testify *for* the state. I don't want you to testify *against* the defendant. I want you to testify *to* the truth.

The witness preparation can be abridged or expanded in proportion to the needs of the case and the time available, but you must do some preparation with the witness. Remember what Quintilian said: "Witnesses are confused, and are drawn into traps by the advocates on the other side; they do more damage by being caught like this than they would have done good by a firm and fearless performance. They must therefore be carefully rehearsed at home and tested by various questions of the kind that the other side may raise."[2] It is of utmost importance that some preparation be done with the witness.

C. CONDUCTING THE DIRECT EXAMINATION

1. THE EXPLORATORY DIRECT EXAMINATION

Although you should never put a witness on the stand without preparing her, you will sometimes find yourself in the position of having to do an exploratory direct examination of a witness. An exploratory direct

---

[2] Id.

examination combines direct examination with the initial witness interview. Each question is an adventure, because you have no idea what the witness will say. Unfortunately, lawyers least able to do the exploratory direct do it more often than more experience lawyers. Young, inexperienced attorneys often wind up in misdemeanor court with heavy dockets of minor, simple cases. The cases move so quickly through the system that the prosecutor hardly has time to breathe, much less prepare. If circumstances compel you to do exploratory direct examinations in a simple trial, begin by looking at the charging document and identify the victim. You have identified your first witness, whose direct examination informs you about the facts of the case sufficiently well enough to tell you which witness on the witness list should be called next. The exploratory direct examination can go something like this:

> Q: Tell us your name please?
>
> Q: And your address?
>
> Q: Do you know the defendant in this case, Arthur Traynor?
>
> Q: Is he present in the courtroom?
>
> Q: Would you mind pointing him out?
>
> Q: Did you come into contact with the defendant on the 12th of January of this year?
>
> Q: Where would that have been?
>
> Q: About what time?
>
> Q: Was that in Camden County, Florida?
>
> Q: Can you describe for us the circumstances under which you came into contact with the defendant on that day?
>
> Q: *Etc. Etc.*

There once was a prosecutor who conducted exploratory direct examinations in the following manner:

> Q: State your name for the record?
>
> Q: Where do you live?
>
> Q: It says here in this information that on the 12th of January of this year Arthur Traynor did then and there unlawfully take, steal, and carry away Vernon Victim's collection of baseball trading cards. What can you tell us about that?

This examination technique can effectively convey the witness's knowledge to the jury, but it is objectionable as overbroad, it gives the witness free rein to say anything (including unhelpful facts) that she wants, and it can also put the jury on notice that the prosecutor knows very little about the facts himself. This was especially true when the witness answered:

A: Nothing.

2. THE EXTEMPORANEOUS DIRECT EXAMINATION

The extemporaneous direct examination is a type of direct which is almost as bad as the exploratory direct. In the extemporaneous direct, you think you know what the witness has to say because you have read the reports and statements, but you have not had time to sit down with the witness and prepare her testimony. Even if you think you know everything the witness has to say, you must prepare her to give direct examination. To illustrate this point, we will recount an experience from the Orlando trial of Theodore Robert Bundy for the murder of Kimberly Diane Leach. One particular morning during the trial, the prosecution witnesses went much more rapidly than anticipated. By noon, the prosecution had called all the witnesses it expected to call during the entire day. The prosecutors reported to the judge that they had no further witnesses and advised that a new group of witnesses should arrive late that afternoon. They asked that the judge recess the trial for the afternoon. The judge refused and advised the prosecutors that they had better be ready to call witnesses at 1:00pm when court reconvened from the lunch break. As the prosecutors returned from lunch, they had a chance encounter with the next day's witnesses, who had arrived early and wanted to check out the courthouse before testifying the next day. The prosecutors rushed the witnesses into the witness room and at 1:00pm began calling them without having prepared them to testify. The testimony of the first witness went like this:

Q: State your name?

A: C.S. Hooker.

Q: And your occupation?

A: I am a Captain of Detectives with the Florida State University Police Department.

Q: Were you so employed during the month of February of 1978?

A: Yes, I was.

Q: During the course of your duties that month, did you have occasion to become involved in the recovery of a white van that had been stolen from the FSU Media Center?

A: Yes, I did.

Q: Can you describe the circumstances under which you became involved in the recovery of that van?

A: As I said, I am Captain of Detectives with the FSU Police Department, and in that capacity, I became involved in the investigation of the Chi Omega murders* * *.

At this point, the prosecutor interrupted the officer's testimony with an expletive, the defense moved for a mistrial on grounds of a violation of the judge's stern warning that the Chi Omega murders never be mentioned in the presence of the jury, and both sides vigorously argued the merits of the motion. Eventually the judge ruled that the error could be remedied with a curative instruction, the prosecution asked for a recess to warn the remainder of the witnesses not to mention the Chi Omega case, and the trial resumed without incident.

3. LEADING QUESTIONS

As we learned in the last chapter, all questions lead. Leading questions suggest to the witness where you want them to go. For example, "State your name" is leading because it suggests to the witness that he has a name. If you do not give the witness some direction, the examination will careen out of control. Questioning should lead to the extent that it suggests the topic, but not to the extent that it suggests the specific answer. Questions are not normally called "leading" if they simply prescribe the field of answers. Only when they narrow the field to a single answer do they become objectionable as leading.

> Q: Where do you live? [Presupposes that witness lives somewhere and leads witness to tell where. Not objectionable.]
>
> Q: Do you live at 325 Pine Street, Anytown, USA? [Presupposes that witness lives in a specific location and directs witness to agree with that location. Objectionable.]

In an interview, the examiner does not know the answer and the questioning is an exercise in discovery. The examiner serves as both the facilitator of disclosure and the audience for disclosure. When the examiner does not know the answer, it is easy to ask non-leading questions. It is impossible to put the answer into the mouth of the witness when you do not know the answer. Direct examination is not an interview. The examiner should already know the answers to the questions. Although the questioner remains the facilitator of disclosure, the judge and jury are the audience for disclosure. Although the audience has changed, the format for questioning has not. Questioning still must proceed from agreement to disclosure. If the question is too suggestive, if it proceeds from disclosure to agreement, it becomes objectionable as leading. When the examiner knows the answer, problems arise. Since the examiner acts as a partner in the disclosure process, the temptation to help the witness becomes almost overpowering. Like the too-helpful parents who elbow the child aside to do the science project themselves, the examiner begins to supply the disclosure and call upon the witness to agree. An uncooperative witness may require leading questions, but they diminish the credibility of a cooperative witness.

4. "AND WHAT HAPPENED NEXT?"

Direct examination, like ballroom dancing, requires cooperation. In ballroom dancing, one dancer leads his partner in a display calculated to entertain the audience. On direct examination, the examiner leads the witness in a display calculated to educate the audience. In order to fully educate, the direct examination must engage the audience's attention. A poorly done direct examination may put the information on the record of the trial, but it does not imprint the information into the consciousness of the audience. The prototypical direct examination identifies the witness, establishes her credentials, and then begins at the beginning and plods unimaginatively from that point to the bitter end, leaving out no detail, whether germane or irrelevant. It is as thorough as it is productive of narcolepsy. Study the following example:

Q: State your name, please.

Q: And your address.

Q: Directing your attention to the 2nd of January of last year, did anything unusual or out of the ordinary happen that day?

Q: And what happened next?

Q: And what happened next?

Q: And what happened next?

Etc., Etc., ad infinitum and *ad nauseam.*

This type of direct examination, repeated daily in the courts of this land, can be called the "windshield wiper" direct. The constant repetition of the mantra, "and what happened next" can be hypnotic. Some lawyers and judges seem to think that "And what happened next?" is leading, because it suggests that something happened next. They seek to repair the question by amending it to: "And what, if anything, happened next?" This question is even more soporific than "And what happened next?" You can do better. You must do better.

5. THE FLASHBACK

Movie directors frequently begin in their stories in the middle at an exciting point and, after thoroughly capturing the audience's attendance, flash back to the beginning. Direct examination can use the same technique.

Q: Were you sleeping in your car during the early morning hours of October the 2nd of last year?

A: Yes.

Q: Did something happen to wake you up?

A: Yes.

Q: What?

A: The Defendant stuck a knife in my groin and pulled it all the way down to my knee. Then he stabbed me repeatedly in the chest and cut my throat.

Q: Why would he do something like that?

A: We had gotten into an argument over a pool game earlier that evening.

6. THE SLOW WALK

When you get to a very important or moving portion of testimony, you can walk the witness slowly through it, dwelling on each and every one of the gory details.

A: The Defendant stuck a knife in my groin and pulled it all the way down to my knee. Then he stabbed me repeatedly in the chest and cut my throat.

[Now you could say "Q: What happened next?" or you could say]:

Q: How many times did he stab you in the chest?

Q: What part of the chest did he stab you in?

Q: Did he stab you in any other parts of the chest?

Q: Did you feel any pain from those stabs in the chest?

Q: Did those stabs in the chest incapacitate you in any way?

Q: How deep was the cut in the throat?

Q: Were you able to breathe after he cut your throat?

Etc. etc.

7. THE FAST FORWARD

A "what happened next" direct examination will eventually get you from point A to point B, but you will oftentimes cover a lot of irrelevant information. With a little forethought, you can craft your questions so that you cover this ground quickly.

Q: When you saw that, what did you do?

A: I went to the police station and reported the crime.

The witness's answer has presented you with the opportunity to fast forward through extraneous detail. You could go through all the details of driving to the police station, parking in the parking lot, going inside the station, and meeting with the officer to report the crime, or you could say:

Q: After you reported the crime, what did you do?

8. TRANSITIONS

In fast forward, the witness's answer has presented you with an opportunity to skim over a lot of irrelevant and potentially confusing detail. You need not wait for the witness to present you with such an opportunity. You can create it yourself. You can omit great hunks of irrelevant chronology by signaling to the witness and the jury that you want to skip ahead to a later time.

A: Then I arrested him.

Now you could have the officer handcuff the defendant, put him in the patrol car, drive him to the jail, book him in, and then advise him of his rights and take a confession, or you could say:

Q: After you took him back to the jail and booked him in, did you advise him of his rights?

9. LOOPING

Opposing counsel do not want you to repeat harmful information. The reason is simple. You must repeat information in order to be sure that it is imprinted upon the minds of the jurors. Although a genius may learn something by being told only once, few jurors are geniuses. Despite the need to repeat information, repetition is arguably objectionable. Judges sustain objections such as "asked and answered," "cumulative," and "repetitive." You must devise a method of repeating information without being repetitive. How can you repeat without being repetitive? You can loop. When you get good information in an answer, you loop back to the good information and incorporate it into your next question.

A: Then he stabbed me again.

Q: When he stabbed you again, where were you hit?

A: I was hit in the shoulder.

Q: When you were hit in the shoulder, did it cause you any pain?

A: The pain was excruciating.

Q: Did this excruciating pain cause you any trouble in moving your arm?

A: My arm was paralyzed.

Q: When you realized that your arm was paralyzed . . .

Etc. etc. etc.

10. TANGIBLE EVIDENCE TRILOGIES

Repetition is the sincerest form of persuasion. After the Second Punic War, the Roman Senator Cato the Elder began every one of his speeches "Carthage must be destroyed." He began his filibuster as a laughingstock, but after years of repetition, he finally persuaded the Romans to destroy Carthage. You must repeat every important point at least three times to ensure that every juror gets it. You can get an occurrence witness to tell her story three times (without drawing an objection) by using a map or chart and photographs. Have the witness recount the story in narrative fashion, then produce the map and have the witness walk back through the testimony a second time showing her (and the defendant's) movements on the chart. Now pull out the photographs and go back through the occurrence a third time having the witness identify the photographs and explain their significance to the event.

11. QUINTILIAN'S CORKSCREW

An uncooperative witness can severely disrupt the cooperative effort of direct examination. When faced with an uncooperative witness, you must coerce cooperation. The coercion available in a free society is not as compelling as might be available under a totalitarian regime, but there are techniques which can be employed that do not contravene the Bill of Rights. Uncooperative witnesses fall into two main categories, those who give too little information, and those who give too much. In Chapter 10 on interviewing and interrogation we first discussed Quintilian's corkscrew, a method of building from smaller to larger admissions until the targeted admissions are corkscrewed out of the witness. Let us now look at this method in more detail.

In a long-ago DWI manslaughter case, a young prosecutor received a telephone call from the medical examiner, who advised that he was about to leave the state, never to return, and if the prosecutor wanted his testimony at the upcoming trial, the prosecutor would have to take a deposition to perpetuate testimony. The prosecutor sought and received permission to perpetuate the medical examiner's testimony, the medical examiner moved out of state, and the case proceeded to trial with the prosecutor anticipating no problem introducing the deposition into evidence. When the judge recessed for lunch at noon of the second or third day of trial, he asked the prosecutor how many more witnesses would be called. The prosecutor told the judge that all he had left was the reading into evidence of the medical examiner's testimony. The defense attorney interposed an objection, and the judge ruled the deposition inadmissible. The prosecutor did not eat lunch that day. He spent the lunch hour frantically searching for someone who could testify to the fact that the victim was dead. He called the fire station, which doubled as the emergency medical services provider, and found the paramedic who had worked the victim's car crash. The prosecutor asked the paramedic to come down to the courthouse, and the paramedic complied. Upon his arrival at the courthouse, the prosecutor told the paramedic that he was going to be called to the stand to testify to the fact of the victim's death. Although the paramedic had determined that the victim was dead, he steadfastly refused to say so under oath. He had been taught in paramedic school that he was not allowed to pronounce someone dead, and he was determined not to voice such an opinion under oath. The prosecutor had no time to find someone else, court was about to reconvene, and something had to be done to prove the victim was dead. The paramedic testified as the prosecution's final witness, and the pertinent portion of the testimony went something like this:

Q: As a paramedic, are you trained to look for signs of life?

A: Yes.

Q: What signs of life are you trained to look for?

A: [Lengthy explanation of the signs of life.]

Q: Did you check the victim for signs of life?

A: Yes.

Q: Did you check the victim's eyes?

A: Yes.

Q: What did you find about the victim's eyes?

A: The victim's eyes were fixed and fully dilated.

Q: Is that a sign of life, or a sign of death?

A: A sign of death.

Q: Did you check the victim's respiration?

A: Yes.

Q: Was the victim breathing?

A: No.

Q: Is that a sign of life, or a sign of death?

A: A sign of death.

Q: Did you check the victim's pulse?

A: Yes.

Q: Did the victim have a pulse?

A: No.

Q: Is that a sign of life or a sign of death?

A: A sign of death.

Q: Did you put a heart monitor on the victim?

A: Yes.

Q: For how long?

A: A full minute.

Q: During that full minute, did the victim's heart beat even once?

A: No.

Q: Is that a sign of life, or a sign of death?

A: A sign of death.

Q: Do you have a policy reference the hauling of dead bodies?

A: Yes.

Q: What is that policy?

A: We don't haul them.

Q: Why not?

A: It ties up rescue vehicles that could be better used hauling sick people.

Q: Did you haul the victim?

A: No.

The prosecutor stopped the examination short of asking for the targeted admission, that the victim was dead, because the paramedic would not have made the admission, and the prosecutor was satisfied that the preliminary admissions proved that fact sufficiently to render asking the final question unnecessary. Had this been a cross-examination rather than a direct, the prosecutor would probably have gone ahead and asked the final question, because the witness would have lost credibility with the jury by refusing to admit the obvious—that the victim was indeed dead. The prosecutor faced one more hurdle resulting from the absence of the medical examiner. On motion for judgment of acquittal the defense attorney asked that the case be dismissed because, although the prosecutor had proven fact of death, he had not proven cause of death. The prosecutor replied that the proof showed the victim in good health prior to the crash and with a 180-degree twist in her neck after the crash. The prosecutor argued, and the judge agreed, that it did not require a medical degree to determine that the victim died of a broken neck sustained during the crash.

12. THE TALKATIVE WITNESS

When a talkative witness seeks to give too much information, you face another set of problems. A talkative witness can make unfortunate statements that result in a mistrial, can be very difficult to control, and can make you look bad when you try to control the witness. The best antidote for a talkative witness comes in pretrial preparation. You must solemnly warn the witness against giving too much information. Sometimes this measure works, but more often the witness proves impervious to warnings. The second technique is the use of headlines. As you begin questioning on a particular subject, headline the subject with a remark such as: "Now may I ask you about the things you saw in the victim's room?" By narrowing the scope of the questions, you narrow the scope of the answer. The third technique is to shorten the questions as much as possible. Short questions demand short answers. If you give enough thought to a line of questioning, you can shorten the questions dramatically. As a last resort, you must call the witness down in open court. You should never do this until you are sure that the judge and jury have reached their limit of tolerance for the witness's talkativeness. You, having previously suffered through the witness's expansive answers, will reach your limit long before the judge and jury. You must not lose patience, because the jury will hold it against you if you become stern with the witness too soon.

D. THE DIRECT EXAMINATION OF THE EXPERT WITNESS

Lawyers both love and fear expert testimony. They love experts because appealing to authority can be very persuasive. They fear experts for the same reason. In the final analysis, an expert is like any other witness. The expert may present more of a challenge than the ordinary witness, but a little homework and a little elbow grease should suffice to meet the challenge. Experts know about all sorts of matters beyond the ken of mere mortals, and it is your duty to learn just enough about those matters to be able to deal with the expert. You do not have to have a Ph.D. in pharmacology to present a pharmacologist's testimony. As a matter of fact, too much knowledge of the expert's field may even be detrimental. If you and the expert are both on a plane of understanding high above the heads of the jurors, you may have difficulty bringing the testimony down to earth enough to make the jurors understand. The most favorable opinion imaginable is useless if it is voiced in hypertechnical jargon.

1. PREPARING TO EXAMINE THE EXPERT

Your first task preparatory to presenting an expert's testimony is to understand the expert's testimony. Typically, material is sent to the crime laboratory and later a report comes to your office setting forth the expert's findings. Do not rely on this report as the key to understanding the expert's testimony. It will be written in tortured terminology and couched in the technical language of the expert's field. It will presuppose facts of which you are unaware and omit information which you need. After you have read the report, you must speak to the expert. She can decipher the technical language, explain what the report really means, and supply the information omitted from the report.

The second task of preparation is to find the simplest, most easily understood explanation of the findings. Make sure the explanation is totally devoid of technical language. This simple explanation forms the backbone of your presentation of the expert's testimony. A really good expert will have already found the simple explanation and will be able to provide you with it. If that is the case, so much the better. If it is not, you must formulate your own. Take your explanation back to the expert and see if she agrees with it. If she doesn't, amend it and revise it until she does. Never try to present a simple explanation that does not enjoy the expert's wholehearted consent. It can be fatal if your expert disagrees with you from the witness stand. When you have such an explanation that the expert is willing to endorse, you are ready to outline your direct examination.

2. LAYING THE PREDICATE FOR THE EXPERT OPINION

Before you can offer an expert's opinion on a subject, you must show that she knows what she is talking about. This need to lay a predicate for the expert's testimony has led to the publication of numerous books of predicate questions for almost any type of expert testimony imaginable.[3] Sometimes the expert will provide the lawyer with a list of proposed predicate questions. Regardless of the field of expertise, the direct examination of an expert should cover three points at a minimum—expertise, examination, expert opinion. Establish the witness's expertise; elucidate the witness's examination; elicit the witness's expert opinion. Often it is helpful to ask the witness to explain how she arrived at that expert opinion; but this step is neither always necessary nor always advisable. In determining whether the explanation should be explored, you should determine how crucial the opinion is to the point to adjudicate. If, for example, you are trying a burglary case and your only real evidence of guilt is the defendant's DNA in a drop of blood found inside the building, the DNA evidence is crucial. Crucial evidence must receive great attention, and the explanation helps to solidify the jury's conviction that the expert knows what she is talking about. If, however, the DNA is found in a place where the defendant admits to being, then the evidence is of lesser importance, and you might decide to omit the explanation. If you know that the defense attorney is given to marathon cross-examinations in which he explores every nook and cranny of the expert's knowledge, you might opt

[3] E.g. Anderson, Ken, and John Bradley, Predicate Questions Manual, Texas District and County Attorneys Association, Austin, Texas, 2005; Salcinas, E.J. Trial Techniques Predicate Questions, National District Attorneys Association, Alexandria, Virginia, 1977.

to allow the defense attorney to elicit the explanation for you on cross-examination. In summary, the direct examination of an expert can be built around four central questions:

Q: Tell us how smart you are? [Expertise].

Q: Did you perform an examination? [Examination].

Q: What did you find out? [Expert opinion].

Q: Why do you say that? [Explanation].

3. CONDUCTING THE EXAMINATION OF THE EXPERT

In order to illustrate these points, let us consider the direct examination of a forensic pathologist. In this case, cause of death was not in issue. The defendant claimed that he shot the victim three times in the back in self-defense. Because of the defense, the expert's opinion needed little explanation, but a thorough recounting of the examination was necessary to rebut the self-defense plea.

DIRECT EXAMINATION

Q: (By Mr. HOPKINS) Tell us your name, please.

A: My name is Terrence Parker Forrest.

Q: And your profession?

A: I'm a medical doctor, I'm a pathologist, and I serve as the Medical Examiner for the Twenty First District of Florida.

Q: As the Medical Examiner for the Twenty First District of Florida, what are your duties?

A: My duties are to under a number of different categories of death, determine the cause of death and the manner of death. And in these circumstances, to perform an autopsy if requested by the State Attorney, or to perform an examination to whatever extent I deem necessary.

Q: How long have you been the Medical Examiner for the Twenty First District?

A: I've been the Medical Examiner for a little over 12 years, and I was Associate Medical Examiner for approximately 10 years before that.

Q: So, then you have approximately 22 years' experience as both Medical Examiner and Associate Medical Examiner?

A: That's correct.

Q: In the course of your duties as a medical examiner, does that include performing autopsies on people who were suspected to be victims of homicide?

A: Yes.

Q: For the purpose of determining the cause of death?

A: That's correct.

Q: What special training have you had to prepare you to perform these duties?

A: Well, I went to medical school, graduated. I served an internship and a residency. I was a general practitioner for six years. And then I went into a pathology residency for four years. I've taken a number of courses in forensic pathology and I've been performing forensic pathology ever since I first located in this area in 1967.

Q: Is Chapman County a part of the Twenty First Medical Examiner's District?

A: It is.

Q: Have you ever been qualified as an expert in court to testify as to the cause of death?

A: Yes, I have many times in this circuit and other circuits in the State of Florida as well as in Federal Court.

Q: Can you put a number on how many times?

A: No, I don't keep account, but it's many, many times over the years.

Q: Would it be more than a hundred times?

A: It would certainly approach a hundred times. I can't—I hesitate to give you an exact figure, but that certainly sounds reasonable to me.

MR. HOPKINS: Your Honor, I'd proffer Dr. Forrest as an expert Medical Examiner qualified to render opinions as to cause of death.

MR. HARRIMAN: We agree, Your Honor.

THE COURT: Dr. Forrest is so designated.

Q: (By Mr. HOPKINS) Dr. Forrest, I would like to direct your attention back to February the 14th of 1994, and ask you if you had occasion to perform an autopsy on a body that was identified to you as being the body of one Larry Sellers?

A: Yes, I did.

Q: And just from a general overview of the body could you determine, in just looking prior to performing anything, any wounds to the body?

A: Yes.

Q: Did you see any wounds?

A: Yes, there were wounds noticeable on the body. Three gunshot wounds were present in the back of the chest.

Q: And were there any other wounds of any significance?

A: There were no other wounds of any significance. There were some minor scratches and scrapes, but not anything of any significance.

Q: Now, the gunshot wounds, would they be what's called in-shoots or entrance wounds?

A: Yes, these are what we refer to as in-shoot wounds or entrance wounds.

Q: And that would be where a bullet entered the body of a person; is that correct?

A: That's correct.

Q: Did you find any exit wounds on the body?

A: There were no exit wounds present on the body.

Q: Then, just from that observation then would you expect to find three bullets in the body?

A: Yes.

Q: Okay. Did you perform an x-ray examination to determine if bullets were in the body?

A: I did.

Q: And were you able to determine from the x-ray examination whether the bullets were in the body?

A: Yes, there were three bullets that were visible on the x-ray of the chest that I had taken.

Q: Now, Doctor, I'm going to discuss each of these in-shoot wounds with you in some detail. Would it assist us if we had a diagram of the human body that we could use to demonstrate these various wounds?

A: Yes, it would. I think it would help the jury, and it would assist me as well.

MR. HOPKINS: I have something here that I've marked as State's Exhibit for identification No. 1. Is there any objection to this, Mr. HARRIMAN.

MR. HARRIMAN: No, sir.

Q: (By Mr. HOPKINS) And this being sort of a schematic diagram of the human body—

A: (Witness nodding head affirmatively)

[The diagram was an enlarged copy of a wound chart regularly used in medical examiners' offices. The diagram depicted a line drawing of front and rear views of the naked body of a man].

Q: —would that be helpful to you?

A: Yes.

M. HOPKINS: We'll offer this into evidence at this time as State's Exhibit 1.

THE COURT: It shall be received as State's Exhibit No. 1.

(WHEREUPON STATE'S EXHIBIT NO. 1 WAS RECEIVED IN EVIDENCE)

Q: (By Mr. HOPKINS): Where would be best to set this up? We'll try it right here to begin with. I'll give you a pen to mark this with. Did you denominate these various in-shoot wounds by any kind of a numbering or a lettering system?

A: I gave the in-shoot wounds a letter designation, different for each one. And then later when I recovered the bullets, I gave them numbers.

[The diagram, which had been blown up to poster size, was placed on an easel].

Q: Now, I'd assume you numbered them "A," "B," "C"; is that correct?

A: That's correct.

Q: Now, the A, B, C order that you numbered them in, did that have any significance as to the order in which these wounds were inflicted on the body?

A: No, it does not.

Q: All right. From your examination of the body, were you able to make any kind of determination as to the order in which these bullets entered the body?

A: No, I was not able to do that.

Q: All right, sir. If you would please step to the diagram, with the Court's permission?

THE COURT: Yes, sir.

Q: (By Mr. HOPKINS) And show us where in-shoot "A," you just mark on the diagram where in-shoot "A" wound would have been.

A: (Witness marking on diagram)

Q: We won't hold you to exact. All right, sir, you've marked, you marked three circles on the back of the body; is that correct?

A: That's correct.

[This question was for record purposes so that any appellate court reading the transcript would be able to follow the examination without having to refer to the chart. It is important to remember that you are playing to more than one audience, not only the judge and jury, but also the appellate court].

Q: And you've designated them "A," "B," and "C," left to right; is that correct?

A: That's correct. This is "A" right here. This is "B" right here. And that's "C" right there.

Q: Now, did you try then to recover the bullets that would have gone through these various bullet entrance wounds?

A: Yes, I did.

Q: All right, sir, let's start with in-shoot number "A." And could you describe for us the path of that bullet, in-shoot "A," and where it went in the body and where it was recovered from?

A: In-shoot "A" went into the body in a path that was from down to up, and slightly from left to right, and from back to front. Just like about this.

Q: And where did it go once it entered the body?

A: It entered the left side of the chest, and it penetrated the lower lobe of the lung on the left, a portion of the upper lung on the left, and to the left side of the heart through the septum in the middle of the heart, and out the right side of the heart, and came to rest within the breast bone in the front.

Q: If you could mark on the front of that diagram where the bullet from in-shoot "A" came to rest.

A: (Witness marking on diagram)

Q: Okay. Now, you've described that going through some pretty important internal organs; is that correct?

A: That's correct.

Q: Was that a fatal shot?

A: Yes, indeed. This was a fatal shot. This caused a great deal of bleeding in the left side of the chest. It caused bleeding around the lung there in the left side of the chest. It caused bleeding around the heart, and it also damaged the heart itself on the way through the heart.

Q: Is that the cause of death of Larry Sellers?

A: In my opinion, Mr. Sellers died because of that gunshot wound to the chest.

Q: Now, you recovered that bullet; is that correct?

A: That's correct.

Q: and did you put a number denomination on that bullet?

A: Yes, I did. The bullet that was recovered from the breastbone was referred to as bullet No. 1, and this was given directly to Officer Jason Pierson, I believe it was, who attended the autopsy at that time.

[At this point, the prosecutor could have shown the bullet to the doctor and had him identify it preliminary to showing the bullet to Officer Pierson when Officer Pierson testified. The prosecutor opted to simply have Officer Pierson testify that he watched the doctor recover the bullet and immediately took it from the doctor after it was marked. This simplified the chain of custody somewhat and made for a more economical presentation].

Q: Was Officer Pierson present during the entire course of the autopsy, if you recall?

A: Yes.

Q: Did he receive all the evidence that you recovered from the body?

A: Yes.

Q: Okay. Let's move then to in-shoot "B," which is closer to the spine in the middle; is that correct?

A: That's correct. This is in-shoot "B" right here. It's much closer to the midline than "A" was, and it's up a little higher, but it's still just to the left of the middle of the back.

Q: Could you describe for us the course of that bullet?

A: This bullet was generally up, but not up here near as "A." And it went from back to the front. And it went fairly straight in that it didn't go through the spine itself but came to lodge in the muscle tissue just by the spine.

Q: From that, I would conclude that it did not penetrate as far as into the body of Mr. Sellers as in-shoot "A" did; is that correct?

A: That's correct.

Q: And do you have any explanation as to why that bullet didn't penetrate as deeply?

A: Well, being closer to the spine it had more muscle mass to penetrate and ligaments and such as such along the spine, and that probably slowed it down more than this one which was a little bit more to the side and had less muscle to go through. But I can't tell you with any degree of certainty exactly why it didn't penetrate as deeply. Of course, bullet "A" once it got through the chest wall and it didn't meet a whole lot of resistance; whereas bullet "B" had resistance and stopped before it came inside of the chest.

[It was not necessary to go into this exposition on bullet penetration, as it was irrelevant to any real issues. Juries, however, become concerned about the oddest issues, and the prosecutor decided to cover this to forestall any potential concern on the jury's part].

Q: Did you recover a bullet then out of in-shoot "B?"

A: Yes, I did.

Q: And what number did you apply to that?

A: That was designated bullet No. "3," and it also was given to Officer Pierson.

Q: Okay. Now, as to in-shoot "B," bullet No. "3," was the wound that was inflicted by that bullet a survivable wound?

A: Yes, it was.

Q: All right, sir. I assume that it was a pretty serious injury. Am I correct in assuming that?

A: Well, certainly it is serious any time we get—you get shot, but it was not as—it was potentially a fatal wound had infection set in and such as that. But at that time, it did not appear to me to have been anywhere as near as serious a wound as "A."

Q: So, but for "A," Mr. Sellers might have possibly been able to survive in-shoot "B"; is that correct?

A: That's my opinion.

Q: All right, sir. Let's move now to in-shoot "C" which is over on the right side. Could you describe for us the path of that bullet?

A: This bullet also went from down to up, and pretty well from back to front, not veering very much to one side or the other. And when it went in, it went in the soft tissue of the side of the back over there. And it went up and it hit the seventh and the sixth and the fifth ribs, breaking all three of them. And it damaged the lung when it broke these ribs and pushed them in, but it didn't enter the chest wall. And came on up and came to rest on the right-hand side about right here in the front. And that's where I recovered that bullet from the chest wall in the front on the right-hand side.

Q: And that would have been approximately in the arm pit area?

A: Yes, very close to the arm pit, along what we call the anterior axillary fold, which is really you might say the front of the arm pit.

Q: All right, sir. So, you got two x's now on the front of that diagram. Would you label the x's as to which in-shoot they relate to?

A: Now, these are not x's. These are the sites where I found the bullet.

Q: All right, sir. I said "x's"—

A: Oh, excuse me

Q: —which is crosses?

A: I beg your pardon. I misunderstood you. Ask me the question again, please.

Q: All right. You had the two crosses there?

A: Right.

Q: Could you label those, those marks there, as to which in-shoot they relate to?

A: That's correct. This relates to in-shoot "A" right here.

Q: Okay.

A: And this one relates to in-shoot "C."

Q: Now, did you also recover that bullet from in-shoot "C?"

A: I did.

Q: And did you number that bullet in any particular numerical order?

A: That bullet was numbered "2."

Q: And then it was turned over also to Jason Pierson?

A: Yes, it was.

Q: Was the clothing of this deceased also turned over to Mr. Pierson—

A: Yes.

Q:—at the autopsy? Okay, all right, sir, would you have a seat please. Okay, for identification purposes, I'm going to show you what's been marked State's Exhibit 2–A for identification and ask you if that's a photograph of the body that was identified to you as being the body of Larry Sellers?

A: Yes, it is.

Q: Did you take that photograph?

A: Yes, I did.

Q: Does that photograph fairly and accurately depict Mr. Sellers as you saw him in the Medical Examiner's office?

A: It does.

MR. HOPKINS: Offer this into evidence, State's Exhibit 2–A. MR. HARRIMAN: No objection, Your Honor.

THE COURT: State's Exhibit 2–A shall be received in evidence.

(WHEREUPON STATE'S EXHIBIT NO. 2–A WAS RECEIVED IN EVIDENCE)

[The prosecutor did not publish this photograph to the jury because it was a simple "mug shot" which was being used to identify the body of Larry Sellers. When Officer Jason Pierson (who knew Sellers personally) took the stand, the photograph would be shown to him to identify Sellers. Having both the doctor and the officer identify the photograph would prove that they were talking about the same autopsy].

Q: (By Mr. HOPKINS) I'm going to show you State's Exhibit 2–B for identification and ask you if you can identify that.

A: Yes, I can.

Q: And what is that?

A: This is a picture of the x-ray. I took a picture of the x-ray on the view box.

Q: And this was an x-ray that you used in helping you to arrive at your conclusions from this autopsy?

A: That's correct.

Q: And does that picture, was that taken by you?

A: The picture was taken by me of the x-ray.

Q: And does that picture fairly and accurately depict the x-ray as you observed it?

A: Yes, it does.

Q: And that's an x-ray of the body of Larry Sellers?

A: Yes.

MR. HOPKINS: Offer this into evidence State's Exhibit No. 2–B.

MR. HARRIMAN: No objection, Your Honor.

THE COURT: State Exhibit No. 2–B was received as offered.

(WHEREUPON STATE'S EXHIBIT NO. 2–B
WAS RECEIVED IN EVIDENCE)

Q: (By Mr. HOPKINS) Now, does this x-ray photograph depict the three bullets that were recovered from the body of Larry Sellers?

A: Yes, it does.

MR. HOPKINS: Your Honor, I request permission to publish this to the jury.

THE COURT: May I see it?

MR. HARRIMAN: No objection, Your Honor.

THE COURT: It shall be published.

(State's Exhibit No. 2–B was shown to the jury)

[The prosecutor had a document camera connected to a television set. He placed the exhibit on the camera platform and displayed the picture to the jury on the television set. This sort of presentation is much more economical of time and effort than passing the exhibits from hand to hand among the jurors].

Q: (By Mr. HOPKINS) Doctor, I'm going to ask you to step over to the television screen.

A: All right.

Q: And show us what is depicted in the x-ray as far as the location of the bullets.

A: It's upside down.

Q: It's upside down? Not being, not having much medical expertise, it would be very easy for me to get it upside down. Is that better?

A: Yes, sir.

Q: Let me see, have I got everything in that needs to be depicted?

A: Yes.

Q: All right, sir. If you would please, show us what that photograph demonstrates.

A: This is a picture of an x-ray of the chest. And you can see the ribs on the left side over here, and you can see the ribs on the right side. This is whiter looking than this because of a lot of blood in there on the left side. This area here is where the heart is. And you see a real light shadow here, you see a real light shadow there, and you see a real light shadow there. Those represent the bullets that were in the body. This one is the one that was by the spine. This is the one that was in the breastbone in the front. And this one is the one that was right by the arm pit over on the right side.

Q: Okay. So, the one that you've indicated last would have been from in-shoot "C"; is that correct?

A: Yes.

Q: And then the upper one, the higher one, would that have from in-shoot "A?"

A: Yes.

Q: And then the lower one would have been, of course, from in-shoot "B"; is that correct?

A: Yes.

Q: Now, you've said something about some build-up of fluid I think in the chest. Could you tell us what that is.

A: This is hazy-looking and lighter in general over here because of a massive amount of blood that's accumulated in the left-side of the chest. And it has tended to push the heart over toward the right.

Q: Okay. Is there anything significant about dislocating the heart in that fashion?

A: It is. That's a very serious problem when at any time enough blood or anything else accumulates rapidly on one side of the chest or the other, and it tends to push the heart and the great vessels to one side or the other, it causes serious problems as far as circulation is concerned.

Q: All right, okay. It could even pinch off the arteries in such a way that blood couldn't get through?

A: It can cause—it can do that. And certainly, in conjunction with the wounds to the heart itself, that's a combination of fatal factors there.

Q: All right, sir. One other photograph, State's Exhibit 2–C for identification. Is that a photograph that you took in the morgue, I mean in the Medical Examiner's office?

A: Yes, it is.

Q: And does that fairly and accurately depict the bullet wounds to the back of Larry Sellers?

A: It does.

MR. HOPKINS: Offer this into evidence, State's Exhibit No. 2–C.

MR. HARRIMAN: No objection, Your Honor.

THE COURT: 2–C is admitted into evidence as offered.

(WHEREUPON STATE'S EXHIBIT NO. 2–C WAS ADMITTED IN EVIDENCE)

MR. HOPKINS: Request permission to publish this to the jury.

THE COURT: Permission granted.

(State's Exhibit No. 2–C was shown to the jury)

[The document camera and television were used again].

Q: (By Mr. HOPKINS) All right, sir, could you explain for us what's depicted in that photograph there?

A: This is Mr. Sellers' back. And this is mainly the back of his chest. Down here would be near the waistline down here, and up here would be the next and the shoulders. And this shows the back of his chest. And this is the center line or midline running down here. Here are the three in-shoot wounds or the three bullet wounds to the back, right here, right here, and over here. This one I designated "A" that we've talked about before. This one, "B" we've talked about. And this is "C" over on the right-hand side of the back of the chest.

[The prosecutor has now had the doctor describe the wounds three times—once with the wound chart, once with the x-ray, and once with the photograph. He has repeated this crucial information three times to the jury, but each time the repetition came from a different vantage point. The differing vantage points render the repetition immune to an asked-and-answered objection or a cumulative evidence objection].

Q: Thank you, Doctor. Based upon—do you have a note as to height and weight of Larry Sellers?

A: Yes, I did. His length was measured to be six feet two inches approximately. And his weight was estimated at 165, possibly 170 pounds.

Q: Based upon your examination, based upon the autopsy that you've performed, do you have an opinion as to the cause of death of Larry Sellers?

A: In my opinion, he died as a result of gunshot wound number or letter "A" to the chest.

Q: And "B" and "C," were they both survivable wounds?

A: They were survivable wounds. It's possible that complications would have set in, but they were survivable wounds under ordinary circumstances.

Q: Potentially fatal, but not necessarily fatal; is that correct?

A: That's correct.

Q: Now, how long after the infliction of these wounds would you expect a person to be able to continue to function in a near-normal fashion?

A: I would think it would be more likely a matter of seconds.

Q: And then from the time of the infliction of the wounds to the time of death, how long a period of time would that take?

A: I think that death was prompt in this instance. And I think that the impairment of the circulation by virtue of the wounds in the heart and the left lung would cause him to die soon after the gunshot wound.

Q: Within a matter of minutes?

A: Yes.

MR. HOPKINS: No further questions.

THE COURT: You may cross-examine.

CROSS-EXAMINATION

Q: (By Mr. HARRIMAN) Doctor, I'm Bernard Harriman. I think we've met before. Nice to see you again. Sir, let me ask you this. First of all, you identified State Exhibit 2–A in evidence. That's Larry Sellers?

A: Yes.

MR. HARRIMAN: Okay, Your Honor, can I, this was not shown to the jury, can I show this to the jury?

THE COURT: You may.

MR. HARRIMAN: Okay, could I just publish this to the jury while I ask you while I ask you a couple more questions. I don't want to say anything. Just pass it down.

(State's Exhibit 2–A was shown to the jury)

[The defense attorney wasted time by using the inefficient method of having the jurors pass the photograph from hand to hand among themselves. The document camera and television were still in the courtroom and could have been used.]

Q: (By Mr. HARRIMAN) Sir, while the members of the jury are looking at that photograph, let me just ask you this. Did you do a gross exam? Is that what it's called when you just look at the body? You know, grossly. Is that the term you use?

A: Well, the examination, that was one, one element of the examination. But the examination actually consisted of a great deal more. And it was more than just a gross examination of the body. The body was opened, and the organs were examined individually and weighed. And it was what I call a complete autopsy.

[The defense attorney here is dividing the attention of the jurors. He's talking over their visual observation of the photograph. As the jurors study the photograph, they are not going to fully absorb the testimony of the doctor. If you pass a photograph from hand to hand among the jurors, stop questioning until they are through examining it].

Q: All right, sir, yes, sir, I understand that. But the gross exam is part of that, that's all I'm asking. Part of the whole, part of the whole exam?

A: Well, the gross examination, you mean the external examination?

Q: Yes, sir.

A: Yes.

Q: That is part of the whole?

A: Right.

Q: Now, would it be fair to say that, you say this gentleman was six foot two or about?

A: He was measured to be approximately 6 foot 2. Now, you have to keep in mind that we have a long stick, and we measure from the heel to the top of the head. And I'll have to admit to you that measuring deceased people on a morgue table is different from having somebody stand up and measure in a doctor's office. And that's why I say approximately.

Q: All right, sir. And about 165, 170 pounds?

A: And that's an estimate on my part. I do not have scales to weigh and I have to estimate the weight.

Q: All right, sir. But would it be fair to say from looking at your file and from recalling independently the exam that you did, that this was a tall, strong man? Would that be, I mean a supple, strong, muscular man? Would that be fair to say?

A: I didn't record an observation as to whether or not he was muscular and large. To me, six feet two is a tall person. And he was medium I would say as far as muscular is concerned or average.

Q: All right.

A: He didn't impress me as being real small or real big.

Q: All right, sir. Okay, that's all I have. Thank you.

THE COURT: Any redirect?

MR. HOPKINS: No, sir. I don't have any redirect. I ask that Dr. Forrest be excused.

MR. HARRIMAN: Agreed, Your Honor.

THE COURT: You may be excused, Doctor. Thank you very much.

The direct examination of a witness consists of two parts preparation and one part presentation. Just as the iceberg has most of its bulk below the surface, the well-done direct examination has most of its bulk done below the surface and outside the courtroom. Of the two parts preparation that occur outside the presence of the jury, the most important part is not what you do alone to prepare yourself. The most important part is what you do with the witness to prepare her to testify.

PRACTICAL EXERCISE

Take the following tape-recorded statement and prepare an abstract of testimony, a direct examination worksheet, and an order of testimony for the witness. The significance of the witness's testimony is as follows: In this case the victim's partially decomposed body was found in a wooded area with a possible cutting wound to her throat. When the van in which she was murdered was recovered, it contained a red "Green Acres" price tag in the amount of $26.00. It is essential to the state's case to put the defendant in that van. The red price tag will be argued as evidence that he was in the van. This witness stands ready to positively identify the defendant as a customer who came into his store shortly before the victim's disappearance and bought a knife bearing a price tag identical to the one in the van. The actual knife was never recovered, but you have a photograph of an identical knife.

Q1: The following interview is taken at 8774 Normandy Boulevard in Jacksonville, Florida, at the Green Acres Sporting Goods Store. The interview will be with Mr. John Farhat, F.A.R.H.A.T. You are the owner?

A1: Yes sir I am.

Q2: Okay. The interview will be in reference to an investigation into the kidnaping of Kimberly Diane Leach, Columbia County, on February the 9th, 1978. Mr. Farhat, tell me your full name please sir.

A2: My name is John Farhat.

Q3: Okay and your address?

A3: [address].

Q4: And your occupation here.

A4: I am the President of Green Acres Sporting Goods, Inc.

Q5: Okay sir. Mr. Farhat, as we have already told you, this is in reference to a purchase made by an individual some few days back here at your store and we showed you a photograph of a red price tag bearing the name Green Acres and the amount $26.00 I believe. Did that photograph—you saw it I believe.

A5: Yes I did.

Q6: Did that appear to be a photograph of the tag that you use here?—

A6: Yes sir.

Q7: Okay. Now recalling back within the last several days do you recall an item in that price range that you may have sold?

A7: Yes sir. I sold a knife which is twenty-six dollars.

Q8: Okay and what kind of knife would that be?

A8: It was a buck knife I believe the name of it, the model name is General.—

Q9: Okay. A Buck Knife and the model General.

A9: It's a sheath knife.

Q10: Okay and tell me in your own words. What you recall about that particular sale.

A10: The man came in. He wasn't uh—I think he got long hair—and he was very polite and he wanted to buy a knife for his friend or a knife like his friend got and we showed him a few models and finally he decided on that General Knife and he paid for it in cash.

Q11: Okay. Was this a white man or a black man?

A11: It was a white man.

Q12: Okay. Could you describe him physically?

A12: As far as I remember he was, he wasn't, you know he didn't have no red cheeks but he was about five eight or nine. He was about between a hundred fifty and a hundred and sixty pounds. He, I think he got blonde hair and he didn't have, he wasn't well-dressed you know. Shaggy clothes you know. Not too good of clothes you know. Just regular clothes.

Q13: Okay and did he, do you recall whether or not he had any facial hair, mustache or anything?

A13: Uh I, I can't remember that.

Q14: Okay.

A14: But he had plenty of hair but I don't know if it was on his face or his head.

Q15: Okay. Do you, can you describe the clothing that he might have been wearing at the time?

A15: It could be a brown clothes you know. Western clothes you know. Something like that.

Q16: Okay. Now do you recall about when this was that he, that this person was in the store?

A16: Uh, now about two weeks ago maybe. About the first week of the month or second week of the month of February 1978.

Q17: Okay. And the time of the day that he was in here?

A17: Uh, could have been around one in the afternoon, something like that. Because I was by myself in the store.

Q18: Okay. There was no one else here but you?

A18: No sir. Nobody was here.

Q19: Did anyone come into the store while he was here?

A19: I don't remember.

Q20: Okay. How long would you say that he was in the store here with you?

A20: Oh, about ten minutes.

Q21: Okay. And did you see any vehicle that he may have been driving?

A21: No sir. I did not look outside.

Q22: And about, did you mention an age. How old you thought this individual may have been.

A22: He could run, with all that hair on him, he could run between say twenty-five and thirty-five years.

Q23: Okay. Now I believe you said he was about five six uh five—

A23: Five eight.

Q24: Five eight.

A24: Five nine. Yeah.

Q25: In what weight range would you say?

A25: One fifty to one sixty, something like that.

Q26: And I believe you said you recalled that he had brown hair. Is that correct?

A26: Yes sir. As far as I remember.

Q27: Okay. Is there anything else that stands out in your mind? Did he wear glasses? Did he wear a hat or anything?

A27: No sir. But he look like he's a you know, he's a sleepy or something or he was really shy.

Q28: Okay. Did uh—

A28: Which I mean he's not the aggressive type you know. He was very polite in his speech.

Q29: Did he have an accent?

A29: No sir.

Q30: Okay. By accent, I mean I have a southern accent

A30: Yes sir. I understand.-

Q31: And—

A31: Yes sir. I don't remember that detail but I don't think so.

Q32: Did he, do you recall if he looked at anything else other than the Buck Knife?

A32: No sir. Just the knives.

Q33: Okay. Was any mention made as to paying with a charge card or anything other than cash?

A33: Not that I, not that I remember. I believe he paid cash.

Q34: Okay. Is there anything else that you recall of this transaction that you had with this individual?

A34: No sir I don't.

Q35: Okay and you believe that it was somewhere within the last couple of weeks?

A35: Yes sir I do.

BY THE EXAMINER: Okay. The date is February 24, 1978. The time is 3:17 P.M. and this interview is concluded.

CHAPTER 12

CONSTRUCTIVE CROSS-EXAMINATION

▪ ▪ ▪

The one who first states a case seems right, until the other comes and cross-examines him.—*Proverbs* 18:17 (NRSV)

A. MISCONCEPTIONS ABOUT CROSS EXAMINATION

1. THE TRIAL OF SOCRATES

The forensic trinity consists of the activities of building, preserving, and destroying, and the common model of the three types of examination fits neatly with each member of the trinity. Conventional wisdom has lawyers building their cases on direct examination, destroying their opponent's cases on cross-examination, and trying to preserve their cases on redirect examination. When most people think of cross-examination, they conjure up visions of the "Perry Mason moment," when a skillful attorney either bludgeons a beleaguered witness into confessing or inflicts fatal wounds upon the witness's credibility. As a matter of fact, the earliest example of cross-examination from world literature fits this destroyer model for cross-examination. When Socrates stood trial on the capital charges of impiety and corrupting the Athenian youth, he had an opportunity to cross-examine one of his accusers, and Plato records that examination in his *Apology of Socrates*.

> Q: Come hither, Meletus, and let me ask a question of you. You think a great deal about the improvement of youth?
>
> A: Yes, I do.
>
> Q: Tell the judges, then, who is their improver; for you must know, as you have taken the pains to discover their corrupter, and are citing and accusing me before them. Speak, then, and tell the judges who their improver is.
>
> A: [No answer].
>
> Q: Observe, Meletus, that you are silent, and have nothing to say. But is not this rather disgraceful, and a very considerable proof of what I was saying, that you have no interest in the matter? Speak up, friend, and tell us who their improver is.

A: The laws.

Q: But that, my good sir, is not my meaning. I want to know who the person is, who, in the first place, knows the laws.

A: The judges, Socrates, who are present in court.

Q: What do you mean to say, Meletus, that they are able to instruct and improve youth?

A: Certainly they are.

Q: What, all of them, or some only and not others?

A: All of them.

Q: By the goddess Here, that is good news! There are plenty of improvers, then. And what do you say of the audience—do they improve them?

A: Yes, they do.

Q: And the Senators?

A: Yes, the Senators improve them.

Q: But perhaps the ecclesiasts corrupt them? Or do they too improve them?

A: They improve them.

Q: Then every Athenian improves and elevates them; all with the exception of myself; and I alone am their corrupter? Is that what you affirm?

A: That is what I stoutly affirm.

Q: I am very unfortunate if that is true. [Argumentative comment omitted]. And now, Meletus, I must ask you another question: Which is better, to live among bad citizens, or among good ones? Answer, friend, I say; for that is a question which may be easily answered. Do not the good do their neighbors good, and the bad do them evil?

A: Certainly.

Q: And is there anyone who would rather be injured than benefitted by those who live with him? Answer, my good friend; the law requires you to answer—does anyone like to be injured?

A: Certainly not.

Q: And when you accuse me of corrupting and deteriorating the youth, do you allege that I corrupt them intentionally or unintentionally?

A: Intentionally, I say.

Q: But you have just admitted that the good do their neighbors good, and the evil do them evil. Now is that a truth which your superior wisdom has recognized thus early in life, and am I, at my age, in such darkness and ignorance as not to know that if a man with whom I have to live is corrupted by me, I am very likely to be harmed by him, and yet I corrupt him, and intentionally, too? that is what you are saying, and of that you will never persuade me or any other human being. [Argumentative comment omitted]. But still I should like to know, Meletus, in what I am affirmed to corrupt the young. I suppose you mean, as I infer from your indictment, that I teach them not to acknowledge the gods which the state acknowledges, but some other new divinities or spiritual agencies in their stead. These are the lessons which corrupt the youth, as you say.

A: Yes, that I say emphatically.

Q: Then, by the gods, Meletus, of whom we are speaking, tell me and the court, in somewhat plainer terms, what you mean! for I do not as yet understand whether you affirm that I teach others to acknowledge some gods * * * not the same gods which the city recognizes. * * * Or, do you mean to say that I am an atheist simply, and a teacher of atheism?

A: I mean the latter—that you are a complete atheist.

Q: That is an extraordinary statement, Meletus. Why do you say that? Do you mean that I do not believe in the god-head of the sun or moon, which is the common creed of all men?

A: I assure you, judges, that he does not believe in them; for he says that the sun is stone, and the moon earth.

Q: Friend Meletus, you think that you are accusing Anaxagoras; and you have but a bad opinion of the judges, if you fancy them ignorant to such a degree as not to know that those doctrines are found in the books of Anaxagoras the Clazomenian, who is full of them. And these are the doctrines which the youth are said to learn of Socrates, when there are not unfrequently exhibitions of them at the theater.

A: I swear by Zeus that you believe absolutely in none at all.

Q: You are a liar, Meletus, not believed even by yourself. [Remainder of examination omitted].[1]

Socrates brilliantly refuted each allegation against him and made Meletus look like a fool. The verdict? Guilty as charged by the slimmest of

[1] Plato, Apology of Socrates, 24e–26e, Ed. Sue Asscher and David Widger. Trans. Benjamin Jowett. 1999. Project Gutenberg. <https://www.gutenberg.org/ebooks/1656>.

majorities. When Socrates tried his hand at final argument during the penalty phase, he again gave a magnificent summation which resulted in a landslide vote for the death penalty. If Socrates did such a marvelous job of destroying Meletus on cross-examination, why did the jury convict him?

2. THE SCOPES TRIAL

Another prototypical example of the destroyer model of cross-examination occurred in the 1925 misdemeanor trial of John Scopes for the crime of teaching evolution. At that trial defense attorney Clarence Darrow baited prosecutor William Jennings Bryan onto the witness stand for "cross-examination" on Bryan's views of Biblical interpretation and evolutionary theory. Darrow attacked Bryan as gleefully and unmercifully as any attorney has ever attacked a witness, and his character assassination of Bryan was immortalized in the McCarthy-era morality play, *Inherit the Wind.* The movie version of Darrow's examination, as depicted by Spencer Tracy, helped to make it the most famous cross-examination in American history. But was it really that good? Darrow's "cross-examination" began with the following exchange.

> Q: You have given considerable study to the Bible, haven't you, Mr. Bryan?
>
> A: Yes, sir, I have tried to.
>
> Q: Then you have made a general study of it?
>
> A: Yes, I have; I have studied the Bible for about fifty years, or sometime more than that, but, of course, I have studied it more as I have become older than when I was but a boy.
>
> Q: You claim that everything in the Bible should be literally interpreted?
>
> A: I believe everything in the Bible should be accepted as it is given there: some of the Bible is given illustratively. For instance: "Ye are the salt of the earth." I would not insist that man was actually salt, or that he had flesh of salt, but it is used in the sense of salt as saving God's people.
>
> Q: But when you read that Jonah swallowed the whale—or that the whale swallowed Jonah—excuse me please—how do you literally interpret that?
>
> A: When I read that a big fish swallowed Jonah—it does not say whale. That is my recollection of it. A big fish, and I believe it, and I believe in a God who can make a whale and can make a man and make both what He pleases.

Q: Now, you say, the big fish swallowed Jonah, and he there remained how long—three days—and then he spewed him upon the land. You believe that the big fish was made to swallow Jonah?

A: I am not prepared to say that; the Bible merely says it was done.

Q: You don't know whether it was the ordinary run of fish, or made for that purpose?

A: You may guess; you evolutionists guess. * * *

Q: You are not prepared to say whether that fish was made especially to swallow a man or not?

A: The Bible doesn't say, so I am not prepared to say.

Q: But do you believe He made them—that He made such a fish and that it was big enough to swallow Jonah?

A: Yes, sir. Let me add: One miracle is just as easy to believe as another.

Q: Just as hard?

A: It is hard to believe for you, but easy for me. A miracle is a thing performed beyond what man can perform. When you get within the realm of miracles; and it is just as easy to believe the miracle of Jonah as any other miracle in the Bible.

Q: Perfectly easy to believe that Jonah swallowed the whale?

A: If the Bible said so; the Bible doesn't make as extreme statements as evolutionists do. * * *

Q: The Bible says Joshua commanded the sun to stand still for the purpose of lengthening the day, doesn't it, and you believe it.

A: I do.

Q: Do you believe at that time the entire sun went around the earth?

A: No, I believe that the earth goes around the sun.

Q: Do you believe that the men who wrote it thought that the day could be lengthened or that the sun could be stopped?

A: I don't know what they thought.

Q: You don't know?

A: I think they wrote the fact without expressing their own thoughts.

Q: Have you an opinion as to whether or not the men who wrote that thought * * *

By Gen. Stewart: I want to object, your honor; it has gone beyond the pale of any issue that could possibly be injected into this lawsuit, expect by imagination. I do not think the defendant has a right to conduct the examination any further and I ask your honor to exclude it.

By the Witness: It seems to me it would be too exacting to confine the defense to the facts; if they are not allowed to get away from the facts, what have they to deal with?

By the Court: Mr. Bryan is willing to be examined. Go ahead.

By Mr. Darrow: I read that years ago. Can you answer my question directly? If the day was lengthened by stopping either the earth or the sun, it must have been the earth?

A: Well, I should say so.

Q: Now, Mr. Bryan, have you ever pondered what would have happened to the earth if it had stood still?

A: No.

Q: You have not?

A: No; the God I believe in could have taken care of that, Mr. Darrow.

Q: I see. Have you ever pondered what would naturally happen to the earth if it stood still suddenly?

A: No.

Q: Don't you know it would have been converted into molten mass of matter?

A: You testify to that when you get on the stand, I will give you a chance.[2]

[Remainder of examination omitted].

The examination continued in the same vein for page after page of transcript, with Darrow and Bryan engaging in a tit-for-tat which did little to advance the case for either side. Although posterity remembers the examination as having thoroughly discredited Bryan, contemporary opinion branded Darrow the loser. If Darrow did such a masterful job of destroying Bryan, why did he come off the loser both at trial and in the eyes of his contemporaries?

---

[2] Linder, Douglas, "Darrow Examines Bryan," Famous Trials. 2006. University of Missouri-Kansas City School of Law. 15 March 2007. <https://www.famous-trials.com/scopesmonkey/2124-day7>. For the full text of the examination, see Younger, Irving, Classics of the Courtroom, Volume III: Clarence Darrow's Cross-Examination of William Jennings Bryan in Tennessee vs. John Thomas Scopes, The Professional Education Group, Inc., Minneapolis, Minnesota, 1988.

3. THE TRIAL OF SUSANNA

Socrates' cross-examination of Meletus does not exhaust the examples of cross-examination from ancient literature. The *Apocrypha* tells the story of a beautiful young woman named Susanna, who went into a private garden to take a bath. Two elders accosted her there and threatened to accuse her of the capital crime of adultery if she did not submit to their sexual advances. She did not, and they did. When she stood trial on their accusation, they testified that they saw her having sexual relations under one of the trees in the garden. A young lawyer by the name of Daniel came to her rescue. Daniel invoked the rule of sequestration and excluded the witnesses from the courtroom. After the witnesses left the courtroom, he called one of the elders to the witness stand and asked him a single question:

> Q: You old relic of wicked days, your sins have now come home, which you have committed in the past, pronouncing unjust judgments, condemning the innocent and acquitting the guilty, the Lord said 'You shall not put an innocent and righteous person to death.' Now then, if you really saw this woman, tell me this: Under what tree did you see them being intimate with each other?
>
> A: Under a mastic tree.[3]

After receiving the elder's answer, Daniel dismissed him and called the second elder. His sole question of the other elder was as poorly worded as the first.

> Q: You offspring of Canaan, and not of Judah, beauty has beguiled you, and lust has perverted your heart. This is how you have been treating the daughters of Israel, and they were intimate with you through fear; but a daughter of Judah would not tolerate your wickedness. Now then, tell me: Under what tree did you catch them being intimate?
>
> A: Under an evergreen oak.[4]

Back in the late 1970's Professor Irving Younger promulgated his famous Ten Commandments of Cross-Examination.[5] Daniel's cross-examination violated at least six of them. Before we disbar Daniel for ineffective assistance of counsel, we need to look at the elders' answers. One said he saw Susanna under a mastic tree. The other said she was under an evergreen oak. Daniel's cross-examination has to have been one

---

[3] Susanna 52–54 (NRSV).

[4] Susanna 56–58 (NRSV).

[5] The commandments are: (1) Be brief. (2) Ask short questions in plain words. (3) Ask leading questions. (4) Do not ask questions to which you do not know the answer. (5) Listen to the answer. (6) Do not quarrel with the witness. (7) Do not allow the witness to repeat his story. (8) Do not permit the witness to explain his answers. (9) Do not ask one question too many. (10) Save the ultimate point for summation.

of the most successful cross-examinations in the history of jurisprudence. Susanna went free and the court ordered the elders executed.

4. THE PURPOSE OF CROSS-EXAMINATION

The bottom line assessment of any courtroom performance is the jury's verdict. The Athenian jury found Socrates guilty. The Dayton jury found Scopes guilty. Darrow and Socrates may have done an excellent job of performing the stereotypical cross-examination, but they lost. Daniel may have done a perfectly dreadful job of asking the questions on cross-examination, but he won. What did Daniel do right that Socrates and Clarence Darrow did wrong? Daniel won where Socrates and Darrow lost because Daniel alone had the proper objective for his cross-examination. Socrates crossed Meletus with the objective of justifying himself and his teachings to posterity. Darrow crossed with the objective of humiliating Bryan. Daniel crossed with the objective of winning. "What," you may ask, "is the purpose of cross-examination if it is not to annihilate the witness?" Before we can answer that question, we should ask ourselves another.

What do you want the jury to be thinking when you finish your cross-examination?

(1) You are brilliant?

(2) You did a good cross?

(3) The witness is a nitwit?

(4) The witness is a liar?

Darrow and Socrates can fairly be said to have achieved objectives 1 through 3, but they still did not prevail. Even if you achieve objective 4, you have not guaranteed success. What you want the jury to be thinking when you end your cross is:

(5) Your side should win.

The jury may think you are the nitwit, the jury may think you did a terrible cross, the jury may think the witness is not only brilliant, she is the fount of all knowledge; but if the jury thinks your side should win, you have done a good cross. Which brings us to the true objective of cross-examination. The ultimate objective of cross-examination is to persuade the jury to find for your side. You can achieve the ultimate objective by setting a series of preliminary tactical and strategic objectives working toward the ultimate objective, but when you set one of the preliminary objectives, you must be sure that, within the dynamics of the case at hand, it will advance you toward the ultimate objective of victory.

We can think of the objectives of cross-examination as having a three-tiered hierarchy. Since the jury will not find for your side unless they accept your case theory, we could restate the ultimate objective as either persuading the jury to accept your case theory or persuading them to reject the defense theory. The hierarchy of objectives for cross-examination would look like this:

Ultimate Objectives

(I) Persuade the jury to accept the case theory.

(II) Persuade the jury to reject the defense theory.

Major (Strategic) Objectives

(A) To build the case theory using favorable facts.

(B) To preserve the case theory by mitigating unfavorable facts.

(C) To destroy the defense theory by exposing fiction.

Minor (Tactical) Objectives

(1) To reemphasize favorable facts brought out on direct.

(2) To bring out additional favorable facts which the witness must admit.

(3) To bolster the credibility of one of your own witnesses.

(4) To create conflict with other witnesses.

(5) To discredit the testimony of the witness.

(6) To discredit the witness.

(7) Other limited objectives dictated by the posture of the case and the wisdom of the cross-examiner.

If you closely review these objectives, you will see that only objectives (5) and (6) of the tactical objectives involve the possibility of a full-frontal assault on the witness's human worth, and only objective (6) necessitates it. Objective (5) can just as often be achieved in a friendly manner by asking such questions as "Q: Would it be fair to say that from your vantage point of more than 100 yards away, looking through heavy foliage at twilight, your ability to observe was somewhat hampered?"

5. THE STEREOTYPICAL CROSS INAPPROPRIATE FOR THE PROSECUTION

Why is it, then, that conventional wisdom looks upon cross-examination as a tool of destruction? Because most cross-examination occurs in the context of a criminal trial, and because most of the cross-examination done in a criminal trial is done by defense attorneys. If the prosecutor has done a good job in the charging stage of the prosecution, the defendant is guilty. If the defendant is guilty, the task on cross-examination becomes one of attacking the case to discredit the evidence of guilt. Because the burden of proof is beyond a reasonable doubt, only a small amount of question may be sufficient for a jury to acquit. Because a criminal defendant has no duty to prove anything, and in many cases has no evidence to prove innocence, the constructive objectives of cross-examination are less often pursued on a defense cross-examination. Because the constructive objectives are so seldom pursued, defense attorneys who do have a viable, provable defense oftentimes damage their case by neglecting the constructive in favor of the destructive. As the saying goes, when your only tool is a hammer, every problem looks like a nail.

Prosecutors do not get as much practice at cross-examination as defense attorneys. If the defendant is guilty, she is not going to have much evidence to present, and you are not going to get much opportunity to cross. When you do get up to cross-examine, most crosses you have seen are destructive crosses, so you instinctively go into destructive mode. You can do immeasurable damage to your case by neglecting the constructive for the destructive. First, unless you completely destroy a witness's testimony, the best that the destructive method can do is to raise doubt. Doubt, being half of the phrase "reasonable doubt," is anathema to a prosecution. Prosecutors crave certainty, because only certainty can erase reasonable doubt. You produce certainty much more readily by the constructive than the destructive. Second, by using the same methods and pursuing the same objectives as the defense did on cross-examination, you validate the defense cross. How must a jury feel when a prosecutor asks them to believe the prosecution witnesses despite the damage done by the defense cross and disbelieve the defense witnesses because they have suffered identical damage by an identical method of cross? Take the example of impeachment by prior conviction. How much credibility would you have if you asked a jury to disbelieve a defense witness because of a single misdemeanor conviction but believe a prosecution witness despite fourteen felony convictions?

B. CONSTRUCTIVE CROSS-EXAMINATION

The lesson of this brief analysis is clear. Although defense attorneys—having no burden of proof and having nothing to prove—can more readily profit using destructive cross-examination, your primary objective on cross-examination should be constructive. In constructive cross-examination, you do not confront the witness head on in an attempt to discredit him. You use the following two step formula:

(1) Take what the witness will give you.

(2) Turn it to your advantage.

1. GIMMIE'S

You can think of constructive cross-examination as cross-examination to gimmie's. Any golfer knows that a gimmie is a shot that his opponent will readily concede. Gimmie's on cross-examination are similar. In constructive cross-examination, a gimmie is a fact which the witness must readily concede. A gimmie has four qualities:

(1) It is favorable.

(2) It must be admitted.

(3) If it is not admitted,

(4) Gotcha!

The witness must give me the gimmie because if she does not, she destroys herself by looking like a liar, a lunatic, or a loser. Gotcha's usually come from one of three areas:

(1) Prior inconsistent statements,

(2) Unimpeachable disagreement, or

(3) Demonstrable illogic.

If a witness has said "the sky was blue," and "the sky was blue" is favorable to your side, you can safely ask the witness to admit "the sky was blue" on cross-examination. If she says "the sky was grey," you can punish her with the prior inconsistent statement. Impeach her with the prior inconsistent statement and then ask for another gimmie. She should be more willing to give you the next gimmie because you have demonstrated an ability to punish her for not supplying the required information. If you have established, or can establish, a fact beyond peradventure, you can safely ask the witness to admit that fact. If she does not she has not harmed your case, she has harmed her credibility.

A witness can look downright foolish if she tries to deny a gimmie with an illogical answer. Illogic comes in three varieties, and of the three gotcha's, it can be the hardest to demonstrate. It can arise from:

(1) Impossibility: Sometimes a witness will make an assertion that is contrary to the laws of nature. No matter how much surface plausibility it has, it just cannot be.

(2) Improbability: Some things a witness says are possible but highly unlikely. If a witness ventures onto the limb of improbability, you can usually saw it off for her.

(3) Implausibility: What the witness says is possible, but people just do not act that way. The witness asserts that she engaged in some sort of nonsensical behavior. You must make sure the jury understands the silliness of the assertion.

2. IDENTIFYING GIMMIE'S

You identify gimmie's by asking yourself a series of three questions, each of which builds upon the previous question.

(1) What must the witness admit? (Primary gimmie).

(2) Given (1), what else must the witness admit? (Secondary gimmie).

(3) Given (1) & (2), what else must the witness admit? (Tertiary gimmie).

Only the primary fact is a true gimmie. If the witness has not already admitted the primary gimmie, she has plausible deniability of secondary and tertiary gimmie's This shows you how to build your line of questioning. You establish the primary gimmie first, and the secondary gimmie must now be admitted. You establish the secondary gimmie, and the tertiary gimmie must be admitted. If you build carefully enough, you can build from gimmie to gotcha by asking a series of questions beginning with seemingly harmless facts and building from them to more and more harmful facts until the witness is cornered into either making an inconvenient admission or looking foolish.

C. PREPARING AND EXECUTING THE CROSS-EXAMINATION

In order to conduct a truly effective cross-examination, you must go through the now familiar three step process of assimilation, assessment, and assembly. You assimilate by learning the facts of the case, learning the witness's testimony, and learning the witness. You assess by asking yourself: Can you build your case with the witness? Must you preserve against the witness's testimony? Should you attempt to destroy the witness? You assemble by asking: What arguments can be made based on the witness's testimony? What gimme's support those arguments? What order of questioning is most persuasive?

You can assimilate by preparing an annotated abstract of the witness's potential testimony exactly as you did for direct examination of your witnesses. You write down in chronological order each material fact to which you expect the witness to testify. You annotate each of the fact points with a reference to deposition, report, or statement supporting your expectation that the witness will testify to that fact. The annotations are essential. They give you a ready reference to quickly find the fact if the witness testifies contrary to your expectation. With the facts at your fingertips, you can easily impeach the witness by prior inconsistent statement.

1. THE CROSS-EXAMINATION WORKSHEET

Once you have gotten your abstract of testimony done, you can put on your thinking cap and decide what you can do with the witness on cross. In order to better answer the three questions of the assessment stage, you should fill out a cross-examination worksheet[6] for your witness. The cross-examination worksheet should contain five sections.

(1) Case Theory: This is the polestar of your cross-examination. Your case theory is the interpretation of the facts which entitles your side to win. It is what the jury must believe in order for you to achieve a conviction. The entire economy of the cross-examination should be aimed at building or preserving your case theory.

(2) Defense Theory: This is the bill of goods the defense is peddling. You must preserve your case theory against the defense theory. As a secondary objective of your cross, you want to undermine the defense theory. Sometimes the best way to destroy the defense theory is simply to hammer home on building and preserving the case theory. The case theory should in and of itself negate the defense theory.

Now that you have a firm idea of what you are trying to prove and how the defense is going to counteract your proof, you use the next three sections to analyze the witness's testimony in light of the forensic trinity.

(3) Build: Here you list the facts that the witness can testify to which bolster your case theory.

(4) Preserve: Here you list the facts that the witness can testify to which undercut the defense theory.

(5) Destroy: Here you list the impeachment material that you intend to use to destroy the witness. If you do a good enough job of building and preserving with the witness, you may decide not to use this material at all.

2. THE TOPICAL PAGE

You are now ready to enter the final phase of your preparation. You decide what arguments you want to base on the witness's testimony, and you prepare topical pages to cover each argument. You take your topical pages and jot down each argument. Each argument is placed at the top of a separate topical page, and each fact supportive of the argument is written down underneath that argument. Each argument then becomes a topic of cross-examination. It is also essential that the references which you noted in your annotated abstract of testimony be included on the topical pages.

---

[6] See Figure 8-5 in Chapter 8.

Now you shuffle and reshuffle your topical pages and place them in such an order as to maximize the effectiveness of your cross.

3. PRIMACY AND RECENCY

As you order your pages, you keep ever mindful of the doctrines of primacy and recency. Just as a crafty boxer steals a round by being very active at the beginning and end of the round, you should structure your cross so as to score heavily at the beginning and end of your cross. The importance of scoring heavily at the outset and at the end has been recognized for centuries, at least since Cicero and Quintilian wrote on the subject.[7] Scoring heavily at the beginning not only impresses the fact finder, it demoralizes the witness. A demoralized witness will usually prove an easier task for cross-examination. If the witness lacks courage, he may become putty in your hands, eager to follow your lead and avoid further embarrassment.

4. PREPARATION SHORTCUTS

Once again, the foregoing is the ideal. Since you live in a less than perfect world, you will seldom achieve the ideal. You can abbreviate your preparation for cross-examination. First you jettison the chronological abstract of testimony, which consumes the greatest part of your preparation time. Work directly from the reports and statements to the cross-examination worksheets. Be sure to annotate the worksheets if you do not prepare an abstract of testimony. If eliminating the abstract of testimony does not give you enough time, eliminate the topical pages. You must never, never eliminate the cross-examination worksheet. This one piece of paper can give you a skeleton from which you can perform a serviceable, if not a stellar, cross-examination. Make sure, however, that as you economize your preparation, you do so because you lack the time, not because you lack the initiative.

5. EXPLORATORY AND EXTEMPORANEOUS CROSS-EXAMINATIONS

Those assistant prosecutors who inhabit the lowest tiers of the hierarchy, have the least experience, and carry the heaviest caseloads seldom have the leisure to prepare. When you begin as an assistant state attorney or deputy district attorney, your division chief will likely give you a cart loaded with banker's boxes full of slim case files and send you to court with the admonition "Go get'em, Tiger!" Frequently, when you ask for guidance, you get the response "You're doing great, keep up the good work!" When you walk into court alone and unguided with ten cases set for

[7] 3 Quintilian, The Orator's Education, 7.1.10–11, Trans. Donald A. Russell, Harvard University Press, Cambridge, Massachusetts, 2001. pp. 157–159.

jury trial, an antechamber full of prosecution witnesses, and no idea which case you will really try after the last-minute pleas are taken, you have not had much time to prepare for cross-examination of the defense witnesses. You may not even suspect who the defense witnesses may be. You may have a list of names, or you may hear the witnesses' names for the first time when the defense attorney calls the witnesses to the stand. You would do well to keep a number of blank cross-examination worksheets handy so that you can deal with the inevitable surprise defense witness. For each of the ten or so cases you have set, you should have an inkling of a case theory. Put four or five blank cross-examination worksheets in each case file with the case theory section filled in. It is a rare judge who will not give you at least a few minutes to interview a witness before the witness testifies. During the few minutes the judge gives you, jot down notes from your interview under the appropriate headings. Think about how the witness fits into the case. After the interview, take some time to go through the three questions: (1) Mrs. Witness, what will you gimmie? (2) Based on that, what else will you gimmie? (3) Based on the first two answers, what else will you gimmie? Note your answers in the appropriate sections of the worksheet. As the witness testifies on direct, jot down additional notes under the appropriate headings. When defense counsel says "No further questions," you are ready to cross-examine. Do not fear these situations. Usually, you face public defenders whose case loads match your own, and who (like you) have spent insufficient time preparing their witnesses to testify. Remember Quintilian's warning about poorly prepared witnesses. They can do the side calling them more harm than good. All you need to do is ask a few pointed questions.

6. THE CASE THEORY

By way of illustrating how the case theory can guide your cross-examination, let us look at an actual trial. Robert Joiner stood accused of murdering Rodney Howard, and it was a case where a pro/con/contra analysis would find many cons. The killing occurred at Joiner's home, all parties to the transaction had freely used beer and marijuana, the victim had battered Joiner's wife, and had knocked Joiner down with a billy club. The violence occurred in Joiner's front yard, and he retaliated by entering his home, arming himself with a shotgun, returning outside, and shooting the victim dead. The prosecution theory held that Joiner intentionally killed as an act of revenge. The defense theory was self-defense. The prosecutor took the case theory and elaborated it into this attention step for his opening statement: "Robert Joiner on April 15, 1995, went and got his shotgun. He loaded the shotgun. He stepped onto the porch of his single wide trailer, raised that shotgun to his shoulder, and shot and killed his good friend, Rodney Howard. And what did he kill him over? A $40.00 bag of pot." The attention step would never be considered for the Pulitzer Prize for literature, but in plain English it: (1) Appealed to logos by clearly stating an unjustified killing; (2) Simultaneously appealed against the defendant's ethos and to the victim's ethos by stating that the defendant was the victim's good friend; and (3) Appealed to pathos by giving the small quantity of marijuana as the trivial cause of the killing.

The defendant had given several exculpatory statements claiming self-defense, but nowhere did anyone ask him about the mechanics involved in actually retrieving and firing the gun. The prosecutor, wishing to argue that the killing was intentional, developed a series of fact points indicating an intentional killing. His topical page supporting the argument for intentional killing looked something like this:

CROSS-EXAM TOPICAL PAGE

ARGUMENT: Intentional Killing

FACT	**REFERENCE**
(1). Went inside the trailer	Taped Statement p. 2.
(2). Got the shotgun	Taped Statement p. 2.
(3). Loaded the shotgun.	Taped Statement p. 3.
(4). Went back outside	Taped Statement p. 3.
(5). Pointed gun	Logical Inference.
(6). Pulled trigger	Logical Inference.
(7). Killed good friend	Taped Statement p. 1.

After deciding upon his argument and arranging the fact points supportive of the argument, nothing was left to do but to ask the questions on cross-examination. Notice that this line of questioning was decided upon long in advance of the trial and was totally independent of the direct examination. No matter what the defendant said on direct examination, this line of questioning should provide a fruitful area of inquiry. The actual questioning went like this:

Q: You went and loaded your gun?

A: Yes, sir.

Q: Broke the breach on it?

A: Yes, sir.

Q: And put a shell in it?

A: Yes, sir.

Q: You walked out on that porch?

A: Yes, sir.

Q: And put the gun to your shoulder?

A: I believe so. I don't remember if I had it actually up to my shoulder or down to my side.

Q: You cocked the hammer back, didn't you?

A: Yes, sir.

Q: And pulled the trigger, didn't you?

A: Yes, sir.

Q: And you killed your good friend, Rodney Howard?

A: Yes, sir.

In this cross-examination, the prosecutor used constructive cross-examination to slowly walk the defendant through each and every simple act of the complex action of retrieving and firing a firearm. Just as the slow walk is effective on direct examination, it performs admirably on cross-examination as well.

7. QUINTILIAN'S CORKSCREW REVISITED

Sometimes the witnesses will give you some opposition and you have to apply Quintilian's corkscrew. The topical method serves admirably for the purpose if you order your questioning properly. Let us review Quintilian's three step procedure for extorting the truth from a witness:

(1) Begin with small admissions. (Gimmie's).

(2) Build to larger admissions. (Gimmie's).

(3) Bombard with damaging admissions. (Gotcha's).

The prosecution team in State of Florida versus Theodore Robert Bundy used Quintilian's corkscrew to neutralize the testimony of a defense medical examiner called to impeach the testimony of the state's medical examiner. Dr. Peter Lipkovic, who examined the body at the crime scene and later performed the autopsy at the medical examiner's office, opined that Kimberly Leach died of homicidal violence to the neck area, type undetermined, accompanied by copious bleeding. Dr. Lipkovic arrived at this conclusion because of the condition of the body, which had been exposed to the elements for approximately two months. Although the body had partially mummified, the neck area was missing. Dr. Lipkovic opined that the neck did not mummify because it had suffered trauma and bled, causing a moist opening in the body which insects attacked and destroyed.

In the charging stage, the prosecutors determined that it would be wise to plead the cause of Miss Leach's death as vaguely as possible in order to avoid any argument that the allegations of the indictment were not supported by the proof at trial. Consequently, after some research, they found two old cases which supported the filing of an indictment alleging cause of death in the following language:

> THEODORE ROBERT BUNDY * * * did murder KIMBERLY DIANE LEACH in some way and manner, or by some means, instrument or weapon to the Grand Jury unknown, thereby inflicting and creating in KIMBERLY DIANE LEACH mortal wounds and injuries or mortal sicknesses, of and from which said mortal wounds and injuries or mortal sicknesses, the said KIMBERLY DIANE LEACH died.[8]

Their circumspection was vindicated when the defense produced a medical examiner, Dr. Joseph Burton, who contradicted Dr. Lipkovic in almost every detail. The defense medical examiner opined that it was impossible to tell what caused the neck area to be missing and impossible to tell the cause of death of the victim.

When the prosecutors took Dr. Burton's deposition, they began to see some hope for neutralizing his testimony. Dr. Burton testified at deposition that, on the basis of his examination of the autopsy report and the crime scene photographs, he could rule out death by accident, suicide, or natural causes. When you rule out accident, suicide, and natural causes, the only thing left is homicide. The prosecutors thus set as their objective for cross-examination to get the doctor to rule out all those manners of death and opine that the death was a homicide committed in some unknown manner. The prosecution team had never heard of cross-examination worksheets or topical pages, but had they done objectives and topical pages for Dr. Burton, the pages would have looked like this:

CROSS-EXAMINATION WORKSHEET

WITNESS: DR. JOSEPH BURTON

CASE THEORY: Theodore Robert Bundy murdered Kimberly Diane Leach in some manner and by some means to the Grand Jury unknown.

DEFENSE THEORY: There is no way to tell how Kimberly Diane Leach died.

BUILD (CONFIRM CASE THEORY)............... REFERENCE

(1) Can rule out accident.. Deposition

(2) Can rule out suicide.. Deposition

(3) Can rule out natural causes.............................. Deposition

(4) Cannot rule out homicide.................................. Deposition

PRESERVE (UNDERCUT CASE THEORY).... REFERENCE

Cannot tell how Kimberly Diane Leach died......... Deposition

[8] Mendenhall v. State, 71 Fla. 552, 72 So. 202 (1916); Houston v. State, 50 Fla. 90, 39 So. 468 (1905).

DESTROY (IMPEACHMENT)............................ REFERENCE

None

CROSS-EXAMINATION TOPICAL PAGE

WITNESS: DR. JOSEPH BURTON

ARGUMENT: Kimberly Diane Leach's death resulted from a homicide.

FACT	REFERENCE
(1) Give hypothetical situation......	—
(2) Based on hypothetical, can rule out accident.	Deposition
(3) Based on hypothetical, can rule out suicide	Deposition
(4) Based on hypothetical, can rule out natural causes	Deposition
(5) Based on hypothetical, cannot rule out homicide.	Deposition
(6) Agree with State's medical examiner that it's a homicide........	Logical inference

Having thus mapped out their strategy for the cross-examination of Dr. Burton, all that was left to do was to execute it. The relevant portion of the cross-examination went like this.

> Q: Assuming only what has been represented to you * * * what would have been your * * * opinion as to the cause of death?
>
> A: Well, this again plays upon one's experience and background [lengthy, marginally relevant exposition omitted] the cause of death was probable violent cause of death, the exact nature could not be determined.
>
> Q: * * * And based solely on what is before you at this point in time, you can * * * rule out natural causes * * *?
>
> A: Natural death would be way down on the list.
>
> Q: All right. And what about suicide?
>
> A: Suicide, in this age group is rare * * *. The circumstances * * * would make suicide * * * far down on the list of probabilities.
>
> Q: I am going to ask you a hypothetical. [Gives extensive statement of facts] what would be your opinion as to cause of death?

A: Well, again, I would be very careful about giving a precise opinion as to specific cause of death.

Q: * * * Could you * * * rule out suicide?

A: I think, within a degree of probability, we could rule it out, yes, sir.

Q: And you have already ruled out [natural causes]?

A: As a probability, yes, sir.

Q: * * * And again * * * could you also rule out * * * accidental death?

A: I think an accident would be a little more difficult to rule out. It would not be the first thing that would come to one's mind, however.

Q: [What's the first thing]?

A: Given the situation as you depicted it, the first thing that would come to mind would be that of a homicide.

Q: * * * Dr. Lipkovic determined * * * the cause of death was homicidal violence, type undetermined * * * Do you have any disagreement with the cause of death?

A: Just plain homicidal violence?

Q: Yes, sir.

A: And no other specifics than that?

Q: Yes, sir?

A: As a specific diagnosis, I would not use that terminology. Having feelings what he is saying, I would probably not disagree with it, no sir.

Q: You would not disagree with that diagnosis?

A: Well, I would disagree with it as a * * * diagnosis * * *, *but not as an opinion based on his experience.* [Emphasis supplied].

Imprecision in the use of terms hampered the effectiveness of the cross. The examiner blurred the distinction between manner of death and cause of death. For example, cause of death can be gunshot wound, but the manner of the infliction of the gunshot wound can be either accidental, suicidal, or homicidal. By conflating the two terms, the examiner had to work much harder to achieve the objective. Every time the examiner said "cause of death" rather than "manner of death" the witness blunted the persuasiveness of the answer by parsing terms. By stating his questions more precisely, the examiner could have been much more concise and forceful.

8. CONSTRUCTIVE CROSS-EXAMINATION, AGREEMENT, AND DISCLOSURE

The examiner in the previous example could have strengthened the cross-examination in another way. He structured his questioning in the customary format. He made a suggestion based upon a presupposed agreement, expecting the witness to adopt the presupposed agreement and make the anticipated disclosure. The key question was:

> Q: Assuming only what has been represented to you [delineates suggested, presupposed facts] * * * what would have been * * * your opinion as to the cause of death? [prescribes a presumed field of responses, leaving disclosure to witness].

The form of the question called upon the witness to make the disclosure, and he did so in a lengthy answer which watered down the impact of the admission. If you are wringing vital admissions from the witness, you want to do so in the clearest, most dramatic fashion possible. Leaving disclosure in the control of the witness does not ensure dramatic, persuasive disclosure. Leaving disclosure in the control of an unfriendly, or even hostile, witness almost ensures that the witness will find some way to neutralize the disclosure. Constructive cross-examination should reverse the customary direction of questioning. It should work from disclosure to agreement. Make the disclosure and call upon the witness to agree. Construct your question so that your question's presupposition is the only option in the presumed field of answers.

> Typical question: Q: What color was the car? [Presupposed fact: the car had color. Presumed field of answers: any imaginable color].

> Constructive cross question: Q: The car was red, wasn't it? [Presupposed fact: the car was red. Presumed field of answers: yes].

When you presuppose a fact in the question and virtually demand that the witness agree, you had better be right. If the witness disagrees, the jury has to decide whom to believe. If they choose to believe the witness, you have moved your case toward an unfavorable verdict. In constructive cross, you must bet on a sure thing. The presupposed fact must be indisputably and undeniably true—a gimmie. In order for a fact to be a true gimmie, if the witness disagrees, she must be vulnerable to retribution through impeachment by prior inconsistent statement, contradiction by undeniable fact, or exposure of the illogic inherent in the denial. The acronym R.I.C.E. will help you remember this. Refusal to admit the presupposed fact exposes the witness to retribution in the form of impeachment, contradiction, or exposure of illogic. Sometimes the mere voicing of the disagreement results in self-executing retribution, as where it is patently illogical or where the disagreement contradicts the testimony of unimpeachable witnesses who have previously testified. In other situations, you will have to work to mete out retribution.

D. STONEWALL TECHNIQUES

When faced with the prospect of admitting an unfavorable fact or disagreeing with it and suffering punishment, many witnesses will attempt to break the horns of their dilemma by stonewalling. When this happens you must penetrate the stonewall. If you properly design your constructive cross-examination the witness can keep you from proving your facts only at the expense of her credibility. You may allow her to sidetrack you, but if you resolutely persevere, you will make your points and lay the foundation for a telling final argument. We will now look at the standard stonewall techniques and then describe available countermeasures for each of them. Other countermeasures may be recommended in various trial advocacy manuals, such as asking the judge to direct the witness to answer the question, entering into a "yes or no" contract with the witness, and other such methods. Asking the judge for help tells the jury that you are too inept to handle the witness by yourself. Entering into a yes or no contract can make you appear overbearing, especially when you follow the contract up with a loaded question or a question which cannot be answered yes or no.

> Q: I'm going to ask you questions which need only be answered yes or no. Will you agree to answer them yes or no?
>
> Q: Are you ashamed that you stole so much money?
>
> Q: Has your electro-shock treatment helped with your problems of bed wetting and fire setting?
>
> Q: Do you still use powdered cocaine, or have you graduated to crack?

When the witness refuses to cooperate and does not give you the answers you want to these questions, you then follow up with:

> BY THE PROSECUTOR: Your Honor, I'd like for you to order the witness to give responsive answers to my questions.
>
> BY THE COURT: Counselor, I'd like for you to ask the witness fair questions.

The countermeasures described below have only to do with the structure of the questions which you ask. If you structure your questions properly, you need not engage in such obvious attempts to control the witness because the questions themselves demand compliance of the witness.

1. DENIAL

The three standard stonewall techniques are denial, diversion, and disguise. Diversion, disguise—and some forms of denial—seek to prevent your proof by distracting your attention from the main point in issue and sending you down lines of inquiry that the witness finds more congenial. Of the three techniques, denial should prove the most ineffective. Remember, on topical cross-examination, you ask only for gimmie's, and gimmie's are facts which the witness can deny only at the expense of her credibility. Denial comes in three types: complete, virtual, and selective.

a. Complete Denial

Complete denial is easily defeated. Remember the acronym R.I.C.E. R. Mete out retribution to the witness; I. Impeach her by prior inconsistent statement; or C. Contradict her with unimpeachable disagreement; or E. Expose the illogic inherent in the denial.

b. Virtual Denial

Most witnesses will be too astute to completely deny the gimmie. They will become creative with their denials, trying to mask the gimmie they find so distasteful. They oftentimes pretend to deny the gimmie through the ploy of virtual denial. In virtual denial the witness takes advantage of a partial inaccuracy in the question's presupposition. Seizing upon this incorrect datum, the witness denies the question in toto. For example:

Q: You went inside and loaded your gun?

A: I didn't go inside and load it.

Here the witness seeks to pull the trick of confounding the questioner by denying the entire question with the mental reservation that, although he went inside and got his gun, it was already loaded. Many jurors will miss the fact that the main point in issue is the fact that he retreated from the conflict, armed himself, and returned to the fray. Many a questioner standing on the threshold of victory will allow this ploy to divert him from victory to defeat.

c. Selective Denial

In selective denial, the witness zeroes in on the part of the question he can safely deny and ignores the distasteful gimmie:

Q: You went inside and loaded your gun?

A: It wasn't my gun.

Here the witness completely ignores the important point and hopes that the questioner will be so discomfitted by the denial, he will forget to follow up. The jury sits there watching the examiner being defeated on question after question with selective denial, and they begin to get the impression that the examiner does not know what he's talking about. Although it is not fatal to your case if the jury thinks you are correct but incompetent, you are in trouble if they begin to think that you are not only incompetent, you are wrong.

2. DIVERSION

Diversion seeks to redirect the inquiry away from the examiner's chosen field of answers and send it down a pathway that the witness finds more congenial. It also comes in three types. They are: deflection, avoidance, and counterattack.

a. Deflection

In deflection, the examiner presupposes uncomfortable facts, and the witness seeks to redirect the inquiry into safer waters. In the following exchange the defendant seeks to redirect the inquiry from his actions to the actions of his victim.

Q: You went inside and loaded your gun?

A: He had slapped my wife and knocked me down with a billy club!

Oftentimes the examiner will allow himself to be thrown off the scent by this simple tactic. He will breeze right past the answer, never realizing that the witness has admitted nothing, and snuck in a self-serving editorial comment. Worse yet, the examiner will take the bait and follow the witness down the false trail the witness has laid.

Q: You went inside and loaded your gun?

A: He had slapped my wife and knocked me down with a billy club!

Q: He only slapped her after she called him a bully, didn't he?

A: She only called him a bully after he grabbed her by the collar and shook her.

Q: He only grabbed her by the collar and shook her after she called him a redneck?

A: She only called him a redneck after he spit tobacco juice on the floor of her kitchen.

By this point the witness has successfully diverted everyone's attention away from the shooting death of the victim to the victim's boorish behavior.

b. Avoidance

In avoidance, the witness either ignores the question asked, and answers the question he wishes he had been asked, or he reinterprets the question so as to call for a helpful answer:

Q: You went inside and loaded your gun?

A: I was so afraid of him that I felt I had to do something to protect my wife.

The same dangers lurk in avoidance as in deflection. Either the examiner will move on to the next question without realizing that the witness has avoided the admission or the examiner will follow the witness down the false trail.

c. Counterattack

The final diversionary tactic is counterattack. The witness turns on the questioner and tries to savage him with a withering retort.

Q: You went inside and loaded your gun?

A: What would you have done if he'd slapped your wife and hit you with a billy club?

The witness seeks to lure the questioner into a tit-for-tat exchange on a battleground where he thinks he can win. In dealing with counterattack, remember the proverb, "Do not answer fools according to their folly, or you will be a fool yourself."[9] Engaging in tit-for-tat with the witness will make you look petty. Losing the tit-for-tat will make you look foolish. It can also sometimes result in you (or another prosecutor) getting to try the case again. In *Gore v. State*,[10] a prosecutor cross-examining a murder defendant allowed a counterattack defense to derail the conviction.

> Apparently because the same prosecutor had previously been involved in prosecuting him, [during cross-examination] Gore "questioned" the prosecutor as to whether the prosecutor had a vendetta against him, and why the prosecutor continued to prosecute cases against him. The prosecutor responded:
>
> > *Because I don't like people who kill women. How's that? You want to know why? Because I don't like people preying on women.* [Emphasis original].
>
> Later in the cross-examination, Gore challenged the prosecutor to take the stand, to which the prosecutor responded:

[9] Proverbs 26:4 (NRSV).

[10] 719 So.2d 1197 (Fla. 1998).

I didn't kill three women, you did.[11] *You see, Mr. Gore, you killed women. That's why you're on the stand.* [Emphasis original].

A. And you're trying to kill me.

Q. I didn't kill anyone.

A. But you're trying to kill me.

Q. *Well, you know what, you're right, I am, because somebody who does what you do deserves to die.* [Emphasis original].

Clearly, it was improper for the prosecutor to express his personal belief about Gore's guilt. [Citations omitted]. To be sure, Gore himself was antagonistic during the questioning, but the conduct on the part of the defendant should not have given rise to this "tit-for-tat" exchange between prosecutor and defendant.[12]

Needless to say, the Florida Supreme Court was not amused by this and other exchanges between the prosecutor and the defendant, and another prosecutor inherited the job of retrying the case.[13] The moral is clear, do not let the witness bait you into a battle of insults or one-liners, you have little to gain and everything to lose.

3. DISGUISE

In the third stonewall technique, disguise, the witness seeks to camouflage the gimmie in one of three ways: explanation, qualification, or obfuscation.

a. Explanation

In explanation, the witness seeks to drown out the uncomfortable admission by accompanying it with some self-serving or irrelevant static:

Q: You went inside and loaded your gun?

A: I had to because that vicious bully had slapped my wife, hit me with a billy club, and threatened to kill me.

b. Qualification

In qualification, the witness seeks to soften the blow of the admission by qualifying it or mitigating it in some way:

Q: You went inside and loaded your gun?

---

[11] Besides being highly improper, this comment by the prosecutor was also misleading. There was no evidence in the record that Gore killed three women. [Footnote by the court].

[12] 719 So.2d at 1201.

[13] Gore v. State, 784 So.2d 418 (Fla. 2001).

A: The shotgun was just inside the door, all I had to do was step inside and grab it.

c. Obfuscation

Obfuscation seeks simply to drown the admission in a sea of irrelevant static:

Q: You went inside and loaded your gun?

A: It wasn't very far down the hall to the bedroom, you know how small single-wide trailers are, and my gun is propped right there by the door for self-defense purposes, so when I staggered back down the hall to get a washcloth to put on my head, I saw the shotgun there and just grabbed it up. There were some shells on the bureau right there by the shotgun—I like to hunt dove, so they were birdshot—so I picked up the shotshell and dropped it in the breech. The gun is an old single-shot twelve gauge that my daddy gave me before he died from cancer last year.

The witness hopes that all the extra verbiage will camouflage the fact that he has admitted to arming himself and loading his gun. By the logic of questions and answers, the obfuscator has admitted the gimmie. You may have proven your point with the obfuscator, but the jury may miss it. Technical proof does not equate to persuasive proof. You must prove the point persuasively.

d. Caveat on Disguise

Explanation, qualification, and obfuscation are not necessarily stonewall techniques. They can be employed by honest-but-talkative witnesses, arrogant witnesses who seek to elucidate their erudition, and timid witnesses who fear that you will cross-examine them unfairly. The stonewall countermeasures set forth below work just as well for these witnesses as for the evasive witness, but your demeanor while employing them with non-evasive witnesses should be one of patience. With evasive witnesses, once you are satisfied that the jury has realized the witness's lack of candor, you may adopt a demeanor of irritation, impatience, or even scorn.

E. STONEWALL COUNTERMEASURES

You must not get thrown off the scent. You must penetrate the stonewall and get at the gimmie. You cannot force the witness to admit the gimmie, but you can force her to confront it. If she confronts it without admitting it, then you win. If she steadfastly refuses to confront it no matter how hard you try, then you win. You must avoid the distraction, isolate the gimmie, and make the witness confront it. You cannot make the witness admit the gimmie, but she can make herself look bad if she denies the gimmie. In order to accomplish this, you must ask the question in such a way as to make it painfully apparent that she is stonewalling. You must be fair, independent, resolute, and effective. You are fair when you ask proper questions politely. Many stonewall techniques are rightfully employed by witnesses who have been asked unfair, impolite questions. For example, the stonewall technique of explanation serves quite well in answering this unfair question:

Q: What were you thinking when you stole the car?

A: I wasn't thinking anything because I didn't steal the car.

You should be independent by asking the witness for an answer and not asking the judge for help. There is nothing more pitiful than a lawyer asking a judge to make the big, bad witness answer the question, unless it is a lawyer who just had the judge refuse his plea for help. You should be resolute by insisting on an answer to your question, and you must continue insisting on an answer until you get it or until it is obvious that the witness will never give it. To be effective, you must shoot the right bullets. Fragile cannonballs contributed to the defeat of the Invincible Armada. They shattered against the hard sides of the English ships instead of penetrating them. Your bullets must be strong enough to knock holes in the stonewall without being flattened themselves. Of course, you shoot bullets in the form of questions. Just as there are a multitude of different bullet types, there are a multitude of question types. Some are effective, some are not. The effectiveness of your bullets depends upon the length, structure, and content of your questions. We will look at just four types of questions and assess them for effectiveness in penetrating the stonewall.

1. OPEN-ENDED QUESTIONS

Open-ended questions have the virtue of eliciting information, but they completely surrender control to the witness. The questioner simply asks an interrogative question and sits back awaiting the favorable answer that seldom comes. When you give the witness free rein, she can editorialize on any subject she wants to.

Q: How did he come to be shot?

A: At an early age he became a bully, constantly beating people up and taking their lunch money away. As he grew older, he continued his violent ways until he was one of the most feared street fighters in the county. After he earned his black belt in Brazilian jujitsu and won the local Golden Gloves tournament in the heavyweight class, he began looking for fights wherever he could find them. His wicked, sinful aggression finally came to an end when he slapped my wife, beat me down with a billy club, and forced me to shoot him in self-defense.

Open-ended questions can be just fine with a candid, nonpartisan witness. If, however, you confront a hostile witness who has enough wit to understand where you are headed with your questioning, she will never let you get there with open-ended questions. You must close your questions as much as possible. Prescribe a narrow field of answers.

2. LONG LEADING QUESTIONS

Lawyers have a great propensity for asking long questions. We have it bred into us from years of higher education, and it is anathema to clear communication.

> Q: Isn't it a fact that, acting with malice aforethought, and with total disregard for the safety of others, you purposely engaged in a series of acts by which you intended to cause the death of the victim, and that series of acts consisted of searching for your weapon, inspecting it to determine whether it was loaded, and loading it?
>
> A: I didn't have malice aforethought, I wasn't disregarding the safety of others, and I didn't intend to kill or hurt anyone. I simply did what I had to do in order to defend myself.

Long leading questions attempt to exert control over the witness, but they lose it by inviting long narrative answers and disagreement in the form of virtual or selective denial.

3. SHORT LEADING QUESTIONS

Long leading questions presuppose multiple facts, each of which serves as an opportunity for the witness to frustrate your effort with virtual or selective denial. The shorter the question, the fewer the facts that can be shoe horned into it. Ideally, the short leading question asks for one fact and one fact only. Short leading questions give you far better ammunition to shoot.

> Q: Did you go for your gun?

The questioner asks a short question which calls for a short answer. Short leading questions exert control and steer the witness toward the desired answer. The normal question form, however, does not exert as much control as you might desire or need. The normal form for a question is auxiliary verb, noun, verb. "Do you like Kipling?" The examiner presupposes that the witness has an opinion on Kipling, but gives the witness the option as to how to answer. On cross-examination to gimmie's, the examiner presupposes a "yes" answer. The context of the question calls for a "yes," but the form of the question does not. In order to be persuasive, not only the context, but the form of the question must call for a "yes." Structure your short leading questions by making a short declarative statement followed by a tag question. A tag question is a phrase added at the end of a declarative sentence to give it the form of a question. For example:

Q: It is hot, [declarative statement] isn't it? [Tag question].

Q: You are fat, [declarative statement] aren't you? [Tag question].

Q: You shot him, [declarative statement] didn't you? [Tag question].

Now, if the question calls for a gimmie, not only the context but the structure of the question demands a "yes" answer. Some examiners add to the compulsion of this form of question by beginning the declarative statement with an intensifier:

Q: It's a fact that [intensifier] you shot him, [declarative statement] isn't it? [Tag question].

The intensifier is not at all necessary, and far from intensifying the question, it can make you look overbearing. Remember, the question calls for a gimmie—a fact known to be true and which an honest witness must admit. Asking for a gimmie demands agreement without the use of intensifiers. Do not use the intensifier unless the witness stonewalls the short leading question.

Q: You shot him, didn't you?

A: He was threatening me and he stole my bong.

Q: It's a fact that you shot him, isn't it?

In this situation the extra compulsion does not appear overbearing because it comes on the heels of the witness engaging in a deflection maneuver.

4. SHORT STATEMENTS

Used properly, tag questions and intensifiers can be powerful tools, but you can form your questions even more powerfully. Dispense with both intensifier and tag question, make the declarative statement, and wait for the witness to agree. End your statement with a period. The court reporter will supply the question mark when he types the transcript.

Q: You went for your gun.

Such a format demands a short answer, and the answer is yes. It exerts maximum control without appearing overbearing. The jury recognizes the statement as demanding a gimmie response, and the witness will disappoint them with anything less than "yes." Tone of voice is essential with short statements. You must be matter of fact. The structure of the question, not the tone of your voice, must demand the agreement.

"Wait a minute," you say, "That's not a question. You can't testify on cross-examination, all you can do is ask questions." Objection overruled.

Grammarians will explain that the short statement is actually an elliptical question in which the tag question ("didn't you?" or "right?") is understood. In cross-examination a "short statement" is really a short leading question on steroids. Now that you are properly equipped with the appropriate ammunition to defeat the stonewall countermeasures, you should make sure that you use the ammunition wisely. You do not shoot quail with a howitzer, and you do not shoot elephants with a pellet gun. Use the least demanding form of the question that the witness will allow. With a cooperative witness, begin asking questions in traditional question format. After you get a rhythm of agreement, you can transition straight to short statements without appearing overbearing. With the slightly less cooperative witness, begin with the tag question format and transition to the intensifier if necessary. After establishing the rhythm of the questioning, go to the short statement format. Using this protocol for shooting your ammunition, you can defeat stonewalling before it starts. When a witness stonewalls long leading questions, the stonewall technique can go unnoticed; but when a witness stonewalls short leading questions, the jury immediately realizes the witness's lack of candor. Now let us look at how to defeat the stonewall techniques if short questions cannot prevent them.

5. COUNTERMEASURES FOR VIRTUAL DENIAL

In virtual denial the witness seeks to defeat the question by denying all the presuppositions in one fell swoop.

Q: You went inside and loaded your gun?

A: I didn't go inside and load it.

As short as this question is, it facilitates virtual denial by asking for three simple facts. (1) going inside, (2) getting the gun, and (3) loading the gun. The better way would have been to prevent virtual denial by asking three questions, one fact at a time, but all is not lost. It is not too late to break the question down into its three component parts and ask them one at a time.

Q: You went inside?

Q: You got your gun?

Q: You loaded your gun?

After going through the three components, move on to your next point, being careful to ask for one fact at a time.

6. COUNTERMEASURES FOR SELECTIVE DENIAL

In selective denial, the witness steadfastly refutes the portion of the question she does not like and ignores the rest.

Q: You went inside and loaded your gun?

A: I didn't load it.

This is somewhat less dishonest than virtual denial, and the questioner does not have to work as hard to make his point. Logicians call selective denial a "negative pregnant." A "negative pregnant," by denying part of a question, implicitly admits the rest. Since few juries have logicians in their ranks, you must make the implicit admission an explicit one:

Q: You went inside and loaded your gun?

A: I didn't load it.

Q: You went inside and got your gun?

A: Yes.

Q: It was already loaded?

A: Yes.

An honest witness will use selective denial to correct faulty presuppositions. When an honest witness does this, however, she explicitly admits the gimmie while denying the faulty presupposition.

Q: You went inside and loaded your gun.

A: I went inside and got my gun, but I didn't load it.

When the witness uses this form of selective denial, you need take no countermeasures. You simply need to be more careful in framing your questions.

Notice that selective denial is a stonewall technique only if you ask a question containing fair presuppositions. If you presuppose too much, selective denial serves as a corrective to the objectionable presuppositions in the question.

Q: You laid in wait for him and shot him, didn't you?

A: I didn't lay in wait for him, but I did shoot him in self-defense.

7. COUNTERMEASURES FOR DIVERSION

The three subtypes of diversion (deflection; avoidance; counterattack) seek the same end, to distract the jury from the gimmie sought by the questioner. Any one of them may be countered by the same method:

Q: You went inside and loaded your gun?

A: I was so afraid of him that I felt I had to do something to protect my wife. [Avoidance].

A: He had slapped my wife and knocked me down with a billy club! [Deflection].

A: What would you have done if somebody slapped your wife and hit you with a billy club? [Counterattack].

Q: You went inside and loaded your gun? [The witness has not answered the question. Because the question has not been answered, you may ask it again. If you meet an "asked and answered" objection, your reply is "asked, but not answered."]

Short questions demand short answers. Long answers to short questions look like excuses.

8. COUNTERMEASURES FOR DISGUISE

The three subtypes of disguise are perhaps the least dishonest stonewall techniques. As we previously noted, explanation and qualification sometimes serve as a necessary defense to unfair questions. Overly talkative witnesses can obfuscate without consciously trying to obstruct the flow of information. You must ask brief, fair questions to ensure that if you come upon explanation, qualification, or obfuscation, they are genuine stonewall techniques. When witnesses deploy them as stonewall techniques, you can handle them all in much the same way:

Q: You went inside and loaded your gun?

A: I had to because that vicious bully had slapped my wife, hit me with a billy club, and threatened to kill me. [Explanation].

A: The shotgun was just inside the door, all I had to do was step inside and grab it. [Qualification].

A: It wasn't very far down the hall to the bedroom, you know how small single-wide trailers are, and my gun is propped right there by the door for self-defense purposes, so when I staggered back down the hall to get a washcloth to put on my head, I saw the shotgun there and just grabbed it up. There were some shells on the bureau right there by the shotgun—I like to hunt dove, so they were birdshot—so I picked up the shotshell and dropped it in the breech. The gun is an old single-shot twelve gauge that my daddy gave me before he died from cancer last year. [Obfuscation].

You could simply reask the question, but it would be better to break it down into its component parts and ask each component separately. The simpler the action called for, the less explanation needed.

Q: You went inside?

Q: You got your gun?

Q: You loaded it?

F. THE HOSTILE WITNESS DIRECT

Hostile witnesses sometimes make use of the stonewall techniques on direct examination. The rules and methods set forth for constructive cross-examination serve admirably for dealing with uncooperative witnesses on direct examination. In the following transcript this sexually violent predator respondent[14]—who was called as the state's first witness—employs several of the nine stonewall techniques. They are identified in the brackets. You may judge for yourself how successful the prosecutor was in employing the stonewall countermeasures.

Q: Your name is Roger Cannon?

A: Yes, it is.

Q: You were convicted in Tift County District Court, Case Number 13043, for child molestation back in—

A: I don't remember back that far, sir. I served all my time on that charge. That's been eighteen, twenty years ago. [Avoidance].

Q: All right, sir. If you'd please listen to the question and let me finish the question, and then you can answer it. All right? You were convicted in Tift County District Court of child molestation back in 1974, were you not?

A: Yes.

Q: I want to show you what's been marked State's Exhibit for Identification, Number 1. And copies have been provided to your attorney. That is a certified copy of your conviction; is it not?

A: Did you say this was Tifton, Georgia?

Q: No, sir. This is a certified copy of your conviction, is it not?

A: I've never saw it before but I'd say that's it.

[State's Exhibit 1 accepted into evidence].

Q: Now, the victim of that case was a young lady whose initials were V.G.?

A: To the best of my recollection, yes, sir.

Q: And you took off your clothes in her presence?

A: That's all a matter of record. [Avoidance].

Q: You took off your clothes in her presence; is that correct?

[14] Several states now have laws providing for commitment of sexually violent predators. These proceedings are conducted under the rules of civil procedure, and the defendant/respondent has no blanket right against self-incrimination. These proceedings seek to involuntarily commit and treat sex offenders posing a threat of recidivism.

A: It's all a matter of record. I don't remember. I can't go back through all of that after twenty years and tell you how it all went.

Q: You were intoxicated at the time this offense occurred. Can you remember that?

A: That's yes.

Q: And you were convicted in Federal court in 1984 of kidnaping; were you not?

A: Yes.

Q: I'm going to show you what's been marked State's Exhibit for Identification Number 2. That's a certified copy—

A: I never saw that before but I guess that's it. [Exhibit received into evidence].

Q: And the victim in that case was a young lady whose initials were W.A.W.; is that correct?

A: Yes.

Q: She was eight years old at the time, is that correct?

A: Yes.

Q: You arranged to take her for the day, did you not?

THE WITNESS: Your Honor, do we have to go back over this, all that? That's eighteen or more years ago and I can't—[A benign form of counterattack. The witness is imputing unfairness to the prosecutor].

THE COURT: Yes, you do. He has that right and you'll go forward.

THE WITNESS: That was—I was—the charges are right. The basics—well, going back into memory after twenty years is cloudy.

Q: You arranged to take her for the day, did you not?

A: Yes, I had her just about every day. [Explanation].

Q: Instead of taking her back at the end of the day, you took her to your home in Camden City, did you not?

A: No, not to my home in Camden City. I took her to Camden City. [Selective denial].

Q: You took her to Camden City?

A: Yes.

Q: And you kept her there in Camden City for six weeks, did you not?

A: Yes, sir.

Q: And during that time you [committed a specific sexual act upon the victim]; did you not?

A: No. [Complete denial. To be impeached by prior inconsistent statement. The prosecutor next lays the predicate for the impeachment].

Q: That never happened?

A: No, and that's not on record, either.

Q: Did you not tell Dr. Sigmund Freud in your—when he came to you and examined you at the prison that you [committed a specific sexual act upon the victim]?

A: No, I did not. [Another complete denial. To be impeached by Dr. Freud's testimony].

Q: Never told Dr. Freud that?

A: No, sir.

Q: That never happened?

A: No, sir.

Q: Now you were also prosecuted in Camden County for lewd assault on a child whose initials were W.A.W.; were you not?

A: Yes.

Q: And you were convicted in Camden County in circuit court of two counts of lewd assault on W.A.W.; were you not?

A: Yes.

Q: I show you what's been marked State's Exhibit for Identification Number 3, which is a certified copy of your conviction in that case, is it not?

A: Yes, sir, that's correct, and that's been eighteen years ago and I also served all my time for that. [Qualification].

[Exhibit received in evidence].

Q: Now, you were also convicted in Bryson County Circuit Court of attempted lewd assault on a child; were you not?

A: Yes, sir.

Q: And the victim in that case was a young lady whose initials were K.S.M.; is that correct?

A: Yes.

Q: I'm going to show you what's been marked for identification as State's Exhibit 4, and this is a—this is a certified copy of your conviction in that case, is it not?

A: Yes.

[Exhibit received in evidence].

Q: Now you were out on pretrial release in that Bryson County case for a period of time, were you not?

A: No. The time difference I don't remember. That's been a long time ago. [Avoidance].

[The prosecutor then established that the Respondent was receiving sex offender treatment during his pretrial release and dropped out of therapy].

Q: And you dropped out of that program; did you not?

A: Yes.

Q: Dr. Goode asked you to come back into treatment; didn't he?

A: He asked me if I was coming back. [Qualification].

Q: All right, sir. Let's see if we've got this straight. You saw Dr. Goode in court.

A: Yes.

Q: He asked you to come back?

A: Yes.

Q: You told him you would?

A: Not exactly, no. [Virtual denial].

Q: You led him to believe you would? [Taking what the witness will give, which is enough to impeach the previous answer].

A: Yes, I guess I did.

Q: And the fact is, you didn't go back into treatment?

A: Yes.

Q: Instead, you went to Georgia?

A: I don't recall. That's been a long time ago, but if that's where I went it's on the record. [Avoidance].

Q: And you took W.A.W., and that was when you assaulted her, was it not, after promising to go back into treatment?

A: I went—I don't know the sequence of when I went back up there. That's been so long ago. [Avoidance. The prosecutor has left off punishing the witness for denying the gimmie's because he believes the witness has so damaged his credibility at this point that no further punishment is necessary].

THE PROSECUTOR: I don't have any other questions.

On constructive cross-examination—cross-examination to gimmie's—you do not have to destroy the witness. The witness either gives you what you want or destroys himself by refusing to admit the obvious. The old saw that "Cross-examination is more often suicidal than homicidal" applies in full force here. You do not want or need to murder a witness who is committing suicide. All you have to do is emulate good Dr. Kevorkian and gently assist the suicide. The stonewall countermeasures serve admirably for this purpose.

PRACTICAL EXERCISE

The cross-examination of Doctor Burton quoted above was quite serviceable, but it could have been conducted much more crisply. Using the cross-examination worksheet and topical page set forth in the text above, draft a series of short questions compelling the witness toward the opinion that the manner of death was homicidal, beginning with the following hypothetical:

> BY THE PROSECUTOR: Doctor, for the purpose of the following series of questions, assume these facts: a twelve-year-old girl disappears from school on the day she was supposed to go with her mother to buy a ballgown for the Valentine Dance, and her partially clothed body is found two months later in a wooded area in another county. The findings at the crime scene and the autopsy results for the body are identical with the findings and autopsy results for Kimberly Diane Leach.

Make the questions as short as possible and as few in number as possible. Should they be leading or open ended? Should you use the interrogative, tag question, or short statement format? Why or why not?

CHAPTER 13

DESTRUCTIVE CROSS-EXAMINATION

■ ■ ■

If it be intended to bring the credit of a witness into question by proof of anything he may have said or declared touching the cause, the witness is first asked, upon cross-examination, whether or not he has said or declared that which is intended to be proved.—The Rule in Queen Caroline's Case[1]

A. REACTIVE CROSS-EXAMINATION

Whenever you cross-examine toward the objective of destruction, you engage in what the National College of District Attorneys calls "reactive" cross-examination. The witness has said something harmful, and you react by attempting to destroy the witness's credibility. If destroyer mode is not the prototype for cross-examination, it is certainly the stereotype. You instinctively want to destroy on cross-examination. When you go into destroyer mode, you have one of three targets:

(1) Discrediting the theory.

(2) Discrediting the testimony.

(3) Discrediting the testifier.

1. DISCREDITING THE THEORY

Either by design or default, every advocate presents a case theory—an interpretation of the facts—to the fact finder. It should succinctly, powerfully state the case, make sense of the evidence, and impel the jury toward a favorable verdict. Some theories do. Some do not. When your adversary presents a plausible theory, you must do something about it. You can make one of three attacks against the opposing theory. You can: (1) Produce confusion, or (2) Prevent confusion, or (3) Promote clarity. ***Producing confusion.*** When confronted with a clear, convincing, compelling theory, the advocate can fall back on the old standby, confusion. Sow enough confusion and that compelling theory no longer looks so clear or convincing. Confusion, however, seldom works to the advantage of the prosecution. It promotes doubt, and doubt forms half of the legal term "reasonable doubt." Prosecutors should confront the objective of producing

---

[1] 2 BR. & B. 284, 129 Eng.Rep. 976 (1820), quoted in State v. Martin, 964 S.W.2d 564, 566–567 (Tenn. 1998).

confusion, not use it. ***Preventing confusion.*** If you fight on the side of the angels, you should be able to present a compelling theory. The defense will respond by calling witnesses to sow confusion in an effort to sell a reasonable doubt theory. You then must prevent or contain the confusion sown by these witnesses. Questioning of the witnesses will consequently aim at restoring order to the chaos created by the defense witnesses' testimony. ***Promoting clarity.*** If you are right, and your theory is just, the defense will most likely present a reasonable doubt theory. Sometimes, however, they will present a competing theory. If you are right and they are wrong, they must present a flawed theory. It may be plausible on the surface, but it must crumble on critical analysis. When your adversary presents witnesses to support such a competing theory, you must clarify. You must ask questions designed to expose the flaws in the competing theory.

2. DISCREDITING THE TESTIMONY

You discredit the witness's testimony by attacking the three A's: (1) Ability to observe, (2) Attentiveness, and (3) Ability to remember. When you attack the witness's testimony through use of the three A's, you can engage in a relatively friendly cross without becoming confrontational. She may climb down from the witness stand thinking warm thoughts about your kindness but thoroughly devastated in the eyes of the jury. When you attack the witness herself, you must prepare for unpleasantries. In questioning a witness's ability to observe, you question her about where she was, how far away she was, what the lighting was, whether she could hear what was being said, any defects in her sight or hearing, and any other matters that you know of which might impair her ability to see, hear, and understand the transaction. When you go after her attentiveness, you point out all the factors which might have distracted her from really paying attention to the event. What she was doing at the time, where her attention was focused, what importance she attached to the things she saw or heard. When you attack the witness's ability to remember, you bring out facts that will cause a jury to question the witness's recollection. In a DUI case, quite frequently the defense witnesses drank as much as the defendant himself. The degree of intoxication of the defense witness then becomes fair game for inquiry. What was the nature of the intoxicant they consumed, the amount of the intoxicant they consumed, the period of time over which they had consumed it, the effect of the intoxicant on the witnesses' memory? Even if the witnesses deny that the intoxicant affected them, you have still laid the groundwork for final argument. "Ladies and gentlemen of the jury, the defense witnesses want you to believe that the six cases of beer they drank had no effect whatsoever on their ability to observe and remember. The last person on earth to know that somebody's drunk is the drunk himself. They say they were fine, but common sense tells us otherwise."

a. The Almanac Trial

Abraham Lincoln did a legendary cross-examination to ability to observe in 1858, when William "Duff" Armstrong stood trial in the Circuit Court of Illinois for the murder of James Metzker. According to the legend of the cross-examination, Charles Allen, the State's star witness, testified on direct examination that he had seen Armstrong strike Metzker in the eye with a slungshot.[2] Allan's testimony was open to question because he made his observation at 11:00pm, from more than 50 feet away, through a stand of trees. On cross Lincoln attacked Allen's ability to observe. Allen insisted he was able to see quite well from the light of the brightly shining moon high overhead. Lincoln proceeded to cross-examine Allen from an almanac which stated that on the night in question, the moon sat on the horizon at the hour of the fight. The courtroom exploded into laughter and the jury acquitted Armstrong.[3] In some versions of the story, Allan broke down and confessed on the stand that he was the murderer. The most famous version of the cross is the examination portrayed by Henry Fonda in the 1939 John Ford movie, *Young Mr. Lincoln.* The story is an example of the "commit and contradict" tactic for cross-examination. You get the witness to commit to a fact, and then you confront the witness with irrefutable proof that the witness is wrong. The problem with almost all versions of the legendary cross is that Lincoln did not confront Allen with the almanac which showed he was wrong about the position of the moon.

What really happened was that Lincoln used a milder form of cross known as "commit and contradict." He did not confront Allen with the almanac, he waited until the defense case and had the judge take judicial notice of the almanac. Then he first used it on final argument and completely stunned the prosecution team.[4] The benefit of this tactic over "commit and confront" is that, a quick-thinking witness confronted with a contradiction can manufacture an explanation which takes the sting out of the confrontation. Waiting until after the witness has left the courtroom to spring the contradiction gives the witness no opportunity to explain or minimize the contradiction. "Commit and confront" can be more spectacular than "commit and contradict," but commit and contradict is safer.

b. The Cold and Rainy Day

Truthful witnesses often destroy their credibility by gilding the lily. They saw what they saw, but they want to fudge their testimony by

---

2 A slungshot, sometimes called a "slapjack," is a small striking weapon consisting of a heavy weight on the end of a strap or flexible handle.

3 Walsh, John Evangelist, Moonlight: Abraham Lincoln and the Almanac Trial, St. Martin's Press, New York, 2000.

4 George R. Dekle Sr. Prairie Defender: The Murder Trials of Abraham Lincoln. Carbondale, IL: Southern Illinois University Press, 2017. pp. 141–151.

claiming an enhanced ability to observe. When Theodore Robert Bundy stood trial for the kidnaping and murder of Lake City Junior High student Kimberly Diane Leach, the prosecution's opening statement began "It was a cold and rainy day. . . ." An elderly school crossing guard took the stand as one of the first witnesses and testified that he saw Bundy lurking around the grounds of the junior high the morning of the disappearance. He gave a credible account of what he saw and manfully withstood a vigorous marathon cross-examination. Defeated and dejected, the defense attorney tried to end on a positive note by cross-examining to a gimmie. He asked whether it was rainy and overcast that day. The guard responded that it was a bright, sunshiny day. Heartened, the defense attorney pursued a lengthy series of questions on the brightness of the sun, the beauty of the morning, the dryness of the air, the singing of the birds, the blooming of the flowers, and the total absence of rain gear on any of the students or teachers that day. The cross probably did not last nearly as long as it seemed to the prosecution team. When defense counsel sat down, the crossing guard left the courtroom completely oblivious to the fact that his credibility lay in tatters on the courtroom floor. In the Bundy case the destruction of the eyewitness required the witness's cooperation.

3. DISCREDITING THE TESTIFIER

You attack the witness herself by giving the jury one of the three D's. (1) Reason to distrust. (2) Reason to dislike. (3) Reason to disrespect. Here we have a clear application of Aristotle's rhetorical trinity. Remember that Aristotle said you persuade by appealing to ethos, pathos, and logos? Reasons to distrust appeal to logos; reasons to disrespect to ethos; and reasons to dislike to pathos. Aristotle taught that only logos was a legitimate tool of persuasion, and ever since his time, ethos and pathos have been logos' disreputable siblings. Modern law reflects Aristotle's teaching. Of the three D's, the law only recognizes distrust as a proper avenue of inquiry on cross-examination. Because the truth of the witness's testimony assumes paramount importance, you must certainly be allowed to explore all logically relevant areas where you might find valid reasons to distrust the witness. Dislike and disrespect are horses of a very different color indeed. No lawbook or case cite recognizes dislike for a witness as a legally sufficient reason to disbelieve that witness. The mere fact that you find someone to be reprehensible or ridiculous does not give you reason to disbelieve her. Dislike facilitates disbelief, but logic tells us that congeniality has nothing to do with credibility. Common sense tells us that if you dislike someone, you want to disbelieve that person. Conversely, if you like someone, you will overlook or ignore all kinds of valid reasons to disbelieve her. Many a defendant has sunk in the storm of a withering cross-examination only to emerge exonerated because the jury found him a likeable liar. To ensure disbelief, you need to give the jury a reason to dislike or disrespect the witness, but you must be subtle. That reason to dislike or disrespect must be admissible for some legally sufficient reason. Character assassination for the sake of assassinating character will only land you in hot water.

Circumspection is the watchword when you employ this type of cross-examination. Consider this case in which the defendant stood trial for murder. The prosecution introduced evidence of a collateral attempted murder as "similar fact evidence." It just so happened that during the collateral attempted murder, the defendant had kidnaped and attempted to murder the victim's two-year-old son. During pretrial proceedings the trial court had ruled evidence of the son's kidnaping inadmissible. On direct the defendant claimed to have fathered the boy. The cross of the defendant included the following exchange:[5]

> Q: Now, let's talk about your son Jimmy for a moment, who you say is your son?
>
> A: Yes. Tina says it too.
>
> Q: by the way, would you tell the ladies and gentlemen of the jury why on the 16th of March 1988, after leaving Tina on the side of the road, you left two-year-old, who you say is your son, Jimmy, locked in an abandoned house in Georgia, naked in 30-degree weather?

This question certainly gave the jury a reason to dislike the defendant. It also gave the Appellate court a reason to reverse the conviction. When you use the last two D's, you must join them firmly to the first. Even then, you must focus on the distrust twin rather than the dislike or disrespect twin. The scalpel is mightier than the meat axe. It is also safer. Fortunately, most reasons to dislike or disrespect also make good reasons to distrust. We shall now look at a few of those reasons.

a. Bias

If a witness dislikes someone on the other side, that witness might have a reason to lie. In the area of bias the fields are white unto harvest. The courts tend to find that just about anything, if counsel presents it artfully, can be evidence of bias. You must always remember, though, that most of the appellate cases finding irrelevant facts to be evidence of bias are cases reversing convictions for cutting off defense inquiry on cross. The playing field is not level; defense counsel can usually get away with murder, while prosecutors are restricted to involuntary manslaughter. If you intend to cross-examine a witness on some exotic form of bias, do your research and have your case law ready. If you expect one of your witnesses will be crossed on an exotic form of bias, do your research and make sure you are ready to oppose it with rock solid case authority.

---

[5] Gore v. State, 719 So.2d 1197, 1199 (Fla. 1998).

Traditional types of bias include: (1) Prejudice by a witness toward a particular group to which the victim or defendant belongs. (2) A special relationship between the witness and the victim or defendant. When you decide to cross in this area, you must do so artfully. You could simply ask the question:

Q: The defendant is your friend, isn't he?

Although this question meets all the requisites for a short leading question—declarative statement consisting of five words followed by a tag question—it is ineffective for two reasons. First, friendship is not so much a fact as a complex factual conclusion drawn from many smaller component facts. The witness can plausibly deny the question because she chooses to define friendship differently than the questioner. Second, merely using a single question to point out the witness's friendship with the defendant does not get the job done. The jury might pick that particular question as the time for their minds to wander and completely miss the point. In order to deprive the witness of plausible deniability and ensure that you drive the point home to the jury, you must craft a series of questions eliciting each component fact which lends credence to the conclusion of friendship and accentuates the closeness of the relationship and the strength of the motive to help the defendant.

Q: Ms. Barmaid, you have known the defendant Mr. Bacchus a long time, haven't you?

Q: You went to high school with him?

Q: You and he attend many of the same social functions?

Q: You have been a guest in his house?

Q: And he in yours?

Q: You consider him a friend?

Q: A good friend?

Q: A very good friend?

Q: You like him?

Q: You like him a lot?

Q: You wouldn't want to see anything bad happen to him, would you?

Q: Now given the length of your relationship, the closeness you feel toward him, and the desire you have that nothing bad happen to him, wouldn't you lie through your teeth to save him?

The last two questions in this series serve as examples of the infamous "one question too many" on cross-examination. If the witness is on her toes, she can craft embarrassing answers to either question. Save these last two questions to ask rhetorically in final argument. You will like the answers you supply yourself in final argument much better than the ones the witness is likely to give.

You can make your point powerfully by connecting your bias cross to voir dire for bias. In small jurisdictions, you frequently have people on the jury panel who know various protagonists in the trial. You ask these prospective jurors all the questions surrounding their knowledge of and friendship toward the protagonists on the opposing side, and they willingly detail their friendship but vow that it will have no influence on their verdict. Of course, they get challenged off the panel. When the witness whom you wish to attack as biased takes the stand, you ask the witness the same types of questions in the same wording. The jurors remember the excusing of their fellows who were asked those same questions, remember that their fellows were excused for bias, and decide that the witness must be biased also.

b. Illogic

Jurors do not like getting hoodwinked any more than anyone else. They do not pay any more attention to imbeciles than anyone else. If you can show the witness's testimony to be illogical, the jury will either dislike or disrespect the witness, and that will reinforce the jury's distrust of the witness. One way to take advantage of illogic is to employ the logical technique of *reductio ad absurdum*. Simply stated, *reductio ad absurdum* says "If A, then B. Not B, therefore not A." You ask yourself, if the witness's testimony is true, what else must be true? Oftentimes the "what else" that must be true is illogical in the extreme. You then construct a series of questions forcing the witness from A to B. The jury sees the illogic of B. The jury then realizes that A, no matter how much surface plausibility it may have, is also illogical. The process works like Quintilian's corkscrew, with the difference being that you do not work toward truth, you work toward the exposure of falsehood. A defendant once claimed that he did not go to Florida to do a drug deal, he was sent to Florida to guard a shaving kit full of money for a friend. His claim seemed quite plausible in the context of his direct examination. He further said that the shaving kit never left his side during the trip. He also stated that while the drug deal was being negotiated (without his knowledge) he was sitting in a bar drinking. If it were true that the shaving kit never left his side, what else must be true? He took the shaving kit to the bar with him. When the defendant climbed out on the limb of implausibility, the prosecutor sawed off the limb by asking if he took the shaving kit to the bar with him. In order to remain consistent, he sheepishly replied that he did. The prosecutor next asked him if anyone else in the bar had a shaving kit with them. To the considerable amusement of the jury, the defendant admitted that nobody else in the bar had a shaving kit.

c. Intoxication

We might find drunks amusing, but we do not find them respectable. We may laugh at them, and the more we laugh, the less likely we are to believe them. Most people, however, find nothing amusing about drunks, and their dislike of the alcoholic feeds their distrust. Be careful, however. This reason to dislike or disrespect is only a reason to distrust under special circumstances. Normally, intoxication only becomes relevant as a reason to disbelieve in two situations. If the intoxication occurred at the time the witness saw the subject matter of her testimony, then intoxication bears on the witness's ability to observe and remember. If the witness testifies while intoxicated, then the intoxication bears on the witness's ability to remember and recount her recollections. In certain types of cases, you do well to give your witnesses sniff tests before putting them on the witness stand just to make sure that they are sober. It takes a long time to live down the embarrassment of having one of your witnesses admit on cross-examination that she is intoxicated. It does nothing to help your chances of getting a conviction, either. Drug use has the same strictures as intoxication. Most jurors will find less reason to laugh at drug users, but more reason to disrespect or dislike them. Nevertheless, cross-examination should be confined to the areas of use at the time of observing and use at the time of testifying.

Trial counsel frequently overlook the fact that reasons to distrust, dislike, or disrespect do not necessarily translate into reasons to disbelieve. Many people are sitting in prison today based on the testimony of completely reprehensible, untrustworthy, disreputable villains. Snitches, accomplices, traitors, and other assorted scoundrels regularly convince juries to convict. A jury may reject a witness's testimony because she is untrustworthy, unlikeable, or unrespectable, but they may not. In order to assure that the jury will reject the testimony, you must also give them a case-specific reason to disbelieve the witness. This comes in the form of a motive to lie in the case on trial or proof of a lie in the case on trial. You have almost certainly clinched the witness's destruction if you give the jury proof of both.

B. CROSS-EXAMINATION OF THE CRIMINAL DEFENDANT

Conventional wisdom says defense attorneys are good on cross and poor on direct, while prosecutors are good on direct, but poor on cross. Maybe. Maybe not. Two things are sure about prosecutors and cross-examination: (1) The inexperienced prosecutor fears the defendant testifying worse than death itself. (2) The experienced defense attorney fears the defendant testifying worse than death itself. Why the paradox? Horace Rumpole, the fictional Old Bailey barrister, says that his greatest impediments to victory are his clients, because when they testify, they insist on blurting out things far better left unblurted.[6]

Could it be that criminal defendants as a class present easy targets for cross-examination? Or could it be that good prosecutors are also good cross-examiners? Cross-examination of the criminal defendant presents the most difficult, most dangerous, most onerous form of cross-examination in the whole field of trial advocacy. Defendants might occasionally blurt out things better left unblurted, but consider this: When the defendant climbs up onto the stand to talk his way out of trouble, the prosecutor typically has no deposition or prior statement. Because the defendant alone among witnesses enjoys the protection of the Fifth Amendment, the prosecutor frequently has no tangible clue what the defendant is going to say. The defendant normally testifies last, so he has heard the whole case and can tailor his story to match. In this situation, if you follow Professor Younger's commandment never to ask a question you do not know the answer to, you will conduct an incredibly short cross. Add to all these difficulties the following: The testimony of the defendant can snatch victory from the jaws of defeat or defeat from the jaws of victory. Many a seemingly ironclad case has sunk under the weight of the defendant's testimony. Many a seemingly lost conviction has been rescued by the defendant's testimony. More than one prosecutor has limped past directed verdict and uttered the silent prayer, "Please put the defendant on the stand."

Whether defendants present easy targets or prosecutors are better cross-examiners than most think, you as a prosecutor should welcome the sight of a defendant climbing up into the witness stand. You should not only welcome it, you should be ready for it. You should prepare to cross-examine the defendant just as you would prepare to cross-examine any other witness. Even if you think there is no way the defendant could possibly take the stand, you should prepare to cross-examine him. If you prosecute long enough, you will confront the fearful spectacle of a defendant, against all expectations, climbing up into the witness stand to sink your case to the bottom of the sea.

How then, can you prepare to cross-examine under such adverse circumstances? You must figure out what the defendant is likely to say and prepare to cross-examine that story. You can look to several places for predictions of the defendant's testimony. You must first look to the facts of the case itself. Each fact pattern has its own logic, and only a finite number of plausible lies can be told in any given fact pattern. If you prop your feet up on your desk, kick back, and think, you can usually deduce what a defendant has to say to talk his way out of trouble. After you have tried a number of similar cases, you notice that the defendants' stories begin to

[6] Mortimer, John, The Second Rumpole Omnibus, Penguin Books, New York, New York, 1988, p. 13.

repeat themselves. Keep track of these stories. They will appear time after time after time, and when you have prepared to cross-examine the story once, you will know what to ask the next time it comes up.

The defense attorney can also tell you much about what the defendant is going to say. Some defense attorneys have a blind faith in their ability to intimidate prosecutors by recounting all the flaws in the state's case. Do not be cowed. The most blustery defense counsel are the ones least likely to want to actually try the case. Do not get angry. Listen to what the attorney says. She is telling you what the defense will be. Do not miss this golden opportunity to take notes and prepare to meet the defenses. Listen to the questions the attorney asks at deposition or pretrial hearings. If the defendant has told her a story, she will try to elicit facts that will support that story. The facts she attempts to elicit will give you a good handle on what the defendant will say. The pretrial motions filed by the defense also give you a good clue as to what the defendant will say. Opposing counsel's voir dire, opening statement, and cross of the State's witnesses also give clues. On voir dire, she will try to condition the jury to be receptive to the defendant's story. If she makes an opening statement, it jolly well better bear some resemblance to the defendant's testimony. When she crosses your witnesses, at least a part of that cross will be done in builder mode, trying to lay the foundation for the defendant's testimony. Once you have an idea of the defendant's story, you prepare to cross-examine that story.

1. THE LIE PRINCIPLE

Almost every jurisdiction has at least one prosecutor who is a deadly cross-examiner. Time after time defendants take the witness stand to recount plausible stories on direct. Time after time the courtroom personnel sit amazed as he demolishes their testimony. Putting your client on the stand against such a prosecutor is always an adventure. Such a prosecutor knows a little-appreciated secret. It is the LIE Principle.

(L) When the defendant takes the witness stand and proclaims his innocence, he's Lying. You did your job in the charging stage. You believe in your case. You do not prosecute the innocent. Well, if the defendant says he is innocent, then he must be lying. You must believe this with all your heart and nerve and sinew. If ever you begin to think maybe the defendant is telling the truth, then you can be assured that the jury has the same thoughts.

(I) If he is lying, then his story will be Illogical. If the truth is that he is guilty, then his lie about his innocence must be fatally flawed.

(E) You can Exploit the illogic. If the jury can see the implausibility, then they will not believe the story.

2. THE LIE PROCEDURE

How do you exploit the implausibility? You follow the LIE Procedure:

(L) Listen. You must, at all costs, listen to the defendant's story. You cannot sit there fretting about what questions you are going to ask. You must listen, and listen intently.

(I) If you listen intently enough, you can Identify the illogic. You sit there and you hear it, and all your being shouts to you, "That doesn't make sense!"

(E) Now that you have identified the illogic, you must Expose it. You must strip all extraneous data from the illogic and make it impossible for the jury to miss.

One anonymous prosecutor in a long-forgotten trial started off his sexual battery case with evidence that his star witness, Meg Tatterson, was calling up sex partners off of the Interstate Highway on her CB radio. One of the truckers bragged to Edward Hyde about his conquest of Meg. Hyde decided he, too, should add Meg to his conquests. Hyde got himself charged with burglary and sexual battery, and he took the stand to testify in his own defense. Hyde testified that Meg had invited him over to her home to have sex. Hyde said he waited until nightfall, crawled through Meg's bedroom window, and engaged in consensual sex with her. Much later in his testimony, he testified that, after satisfying both himself and Meg, he went home and knocked on the door to have his mother let him in. What is wrong with this picture? He crawled through Meg's window but knocked on his own door? On cross-examination the prosecutor took these two incidents, placed them side by side, and let the jury draw their own conclusions.[7]

Q: When you got home, what did you do?

A: Knocked on the door.

Q: When you got to Meg's, what did you do?

A: Crawled through her window.

Q: You knocked on your own door?

A: Yes.

Q: But you crawled through Meg's window?

A: Yes.

Q: You knocked on the door of the house where you lived?

A: Yes.

---

7 Anecdotal reconstruction.

Q: But you crawled through the window of the house where you'd been invited?

A: Yes.

The jury found Hyde guilty of both burglary and sexual battery.

3. THE LIE PROLOG

A quick witted, resourceful cross-examiner can simply listen to a direct examination and unfailingly find the flaw—if he is always at the top of his game. He must never be fatigued, weighted down by other cares, or otherwise operating at less than full potential. There is a better way of taking advantage of the LIE Principle than engaging in extemporaneous use of the LIE Procedure. The LIE Procedure should begin pretrial with the LIE Prolog.

(L) Learn the facts of the case.

(I) Identify the lie the defendant must tell to extricate himself from those facts.

(E) Engineer a cross-examination that will exploit the lie's illogic.

4. THE MISSOURI METHOD

Sometimes the illogic is buried in physical improbabilities or impossibilities which can be overlooked in oral testimony. If this is the case, you must make use of the Missouri method—ask the witness to "show me" how it happened. Before you deploy the Missouri method in a courtroom, you need to do some experimentation outside the courtroom to make sure that the witness's testimony is truly improbable or impossible. Nothing could be more embarrassing than to ask a witness to "show me" and then have the witness give a perfect demonstration of the action you thought impossible. Young Harry Goodman once shot up a bar with a pistol that he "forgot" he was carrying. He testified that as he danced on the barroom floor, he heard a scuffle and turned around to see his brother being attacked by a number of men. He said that as he turned around, the pistol in his coat pocket swung around and hit him on the leg, reminding him of its presence. He then produced the pistol and shot two of the men. Cross-examination proceeded in the following fashion:

Q: You forgot you had the gun in your pocket?

A: Yes, sir.

Q: Now, kind of like I've got it in my pocket right here? [The prosecutor places the pistol in his coat pocket].

A: Yes, sir.

Q: So the first inkling that you had a gun was when you swung around?

A: Yes, sir. Because really I was dancing, but I wasn't really moving. [The witness has just realized that if he had been gyrating on the barroom floor, as he had just testified, the pistol would have given constant reminders of its presence by banging repeatedly against his leg].

Q: You weren't moving while you were dancing?

A: No, sir, I was just like when I dancing. [The witness is becoming tongue tied].

Q: Can you demonstrate how you were dancing?

A: [Demonstrating] When I was dancing, the only thing I was doing was just like this here, just clapping my hand. I wasn't really moving.

Q: Any particular name for that dance you were doing?

A: [No answer].

Q: You knew that gun was in your pocket, didn't you?

A: [No answer].

Q: You never forgot that gun was in your pocket, did you?

A: [No answer].

C. PRIOR INCONSISTENT STATEMENTS

"That's not what you told me before!" How many times have you heard that angry statement in everyday arguments? When those you deal with cannot keep their stories straight, you not only dislike them, that dislike helps to deepen your distrust. Impeachment by prior inconsistent statement might just be the most common form of impeachment in the courts of this land. It is only natural to assume that if someone previously said something different from his testimony, then you have reason to question his credibility. Before you launch off into an impeachment by prior inconsistent statement, however, be sure the prior statement is really inconsistent. As you read these words, somewhere in this great land some clueless attorney is enthusiastically attempting to impeach a witness with a prior consistent statement. Consider the long-ago case in which a woman testified that she had been shot in the chest. At deposition she had said she was shot in the shoulder. The defense attorney (a Mensa member) made this "inconsistency" the centerpiece of his cross-examination. The woman crumbled under the lawyer's verbal onslaught. When he finished, she had been reduced to tears, and he sat down triumphant. The prosecutor rose for redirect and asked a single question: "Ma'am, would you please put your finger on the exact place where you were shot?" The woman took her finger and placed it on a portion of her torso which could fairly be called either chest or shoulder.

When you impeach by prior inconsistent statement, the inconsistency should not be minor. There is a slang term that succinctly describes impeachment with minor inconsistencies—nitpicking. Nobody likes a nitpicker. Nitpickers are tedious, boring, and irritating. Impeachment with minor inconsistencies can be justified (or at least excused) if it is done for one of four reasons.

(1) To rattle the witness. Some witnesses, especially professional witnesses, live in horror of being impeached by prior inconsistent statement. If a witness can be shaken by a few minor impeachments, then that witness will likely become much more compliant and agreeable in answering your questions

(2) To rattle opposing counsel. Some lawyers, mostly rookies, go to pieces over the impeachment of their witnesses on any point, no matter how inconsequential. If such impeachment can unnerve opposing counsel, then she is going to be far less effective for the remainder of the trial.

(3) As an act of desperation. If your case is falling apart, the opposing witnesses are killing you, and it is beginning to look more and more like you will have to put another tally in the "L" column, you can do one of two things. You can tuck your tail between your legs and meekly take your whipping, or you can fight with whatever ammunition is available. In this case, if you can impeach with minor inconsistencies, you do so.

(4) The most compelling reason to impeach with minor prior inconsistencies is that there are myriads of minor inconsistencies. Suppose the witness gets through her testimony with the major portions of her story consistent, but the conflicts as to details are too numerous to be explained by the normal vagaries of memory. When this happens, you can bleed the witness dry with a thousand small cuts rather than decapitating her with a mighty chop.

1. THE RULE IN QUEEN CAROLINE'S CASE

It is possible to impeach by prior inconsistent statement in one of two ways—either get the witness to admit making the statement or simply offer up extrinsic evidence of the statement. Good manners dictate that you ask the witness about the statement first before offering up evidence of the statement, and that has been the rule since Queen Caroline's Case was decided in 1820.[8] In the somewhat later case of *Moore v. Bettis*,[9] The Tennessee Supreme Court endorsed the wisdom of this requirement in the following words:

> It would be manifest injustice to the party and the witness to impeach his character, by proof of statements made on other occasions, without first calling his attention to them, and giving him an opportunity to explain their true nature and character. It might appear from such explanation, that the conversation or statement was unimportant in itself, or that it had been wholly misunderstood, or misconceived by the impeaching witnesses. If, then, it be proposed to contradict and impeach the witness, by proving that he had made statements out of court different from those to which he now testifies, it is first necessary to ask him as to the "time, place and person, involved in the supposed contradiction," and not generally, whether he had ever said so and so, or always made the same statement.

Over the years a standard sort of format evolved for confronting the witness with the prior inconsistent statement. Rule 613(a)(1) of the Texas Rules of Evidence Section 24–9–83, Ga.Code, provides a clear statement of the traditional format:

> When examining a witness about the witness's prior inconsistent statement—whether oral or written—a party must first tell the witness:
>
> **(A)** the contents of the statement;
>
> **(B)** the time and place of the statement; and
>
> **(C)** the person to whom the witness made the statement.[10]

Some statutes and rules simply state that the witness should be confronted with the circumstances of the prior inconsistent statement,[11] or that the examiner should fairly draw her attention to the statement.[12] Because it is of ancient vintage, and because it requires careful attention to detail, the Rule in Queen Caroline's Case has fallen somewhat into disfavor.[13]

---

[8] 2 BR. & B. 284, 129 Eng.Rep. 976 (1820), quoted in State v. Martin, 964 S.W.2d 564, 566–567 (Tenn. 1998).

[9] 30 Tenn. 67, 1850 WL 2050, *2 (1850).

[10] Accord. Colo.R.Evid 613(a); Ga.Code § 24–9–83; Ky.R.Evid. 613(a).

[11] E.g. Ala.R.Evid. 613(b).

[12] La.Code Evid. Art. 613.

[13] Starr v. Morsette, 236 N.W.2d 183, 188 n. 2 (N.D. 1975).

2. THE FEDERAL RULE

Rule 613, Fed.R.Evid., which many states have promulgated almost verbatim,[14] allows extrinsic evidence of the statement without telling the witness the substance of the statement.[15] This makes no sense. How can a witness explain or deny a statement when she does not even know what it is supposed to be? By allowing explanation after the introduction of extrinsic evidence.[16] This results in a cumbersome presentation, as exemplified by the Alaskan case of *Active v. State*,[17] where the state impeached a witness on rebuttal without laying a predicate on cross-examination. This required a surrebuttal where the defense witness was recalled and asked to explain or deny the statement. The prosecutor occasioned a waste of much time, energy, and effort by not confronting the witness on cross-examination. If he had confronted the witness on cross, she may have admitted the statement, and the rebuttal witness would not have been necessary. Even if she denied the statement and the rebuttal witness testified, no surrebuttal would have been necessary. Old law is not necessarily unwise law, and many authorities have begun to recognize the wisdom of Queen Caroline's Rule. In *Mercer v. United States*,[18] the court acknowledged that the rule did not require confronting the witness with the prior inconsistent statement but held that she should have been shown the statement while she was testifying so that she could explain or deny it. Tennessee promulgated Rule 613, Fed.R.Evid., almost verbatim, but when the Tennessee Supreme Court confronted the anomalies arising from the rule in *State v. Martin*,[19] they had this to say:

> We note that Rule 613(b) of the Federal Rules of Evidence is identical to Rule 613(b) of the Tennessee Rules of Evidence. The federal advisory comments, however, state that a foundation may either be laid before or after an offer of the extrinsic evidence. While there exists a split of authority as to the timing of the foundation, several circuits have clearly expressed a preference for the traditional approach in light of the difficulties the change has caused. See *U.S. v. Bonnett*, 877 F.2d 1450, 1462 (10th Cir.1989) (preferring traditional approach so trier of fact can "observe [witness] demeanor and the nature of his testimony as he denies or explains his prior testimony."); *Wammock v. Celotex*, 793 F.2d 1518 (11th Cir.1986) (holding "[r]ule 613(b) does not supplant the traditional method of confronting a witness with his inconsistent statement prior to its introduction."); *U.S. v.*

14 E.g. Tenn.R.Evid. 613.

15 613(a).

16 613(b).

17 153 P.3d 355 (Alaska App. 2007).

18 724 A.2d 1176 (D.C. 1999).

19 964 S.W.2d 564 (Tenn. 1998).

> *McGuire*, 744 F.2d 1197, 1204 (6th Cir.1984) (stating "[w]e do not approve of the government's not informing the defendant of this evidence, which we view as a questionable trial tactic."); *U.S. v. Barrett*, 539 F.2d 244, 254 (1st Cir.1976) (noting traditional foundational good practice though not required).[20]

Then the Court reinterpreted Tenn.R.Evid. 613 to require a Queen Caroline predicate. Kentucky first considered promulgating the Federal Rule verbatim but redrafted the rule to reinstate Queen Caroline's predicate.[21]

3. MEETING THE LEGAL REQUISITES OF QUEEN CAROLINE'S PREDICATE

Whether your jurisdiction requires the Queen Caroline predicate or not, you should lay it before offering extrinsic evidence of the prior inconsistent statement. It is cleaner, more economical of time, and much more fair than the Federal method. The only reason not to do so would be that you learned of the prior statement after the witness testified and was released from subpoena. To do a proper Queen Caroline impeachment, you must use the five W's:

When said: Give the witness the date and time of the statement.

Where said: Give the witness the location of the statement. Date, time, and place need not be exact, but you must give as close an approximation as possible.

Who heard: Give the witness the identity of whoever heard the statement.

What said: Give the witness the substance of the statement.

Whether said: Ask the witness to admit or deny making the statement.

Most state rules of evidence provide that the witness must be afforded an opportunity to explain the inconsistency. Some lawyers feel this provision requires them to ask the witness to explain the inconsistency. It only means that the witness can explain it if she wishes, but counsel is not required to ask. Counsel is simply prohibited from cutting the witness off if she tries to explain it. Do not ask for an explanation, but do not try to stop the witness if she volunteers one.

Never undertake to impeach by a prior inconsistent statement which you cannot prove up. Some lawyers do this in the hopes that: (a) the witness will meekly admit it, or (b) the jury will believe the statement was made anyway. Acting on the first hope is wishful thinking. Acting on the second

---

20 Id. at 567–568.

21 Burchett v. Commonwealth, 98 S.W.3d 492, 510 (Ky. 2003) (Keller, J., concurring opinion).

is unprofessional conduct. The greatest temptation to do this will come when you have a one-on-one interview with the witness and she says something only your ears hear. You cannot blurt out "But didn't you tell me thus and so?" You cannot become a witness without running afoul of ethical requirements. Moral: Always try to have a second party present at a witness interview, so that the second party can testify to the inconsistency.

4. REQUISITES OF A PERSUASIVE QUEEN CAROLINE'S PREDICATE

A legally proper Queen Caroline impeachment by prior inconsistent statement must comply with the five W's. But you want more than a legally proper impeachment. You want an effective impeachment. To do an effective impeachment, you must do more than just meet the bare bones legal essentials. An effective impeachment covers the five R's:

Retrieve: In order to do an effective impeachment by prior inconsistent statement, you must be able to retrieve the statement from your files so that the impeachment may be done precisely. Do not fumble for the prior, have it handy. Countless lawyers have left countless witnesses unimpeached because they simply could not find the prior in the volumes of paperwork in the case file. Countless more have botched an impeachment for the same reason. If you cannot find the prior inconsistent statement, do not try to recite it to the witness from memory. You will get it wrong, and when you find it in your papers you will have egg on your face. You must work out a system for identifying these nuggets and finding them quickly in the heat of combat. The annotation system described in Chapters 8, 11, and 12 is just such a system.

Repeat: Have the witness repeat the fact that you want to impeach. You want to do this in order to put the present testimony as close as possible to the prior statement. This should highlight to the jury the inconsistency between the two statements.

Refute: Meet the legal requirements for the prior inconsistent statement and confront the witness with it.

Remind: If the witness was under oath, remind her of her oath. In many jurisdictions, if the prior inconsistent statement was made under oath in a legal proceeding, the prior inconsistent statement is substantive evidence.[22] Even if it is not substantive evidence, the fact that it was made under oath should impress the jury.

---

[22] E.g. West's Fla.Stat.Ann. § 90.801(2)(a).

Reference: Where you can, identify the document the statement comes from (deposition, statement, transcript, etc.) and the page and line numbers where the statement can be found. We will discuss the reason for this a little later.

5. LAYING QUEEN CAROLINE'S PREDICATE

The easiest and most effective impeachments by prior inconsistent statement come from transcripts of testimony. Impeachment from a transcript should go something like this impeachment of a young woman who claimed to have accidentally stabbed her husband in the groin while slicing sausage.[23]

Q: As far as drugs are concerned, did you consume any drugs?

A: Yes, me and Edward [the victim] did.

Q: What did you consume?

A: We both did some coke.

Q: Crack?

A: No.

Q: No crack?

A: No, sir.

Q: It was powder?

A: Yes, sir.

Q: You're sure that you consumed no crack? [Repeat].

A: I'm absolutely positive. I've never done that.

Q: Do you remember testifying before the grand jury on May the 1st, 1996?

A: Yes, sir.

BY THE PROSECUTOR: I'm on page 11, counsel. [Reference].

BY THE DEFENSE ATTORNEY: Give me just a moment to catch up.

Q: (BY THE PROSECUTOR) Do you remember being placed under oath that day? [Remind].

A: Yes.

Q: Do you remember swearing to tell the truth?

A: Yes.

---

[23] Actual trial transcript.

BY THE PROSECUTOR: Are you caught up, Mr. Fender?

BY DEFENSE COUNSEL: Yes. What line?

BY THE PROSECUTOR: We're down to line 19. [Reference].

Q: (BY THE PROSECUTOR) Do you remember being asked these questions and giving these answers? [Refute].

> Q: What sort of drugs did you consume while you were riding in the woods?
>
> A: Cocaine.

A: Right.

Q: (continuing)

> Q: Would that be powder cocaine or crack cocaine?
>
> A: Powder and crack.

A: No, sir. I did not say that.

Q: You did not say that?

A: No, I did not * * *. That's not what I—if that's what that says, then I did not understand what they say. I did not hear them say "crack." I would not have said that. I've never done it or even seen it.

Q: The question is, do you remember being asked this question:

> Q: Would that be powder cocaine or crack cocaine?

And do you remember giving this answer?

> A: Powder and crack.

A: No, sir. All I would have said is powdered. I may have said no crack or something, but, no, no, sir, I wouldn't have said that.

The defendant had thrice previously been impeached by prior inconsistent testimony, and would be impeached five more times from transcripts of her testimony. Notice the prosecutor's giving the page and line to the defense attorney. This shows the prosecutor to be fair. It also gives immediate authentication to the prior statement. The jury sees the defense attorney pick up the transcript, turn to the page and line, and read along. The jury correctly expects that if you do not give the statement accurately, the defense attorney will object. The defense attorney's lack of objection validates your assertion.

Even when you do an impeachment by prior inconsistent statement right, you can usually do it better. You want to put the present statement as close as possible to the prior inconsistent statement. The legal predicate you must lay gets in the way. It usually goes like this:

Q: Now, Mr. Witness, you just testified that the grass was brown?

Q: Do you remember having your deposition taken?

Q: Do you remember that it was taken on January the 2nd of last year?

Q: Do you remember that it was taken in the conference room at the law office of Hammerknocker and Thumbtacker here in Metropolis?

Q: Do you remember that I was present?

Q: Do you remember that opposing counsel was present?

Q: Do you remember that a court reporter was there taking down the testimony?

Q: Do you remember raising your right hand?

Q: Do you remember swearing to tell the truth?

Q: Do you remember being asked questions?

Q: Do you remember giving answers?

Q: Opposing counsel should note that I am at Page 23, lines 4 and 5 of that transcript. Do you remember being asked the following question and giving the following answer?

> Q: What color was the grass?
>
> A: The grass was green.

Q: And you were under oath when you testified the grass was green?

You need to get the conflicting statements a little closer together. You can do it. Do it this way:

Q: You just said the grass was brown?

Q: Do you remember in your deposition given at the office of Hammerknocker & Thumbtacker on January 2nd, testifying as follows—I'm on Page 23, lines 4 & 5—

> Q: What color was the grass?
>
> A: The grass was green.

Q: You were under oath when you testified that the grass was green?

6. GETTING THE WITNESS TO ADMIT LYING

Oftentimes, when a defendant is first confronted with an accusation, he will tell a story which he thinks fits the known facts. Later, after more and more incriminating evidence is compiled, he realizes that his story is unlikely to be believed because of the great weight of contrary evidence. He must change his story. When he changes his story, you can impeach him by prior inconsistent statement and he must admit that his first story was untrue. This provides a golden opportunity for you to cross-examine to the topic (argument) of "liar, liar." Darryl Lee LeBarron stood accused of murdering Randy Hardmann by stabbing him with a knife during a drunken brawl in Hardmann's front yard. The defendant claimed he killed in self-defense when the victim attacked him with a knife. Unfortunately for LeBarron's defense, he had made prior inconsistent statements to the effect that he had not seen a knife. On cross-examination the prosecutor began by fixing his testimony firmly that he saw a knife. He then continued:[24]

> Q: Now, in truth and fact, Mr. LeBarron, during that second confrontation, you never saw a knife, did you?
>
> A: Yeah, I did see a knife.
>
> Q: Do you remember giving a tape-recorded statement to Ms. Janet Trout?
>
> A: Yes, I do.
>
> [At this point a transcript of the statement was produced and given to the defendant].
>
> Q: Then if you'll flip it over to about the third page maybe, let me take a look. The second page, right down toward the bottom when Ms. Trout was asking you about the fatal confrontation, do you remember her asking you this question and you giving this answer? QUESTION: "Did you see the knife at that point? ANSWER: I never saw the knife at all except for when he come out to the front porch, and he was waving it."
>
> A: Yes, I did.
>
> Q: You raised your right hand and swore that the statement was true?
>
> A: Yes.
>
> Q: And so you swore under oath that the statement, "I never saw the knife at all except for when he come out on the front porch, and he was waving it," was true; did you not?
>
> A: Yes.
>
> Q: And that is the truth, isn't it.
>
> A: No.

[24] Transcript condensed for clarity.

Q: It's not?

A: No.

Q: You knew it wasn't true when you said it?

A: Yes.

Q: You told Ms. Trout something you knew to be untrue?

A: Yeah.

Q: You lied?

A: Yeah.

Q: You lied to Ms. Trout?

A: Yeah.

Q: And the reason you lied to Ms. Trout was—

A: Was because I was upset and afraid of going to jail. It was the first time I had ever been in trouble.

Q: So you were telling her a lie that you thought might help keep you from going to jail; is that right?

A: Yeah.

Q: You were telling her a lie that you thought might help you through this criminal prosecution, isn't that right?

A: Yes.

Q: And you thought that saying, "I never saw a knife at all except for when he come out to the front porch, and he was waving it," would help you avoid criminal prosecution is that right?

A: Right.

Q: Let's look on the second page of the statement.

A: (Witness perusing papers).

Q: And I believe right down toward the bottom of the page, do you recall Ms. Trout asking you this question and you giving her this answer: "QUESTION: Okay. At that point in time, did you have a knife in your hands? And your answer: No ma'am. I never had a knife in my hands at all. I don't carry knives. I don't carry weapons. I don't need them."

A: What's your question?

Q: Do you remember being asked that question and giving that answer?

A: Yeah.

Q: And you swore under oath that the answer was true?

A: Yes.

Q: So your statement "I never had a knife in my hands at all" that was a lie, wasn't it?

A: That was a lie.

Q: And your statement: "I don't carry knives," that was a lie, wasn't it?

A: I don't carry knives except for work.

Q: You didn't tell Ms. Trout "I don't carry knives except for work" did you?

A: No.

Q: You told Ms. Trout, "I don't carry knives," didn't you?

A: Yes, yeah.

Q: And that was a lie, wasn't it?

A: Yeah.

Q: And then you said: "I don't carry weapons," and that was a lie, too, wasn't it?

A: Yeah.

[The prosecutor asked the defendant about a number of other prior inconsistent statements, each of which the defendant proclaimed to be a lie and then concluded the examination with this series of questions].

Q: Do you have any idea how many separate, individual lies you have told the police—

A: No.

Q:—As it relates to this case?

A: No.

Q: But it's a lot, isn't it?

A: Yeah.

Q: And the reason for telling all of those lies, and some of them under oath, was to try to get yourself out of a tight spot in this case; is that right?

A: Yeah.

BY THE PROSECUTOR: I have no further questions.

The "liar, liar" technique, when stripped to its barest essentials involves the following progression:

(1) Get the defendant to say that a prior inconsistent statement is untrue.

(2) Get the defendant to say that she knew it was untrue when she made it.

(3) Get the defendant to admit that she lied.

(4) Get the defendant to admit that she lied in order to mislead the listener. (Why else does someone lie?)

(5) Get the defendant to admit that she lied to get out of trouble.

(6) Argue to the jury that they cannot trust the story of a person who has admittedly tried to lie her way out of trouble in this case. There are no assurances that she hasn't just thought up a better lie to tell.

The question sequence should go something like this:

Q: It wasn't true?

Q: You knew it wasn't true?

Q: You lied?

Q: You lied to Officer Friendly because you wanted to mislead him?

Q: You wanted to mislead Officer Friendly so you could get out of trouble?

Remember four caveats about the "liar, liar" technique. First, some judges get very nervous when a prosecutor puts "liar" and "defendant" in the same sentence.[25] They will almost automatically declare a mistrial. Have your case authority ready for such an eventuality. Even if you have the case law, some judges will not care what the case law says, they simply will not allow you to call the defendant a liar. If they will not allow it, then you cannot do it. The judge may, however, allow you to use euphemisms for liar. If she will, do so. Second, before you can call someone, especially the defendant, a liar, there must be a firm basis in the record for it.[26] There must be evidence suggesting that the witness is in fact lying. Mere conflict in testimony does not prove mendacity. People observing and interpreting their observations from different vantage points make different reports of the same incident. Third, as a prosecutor you may not make the argument

[25] See, e.g. State v. Floyd, 10 Conn.App. 361, 523 A.2d 1323 (1987); People v. Mitchell, 35 Ill.App.3d 151, 341 N.E.2d 153 (1975).

[26] E.g. People v. Parisie, 5 Ill. App.3d 1009, 287 N.E.2d 310 (1972); Vargas v. State, 627 S.W.2d 785 (Tex. App. 4th Dist. 1982).

"convict him because he's lying" or try to turn the trial into a "lying contest" between the defendant and the state's witnesses.[27] The argument should be "disbelieve him because he's lying. Convict him because the state's evidence proves guilt beyond a reasonable doubt." Fourth, make the point and move on. Do not make the "liar, liar" issue the centerpiece of your presentation. Virtue taken to extreme can become vice. In *State v. Pabst*,[28] the Kansas Supreme Court reversed a conviction where the prosecutor called the defendant a liar on eleven separate occasions. They may have held differently if he had not made such excessive reference to the defendant's mendacity.

D. COMPARATIVE CROSS-EXAMINATION

Sometimes the witness's testimony is not internally inconsistent, but inconsistent with the testimony of others. You can totally destroy a witness's credibility by comparing the conflicts between the testifying witness and other witnesses. Consider the following examination from *Plymale v. Commonwealth*.[29]

> Q: In other words, if I understand you correctly, every witness for the Commonwealth, nearly every witness for the Commonwealth, who has taken this stand, and who has testified to anything that is against you, is guilty of perjury or is guilty of falsifying?
>
> A: I have not said that.
>
> Q: Sheriff Thompson has falsified?
>
> A: He has.
>
> Q: Kenneth Rogers?
>
> A: Absolutely.
>
> Q: Mr. Lewis Goode has falsified, hasn't he?
>
> A: Whether that was intentional—
>
> Q: He did not tell it as you know it. William Craft has falsified?
>
> A: Yes, sir, he has.
>
> Q: When Mr. Thompson told you what had happened to Mr. Deal was a serious thing, you said I know it is. You knew that much didn't you?
>
> A: I sure did.

27 Bowman v. State, 710 N.W.2d 200 (Iowa 2006).

28 268 Kan. 501, 996 P.2d 321 (2000).

29 195 Va. 582, 79 S.E.2d 610 (1954).

Q: And you also told him, I have no sympathy for the old son-of-a-bitch?

A: I did not.

Q: And Mr. Thompson is lying then?

A: He absolutely is.

Q: You will put your word against his?

A: Yes, sir, I will.

Q: As a matter of fact, Mr. Plymale, did you ever make any denial of it before Mr. Thompson and Mr. Goode?

A: I did.

Q: Then on that point Mr. E. A. Thompson and Mr. Lewis Goode they are falsifying?

A: They are.

Q: So, again, I say that all of these witnesses who have said anything that is against you have strained the truth and are trying to frame you in this matter?

A: Not all the witnesses.[30]

Cross-examination in this vein can have a devastating effect on a witness's credibility. Too devastating. It is improper. How is it improper? If you are questioning witnesses who are under the rule of sequestration, then you violate the rule when you tell the testifying witness what another witness has said. This objection does not apply to the defendant, because he has been in court the whole time and heard all the witnesses testify. There are other problems, however. It is the jury's job to decide who is telling the truth and who is not. Asking one witness to opine on the truthfulness of another witness invades the province of the jury. Another problem: This is opinion testimony, and not even an expert witness can give an opinion on the veracity of a witness.[31] You impeach witnesses by certain standard methods,[32] and having one witness opine on the truthfulness of another is not one of them. Can we salvage this type questioning? The

[30] 195 Va. at 592–594, 79 S.E.2d at 616.

[31] Plymale v. Commonwealth, 195 Va. 582, 594, 79 S.E.2d 610, 616 (1954) ("[N]o witness, much less the accused, should be required so to characterize the testimony of another witness"); Boatwright v. State, 452 So.2d 666, 668 (Fla. App. 4th DCA 1984)("During cross-examination of a key defense witness, the prosecutor skillfully established the differences between the witness's testimony and that of earlier state witnesses. Up to that point, the cross-examination was perfectly legitimate. Then, over defense objection, the prosecutor asked the witness whether each of the earlier witnesses had been lying. This effort to isolate and thereby discredit the witness is improper for a number of reasons").

[32] Prior inconsistent statement; prior conviction; and testimony as to the witness's reputation for truth and veracity.

Plymale prosecutor asked, "Q: Then on that point Mr. E. A. Thompson and Mr. Lewis Goode they are falsifying?" What if he had asked

> Q: Then on that point Mr. E. A. Thompson and Mr. Lewis Goode they are
>
> a. wrong?
>
> b. not accurate?
>
> c. mistaken?

Does this render the line of questioning unobjectionable? These words could be considered euphemisms for "lying," but some jurisdictions will allow such questioning. Florida courts have held that "Asking whether another witness is 'wrong,' 'not accurate,' or 'mistaken' is very different from asking whether the witness is a liar."[33] The Michigan Court of Appeals dealt with a challenge to such questioning in the following language:

> We find no merit in defendant's claim that the prosecutor engaged in misconduct by asking defendant whether he disputed specific points of other witnesses' testimony. * * *
>
> [T]he prosecutor did not ask defendant to comment on the witnesses' credibility; she only asked whether the defendant had a different version of the facts. * * *
>
> It is not improper for the prosecutor to attempt to ascertain which facts are in dispute.[34]

The West Virginia Supreme Court voiced the paradox best when it said that, although "it is objectionable on cross-examination to require a witness to state whether another witness' testimony is true or false, since this is the ultimate question that a jury must decide," but the court held that it is perfectly proper "to direct a witness to specific previous testimony of another witness and ask the witness whether he agrees or disagrees with such testimony."[35] If your jurisdiction allows such questioning techniques, by all means use them. You would be foolish to eschew use of court-approved techniques. Have your case law readily accessible if you embark upon such impeachment and be very careful to use the exact language approved in the appellate decisions governing your jurisdiction.

There is, however, a safer and more subtle way to achieve this objective. Jot down key points of the other witnesses' testimony that you expect the witness to disagree with. Try to write the points down in exactly

---

[33] Joseph v. State, 868 So.2d 5, 8 (Fla.App.4th DCA 2004).

[34] People v. Ackerman, 257 Mich. App. 434, 449, 669 N.W.2d 818, 827 (2003).

[35] State v. Atkins,163 W.Va. 502, 519, 261 S.E.2d 55, 65 (1979).

the same language as testified to by the witness. If Otto Otherwitness said "The sheen of the grass was green," then you ask the witness:

Q: You say the grass was brown?

Q: Then the sheen of the grass was not green?

The jury recalls the testimony of Otto and decides that the witness is calling Otto a liar. The witness is impeached and there is no hint of reversible error. Consider the example of an old resisting arrest case where the defense called numerous witnesses. The defense witnesses' testimony was in irreconcilable conflict. Every witness told a completely different story about what happened. The prosecutor knew that the defendant had to testify contrary to most of his witnesses, so he made copious notes in the witnesses' own language on key points of their testimony. When the defendant testified, the prosecutor examined him by going down the list and, in the defense witnesses' own words, asking the defendant about the various points of the testimony. After denying several statements made by his witnesses, the defendant became agitated, turned to the jury and volunteered the following: "Ladies and gentlemen of the jury, my witnesses lied. I don't know why they lied, but don't hold it against them. They was just trying to help." Needless to say, they did not help at all.

E. IMPEACHMENT BY PRIOR CONVICTION

The different jurisdictions vary widely as to precisely how and under what circumstances you may impeach by prior conviction. In some jurisdictions you may not impeach at all for prior convictions of any kind.[36] In some jurisdictions, you may impeach with a conviction of any crime,[37] including misdemeanors.[38] Some jurisdictions will allow impeachment only for crimes involving dishonesty or false statement;[39] some only for felonies.[40] Most jurisdictions will allow impeachment for felonies or crimes involving dishonesty or false statement,[41] but sometimes they place hedges of prerequisites and qualifications around the impeachment. The Federal Rule requires that crimes involving dishonesty or false statement can be used only if it can readily be determined that establishing the elements of the crime required proof of dishonesty or false statement.[42] Some jurisdictions require a preliminary finding by the judge that the probative value of the impeachment outweighs the prejudicial effect.[43] Some set time

---

36 Mont.R.Evid. 609.

37 N.J.R.Evid. 609.

38 Mass.Gen.Laws Ann. c.233, § 21.

39 Alaska R.Evid. 609(a); Kansas Stat.Ann. 60–421.

40 Nev.Rev.Stat. 50.095.

41 See, e.g., Ark.R.Evid. 609(a); Del.R.Evid. 609(a).

42 Fed.R.Evid. 609(a)(2).

43 Alaska R.Evid. 609(c); Del. R.Evid. 609(a).

limits on the use of convictions, with ten years being the usual period;[44] Some shorten the period to five years for any conviction,[45] but some reserve the five year limit for misdemeanor convictions only.[46] Some jurisdictions distinguish between impeachment of parties and impeachment of mere witnesses, with more stringent protection for parties than witnesses. Kansas allows such impeachment of the defendant only if the defendant first introduces evidence supporting her credibility.[47] Maine requires a judicial weighing of the probative value before allowing such impeachment of a criminal defendant or a party to a civil case.[48] Mississippi requires a weighing of probative value for impeachment of parties by felony conviction, but allows per se impeachment for crimes of dishonesty or false statement.[49]

What does all this mean? It means that modern law still gives credence to Aristotle's dictum that arguments to character (ethos) will likely mislead. It also means that impeachment by prior conviction, especially of a criminal defendant, will be looked upon with a jaundiced eye by trial judges and reviewing courts. Prosecutors derive great pleasure from impeachment by prior conviction, but the value of this type of impeachment can be greatly overrated. First, trial judges will be reluctant to allow it unless it is done in the most circumspect manner possible. Second, appellate courts will reverse if it appears that there is the least bit of overreaching in the introduction of such evidence. Third, all the strictures placed upon such impeachment serve as a powerful antivenin to the toxicity of the impeachment. For example, in a sexual battery case, evidence that the defendant has previously been convicted of sexual battery could devastate the defense, but most jurisdictions do not allow the nature of the offense to be published to the jury—all that most juries will hear is that the defendant was previously convicted of "a felony." This restriction makes very good sense. It is the fact of the felony conviction that legally impeaches, not the nature of the conviction. In most jurisdictions you will be reduced to a ritual asking of specific questions. You cannot ask what the crimes were. You cannot ask the circumstances of the crimes. You can only ask whether the witness has ever been convicted of a felony or of a crime involving dishonesty or false statement. Here, then, is the litany, which you should follow verbatim if you want to avoid a mistrial or reversible error:

Q: Mr. Witness, have you ever been convicted of a felony?

44 Ark.R.Evid. 609(b); N.D.R.Evid. 609(b).

45 Alaska R.Evid. 609(b).

46 Mass.Gen.Laws Ann. c. 233, § 21.

47 Kansas Stat.Ann. 60–421.

48 Maine R.Evid. 609(a).

49 Miss.R.Evid. 609(a).

Q: How many times?

Or

Q: Mr. Witness, have you ever been convicted of a crime involving dishonesty or false statement?

Q: How many times.

Sometimes a witness has convictions for both felonies and crimes involving dishonesty or false statement. Some crimes may be both a felony and a crime involving dishonesty or false statement. You cannot properly "double up" the crimes, making it look like the witness has been convicted of more crimes than he actually has. In that case you should amend the dishonesty question to state "have you ever been convicted of a misdemeanor involving dishonesty or false statement?" Suppose the defendant stands convicted of one count of felony worthless check. Here you must make a tactical decision. Which sounds better, "convicted of a felony" or "convicted of a crime involving dishonesty or false statement?" You decide. You cannot have it both ways. Make your decision based on the dynamics of the case and then inform defense counsel which of the two litanies you intended to use. You do this because a lawyer comes close to malpractice if she does not coach her witnesses on how these questions will be asked and how they should be answered. One example will illustrate the point. Years ago, a man stood trial for burglary. Although he had been caught sitting on a bag of burglar tools on the roof of the building, he insisted on his constitutional right to trial by jury but ignored his equally important right to remain silent. On cross-examination the prosecutor asked him if he had ever been convicted of a crime. The uncoached defendant replied, "I did time once for manslaughter, but I didn't kill him. I just stabbed him. He died in the hospital." It is only right to advise counsel how you are going to ask the question so that she can properly prepare her witness to answer it. If you withhold this information you might gain some sort of an advantage in the confusion that could follow from the witness fumbling the answer, but it would be unfair. Remember, a prosecutor may strike hard blows, but they must be fair.

When doing an impeachment by prior conviction, what the case law says is not nearly as important as what the trial judge says. If a trial judge does not let you perform impeachment in a certain way, it makes no difference what the case law says. You do not have the right to appeal and there is nothing you can do except adhere to the judge's ruling. The case law comes into play if the judge allows you to do the impeachment, because the defendant has the right to appeal. It had better be done right, or it is going to get reversed. Before undertaking to impeach by prior conviction, learn all the ramifications and pitfalls of the law of your jurisdiction and observe them rigidly. Do not try to expand the horizons of the law with inventive interpretations, just do the impeachment as circumspectly as possible. It may not be as spectacular as you might have hoped, but it should withstand appellate scrutiny. Remember, under the usual strictures placed on impeachment by prior conviction, it is not the fact of the conviction that impeaches so much as the witness's reaction to being confronted with it. The witness's reaction may open a door for further inquiry that would otherwise have been forestalled, but be careful. Do not charge through the door—tiptoe through it.

PRACTICAL EXERCISE

You have five certified copies of five felony convictions bearing the name of the defendant and a lab report stating that the fingerprints on the certified copies match the fingerprints of the defendant. On cross-examination, the defendant only admits three prior felony convictions. How do you go about impeaching his admission? Map out a presentation which will prove the defendant is lying about his number of convictions. In planning the cross-examination, you may refer to the Roger Cannon cross set out in Chapter 12, but remember that Cannon's convictions were not merely impeachment, they were substantive evidence in a sexually violent predator prosecution.

CHAPTER 14

VOIR DIRE

■ ■ ■

We have a criminal jury system which is superior to any in the world, and its efficiency is only marred by the difficulty of finding twelve men every day who don't know anything and can't read.—Mark Twain

A. OBJECTIVES OF THE VOIR DIRE EXAMINATION

What are the attributes of an ideal juror? Conventional wisdom says a good prosecution juror must be "middle, middle, middle." Middle class, middle aged, middle of the road. Maybe. Maybe not. We all believe that we can decide issues impartially, and most of us strive mightily to do so. But we are the slaves of our experiences. We look at our world through the dual lenses of prior experience and preconception. We can reach conclusions at variance with those prior experiences and preconceptions, but we require more convincing. That middle class, middle aged, middle of the road juror who looks so good on paper may have a prior experience giving rise to an ingrained preconception fatal to your case.

Ancient rhetoricians taught that the orator's first task was to render the jury attentive, receptive, and well disposed. These are the characteristics of an ideal juror—attentive to your evidence, receptive to your case theory, and well-disposed toward your side. In ancient times, when juries were imposed upon the litigants, the first thing advocates did to produce these three qualities was to flatter the jury. As we will learn in the chapters on final argument, they devoted the beginning of the speech almost exclusively to the task courting the jury. In the modern courtroom, before the first lawyer makes the first speech, litigants have a method of making the jury attentive, receptive, and well disposed. It is called jury selection. In jury selection, you should not be so much concerned with rendering inattentive jurors attentive, unreceptive jurors receptive, and disapproving jurors well-disposed as you are with obtaining jurors who are already attentive, receptive, and well-disposed. You do this through the threefold process of selection, rejection, and protection.

1. SELECTION, REJECTION, PROTECTION

In the process of selecting, rejecting, and protecting, you want to discover the good and bad jurors, defend the good jurors against dismissal, and dismiss the bad jurors. Selection identifies good jurors. Protection tries to indoctrinate them to survive a challenge for cause and to force the opposition to waste peremptory challenges in dismissing them. The goals of rejection form the opposite side of the coin of selection and protection: you want to identify bad jurors, to lay the groundwork for a challenge for cause against those bad jurors or failing that to establish on the record a constitutionally defensible reason for exercising a peremptory challenge. The Supreme Court ruled in *Batson v. Kentucky*[1] that peremptory challenges could not be exercised based upon the status of a prospective juror as a member of an ethnic minority. From that acorn of precedent has grown a mighty oak of case law condemning the exercise of peremptory challenged based on race, gender,[2] and ethnic origin.[3] Since everyone has a race, a gender, and an ethnic origin, a peremptory challenge of any juror is subject to being attacked as motivated by prejudice. The prophylaxis for such an attack is to set forth on the record a series of questions exploring the factors which you find objectionable in the juror. When opposing counsel attacks your peremptory challenge of that juror, your statement of prejudice-neutrality will not have to stand on its own legs, the record of your questioning will fully support it. Suppose, for example, you challenge a Lower Slobbovian social worker without asking him anything other than his occupation. Opposing counsel objects that you have arbitrarily and invidiously targeted Lower Slobbovians and demands a race-neutral reason for your peremptory challenge. The judge asks you why you challenged the prospective juror, and you say, "He works in a profession that is more into helping people than it is into hurting them." The judge grants the challenge. You get a conviction, and the defense appeals. You could find your conviction in deep trouble on appeal. Because you asked the juror no questions on the subject, you have left yourself open to the criticism that your race-neutral reason is a pretext. Ask the juror some questions before you exercise the peremptory.

> Q: Now, Mr. Slobovnikov, as a social worker, you are geared toward helping people, aren't you?
>
> Q: And as a matter of fact, you help people who are in pretty much the same situation as the defendant, don't you?
>
> Q: Some of them are even charged with the same kind of crimes as the defendant, aren't they?

---

1 476 U.S. 79, 106 S.Ct. 1712 (1986).

2 J.E.B. v. Alabama ex rel. T.B., 511 U.S. 127, 114 S.Ct. 1419 (1994).

3 Hernandez v. New York, 500 U.S. 352, 111 S.Ct. 1895 (1991).

> Q: Now, in this case you understand that you are not going to be asked to help the defendant?
>
> Q: You're going to be asked to render a fair verdict?
>
> Q: When you go back in that jury room, would your profession as a helper, and your experience helping people like the defendant, and your experience helping people charged with crimes like the defendant is charged with, would all that maybe get in the way of your being able to weigh the evidence in this case?
>
> Q: Would all that maybe make you want to help the defendant no matter what the evidence may be?
>
> Q: Could you set all that aside and render a fair and impartial verdict based only on the law and the evidence that you hear inside this courtroom?

You may not have to give a race-neutral explanation for the exercise of that peremptory. You may lay the groundwork for a challenge for cause.

Of the three goals of selection, rejection, and protection, rejection is most nearly attainable. If you can identify the bad jurors, you can usually make a record for a constitutionally viable reason for exercising a peremptory challenge. Your opponent can do the same for your good jurors. As you identify and eliminate good jurors for the opposition, the opposition is doing the same with your good jurors. The usual result? A less-than-ideal jury for either side, but most often a jury that both sides feel they can work with.

2. THE DEFENSE'S EDGE

In most situations, the defense has a slight edge in jury selection, because selecting an ideal jury is not always the defense's sole goal of jury selection. In most trials, the primary objective of selecting the ideal jury is impeded by secondary objectives. Oftentimes the prosecutor has a heavy trial docket and more than one jury to select out of a too-small panel of prospective jurors. The decisions made in the selection of the first jury will have a profound impact on the selection of the later juries. If the defense has as a secondary goal the prevention of selecting any jury, then your compulsion to get some jury, any jury, will cause you to settle for a less-than-ideal jury. The defense's secondary objective of selecting no jury makes you feel compelled to take the risk of accepting a questionable jury. This can be especially true when picking the last jury out of a depleted panel. Many times, a prosecutor in a small jurisdiction will confront the prospect of accepting an unsatisfactory jury or busting a panel.[4] The

[4] To "bust the panel" means to exhaust the supply of prospective jurors without being able to select a jury. This may not occur in Megalopolis, but it is a constant danger in small jurisdictions throughout the nation.

compulsion to move the docket often causes the prosecutor to accept the unsatisfactory jury. Sometimes you have no alternative, but sometimes you do. Busting the panel is a viable alternative to an unsatisfactory jury. It makes court personnel and witnesses unhappy, but anger is temporary. An acquittal by a bad jury is forever.

3. "LEADING" QUESTIONS

Once you have identified a favorable juror, you can be sure that your adversary will attempt to lead the juror into saying something to form the basis of a challenge for cause. Remember, questioning is a cooperative process. Jurors for the most part try to cooperate in answering questions. This means they will be receptive to the presuppositions in the lawyers' questions. You can be sure that your adversary's questions will be loaded with presuppositions that the jurors cannot be fair. You must perform a preemptive strike, asking questions containing presuppositions that the jurors can be fair.

By the Defense:

> Q: It would be very difficult for you to set aside your previous negative experience with the burglary of your house in deciding your verdict in this case, wouldn't it?

When a juror answers this question, the natural tendency of a friendly witness to help the examiner will lead the witness to agree. Once the juror has agreed that it would be hard to set aside prejudices, this answer will stand in the way of the juror committing to set the prejudices aside. The prosecution, however, has the first opportunity to question the juror, and can ask a question like the following one.

By the Prosecution:

> Q: Understanding that the burglary to your home happened many years ago and has nothing to do with this matter, can you set that incident aside and not let it affect how you decide your verdict in this case?

This question presupposes that she can set it aside. Having adopted the presupposition and stated that she can set the incident aside, when the defense attorney asks if it would be difficult, the juror will most likely acknowledge the difficulty but assure counsel that she can set the matter aside. Most people want to be honest. Most jurors want to do the right thing. If a juror has a genuine impediment to fairness, she will answer your question in the negative.

Of course, when you have identified bad jurors, you work in the other direction. But while working in the other direction, you recall the component-fact technique of cross-examination described under the topic of bias in Chapter 13. You take the negative fact, break it down into as many component parts as possible, and walk the juror through each one of them. By the time you get to the final question about not being able to be fair, you might not have convinced the juror, but you may have convinced the judge, and you certainly have laid a record for a race/gender neutral peremptory challenge.

Once committed in a particular direction, a juror will be loath to change directions. Defense counsel may occasionally browbeat a juror into creating a sufficient record for either making or defeating a cause challenge, but in the process, they may also have alienated the rest of the panel. Once a juror takes a stand on a subject, you may nudge a little, but do not shove. The defense attorney, by trying to shove the juror off the stand she has taken, offends the other jurors. It is not wise to offend the jury. Even if they do not consciously seek revenge with the verdict, they will be subconsciously predisposed against the offending lawyer.

If a juror rejects your presuppositions, it is a waste of time on your part to try to browbeat the juror into saying the magic words which you believe will lay the groundwork for making or defeating a cause challenge. If you have a favorable juror who is displaying an attitude that will not survive a challenge for cause, you need to face reality and agree to the cause challenge. If a bad juror steadfastly refuses to admit bias, then that is what peremptory challenges are for. If you readily concede proper challenges for cause from the other side, you build credibility with the judge, who should be more receptive to your arguments when you make your challenges for cause.

B. PREPARATION FOR THE VOIR DIRE EXAMINATION

1. THE VENIRE

When the court clerk draws the list of potential jurors from the jury pool (or when the computer generates the list), they are listed on a document commonly called a venire. The venire can contain more or less information about the juror, but it usually includes name and address. Some clerk's offices will provide counsel with advance copies of the venire. If you can get an advance copy of the venire, get it. Depending on how large or small your jurisdiction may be, you can do several things with the venire. One of the things you can do is check the driving records of the prospective jurors and at least do a cursory check of the jurors' criminal records in your county. If the county is small enough, law enforcement officers, victims, and victims' families may very well know some of the prospective jurors. In that case, you would do well to have these people come to the office and review the venire. They can give you invaluable information about the jurors they know. If you do this with victims, you must strongly caution them that they are not, under any circumstances, to contact the prospective jurors and try to lobby them pretrial. When you discuss the venire with your informants, ask them for more than a thumbs-up, thumbs-down assessment. You want some personal history on the jurors from your informants, and you must get your informants' reasons for why they think a particular venireperson would make a good juror or a bad juror. Firstly, if they think the person would make a bad juror, you must know why so you can use it as a prejudice-neutral reason for exercise of a peremptory. Secondly, you may strongly disagree with their reason for thinking the person would make a good juror.

The foregoing paragraph was written before the explosion of social media on the internet. Of course, social media can serve as an invaluable indicator of a juror's predispositions. In addition to social media, you can search websites like the Department of Corrections offender webpage, the sexual predator/sex offender database, records of civil suits in the court clerk's online webpage. The fields are white unto harvest with previously inaccessible data which can be mined for information relevant to a potential juror's prejudices and predispositions.

2. JUROR QUESTIONNAIRES

Many jurisdictions now send out juror questionnaires with the juror summons. These questionnaires can be as brief as ten to fifteen questions or as lengthy as the 15-page, 51 question "Juror Questionnaire" used in capital murder cases in the California[5] Questionnaires can prove invaluable assistance in jury selection, and can expedite the voir dire process—if counsel will read them. Too often the lawyers waste valuable time asking questions that have already been answered on the questionnaires. If you can get access to questionnaires in a timely fashion, do so. If you get them, study them. Place them in a three-ring binder in alphabetical order so that they will be ready at hand and easily retrieved for ready reference during voir dire.

3. THE OUTLINE

There are generic questions which should be asked in almost any criminal case, and there are issue-oriented questions which pertain only to specific types of cases. Make an outline of the standard topics of inquiry to use with all cases, leaving plenty of blank spaces for questioning on special topics. A generic voir dire outline could include the following topics:

(1) The jurors' knowledge of the defendant, the victim, the attorneys, and any courtroom personnel.

[5] Juror Questionnaire for Criminal Cases/Capital Case Supplement (JURY-002). <https://selfhelp.courts.ca.gov/jcc-form/JURY-002>.

(2) The jurors' knowledge of any potential witnesses.

(3) The jurors' knowledge of anything having to do with the circumstances of the crime.

(4) Any prior court contact the jurors may have had—as a party, defendant, victim, witness, juror, ANYTHING.

(5) Verdict based on evidence.

(6) Irrelevance of feelings of bias, prejudice, and sympathy.

(7) Burden of proof.

(8) Reasonable doubt.

(9) Vital statistics.

(10) Case-specific topics.

Keep copies of the outline handy and use it for planning and executing your voir dire. Go back to the case theory worksheet and look over the pros and cons of the case. There should be issues on that worksheet that might cause jurors difficulty in being fair and impartial. Having identified those issues, you must craft a series of questions to reveal whether the jurors will be biased by any of the issues. Note these topics onto the voir dire outline. You are now almost ready to conduct the voir dire examination.

C. PERFORMING THE VOIR DIRE EXAMINATION

Because the actual mechanics of voir dire differ markedly from jurisdiction to jurisdiction and from courtroom to courtroom within the same jurisdiction, it is difficult to formulate a one-size-fits-all model for voir dire examination. What follows is a generic description keyed to a smaller jurisdiction. In smaller jurisdictions, the jury panel reports to the courtroom where the trial will be held, the trial judge asks them the preliminary qualifying questions. Then the prosecutor announces the style of the case set for trial, prosecution and defense announce ready for trial, and the judge directs the clerk to draw a panel of jurors. As the jurors names are drawn, they take their seats in the jury box and the judge, clerk, and both counsel furiously note down which juror is sitting where on a seating chart. The jury box is filled with prospective jurors, and then the lawyers conduct voir dire examination of the jurors in the box with the other prospective jurors listening. As challenges are exercised, jurors return to the audience to await the selection of the next jury, and new jurors are periodically called into the box to fill the empty seats. To keep track of who is sitting where, you need a seating chart with sufficient space to allow for note taking under the juror's name. If the case is being tried in an older courtroom built when all jury boxes contained twelve seats configured into two rows, the lawyers take a legal pad, turn it sideways, and draw five evenly spaced parallel lines down the page. This divides the page into six equal columns. The lawyers then bisect the parallel lines with one perpendicular line, dividing the page into twelve cells representing the twelve seats in the jury box. As the jurors are called and seated, their names are written at the top of the cell corresponding to their seat in the box, and notes of their answers are written in the cells under their names. When a juror is excused, her name and notes are crossed out and the new juror's name and notes are entered into the cell. When this page becomes too littered with notes and crossed off names of challenged jurors, the lawyer flips to the next page, draws twelve more cells, transfers the names of the surviving jurors to the new page, and continues the process.

1. A GENERIC VOIR DIRE

Sometimes the judge will conduct a preliminary examination of the jurors and then turn the process over to the lawyers; sometimes the judge will simply allow the lawyers to start the questioning. After the judge does the preliminary examination, the prosecutor customarily goes next in asking the questions, followed by the defense attorney. The more crisply and efficiently you conduct your voir dire, the more likely the judge will be to put all the preliminary questioning in your hands. Be crisp and efficient. You want the judge to do as little of the preliminary questioning as possible. The more you do of the questioning, the better you will come to know the jurors, and the better you will like the form of the questions. The following model voir dire assumes that the judge has simply read the information to the jury, has explained the process of voir dire to them, and has completely turned the preliminary questioning over to you.

> BY THE PROSECUTOR: Good morning, ladies and gentlemen, as the judge said, my name is Stanley Hopkins, I am an assistant state attorney, and I will be representing the state today in this case, which is the State of Florida versus Red Brown. Mr. Brown is the gentleman seated over there at counsel table next to his attorney, Mr. Dee Fender. It will be my privilege at this time to ask you a few questions touching upon your qualifications to sit as a fair and impartial jury. I don't mean by these questions to embarrass you or to be nosey or to pry into your affairs, and I apologize in advance if I offend anyone with any of these questions, but there are a number of questions which must be asked to seat as fair and impartial a jury as possible.
>
> Q: Now the first question I'd like to ask is, do any of you know me. When I say "know," I mean that in the broadest sense. Have any of you ever seen or heard of me, bumped into me on the street, or read about me in the paper? Just raise your hand if you have, and we'll explore your knowledge of me in more detail. [If there is a yes from anyone, follow up on it].

Q: Same question as to Mr. Fender, do any of you know him or know of him in any way?

Q: Same question as to the defendant. Do any of you know Mr. Brown or any member of his family in any way whatsoever?

Q: Did each of you hear and understand the information when it was read to you by Judge Wisdom?

Q: Then each of you understands that Mr. Brown is charged with battery upon Hugh Glass?

Q: Does each of you understand that Mr. Brown is not being sued for money, he is being charged with a crime?

Q: Does each of you understand that because he is charged with a crime, the burden of proof is on the state to prove him guilty of that crime?

Q: Does each of you understand that Mr. Brown does not have to prove himself innocent, that he doesn't have to prove anything?

Q: Does each of you understand that the burden of proof that the state must carry in proving Mr. Brown guilty is proof beyond a reasonable doubt?

Q: You understand that isn't proof beyond a shadow of a doubt or beyond all doubt, but simply proof beyond a reasonable doubt?

Q: At the appropriate time, Judge Wisdom will give you the legal definition of reasonable doubt. When he does, can you follow his instructions and hold the state to that standard of proof?

Q: Juror Jones [addressing the first juror on the left on the front row], if at the close of the evidence, you are satisfied beyond a reasonable doubt that the defendant is guilty, could you and would you vote to return a verdict of guilty?

Q: Juror Smith [addressing the second juror on the left on the front row], if at the close of the evidence, you are satisfied beyond a reasonable doubt that the defendant is guilty, could you and would you vote to return a verdict of guilty?

Q: Juror White [addressing the third juror on the left on the front row], would you? [Continue juror by juror down the front row asking each juror this question individually. When you finish on the front row, go to the second and repeat the process until each and every juror has committed to finding the defendant guilty upon a showing of guilt beyond a reasonable doubt].

Q: Juror Jones [going back to the first juror], if on the other hand, you are not satisfied, but you have a reasonable doubt as to the defendant's guilt, can you give him the benefit of that reasonable doubt and vote not guilty?

Q: Juror Smith, can you?

Q: Juror White, can you? [Continue until each juror has indicated an ability to find the defendant not guilty upon a failure of proof beyond a reasonable doubt].

Q: I am now going to ask if any of you have had any contact with the court system. When I say "court contact" I mean any kind of contact at all. If you got a traffic ticket, sued someone or got sued, got divorced, got subpoenaed as a witness, were the victim of a crime, had a close friend or relative involved as a victim or a defendant in a lawsuit, got arrested, any kind of contact at all. Have any of you had any contact of any kind with the court system? Just raise your hand if you have. [Almost everyone should raise their hand. Explore with each of them the nature of their contact, again being careful to stay away from particulars and focusing on feelings].

[If the juror's court contact is not problematical, ask the following questions].

Q: Juror Jones, was there anything about your contact with the court that gave you any bad feelings about the court system?

Q: Are those feelings such that you can set them aside and not let them have any part in the verdict you render in this case?

[If the contact was bad, ask questions to the following tenor].

Q: I would imagine that you weren't particularly happy about being arrested, were you?

Q: That probably made you angry, didn't it?

Q: Did you feel like you were being mistreated?

Q: You understand the charge in this case is very similar to the charge you were arrested for?

Q: Now, given the fact that you were angry about being arrested, that you felt you were mistreated, and that this charge is very similar to the one you were arrested for, do you feel that all those facts might be difficult to set aside?

Q: Do you feel that those facts might interfere with your ability to fairly weigh and evaluate the evidence in this case?

Q: Do you feel that you might have trouble sitting as a fair and impartial juror in this case?

Q: Do you feel that, although you'd be perfectly able to sit on another type of case, you probably shouldn't be sitting on this one?

[Ask questions to this tenor as long as the juror agrees with you, elaborating on the juror's difficulty in sitting. Eventually you will have laid the groundwork for a challenge for cause. Failing that, you will have established on the record a prejudice-free reason for the exercise of a peremptory challenge. Caveat: If the juror denies being prejudiced by the previous incident and you believe her, you might consider the possibility of keeping her on the jury. Once you believe you have a solid cause challenge, go up to the bench and make it. There is no use wasting further time with voir dire of a witness you are certain will not serve. If the judge denies the cause challenge, do not immediately exercise a peremptory, wait until the judge calls for peremptory challenges].

Q: Have any of you read anything about this case in the paper, heard about it on the radio or TV, or heard anyone talking about the case? [If anyone admits to knowledge, explore the extent of that knowledge without having the juror recite exactly what it is she knows. Remember that the rest of the panel is listening. You don't want them poisoned by the juror's answers].

Q: You understand that you will be called upon to base your verdict in this case upon the evidence as it comes to you in this courtroom and upon the law as the judge instructs you, and that you must base your verdict on those two things and those two things alone?

Q: Can you set aside anything you may have heard outside this courtroom and base your verdict solely on the law and the evidence as you see and hear it inside this courtroom?

Q: There are a number of persons who may be called as witnesses in this case. I am going to call off the names of those persons to see if you know them. Remember, though, just because I call their name, that doesn't mean they're going to testify. As I call these names off, if you know any of the witnesses, just raise your hand.

Hugh Glass, who is the victim alleged in the case.

Officer B. Friendly, a deputy sheriff with the local sheriff's department.

Athelny Jones, a jailer at the county jail.

Daisy Glass.

Cora Brown.

BY THE PROSECUTOR: [speaking to defense counsel] Mr. Fender, have I left out any names? [If defense counsel is still hiding any defense witnesses, this usually flushes them out].

Q: Juror Jones, you raised your hand indicating that you knew Officer Friendly. Do you know him well, or is he an acquaintance, or just someone you know when you see him? [If the juror says she knows him well, explore a little further. If the juror says the witness is only an acquaintance or someone she knows by sight, ask no further questions about the relationship].

Q: You understand that if you are selected as a juror, you must set aside your knowledge of Officer Friendly, and you must weigh and evaluate his testimony just as you would the testimony of any other witness. Can you do that?

[Here ask case-specific questions. After asking case-specific questions, individually ask the jurors about their vital statistics].

Q: Juror Jones, how long have you lived in Camden County?

Q: Before that, where did you live?

Q: What sort of work do you do?

Q: How long have you done that kind of work?

Q: Are you married?

Q: What sort of work does your spouse do?

Q: Do you have any children? [Ask about the children's age, education, and/or employment].

Q: I am about to finish up with my questions and Mr. Fender will be getting up to ask you some questions, but before I sit down, I'd like to ask one final question. Can any of you think of any reason at all why you could not sit as a fair and impartial juror in this case?

BY THE PROSECUTOR: No further questions at this time.

2. MAKING THE CHALLENGES

After all the questions have been asked, the judge will call upon counsel to make peremptory challenges. Usually, the prosecution goes first on the first round of peremptories, followed by the defense, and the order is reversed for the second round of peremptories. Study the jurors and decide who needs to be rejected. If you have more than one, establish a "batting order" with the most unacceptable juror in the number one spot and the least unacceptable juror in the last spot. You only have a limited number of peremptory challenges; you must conserve them and use them wisely. Exercise your peremptories one at a time. Defense counsel just might burn one of her peremptory challenges on a juror you do not like. If this happens, you are two peremptories ahead—the one you saved, and the one defense counsel burned. Try to save at least one peremptory challenge against the possibility that a slot opens, and one final juror is called out of the audience. This final juror will likely be perfectly horrible, but immune to a challenge for cause. One law that almost always comes into play during the trial of a case is Murphy's Law. If you are still saving that one last challenge, you can get rid of the juror and hope that another perfectly horrible juror does not take her place.

D. INDIVIDUAL VOIR DIRE

While jurors are usually questioned *en masse*, some issues are better handled through individual voir dire outside the presence of the other jurors. In high profile capital murder cases, the parties usually employ individual voir dire to inquire into the jurors' feelings about the death penalty and the juror's prior knowledge of the facts of the case. The following transcript sets forth the individual voir dire of a potential juror in a capital murder case.

> BY THE PROSECUTOR: Good morning, Mr. Juror, I will be presenting the evidence on behalf of the state in this case today, and I will be asking you about a couple of issues before we get into the rest of the voir dire of the jury.
>
> The two areas that I want to ask you about, are the areas of pretrial publicity and your views on the death penalty.
>
> First, I'd like to ask you, have you read or heard anything about this case outside the courtroom?
>
> BY THE JUROR: Very little, a little bit, but very little.
>
> BY THE PROSECUTOR: Could you set aside what you heard outside the courtroom and base your verdict in this case solely on the evidence as it comes to you from the witness stand and the law as the judge instructs you? [The prosecutor does not inquire into the particulars of the juror's knowledge because the pertinent question is not what the juror knows but whether the juror can set it aside].
>
> BY THE JUROR: I'm sure that I could, I haven't heard that much to know enough to bias me in any way.
>
> BY THE PROSECUTOR: You say, you have not heard enough about it to bias you in any way, is that correct?
>
> BY THE JUROR: Right.

BY THE PROSECUTOR: Okay, the second area is your views on the death penalty, whether you favor or oppose it, or just what kind of views you have?

BY THE JUROR: I definitely favor capital punishment. [The prosecutor now believes he knows all he needs to know as to whether the juror can render a guilty verdict and recommend the death penalty. This belief is due as much to the juror's demeanor as to his diction while answering the question. The inquiry isn't over, because the juror needs to be insulated from the leading questions that will be asked by defense counsel in an effort to get the juror to say something which will be the basis of a challenge for cause].

BY THE PROSECUTOR: In Florida, every first-degree murder case is divided into two stages, in the first stage, the jury just decides the issue of guilt or innocence, and only in that second phase of the trial, if the jury finds the defendant guilty of murder in the first degree, in the second phase of the trial they decide the issue of whether they ought to recommend the death penalty.

Could you sit through the first phase of the first-degree murder trial and decide the issue of guilt or innocence, without regard for what the penalties may be, without letting that play a part in your verdict?

BY THE JUROR: I think so, yes sir.

BY THE PROSECUTOR: In the second phase of the trial, or the second phase of a first-degree murder trial, the jury is instructed on aggravating and mitigating circumstances by the judge, and the state and defense will have an opportunity to introduce evidence of aggravating and mitigating circumstances, and the judge tells the jury how to weigh and evaluate those circumstances in arriving at a recommendation to the court as to what penalty ought to be imposed.

Now the question that I'm leading up to asking you is, if you were sitting as a juror in the second phase of a first-degree murder trial, could you follow the judge's instructions and weigh and evaluate the aggravating and mitigating circumstances and render a recommendation to the judge. [This question is impossibly complex. It should be simplified. The question is so lengthy because the prosecutor is asking questions off the top of his head without having scripted the questions ahead of time].

BY THE JUROR: Yes, sir.

BY THE PROSECUTOR: And could you follow those instructions, even if you felt that the law ought to be some other way?

BY THE JUROR: Yes, sir.

BY THE PROSECUTOR: If, under the law, you felt that the law called for the imposition of the death penalty, could you vote to recommend the death penalty?

BY THE JUROR: Yes, sir.

BY THE PROSECUTOR: If you felt under the weighing of the aggravating and mitigating circumstances, that the law called for the imposition of life in prison, could you vote for that?

BY THE JUROR: Yes, sir.

BY THE PROSECUTOR: I don't have any further questions.

BY THE DEFENSE: I'm Dee Fender, I'm a lawyer with the Public Defender's Office, and I represent Peter Carey in this case. This is Mr. Carey to my immediate right, and the man to my immediate left is Mr. Aaron Advocate, who will be helping me in this trial.

First, I want to make it plain, that this screening process that we're going through, is a process that is followed in virtually every capital case, because many people have strong feelings about the death penalty.

If one or more of the charges is a capital charge, it is common for the jurors to be screened regarding their feelings about the death penalty.

Do you understand that?

BY THE JUROR: I understand that.

BY THE DEFENSE: We don't mean to in any way imply that my client is guilty of any of these charges, that's the matter for the jury to decide at the trial, and that will be the first order of business for the jury to listen to all the evidence and render a verdict consistent with the evidence and the law regarding his guilt or innocence of murder, kidnaping, and robbery. Okay?

BY THE JUROR: Okay.

BY THE DEFENSE: And as Mr. Hopkins was saying, only if the jury should return a verdict of guilty of first-degree murder, is when we'd go into the second phase of the trial.

BY THE JUROR: Yes, sir.

BY THE DEFENSE: Now, you said, you began by saying that you are definitely in favor of capital punishment. Do you feel that it is an appropriate sentence in every murder case?

BY THE JUROR: No, sir, I do not. There are circumstances to all of them.

BY THE DEFENSE: What about cases of premeditated murder, do you feel that it is always appropriate in premeditated murder? [The prosecutor should have insulated the juror against this question by getting the juror to understand that the death penalty is not appropriate for "unaggravated" cases involving simple premeditation and nothing more].

BY THE JUROR: In most cases, yes sir, if it is premeditated.

BY THE DEFENSE: Again, you said, most cases, so that would depend on the circumstances?

BY THE JUROR: On the circumstances, if he was sane and so forth and knows what he is doing.

BY THE DEFENSE: All right, the law in Florida is that whether the death penalty is appropriate for first-degree murder cases would depend on the presence or absence of certain circumstances that would have to be proven in court.

BY THE JUROR: Right.

BY THE DEFENSE: Even if it is a first-degree premeditated murder, the law is that does not in and of itself justify the imposition of the death penalty.

BY THE JUROR: Not necessarily, no sir.

BY THE DEFENSE: You may find that your views regarding the appropriateness of the death penalty in a given situation are at odds with or different from what the law actually is.

My question to you is, are your personal feelings about the death penalty so strong that you would have difficulty setting them aside and basing your recommendation or judgement in this case strictly upon the law and evidence?

BY THE JUROR: No sir, most definitely not, because the law and the evidence is what determines it.

BY THE DEFENSE: For instance, in Florida the legislature by statute has spelled out the various categories of what we call aggravating circumstances.

Those are circumstances that would tend to justify the imposition of the death penalty and they all set for forth some mitigating circumstances and decreed that the defendant may offer evidence of those mitigating circumstances and of any other matter, which may reasonably be said to be mitigating.

All that we can ask you at this point is, as far as you know, do you feel that you can be completely fair and impartial in this case?

BY THE JUROR: I think so.

BY THE DEFENSE: Anything about your background or your feelings toward the death penalty that would render you somewhat less than impartial?

BY THE JUROR: No sir, I don't think so.

BY THE DEFENSE: I have no further questions.

BY THE COURT: Mr. Hopkins, any further questions?

BY THE PROSECUTOR: No sir.

PRACTICAL EXERCISE

You are prosecuting a case involving charges of racketeering, drug smuggling, kidnaping, conspiracy to murder, and murder for hire. In brief, a drug smuggling ring consisting of police officers has hired two hit men to kill an agricultural inspector who arrested one of their mules.[6] The murder has been carried out, and five years have passed without an arrest. The victim's body was discovered in a small rural county with an unprofessional sheriff's department, and the crime scene was completely ruined. You have absolutely no physical or scientific evidence whatsoever. Two defendants in unrelated drug cases have been arrested and are facing hefty sentences. They agree to testify concerning their limited knowledge of the murder for hire, but only if they receive probationary sentences. Based on their cooperation, you have arranged for a drug sting operation in which the second-in-command of the drug ring is arrested. The second-in-command agrees to plead guilty to second-degree murder in return for a life sentence and further agrees to testify against the kingpin, the underlings, and the hit men. Nine members of the drug ring have been arrested based on the second-in-command's testimony, and three of them have agreed to testify for reduced sentences. You are trying the kingpin, two hit men, and three other underlings who helped to plan the murder. Although you have a solid drug smuggling case, the evidence of guilt of the murder conspiracy (and the murder itself) rests exclusively on accomplice testimony. On the eve of the trial, the second-in-command suffers a massive heart attack and dies, thereby creating a huge hole in the proof you expected to adduce. You immediately enter into very lenient plea bargains with two more underlings, and now only the kingpin, one underling, and the two hit men remain for trial. What issues do you see that might cause jurors difficulty? What sort of questions do you ask to ferret out and deal with any potential prejudice on the part of the potential jurors?

---

[6] A "mule" is a driver who hauls large quantities of drugs for a drug smuggling operation.

CHAPTER 15

OPENING STATEMENT

■ ■ ■

You never get a second chance to make a first impression—Anonymous

Tell them what you're going to tell them; tell them; and then tell them what you told them.—Anonymous

A. THE GENERIC OPENING STATEMENT

Custom and usage dictate the overall arrangement of our presentation to the jury. We begin with an opening statement, then we present the evidence in our case in chief. The defense then presents evidence, and we sum up the case with final arguments. The opening statement is neither evidence nor argument,[1] but it gives the jury an overview of the evidence so that they can better understand the context of the evidence as it comes in at trial. The opening statement gives the advocate his first opportunity to present the case in a coherent, compelling fashion, and it should not be missed. Many prosecutors, carrying heavy dockets of simple cases, feel that the simplicity of their cases allows them to skimp on opening statement or even omit it altogether. After all, so the reasoning goes, a case with only two or three witnesses more or less explains itself. Other prosecutors with heavy dockets feel they are too ignorant of their cases to make an opening statement. Judges have, on occasion, entered a judgment of acquittal or directed verdict after the prosecutor gave a legally insufficient opening statement,[2] and a directed verdict or judgment of acquittal entered after opening statement ends the prosecution for all time.[3] Some prosecutors avoid this danger by reading the indictment or information at the beginning of opening statement, while others avoid it by omitting the opening statement altogether. A prosecutor makes a capital mistake to omit the opening statement, but an even bigger mistake to make a poor one. Consider the following opening statement.

---

[1] Juhasz v. Barton, 146 Fla. 484, 1 So.2d 476, 488 (1941); State v. DelCastillo, 411 N.W.2d 602, 604–605 (Minn.App. 1987); State v. Torres, 16 Wash.App. 254, 554 P.2d 1069 (1976).

[2] Commonwealth v. Lowder, 432 Mass. 92, 731 N.E.2d 510 (2000); Coday v. State, 179 S.W.3d 343, 360–361 (Mo. App.S.D. 2005).

[3] United States v. Ingraldi, 793 F.2d 408, 414 (1st Cir. 1986); State v. Lynch, 79 N.J. 327, 399 A.2d 629 (1979).

Good morning, ladies and gentlemen of the jury, as you learned during voir dire this morning, I am Anthony Jones, and I am the assistant state attorney, who will be prosecuting this case for the state today, which is the case of the State of Florida versus Henry Baker. It will be my privilege now to address you in a few words of opening statement. What is an opening statement? An opening statement is not evidence, and you should not consider it to be evidence, it is merely the attorneys' statement about what they expect the evidence to show during the course of the trial. You could consider it as a road map, or a guide, which will help you to understand the evidence as it is presented to you during the course of the trial. After I have made my opening statement, Mr. Dee Fender will have an opportunity, if he desires, to make an opening statement on behalf of the defendant. After opening statements have been made, I will then call the witnesses on behalf of the state, and they will be examined and cross-examined. I will ask the witnesses questions first on direct examination, and Mr. Fender will then be allowed to cross-examine the witnesses. After all the witnesses have testified and both sides have rested, Mr. Fender and I will again have the opportunity to address you in final argument. Then the judge will instruct you on the law of the case, and you will be allowed to retire and deliberate upon your verdict.

The first witness the state will call to the stand will be Officer Tobias Gregson of the Police Department. Officer Gregson will be sworn to tell the truth and he will testify that he was on routine patrol on the date in question when he observed the defendant's vehicle driving in an erratic pattern on Main Street at about 2:00am. Officer Gregson will testify that this irregular driving pattern caused him concern as to whether or not the defendant might be driving under the influence of alcohol to the extent that his normal faculties were impaired. Officer Gregson will testify that he activated his emergency lights and initiated a traffic stop of the vehicle driven by the defendant. Officer Gregson will tell you that upon making the stop and exiting his vehicle, he approached the driver's side window of the defendant's vehicle. Officer Gregson will then describe for you the various signs of impairment that he observed the defendant displaying. Officer Gregson will testify that he caused the defendant to exit his vehicle and perform several field sobriety exercises. Officer Gregson will tell you that the defendant was unable to perform those exercises in a satisfactory fashion, and he will testify that he decided to effectuate an arrest upon the defendant for the offense of driving under the influence of alcohol to the extent that his normal faculties were impaired. Officer Gregson will then testify that he took the defendant to the police station for the administration of an intoxilyzer to determine the extent of the defendant's impairment.

The next witness the state will call is Victor Hatherly, a certified intoxilyzer operator with the Police Department, who will testify to the various maintenance procedures for the intoxilyzer used by the Police Department. Officer Hatherly will testify that he advised the defendant of the necessary implied consent warning and further complied with the necessary formalities for the administration of an intoxilyzer test upon the defendant. Officer Hatherly will then testify and share with you the results of the intoxilyzer test.

At the conclusion of the evidence, we will again have the opportunity to address you in final argument and the judge will instruct you on the law. You will then retire to deliberate upon your verdict. When you have arrived at a verdict, you will be called back into the courtroom to publish that verdict, and that verdict should find the defendant guilty as charged of driving under the influence of alcoholic beverages to the extent that his normal faculties were impaired. Mr. Fender will now have an opportunity to address you in opening statement, and I ask that you give him the same courteous attention that you gave me.

This opening statement not only demonstrates that you can make an opening statement without informing the jury of any pertinent facts of the case, but that you can make an opening statement without even knowing the facts of the case. This opening fits the facts of almost any DUI case. It has told the jury absolutely nothing and has given them absolutely no reason to think that the defendant ought to be convicted. The opening statement tells the jury how the trial will be conducted, but it does not tell the jury anything about the evidence. Jones opened with an uninspiring warning to the effect that what he was about to tell them was not evidence. He might as well have stood up and advised the jury that now would be a good time to take a nap, because he was about to make some inconsequential noise. Jones then launched off into a witness-by-witness recitation of each witness's testimony, prefacing each and every sentence with a variation of the phrase "Officer [insert name here] will testify that [insert fact here]." Fortunately, he had only two witnesses. If he had five to ten witnesses, the opening statement would not only have been soporific, it would also have been confusing. Jones then wound up his masterpiece with a description of how final arguments, jury instructions, and jury deliberations would be conducted, and concluded with an admonition to listen carefully to what his opponent had to say. An excellent case might survive an opening statement like this, but a weaker case will crumble under the weight of such a performance. Jones not only can do better, he must do better.

> Ladies and gentlemen of the jury, during the early morning hours of January 23 of this year, Henry Baker, a man with a Master's Degree from State University, couldn't say his ABC's. He couldn't find his driver's license. He couldn't walk a straight line. And he couldn't keep his car under control. He couldn't do any of these things because he had a blood alcohol level of 0.23. He was too impaired by alcohol to drive a car.
>
> Early that morning, Mr. Baker walked out of the Watering Hole Inn and got into his 2006 Ford Escalade. He cranked the car and drove onto Main Street, where he was spotted by Officer Tobias Gregson. Officer Gregson watched as Baker pulled out of the parking lot across a flowerbed and over the curb onto the street. Officer Gregson watched as Baker drove into the left lane of Main Street, overcorrected, and ran back up on the curb and onto the sidewalk. Officer Gregson fell in behind Baker as he swerved down Main Street and ran the red light. Officer Gregson turned on his blue light and stopped Baker. When Officer Gregson asked Baker for his driver's license, Baker gave him a credit card that had Baker's picture on it. Gregson smelled alcohol on Baker's breath, so he asked him to do some field sobriety exercises. When Gregson asked Baker to say the alphabet, he sang "A–B–C–Z–Q–R–P." When Gregson asked Baker to walk a straight line, he staggered. Officer Gregson took Baker to the police station and had him take an intoxilyzer test. Baker blew a 0.23, over twice the legal limit.
>
> Henry Baker couldn't say his ABC's. He couldn't find his driver's license. He couldn't walk a straight line. And he shouldn't have been driving a car. When you hear all the evidence, you will be satisfied beyond a reasonable doubt that Henry Baker is guilty of driving under the influence of an alcoholic beverage to the extent that his normal faculties were impaired.

In fewer than half the words of the first opening, the second opening actually tells the jury what happened. It not only tells them what happened, it does so in a way that strongly suggests to the jury that Baker should not have driven that night. How does the second opening succeed where the first fails? Let us begin by examining the case theory. Both openings had the same case theory: Baker was too drunk to walk a straight line, let alone drive a car, because his blood alcohol level was 0.23. In the first opening, the jury had to listen intently to the entire opening statement in order to discern the case theory, and they still couldn't find it. They were going to have to wait for the testimony to unfold to learn the case theory.

In the second opening, the prosecutor put the case theory to the jury in the first brief paragraph of the opening statement. After setting forth the case theory, the second opening gave a succinct statement of the facts supporting the case theory. After giving the statement of facts, the prosecutor closed by repeating the case theory and assuring the jury that they would be satisfied beyond a reasonable doubt of the defendant's guilt. The opening followed a simple pattern. Tell them what you're going to tell them; tell them; and then tell them what you told them. This pattern not only serves as a good model for an opening statement, it serves as a good model for the entire forensic presentation. In the opening statement you should tell them what you are going to tell them. In your case in chief, you should deliver the goods by telling them. And in your final argument, you should tell them what you told them.

B. THE PARTS OF AN OPENING STATEMENT

This simple scheme for opening statement—tell them what you're going to tell them, tell them, and tell them what you told them—follows the basic outline for a forensic presentation recognized more than 2,000 years ago by Aristotle. Aristotle taught that a forensic speech had four parts—the introduction, the statement of the case, the argument, and the conclusion.[4] The purpose of the introduction is to make the jury attentive, receptive, and well disposed; the statement of the case sets out what is sought to be proved; the argument seeks to prove it; and the conclusion summarizes the argument and attempts to stir the jury to accept the argument. Modern criminal procedural eliminates argument from the opening statement.

> An opening statement should not be argumentative, inflammatory, misstate what will be contained in the evidence, or contain expressions of the personal belief of the prosecutor.[5]

The modern rules for opening statements thus reduce Aristotle's model to a three-part presentation—introduction, statement of the case, and conclusion. By the time the trial reaches the opening statement, the attorneys have had somewhat of an opportunity, through jury selection, to render the jury attentive, receptive, and well disposed. The introduction to the opening statement should continue this process. Because you are not supposed to argue in opening statements, the body of the speech should be a clear, concise factual recitation of the anticipated evidence. The conclusion should end the speech with a powerful statement that gets the speaker back from the lectern to counsel table without losing the effect of the rest of the speech and leaves the jury ready to hear the evidence which

---

[4] Aristotle, Rhetoric, 1414b, The Complete Works of Aristotle, 2:2254. Princeton University Press, 1984.

[5] State v. Torres, 16 Wash.App. 254, 258, 554 P.2d 1069, 1072 (1976).

will confirm the facts given in the opening. The National College of District Attorneys recommended this structure for an opening, calling the three parts of the speech the attention step, the fact narration, and the exit line.

1. THE ATTENTION STEP

The doctrine of primacy and recency teaches that the first thing someone sees or hears is the thing that is remembered best, and the last thing observed is what is remembered second best. Boxers take advantage of this teaching with a maneuver called "stealing a round." Each round of a fight is scored separately, and the judges total the scores for each round separately to determine the winner of the fight. Boxers will therefore attempt to steal a round with a flurry of activity at the beginning and end of a round, believing that the judges will be more impressed with what happens first and last than with what happens during the middle of the round. You should seek to win the opening statement by the same method. At no time during the course of the trial will the jury be more fully attentive to what you have to say than during the first minute or so of your opening statement. If you can convict the defendant with the first twenty-five words or less of the opening statement, you have made a giant stride toward winning the case.

The National College of District Attorneys taught that there are three types of effective attention steps, any one of which can provide a powerful beginning to the opening statement. They are the fact capsule, the value-based theme, and the descriptive characterization. The fact capsule gives the jury a succinct statement of the case. It is usually a simple statement of the case theory, worded so as to state the case theory as powerfully as possible. The value-based theme sets the stage for the introduction of the case theory by evoking deeply held values common to all human beings and relating those values to the case theory in such a way as to impel the jury toward a favorable verdict. The descriptive characterization dwells on the pathos of some aspect of the case, rendering the jury receptive to the case theory. Depending upon the nature of the case and the advocate's skill, any one of the three could prove highly persuasive. The value-based theme is the most generic of the three types of attention steps and can be adapted to case after case.

Whatever form the attention step takes, it must be stated with brevity, clarity, and verity. The attention step should sound more like a primary reader than a James Joyce novel, a philosophical treatise, or a legal brief. The days of bombastic oratory may not be dead, but they are certainly moribund. Compare the following fact capsules.

> (1) Acting from a premeditated design and with malice aforethought, Peter Carey inflicted multiple gunshot wounds in and upon the bound and gagged body of Lucy Ferrier, thereby

causing her to languish and thereafter to die subsequent to his departure but prior to the arrival of an advanced life support unit from the local emergency rescue service.

(2) In an act of unparalleled brutality and cold, calculated premeditation, Peter Carey armed himself with one of the most terrible instruments of destruction known to man, a twelve gauge shotgun, and he used that terrible instrument to propel three loads of triple aught buckshot—three messengers of death—into the helpless body of Lucy Ferrier as she lay bound and gagged on the floor of her modest kitchen. After performing this vicious act of premeditated murder, Carey left Lucy languishing in terrible pain and spilling her lifeblood onto the floor. The mission of mercy performed by the heroic paramedics from our local emergency rescue service proved unsuccessful, for Lucy had succumbed to the grievous wounds inflicted by this mad-dog killer prior to their arrival.

Fact capsule (1) might make a good statement of the case for a legal brief, but it buries the pathos of the deed in tortured sentence structure and polysyllabic diction. Fact capsule (2) could have been copied from the pages of a dime novel. It is so highly argumentative that it has no place in an opening statement. It might even provoke the judge to declare a mistrial. Now look at fact capsule (3).

(3) Peter Carey hogtied Lucy Ferrier. Then he took a shotgun, and he shot her in the chest. Then he reloaded and shot her in the chest again. Then he reloaded and shot her in the chest again. Then he walked off and left her dying on the floor of her kitchen.

Fact capsule (3) is a simple, plain-spoken statement of what happened. Where fact capsules a and b have a Flesch-Kincaid Grade Level of 16, fact capsule (3)'s grade level is 3.9. Unlike fact capsules (1) and (2), fact capsule (3) has no adjectives or adverbs, and every sentence is a simple sentence. Fact capsule (3) can be understood by the least intellectual grammar school dropout or the most accomplished member of Mensa. And—fact capsule (3), for all its simplicity, is more powerful than either capsule (1) or (2). When the facts themselves are such that they stir the emotion, why gild the lily?

The value-based theme begins by evoking a strongly held value, belief, need, or emotion common to most people and associates that value, belief, need, or emotion with the case theory. Usually this is accomplished by stating some proverb or aphorism and relating it to the case theory. Since these proverbs and aphorisms state universally held beliefs, needs, and values, they can be used over and over again in a variety of cases. For example, consider the following value-based themes.

(1) Ladies and gentlemen, this is a case about choices and consequences, Duncan Ross chose to break the law, and now he must face the consequences.

(2) There's an old saying that three people can keep a secret if two of them are dead. The secret that brings us to court today involves three people—Duncan Ross, his wife Virginia, and his girlfriend Irene Adler—and only his wife is dead.

(3) Suspicion always haunts the guilty mind, and Isa Whitney's mind was haunted with fear. He feared arrest because he was setting up a sale of cocaine to some new purchasers. His fears were justified because those purchasers were undercover officers working with the drug task force.

(4) There's a proverb that says, "the wicked flee where none pursue," and that's what Jonathan Small did. Before anyone even knew that he had killed Jack Mortimer, Small had emptied Mortimer's bank account and fled to the other side of the continent.

Theme (1) works well with crimes which do not generate a great deal of pathos, and prosecutors often use it in DUI prosecutions. The defendant called the tune when he decided to drive drunk, and now he must pay the piper. Theme (2) works well in cases built on the testimony of accomplices. It strikes home with the common experience of the listener and serves to bolster the accomplices' testimony before they ever take the stand. Themes (3) and (4) argue without being argumentative. They recite facts which silently speak of guilt. Prosecutors with fertile imaginations can conjure up many more value-based themes to apply to the facts of their cases.

The descriptive characterization is more case-specific than the value-based theme, and its effectiveness depends wholly on how well the characterization strikes home. Consider the following.

(1) "I can't believe you shot my husband!" "He was threatening me, and he stole my bong." Having thus explained why he had shot his brother, Adam Cain walked outside, got in his car, and drove off, leaving his brother dying on the kitchen floor.

(2) In many ways, Lucy Hebron was a normal little eight-year-old. She played with dolls, she loved to skip rope, and she said her prayers every night. But her prayers weren't like other little girls'. She didn't pray "God bless Mommy and Daddy." She prayed "Please make Daddy stop."

(3) It was a cold and rainy day.

Characterization (1) failed. It sought to stir pathos over killing someone because he stole a pot pipe. It missed the mark because the jurors were taken, not by the motive for the shooting, but the wife's expression of disbelief. If she couldn't believe Cain had shot her husband, why should they? Characterization (2) may not have rendered the jury well-disposed to the prosecution, but it certainly rendered them ill disposed toward the defendant. Characterization (3) mimics what is reputed to be the worst opening line in all of English literature,[6] but it was the descriptive characterization which opened the State of Florida versus Theodore Robert Bundy. The descriptive characterization does not have to be great literature if it strikes home to render the jury attentive, receptive, and well disposed.

No matter what type of attention step you choose, you must remember that you cannot be argumentative, you cannot be inflammatory, you cannot express personal opinion, you cannot misstate the evidence. In your attention step, and in the entire body of the opening statement, you must calmly and clearly state the facts in such a way that the facts argue themselves.

2. THE FACT NARRATION

The next section of the opening statement consists of simply telling the jury about your case. Speak plain words in simple sentences. Never use a three-syllable word where a two-syllable word will do. Never use a two-syllable word where a one syllable word will do. Speak in active voice. Passive voice has this fault—it is passive. Compare the following two sentences.

(1) James Damery was victimized by John Clay's caption and asportation of the motor vehicle which was entrusted to Damery's care, custody, and control by James McCarthy.

(2) John Clay stole James McCarthy's car from James Damery's garage.

Give the jury a fact narration, not a procedural overview. Do not say "We will call so-and-so who will testify to thus-and-such. Then we will call what's-his-name who will testify to whatever. Then we will call. . . ." This sort of delivery destroys the force of the presentation. Tell a story and tell it from a vantage point different from the jury's point of view. Do not tell them what they will see and hear from the jury box. Tell them what somebody saw and heard and felt and smelt while the crime occurred. You can tell the story from the vantage point of the defendant, the victim, or one of the witnesses, or you can tell the story from the vantage point of the all-seeing eye. Some call this last vantage point the "God's eye view," others

---

[6] "It was a dark and stormy night * * * *," Sir Edward George Bulwer-Lytton, Paul Clifford, Whitefish, Montana: Kessinger Publishing, 1942, p. 1.

call it the "Greek chorus" vantage point.[7] Whatever vantage point you use to tell the story, stick to it and give the jury a clear, concise, factual recitation of the evidence. Writing classes taught us not to be redundant, repetitive, or repetitious. We therefore seek to avoid using the same word over and over during a composition or a speech. Slavish adherence to this precept can sow confusion with the jury. In an opening statement, when you refer to people, places, or things, you should always call them by the same name. If you refer Duncan Ross as "the defendant" in one place, "Ross" in another, and "the perpetrator" in another, the listener just might think you are talking about three different people. When you have multiple actors referred to with multiple names, you have a recipe for disastrous misunderstanding. Remember, an opening statement is not an exercise in great literature, it is an exercise in persuasion. The jury cannot be persuaded if they do not understand what you are talking about. On the other end of the spectrum, overuse of pronouns also confuses the issues. "He could tell he wasn't very happy with him because when he hit him, he took his money, and then he ran away from him." Who wasn't happy with whom? Who hit whom? What really happened here? Consider the following factual narrative.

> Peter Carey fell out with his girlfriend, Lucy Ferrier. He got so mad that he went and stole his brother's shotgun and a box of shotgun shells. He took that shotgun and got on his bicycle, and he rode all the way across town to Lucy's home. He walked up and knocked on Lucy's front door, and when her son Vic answered the door, Carey pushed his way into the house. Carey tore the phone off the wall and pushed Vic into a closet. He tied Vic up with the phone cord and went back into the kitchen, where he grabbed Lucy and tied her up, too. Then Carey broke open the breach on the shotgun and put a shell in the chamber. He closed the shotgun and stuck it to Lucy's chest. He pulled the trigger, and a load of buckshot tore into Lucy's chest. Carey broke open the breach of the shotgun, pulled the empty shell out, and put in another. He closed the breach and stuck the shotgun to Lucy's chest again. He pulled the trigger again, and another load of buckshot went into her chest. Carey reloaded the shotgun one more time, shoved the gun up against Lucy's chest, and shot her again. Then he threw the shotgun onto the floor and went and got back on his bicycle and went home. When Vic got himself untied, he ran into the kitchen and found Lucy still alive, but just barely. Vic ran next door and called 911. When rescue got there, they found Lucy dead. Vic told the police what had happened, and Officer Tobias Gregson went to Carey's house, where he arrested Peter Carey. Officer

[7] Greek tragedies customarily had a chorus, a group of actors who were omniscient and who informed the audience of previous history and of happenings offstage.

> Gregson advised Carey of his rights, and Carey told Officer Gregson he killed Lucy because she spent too many of his "dead presidents." The medical examiner performed an autopsy on Lucy, and he determined that Lucy died from three short range shotgun blasts. He ruled the death a homicide. Officer Gregson collected the shotgun shells and the shotgun, and he sent them to the crime lab in the state capital. At the crime lab, a fingerprint examiner found five of Carey's fingerprints on the shotgun, and one of Carey's fingerprints on one of the shotgun shells. The firearms examiner determined that the empty shotgun shells were fired from the shotgun. The firearms examiner looked at the shotgun pellets and wadding that the medical examiner took from Lucy's body and compared the pellets and wadding to the empty shotgun shells. The pellets and wadding were of the same type as would have been loaded into that brand of shotgun shell. Officer Gregson also collected Carey's clothing, and submitted that to the lab, too. A serologist at the lab found blood spatters on Carey's clothing and compared those blood spatters with the DNA of Lucy Ferrier. The DNA of the blood on Carey's clothing matched Lucy's DNA.

This fact narrative has a Flesch-Kincaid Grade Level of 8.16, and only 3% of the sentences are in the passive voice. It has all three of the requisites of a good forensic presentation—brevity, clarity, and verity. You could take these facts and spin them into an opening statement running to thousands of words, but you could hardly state the case more succinctly or more forcefully. The only thing left to do now is to give the exit line, go back to counsel table, and sit down.

3. THE EXIT LINE

The doctrine of primacy and recency comes back into play with the exit line. You must say something memorable. You cannot trail off with a comment like "Well, that's about all I have to say about that." Some lawyers have a stock closing that they apply to all cases, ". . . and at the conclusion of the evidence, ladies and gentlemen, you will be satisfied that my client should prevail in this lawsuit." A good recency strategy is to repeat the case theory. Some prosecutors repeat the case theory and close out with a canned sentence appropriate to all occasions.

> Peter Carey hogtied Lucy Ferrier. Then he shot her in the chest. Then he reloaded and shot her in the chest again. Then he reloaded and shot her in the chest again. Then he walked off and left her dying on the floor of her kitchen. At the conclusion of the evidence, you will be satisfied beyond a reasonable doubt that Peter Carey is guilty of Murder in the First Degree. [Silently look each juror in the eye and then turn and walk to counsel table].

4. PUTTING IT ALL TOGETHER

The fact narration should flow logically from the attention step, and the exit line should grow naturally out of the fact narration. All three parts of the opening statement should form a seamless whole with a single message. The following example should illustrate the point.

> **Attention Step:** Robert Joyner on April 15, 1995, went and got his shotgun. He loaded the shotgun, stepped out onto the front porch of his single wide trailer, raised that shotgun to his shoulder, and he shot and killed his good friend, Rodney Howard. And what did he kill him over? A $40.00 bag of pot.
>
> **Fact Narration:** Joyner and Howard planned on getting together that night and going halves on a bag of pot. Howard and his girlfriend went to Joyner's trailer, where they met with Joyner and his wife and another woman named Roberta Swensen. They spent the evening talking, arguing, and getting drunk. Since everyone was drinking heavily, no two of them remember exactly the same thing. The gist of what happened, though, is as follows:
>
> Joyner argued with Howard. Howard argued with Swensen. Everybody seemed to be arguing with everybody else. Joyner's wife got so drunk she took off her shirt and bra, and there was an argument about that. Joyner and Howard finally made up enough to go off and buy the pot. When they got back to the trailer, they argued over the division of the pot. The argument wound up outside, where Joyner and Howard got into a fist fight. Joyner's wife and Roberta Swensen joined in the fight on Joyner's side. Howard picked up a stick and hit Joyner. Swensen got the stick away from Howard, and Joyner went back inside the trailer.
>
> While Howard was getting ready to leave, Joyner was getting ready to get even. He got his shotgun, loaded it, and stepped onto the porch. As Howard opened his car door to get in and drive off, Joyner raised the shotgun and fired. He shot from a distance of about 25 feet, and the blast tore into Howard's chest, and went through his heart, lungs, and aorta. Howard said to his wife, "Amy, they've shot me. I'm going to die." He then stumbled away from the car and fell down.
>
> While Amy Howard was trying to help her fallen husband, Joyner was going back inside and putting up his shotgun. When the law got there, he was sitting on the living room sofa.
>
> **Exit Line:** Robert Joyner on April 15, 1995, went and got his shotgun. He loaded the shotgun, stepped out onto the front porch of his single wide trailer, raised that shotgun to his shoulder, and he shot and killed his good friend, Rodney Howard. And what did

he kill him over? A $40.00 bag of pot. At the conclusion of the evidence, you will be satisfied beyond a reasonable doubt that Robert Joyner is guilty of Murder in the Second Degree with a Firearm.

C. VERBATIM OR OUTLINE?

Should you write your opening statement out word for word? Or should you simply outline it? At least since the time of Cicero, advocates have differed on which is the better method. Cicero believed that the advocate enhanced his eloquence by writing his speeches out word for word, but he would have been scandalized if an advocate read his speech word for word.[8] The danger that you might read the opening statement is the best argument against writing it out word for word. An advocate who reads the opening statement will convince no one, but he might put some of the jurors to sleep. If you have written out your opening word for word and feel tempted to read it to the jury, reach across your body and place your right hand on the left side of the lectern. Then step to the left until your right hand is at your right side, still on the lectern. You will now be out from behind the lectern, and your notes will be out of your line of sight. As you look at the jury to give your opening, your text will be off to your right and unavailable to read. If you become stuck, and it is absolutely necessary to look at your text to refresh your recollection, pause and step behind the lectern, look at your text, and then step back to the left of the lectern and resume your opening. Those who have had experience with trial team in law school sometimes think that notes are anathema, and that the presentation must appear to be given extemporaneously. Whatever you do, do not try to deliver an extemporaneous opening statement to a real jury. You may think that the case is simple and think that you know the facts cold, but you will inevitably omit saying something important or say something you will regret bitterly. A presentation delivered flawlessly and without notes may make the audience think you have great skill, but you had better not be trying to convince the jury how good you are. You had better be trying to convince the jury how good your case is. What the jury thinks of you matters very little compared to what they think of your case.

PRACTICAL EXERCISE

Review the fact pattern set out in the Practical Problem at the end of Chapter 8. Write three separate attention steps for the opening statement in your case. One should be a fact capsule, one a descriptive characterization, and one a value-based theme. Decide which of the three attention steps is the most powerful and write an opening statement for the case using that attention step.

---

[8] 3 Cicero, De Oratore, 1.33.150, Harvard University Press, Cambridge, Massachusetts, 1942, p. 103.

CHAPTER 16

FINAL ARGUMENT

■ ■ ■

The art of inventing and arranging arguments is, as has been said, the only province that rhetoric can claim entirely and exclusively.—Richard Whately[1]

A. A PROPER PERSPECTIVE ON FINAL ARGUMENT

Final argument is so highly regarded as a persuasive tool that if you asked many lawyers how to begin preparing for a trial, they would tell you to write your final argument before doing anything else. Lawyers who do this get the cart before the horse. A final argument is a confirmation of something. How can you prepare a confirmation before you have prepared the subject matter of that confirmation? Aristotle taught that the statement of the case comes first and then comes the argument. You could say that the ABC's of preparing your case presentation consist of ascertaining your case theory; building an opening statement around your case theory; and confirming your case theory in final argument. You should think of the case theory, opening statement, and final argument as a unified whole, with an interruption between opening statement and final argument for the presentation of evidence.

1. INVENTION (OR DISCOVERY) OF ARGUMENTS

The prosecutor presents a factual history to the jury which shows the defendant guilty of the crime charged. Ideally, the prosecution puts on such a compelling case that no argument is necessary, as when Cicero convicted Verres by simply calling witnesses and making no argument at all.[2] Much more often the prosecutor must persuade the jury that the facts presented show the defendant's guilt. At some time in your career as a prosecutor you will sit down before a trial and order your witnesses, arrange the evidence, write the direct examinations; and then sit dumbfounded as you try to think of something, anything, to say in final argument. Worse yet, you will

[1] Elements of Rhetoric Comprising an Analysis of the Laws of Moral Evidence and Persuasion with Rules for Argumentative Composition and Elocution, Kessinger Publishing Company, Whitefish, Montana, 1854/2005. p. 38.

[2] Plutarch, Life of Cicero 7.4–5. Ed. Thayer, Bill. Trans. Perrin, Bernadotte. 2005. University of Chicago. 30 March 2007. <http://penelope.uchicago.edu/Thayer/E/Roman/Texts/Plutarch/Lives/Cicero*.html>.

not have given the matter any thought until you have rested and the judge says, "Counselor, you may address the jury." As you sit there with an empty feeling in your stomach wondering what you are going to say, remember that you had fair warning. You must prepare your arguments in advance of trial, and if you follow the advice of this manual, your argument will almost write itself. Preparation for final argument begins the moment you become aware of the case, as you begin to assimilate, and assess the facts, and as you assemble your best case from those facts. Your final argument ought to flow naturally from the stream of your evidentiary presentation, your opening statement, and your case theory.

Begin to write your final argument by reviewing your case theory, the defense theory, and the point to adjudicate. Is the case a whodunnit, a whydunnnit, or a what-of-it? Is it honorable, dishonorable, doubtful, or trivial? All these matters were discussed in detail in Chapter 7, but you must revisit them. You have built your opening statement to confirm the case theory and carry the point to adjudicate, and you have marshaled the evidence toward that same end. You must now review that evidence and determine what arguments to make. If you did your job in the charging stage and the case has not fallen apart between arrest and trial, the evidence will support a number of arguments to confirm the case theory and carry the point to adjudicate. The arguments must be persuasive, they must be plausible, but above all, they must be firmly rooted in fact.

All arguments can be classified in categories that the ancients called *topoi*, or topics. Some of the common topics of invention are: definition and division, comparison and contrast, relationship, circumstance, and testimony. Almost all persuasive arguments will speak to one or more of these topics. We will discuss and define these topics later, but first we must discuss how to build arguments.

2. EXAMPLE AND ENTHYMEME

Aristotle taught that the two types of arguments were the example and the enthymeme.[3] The example proves the most primitive form of argument, and the one we most instinctively use. "But, Mom, everybody else's parents let them go to the skating rink on Friday nights." To which Mom replied with a counterexample, "If your friend's parents put them in jail on Friday night, would you want to go to jail, too?" Although Aristotle did not define the enthymeme, he said the enthymeme was to rhetoric what the syllogism was to logic. The enthymeme then is a rhetorical syllogism. The enthymeme differs from the syllogism in two ways. We find the most obvious difference in the way they are stated. A syllogism states two premises (major and minor) and a conclusion. An enthymeme usually

[3] Aristotle, Rhetoric, 1356b, The Complete Works of Aristotle, 2:2156. Princeton University Press, 1984.

states only one premise and a conclusion. Many books on logic illustrate the structure of a syllogism with the following example:

Premise 1: All men are mortal.

Premise 2: Socrates is a man.

Conclusion: Socrates is mortal.

The enthymeme, however, has this structure:

Premise: Socrates drank hemlock.

Conclusion: Socrates committed suicide.

One of the premises is missing from this enthymeme. If we supply it, the enthymeme looks like this:

Premise 1: Hemlock is a poison.

Premise 2: Socrates drank hemlock.

Conclusion: Socrates committed suicide.

An enthymeme has as many premises as a syllogism, it simply elides or suppresses one of the premises in much the same way as the short statement elides the tag question. Because the arguer usually suppresses the weaker of the two premises in an enthymeme, you can often defeat the enthymeme by simply stating the suppressed premise. For example, your opponent tells the jury "That Greek Socrates is a liar!" You defeat the argument by demonstrating the full structure of the enthymeme, stating its suppressed premise. "My learned colleague seeks to discredit Socrates by telling you that he is a Greek and therefore a liar. He bases his argument on the prejudiced assumption that all Greeks are liars."

The second distinction between syllogism and enthymeme is more subtle but at the same time more profound. We state both syllogism and enthymeme in the language of deductive reasoning. With a valid syllogism, if the major and minor premises are certainly true, the conclusion must also be true. The premises of an enthymeme, unlike the premises of a syllogism, are open to question. If the enthymeme's premises are only probably true, then the conclusion can at best be established as probably true. Further, in an enthymeme, even if the major and minor premises are certainly true, then the conclusion is only probably true. The logician can give absolute proof of a proposition with one valid syllogism. One deductively valid enthymeme does not conclusively prove anything. Look back at the example enthymeme above. That hemlock is poison and that Socrates drank hemlock can both be true without conclusively proving that Socrates committed suicide. He may have thought the hemlock was harmless and accidentally killed himself. He may have been forced to drink the hemlock by the Athenian government as punishment for a crime. An enthymeme can show a proposition to be more or less probable depending on the persuasiveness of the premises, but it can never serve as absolute proof.

3. COMPOUNDING ENTHYMEMES

Where logical proof is satisfied with a single syllogism, rhetorical proof requires a series of enthymemes. How many enthymemes get you to absolute proof? An infinite number cannot get you to absolute proof. Fortunately for the prosecution, you do not need absolute proof. You only need proof beyond a reasonable doubt. So how many enthymemes get you to proof beyond a reasonable doubt? It depends on how persuasively you state them and present them. A series of enthymemes can make a powerful case. Each individual enthymeme may fail to persuade, but taken as a whole, they produce conviction. In discussing this use of enthymemes we will use the mid-twentieth century case of State of Florida versus Enoch Drebber. On a dark night in the winter months, a big, burly man with a raspy voice broke into an elderly lady's home and raped her. The rapist, who was completely bald, cut his finger on the broken glass at the point of entry and bled profusely. During the rape he told the lady he lived nearby, but he was originally from "up north." The sheriff, while investigating the case, came upon Enoch Drebber, a big, burly, bald man with a raspy voice and a cut on his finger who lived near the victim's house. Upon being interviewed, Drebber said he would not deny committing the rape because he had done time up north for another rape. Drebber added that he needed help with his problem. Since this case predated DNA evidence, all that could be done with the bloodstain was to determine its ABO type. Serological examination showed that Drebber had Type O blood, the same as the blood found at the point of entry. The prosecution had the following enthymemes available for argument:

Premise 1: The rapist was a big, burly bald male.
Premise 2: Enoch Drebber is a big, burly bald male.
Conclusion: Enoch Drebber is the rapist.

Premise 1: The rapist had a raspy voice.
Premise 2: Enoch Drebber has a raspy voice.
Conclusion: Enoch Drebber is the rapist.

Premise 1: The rapist cut his finger.
Premise 2: Enoch Drebber cut his finger.
Conclusion: Enoch Drebber is the rapist.

Premise 1: The rapist had type O blood.
Premise 2: Enoch Drebber has type O blood.
Conclusion: Enoch Drebber is the rapist.

Premise 1: The rapist lived near the victim.
Premise 2: Enoch Drebber lived near the victim.
Conclusion: Enoch Drebber is the rapist.

Premise 1: The rapist came from "up north."
Premise 2: Enoch Drebber comes from "up north."
Conclusion: Enoch Drebber is the rapist.

Premise 1: A man who has raped before will likely rape again.
Premise 2: Enoch Drebber has raped before.
Conclusion: Enoch Drebber is the rapist.

Premise 1: Someone who "needs help" because he raped before is likely a rapist.
Premise 2: Enoch Drebber "needs help" because he raped before.
Conclusion: Enoch Drebber is the rapist.

Premise 1: An innocent man would deny committing the rape.
Premise 2: Enoch Drebber "won't deny" committing the rape.
Conclusion: Enoch Drebber is the rapist.

The defense undertook to deny the prosecution four of the available enthymemes by moving to suppress Drebber's statement. At suppression hearing, the judge suppressed two of the state's enthymemes. He would not allow evidence of the previous rape, and he would not allow evidence that Drebber "needed help." He would only allow evidence of Drebber's statements that he "would not deny" the rape and that he "came from up north." At trial the victim could only say that Drebber looked and sounded like the rapist, but she could not positively identify him. At trial the prosecution compounded the available enthymemes into a series of arguments in the following fashion.

> We know the rapist was a big, burly, bald man with a raspy voice, type O blood, and a cut finger. We know the rapist lives near the victim and came from up north. Now of all the people with type O blood, who is a big, burly, bald man? Who has a raspy voice? Who cut his finger? Who lives near the victim? Who came from up north? Who "won't deny" committing the rape? Enoch Drebber, that's who!

B. THE TOPICS OF INVENTION

A simple serial statement of the enthymemes might carry the day, but the topics of invention give numerous ways of stating the enthymemes more persuasively. The wise advocate will consider all available topical forms for presenting the available arguments. At the risk of becoming tedious, we will take the arguments from the Drebber case and recast them in the forms of several representative common topics.

1. DEFINITION AND DIVISION

Definition and Division are two closely related topics whereby the advocate argues either from the whole to the part or the parts to the whole.

They are argument forms that are very useful in delineating the issues to be tried.

Division: In order to prove the defendant guilty of rape, we need to prove four things—that someone had carnal knowledge of Lucy Ferrier, that Lucy did not consent, that force was used to achieve carnal knowledge, and that Enoch Drebber is the one who did it. There is no argument about the first three elements of the crime. Both sides agree that Lucy was raped. The only question is "Did Enoch Drebber do it?" Lucy says he sure looks and sounds like the rapist. And there's no argument that the rapist was a big, burly, bald man from up north who had a raspy voice, type O blood, and a cut finger. There's also no argument that the rapist lived nearby. And when the sheriff asked him about the rape, Enoch Drebber wouldn't deny it. Did he do it? You bet he did.

Definition: What do we know about the rapist? He was a big, burly, bald man who looked a lot like the defendant. He had type O blood. He had a raspy voice. He cut his finger. He lived near Lucy, but he originally came from up north. Who in all of Camden County meets all of these specifications? Enoch Drebber, the man who won't deny being the rapist.

2. COMPARISON AND CONTRAST

Comparison and Contrast look at one thing and compare it to another. Are they similar? Are they different? The enthymemes argued above under the topic of division could just as easily have been argued under the topics of comparison or contrast.

Comparison: Let's look at the rapist and then let's look at Enoch Drebber and see what we come up with. The rapist was a big, burly, bald man. So is Enoch Drebber. The rapist had a raspy voice. So does Enoch Drebber. The rapist cut his finger. So did Enoch Drebber. The rapist has type O blood. So does Enoch Drebber. The rapist lives near Lucy. So does Enoch Drebber. The rapist came from up north. So does Enoch Drebber. The rapist raped Lucy Ferrier. Enoch Drebber won't deny raping Lucy Ferrier. Are the rapist and Enoch Drebber one and the same person? Of course they are!

Contrast: Drebber's attorney, Mr. Dee Fender, says that 60% of the population has type O blood, therefore 60% of the population could have raped Lucy Ferrier. Well, 60% of the population aren't big, burly, bald men. Drebber is. Sixty percent of the population don't look like the rapist. Drebber does. Sixty percent of the population don't have a raspy voice. Drebber does. Sixty percent of the population didn't cut their finger. Drebber did. Sixty percent of the population don't live near Lucy. Drebber does. Sixty percent of the population don't come from "up north." Drebber does. Sixty percent of the population didn't rape Lucy. Drebber "won't deny" raping Lucy. Could 60% of the population have raped Lucy? No, Enoch Drebber raped Lucy Ferrier.

3. RELATIONSHIP

Relationship arguments deal with cause and effect, antecedent and consequent, contraries, and contradictories. Cause and effect argues that because a thing exists, its likely cause must exist also. "There is a bullet in the victim's body. The victim must have been shot." Antecedent and consequent argues to or from the likely consequences of a given action. It is usually voiced in an "if . . . then" argument. Contraries considers incompatibility. One thing may not rule out another, but it makes it much less likely. "If it were summer, there would not be snow on the ground." Contradictories are similar to contraries, but the two things considered are not merely incompatible, they are mutually exclusive. "Either he did it or he didn't."

Cause and effect. Doctor Killam did a swab of Lucy Ferrier's vagina. The crime lab found semen in the vaginal swab. Sexual intercourse is the usual way that semen gets into a vagina. This tells us that Lucy was raped.

Antecedent and consequent. Lucy Ferrier was raped by a big, burly, bald northerner with a raspy voice, type O blood, and an injured finger. If Enoch Drebber raped Lucy, you'd expect him to fit that description. He does.

Contraries. An innocent man would deny raping Lucy Ferrier, but Enoch Drebber said he wouldn't deny raping her. He must have raped her.

Contradictories. If Enoch Drebber was a small, skinny, longhaired man from down south, we'd know he was innocent, but he isn't—he's a big, burly, bald man from up north. If Enoch Drebber had a healthy finger, we'd know he was innocent—but he cut his finger. If Enoch Drebber had type A blood, we'd know he was innocent—but he has type O blood. If Enoch Drebber lived on the other side of town, we'd know he was innocent—but he lives near Lucy Ferrier.

4. CIRCUMSTANCE

Circumstances deals mainly with past and future fact. "The best predictor of future action is past action. He did it before. He'll do it again." If the judge had not manicured Drebber's statement by ruling the prior rape inadmissible, the prosecution would have had an excellent argument from past and future fact. Another argument to circumstance is the argument to possible and impossible. Since forensic rhetoric deals most often with probabilities, it may be helpful to think of this topic as probable and improbable.

> **Past and Future Fact.** Drebber told the sheriff that he wouldn't deny raping Lucy. Now why wouldn't he deny committing the rape? Because he knew that the sheriff would see that denial for the lie that it was when it came to light that Drebber had done the same thing before. As a matter of fact, he even admitted he had a problem. Now someone who has raped before, someone who has a problem with raping people, that is someone who would rape again. He did it before back up north where he came from. He did it again that night in Lucy Ferrier's home.

> **Probable and Improbable.** Ladies and gentlemen, what is the likelihood that two big, burly, bald northerners with a raspy voice, type O blood, and a cut finger lived near Lucy Ferrier? If Enoch Drebber didn't rape Lucy, there has to be another one out there living near Lucy. The sheriff looked and he didn't find anyone but the defendant. Either Enoch Drebber or his mysterious disappearing twin brother raped Lucy Ferrier. Enoch Drebber doesn't have a mysterious disappearing twin brother. Enoch Drebber raped Lucy Ferrier.

Repetition can be a powerful teaching tool. It can also be a powerful persuader. Adolph Hitler said that if a lie is told often enough, people will begin to believe it. If repetition serves so well to convince the audience of a lie, how much better must it serve to convince them of the truth? The different topical forms provide a way to recast and restate the same arguments multiple times without appearing redundant.

5. TESTIMONY

Up to this point, we have discussed only topics which speak to the ultimate issue of guilt or innocence. For these topics to have any persuasiveness at all, the premises which form their basis must be accepted as true by the jury. Therefore, you often need to argue the truth of the premises upon which you want to base your arguments. The topic of testimony can speak to the ultimate issue of guilt, but it can also speak to the preliminary issue of whether to believe the premises forming the basis of arguments to guilt or innocence. For example, arguing that the victim positively identified the defendant argues to the ultimate issue of guilt, but arguing that the victim is worthy of belief argues the preliminary issue of whether to believe the positive identification. The term "testimony" seems straightforward enough, but when applied to topics, it encompasses more than merely what the witnesses said. The topic of testimony includes oaths, witnesses, authorities, and maxims.

a. Witnesses

When we think of testimony, we are most likely to think of witnesses. Inconsistency is the most commonly voiced argument against the credibility of witnesses. As we saw when we discussed cross-examination, a witness's testimony can be internally inconsistent, inconsistent with other witnesses, or inconsistent with firmly established facts.

> **Internally inconsistent.** How can we believe John Welch? On direct examination he testified that he saw the defendant drink two beers. On cross-examination he revised that number up to a six pack. At deposition he admitted the defendant drank two six packs! Was it two beers, six beers, or twelve beers? If he told us the sun was shining, we'd best break out our umbrellas.

> **Inconsistent with other witnesses.** The convenience store clerk said Baker bought two six packs. Baker admitted to Officer Gregson he drank two six packs. How can we possibly believe John Welch when he says Baker only had two beers?

> **Inconsistent with facts.** John Welch says Henry Baker only drank two beers, but Officer Gregson found six cold, wet, empty beer cans in the front floorboard of Baker's car. Who else was in the car with Baker when he was stopped? Nobody. Who else could have drunk those four extra beers? Nobody!

Just as inconsistency can be argued as a reason to disbelieve, consistency can be argued as a reason to believe.

> **Internal consistency.** Little eight-year-old Lucy Hebron has gotten up on the stand and told us on direct examination what Joseph Stangerson did to her. And when Dee Fender cross-examined her, she told him exactly the same thing. Which is exactly what she told her mother when she first reported the attack; and exactly what she told the doctor who examined her; and exactly what she told on deposition. How could she be so consistent with so many tellings? Because she's telling the truth.

> **Consistency with other witnesses.** Why should we believe Lucy Hebron when she says Joseph Stangerson molested her? Sara Stangerson testified that he did exactly the same thing to her. Lucy's cousin Olivia testified he did exactly the same thing to her. Lucy's sister Veronica testified he did exactly the same thing to her. With such a host of witnesses saying exactly the same thing, how can we disbelieve Lucy?

> **Consistency with established fact.** Lucy Hebron testified how Joseph Stangerson molested her, and she described not only Stangerson's bedroom, but a scar on his hip. How could she have known what his bedroom looked like unless she's telling the truth? How could she have known about that scar unless she's telling the truth? And what kind of injuries did the doctor find when he examined Lucy? Exactly the kind you'd expect to find if she was telling the truth.

Let us now consider two often overlooked aspects of the topic of witnesses—consistency as a reason to disbelieve and inconsistency as a reason to believe. An example from a long-ago child molestation case against a gentleman we will call Basal McKinney should suffice to make the point. In the McKinney case, the defense mounted a standard sort of attack on the victims' mother, claiming that she procured the children's testimony against their stepfather. The defense presented a number of defense witnesses, each of whom undertook to assassinate the mother's character. The prosecutor soon noticed that each witness said the mother was "controlling and manipulative." After picking up on this overly consistent detail, the prosecutor asked one of the witnesses to define "manipulative." The witness could not even begin to guess what the word meant. The very next witness to testify varied from the script, characterizing the mother as "controlling and panipulative." The prosecutor refrained from asking the witness to define "panipulative," but satisfied herself with having the witness repeat the term "panipulative" several times. This incident serves as a painful reminder that a too-consistent story most likely results from collusion. In another old cattle rustling case a civilian witness testified to a lengthy conversation she had with the defendant in which he purportedly confessed to stealing cattle from the victim. The defense attorney detected a change in the witness's voice as she recounted the confession. It assumed a singsong tone absent during the rest of her testimony. On cross-examination the defense attorney had the witness repeat the confession several times. The prosecutor was content to allow this repetition of harmful evidence until he noticed that the witness used exactly the same words and the same singsong voice each time she recited the defendant's "confession." The jury readily accepted the defense argument that the witness had memorized her testimony. In another murder case, the defendant convicted himself by repeating defense counsel's opening statement almost word-for-word on direct examination. Too-consistent testimony most likely is rehearsed testimony.

The proverb may say that there is safety in a multitude of counselors,[4] but the experienced prosecutor knows there is confusion in a multitude of witnesses. No two people ever view the same traumatic event the same

---

[4] Proverbs 11:14 (KJV).

way, and no two people ever give 100% consistent accounts of an event. Minor inconsistencies mean nothing, but they have freed more guilty defendants than almost any other form of evidence. The defense argues that inconsistencies equal reasonable doubt, and oftentimes you are hard put to answer the charge. In such a situation you must demonstrate that minor inconsistencies in recounting an event do not mean that the event did not occur. The old movie *Gigi* gives you an excellent example for combating such defense arguments. In the movie, Maurice Chevalier reminisces with an old flame about their first date. They sing a duet recounting the details of the date and she contradicts him in every detail. He says they met one time. She says another. He says he was on time. She says he was late. He says they dined with acquaintances. She says they dined alone. He says they were serenaded by a tenor. She says the singer was a baritone. None of these discrepancies should give rise to any reasonable doubt about whether they had a dinner date at which they were serenaded by a male singer. More than one prosecutor has saved more than one case by reciting this song for a jury.

b. Oaths

In the modern courtroom almost all witnesses are placed under oath, but it was not always so. Because the penal sanctions[5] attached to oaths served as a voucher for sworn statements, witnesses who testified under oath could be argued as more believable. In the modern courtroom, oaths as a topic come into play most often with out-of-court statements made under oath. If the defendant not only confessed, but confessed under oath, the oath may be argued as adding weight to the confession.

> How do we know Henry Baker drank two six packs of beer? When Officer Gregson questioned him, Henry Baker raised his right hand and swore to tell the truth, and he testified that he drank two six packs before getting behind the wheel of his car. That's not an offhand comment. That's a sworn statement under oath, and we can be sure that Baker wouldn't have said it if it wasn't true.

With impeachment by prior inconsistent statement, prior statements made under oath impeach more persuasively than prior inconsistent statements made in offhand conversation. Many jurisdictions recognize the persuasive nature of prior inconsistent statements under oath by excluding them from the hearsay rule.[6]

---

[5] Today the secular sanctions make statements under oath more persuasive. In ancient times, the divine sanctions for the sin of false swearing were a weightier consideration.

[6] Fed.R.Evid. 801(d)(1)(A), Accord: West's Fla.Stat.Ann. § 90.801(2)(b); Idaho R.Evid. 801(d)(1)(A). Some states which have adopted this rule exclude all prior inconsistent statements from the hearsay rule, whether sworn or not. See, e.g. Alaska R.Evid. 801(d)(1)(A); Del. R.Evid. 801(d)(1)(A). Arkansas excludes unsworn prior inconsistent statements from the hearsay rule in civil trials but only excludes testimonial prior inconsistent statements in criminal trials. Ark. R.Evid. 801(d)(1)(I).

> Today John Welch testified that Henry Baker had only two beers, but we know that Baker had more than that. How do we know? When Welch testified last month at deposition, he swore under oath that Baker had downed two six packs. Baker didn't have just two beers, he had twelve!

c. Authorities

In deciding weighty matters, we almost instinctively look to those reputed to have greater knowledge than we. When arguing a crucial point made by expert testimony, you should never resort to simply saying "The expert says it. You believe it. That settles it." The expert should be able to give a rational, logical, easily understandable explanation of how she arrived at whatever conclusion she reached. Many experts almost instinctively recoil from giving simple explanations, shrouding their testimony in a cloak of hyper-technical jargon. To explain the experts' reasons for obfuscation, we will use an example. When Sherlock Holmes once explained to a client how he could tell at a glance that the client had done manual labor, took snuff, was a Freemason, had been to China, and had recently done a lot of writing, the client responded, "Well, I never! I thought at first that you had done something clever, but I see that there was nothing in it, after all."[7] Such experts, like Holmes, fear that their reputations will "suffer shipwreck if [they are] so candid."[8] You must penetrate the fog of obfuscation and find a way to bolster the expert's opinion with a clear, cogent explanation of how she arrived at that opinion—both in testimony and in argument. This is especially true if the authority speaks on an issue close to the point to adjudicate. If the authority merely speaks to a preliminary or undisputed point, a lengthy explanation will detract from the main issue.

d. Maxims

Maxims, proverbs, and aphorisms do not usually spring to the modern mind when we think about the topic of testimony; but the ancients saw maxims as a type of testimony given, not by flesh and blood witnesses, but by the common experiences of all humans everywhere. We have previously discussed how the maxim "three people can keep a secret if two of them are dead" can serve, just by its recitation, to bolster the credibility of accomplice testimony. Do the witnesses conflict as to the time of an incident? Has the defense made this conflict the centerpiece of a reasonable doubt argument? You often need say no more than "the man with one watch always knows what time it is, but the man with two watches is never sure." Books of quotations, the Bible, Shakespeare, current events, movies, all can be the

---

[7] Arthur Conan Doyle, "The Red Headed League," The Complete Sherlock Holmes, Gramercy Books, New York, New York, 2002. p.75.

[8] Id.

source of maxims which offer "testimony" in support of your position. You can even make up maxims to make your points. "If it doesn't fit, you must acquit." Aristotle thought maxims especially adapted to persuading unintelligent jurors, if you could just discern their preconceptions and choose maxims which reinforced those preconceptions.[9]

6. SIGNS

Ancient rhetoricians recognized many different topics of invention. Some of them, torture and rumor for example, have no place in the modern courtroom. Modern advocates will immediately recognize and readily admit the importance of the topics covered so far, but they will be mystified by the term signs. What the ancients called signs moderns would call circumstantial evidence. Aristotle recognized two classes of signs. infallible signs were conclusive proof, but fallible signs were only persuasive.[10] Quintilian held that there were three types of signs relevant to the courtroom. Signs which were conclusive of guilt,[11] signs which gave rise to a greater or lesser probability of guilt,[12] and signs which were merely consistent with guilt.[13] A conclusive sign, settles the point. There is no need for further argument. A confirmatory sign gives rise to a probability, but it does not carry the day. It needs help from other signs, enthymemes, and examples to persuade the jury. The Enoch Drebber case we have been discussing throughout this chapter illustrates a case in which a number of confirmatory signs were used as the raw materials for enthymemes and grouped together to obtain a conviction. Consistent signs really prove little, but they do add some weight to confirmatory signs.

Fingerprints, for example, are conclusive signs that the defendant touched an object. They are seldom conclusive of guilt. They may, however, be confirmatory of guilt or consistent with guilt. Suppose you have a convenience store robbery in which the robber slashes the cashier's throat and murders her. In the cash drawer you find the defendant's fingerprint formed in the victim's blood. This is as near a conclusive sign of the defendant's guilt as one can imagine. Suppose a rural mail carrier disappears from her route. Her last delivery was made to Edwin Drood's mailbox. Investigators find Drood's fingerprint on a piece of undelivered mail in the victim's car. This fingerprint constitutes a confirmatory sign of the defendant's guilt. He has some wiggle room for evading responsibility, but the fingerprint gives rise to a high probability of guilt. Suppose again two men are found shot to death in their automobile behind the apartment

[9] Rhetoric, 1395b, The Complete Works of Aristotle, 2:2223, 2224. Princeton University Press, 1984.

[10] Id. at 1357b.

[11] 2 Quintilian, The Orator's Education, 5.9,1–2, Trans. Donald A. Russell, Harvard University Press, Cambridge, Massachusetts, 2001. p. 359.

[12] Id. at 5.9.8–11.

[13] Id. at 5.9.12–14.

house where Roger Shelnut, who runs a car detailing business, lives. Shelnut's fingerprints are found on the passenger side sun visor of the car. These fingerprints are merely consistent signs. They could have been left in the car when Shelnut killed the victims, or they could have been left in the car at some other time.

Gunshot wounds conclusively prove that the victim was shot, but the nature of the gunshot wounds may be more or less conclusive as to what was in the mind of the defendant at the time of the shooting. In the last chapter's Peter Carey hypothetical, the defendant hogtied his girlfriend and shot her in the chest three times with a single shot, break action shotgun. This comes very close to being a conclusive sign of premeditation. Suppose Calvin Lindsey holds a shotgun within four feet of his victim's temple and fires one shot into the victim's head. He then turns and holds the shotgun inches from the face of the victim's sister and shoots her once in the head. The way the first victim was shot is arguably only a consistent sign of premeditation, but the shooting of the second victim is a highly confirmatory sign of premeditation. Suppose Donovan Walton shoots his girlfriend once between the eyes from a distance of twenty yards. This is merely consistent with premeditation—it could have been a lucky (or unlucky) shot.

Circumstantial evidence rarely constitutes a conclusive sign of guilt. Usually when you encounter a conclusive sign, it is conclusive as to only an element of the crime or a single material fact in issue. Confirmatory signs are quite common, but they need help from other evidence for conclusive proof of guilt. Consistent signs are most plentiful, but they prove little. They do, however, help other evidence in proving guilt. When the sign is not conclusive, it is open to varying interpretations. Prosecutors' biggest failure in evaluating circumstantial evidence comes in the failure to consider innocent interpretations. As Sherlock Holmes would say:

> Circumstantial evidence is a very tricky thing. It may seem to point very straight to one thing, but if you shift your own point of view a little, you may find it pointing in an equally uncompromising manner to something entirely different.[14]

For example, an uncritical prosecutor confronting the mail carrier murder discussed above might take the defendant's fingerprint on the piece of undelivered mail as a conclusive sign of guilt. It is not. There was a very innocent explanation. The letter might have been delivered to the defendant by mistake, and he put it back into his mailbox for the carrier to deliver properly. The fingerprint is still a confirmatory sign, but the jury's assessment of its value as proof of guilt can be greatly influenced by an

[14] Arthur Conan Doyle, "The Boscombe Valley Mystery," The Complete Sherlock Holmes, Gramercy Books, New York, New York, 2002. p.88.

eloquent defense attorney. What do you do to forestall this possibility? Again, Sherlock Holmes shows the way:

> One should always look for a possible alternative and provide against it. It is the first rule of criminal investigation.[15]

Holmes might have overstated the importance of this dictum, but not by much. More circumstantial evidence cases are lost because the prosecution failed to see the innocent interpretation than for almost any other reason. If you fail to see the innocent explanation, the defense attorney will be glad to point it out for you in final argument. By that time, there will be little you can do to salvage your case. In the mail carrier murder, the prosecutor did not wait for final argument to identify the weakness. He identified the weakness and made some inquiry. He found out that the crime lab had quit looking for fingerprints on the undelivered mail when they found the first one. The prosecutor asked the lab to process the remaining mail. Further processing revealed the defendant's fingerprints on several additional pieces of undelivered mail, and the defendant's innocent explanation was destroyed before it was ever voiced. One piece of mail might have been misdelivered, but not the whole load. Looking for the innocent explanation and providing against it turned a sign which was only moderately confirmatory into a near conclusive sign.

Prosecutors will be tempted to argue confirmatory signs as conclusive. Defense attorneys will argue confirmatory signs as merely consistent. You can quickly ruin your credibility by overstating the strength of your evidence. The way to bolster circumstantial evidence is not to overstate its implications, but to explain how it fits with other circumstances. Circumstantial evidence is strongest when it is connected to other circumstances. Each single circumstance constitutes a sign of guilt which can be used as the premise of an enthymeme indicating guilt. Multiple circumstances constitute multiple signs, and the multiple signs must be argued together to satisfy the jury beyond a reasonable doubt. The best kind of circumstances are corroborated by eyewitness testimony. The Enoch Drebber case serves as an excellent example of this point. In that case, the victim's tentative identification of Drebber as looking and sounding like the rapist, considered with all the circumstances, satisfied the jury beyond a reasonable doubt of his guilt.

C. SHAM TOPICS

Just as there are valid topics of argument, there are a number of spurious topics which can be used and which you must be deal with as they arise. A non-exhaustive listing of those topics would include: divide and conquer; the straw man; the perfectionist fallacy; the *ad hominem* fallacy;

[15] Arthur Conan Doyle, "The Adventure of Black Peter," The Complete Sherlock Holmes, Gramercy Books, New York, New York, 2002. p.241.

the appeal to pity; and shifting the issues. In the divide and conquer argument, the arguer takes each individual enthymeme and demonstrates that it, standing alone, cannot carry the day in proving the prosecution case beyond a reasonable doubt. You frequently hear the divide and conquer argument in a circumstantial evidence case, and the defense attorney in the Enoch Drebber case could have easily used the divide and conquer maneuver. In answer you must remind the jury that, although no single argument carries the day, all the arguments taken together certainly do. In the strawman fallacy, the arguer takes an easily refuted fact or argument, refutes it, and then pretends that she has defeated the entire case. In the Theodore Robert Bundy case, a single eyewitness saw the actual abduction of Kimberly Leach, but the eyewitness gave very weak testimony. The defense devoted much time to criticizing the weakness of that witness's testimony and argued that the prosecution case fell apart without it. This argument was easily countered in much the same fashion that the divide and conquer maneuver is countered, by calling the jury's attention to all the other facts of the case. The perfectionist fallacy works off of two universal truths: first, that nothing is perfect; and second, that all the affairs of humans are open to some doubt. The perfectionist seizes upon the imperfections in the prosecution case (e.g., no fingerprints), and argues that these imperfections give rise to reasonable doubt. If the prosecution case rests largely on circumstantial evidence, the perfectionist points to the gaps in the case and argues the uncertainties inherent in all circumstantial evidence cases as reasonable doubt. As a counter to this argument you could use the example of the jigsaw puzzle. "You don't need all the pieces of a jigsaw puzzle to get the picture, and ladies and gentlemen, we have put together more than enough pieces to show the defendant guilty." The television game show *Wheel of Fortune* makes a good analogy. "Ladies and gentlemen, if the category is judicial findings and the first letter is G and the last three letters are LTY, you don't need to buy a vowel to know that the verdict is guilty." The *ad hominem* argument has freed more guilty defendants than almost any other argument. It is closely allied to the appeal to pity and shifting the issues. In many cases where the overt defense is "self-defense," the covert defense is "he had it coming." The defense tries to make the victim look as evil as possible and the defendant as pitiful as possible and then suggests ever so subtly that the real issue in the case is whether the victim deserved what he got. Thus the issue gets shifted from guilt or innocence to some other issue more congenial to the defendant. Headlines like "Battered Spouse or Deliberate Murderer?" demonstrate this shift of issues. A defendant can be both a battered spouse and a deliberate murderer. "Ladies and gentlemen, the defense attorney suggests to you that the victim had it coming. Whether he did or didn't is irrelevant. The defendant had no right to bring it to him. When we get back to the real issue here, it's obvious that the defendant is guilty."

Every argument must move the jury toward returning a favorable verdict. When we accentuate the "adversarial" in the adversarial system, we sometimes lose sight of the fact that injuring the opponent does not necessarily advance our case. Disparaging someone on the defense side simply because she happens to be on the defense side makes no sense. You are not fighting opposing counsel. You are trying your case. The argument has to serve a constructive purpose of moving the case toward a favorable verdict. You have formulated your case theory. You have discerned the defense theory. The tension between the two theories has given you the point to adjudicate. Your arguments must aim at one of three major objectives. (1) To persuade the jury to accept your case theory. (2) To persuade the jury to reject the defense theory. (3) To persuade the jury to resolve the point to adjudicate in your favor. If an argument does not contribute directly or indirectly to one of those three aims, you probably should not make it.

D. THE PARTS OF A SPEECH

Once you have discovered the best arguments and composed them as forcefully as possible, you must arrange them into the unified whole of final argument and deliver them as persuasively and as memorably as possible. Aristotle's arrangement of the forensic speech called for an introduction, a statement of the case, an argument, and a conclusion. The *Rhetorica ad Herennium* elaborated upon Aristotle's format by subdividing the argument into six parts. The *Rhetorica's* parts of a forensic speech were:[16]

(1) Introduction

(2) Statement of Facts

(3) Division

(4) Confirmation

(5) Refutation

(6) Conclusion.

As rhetorical literature proliferated, authors parsed the speech into more and more complex subdivisions, but we need not complicate the speech further than the six parts outlined above.

1. THE INTRODUCTION

The Introduction seeks to render the jury attentive, receptive, and well-disposed. When modern lawyers begin their final argument by thanking the jury for not going to sleep and paying attention to the case, they attempt to do what lawyers have done for more than two thousand

[16] 1 [Cicero], Rhetorica ad Herennium, 1.3.4, Harvard University Press, Cambridge, Massachusetts, 1954. p. 9.

years. In the modern final argument, you need not dwell on the introduction. The jury should have already been rendered attentive, receptive, and well-disposed during the course of the trial. If you need to do a lot of buttering up of the jury at this late date, you are in deep trouble. In most cases you can safely dispense with the introduction or amalgamate it with the statement of facts.

2. THE STATEMENT OF FACTS

The Statement of facts consists of a brief, clear, believable statement of the facts of the case. Here you will elaborate your case theory into a memorable statement that (hopefully) reconfirms the jury's feeling that the defendant is a person who ought to be punished. If you have a short and simple case, you might safely omit the statement of facts, but this is usually a mistake. Giving a statement of facts immediately on the heels of a one-or-two witness case may be superfluous, but you can compose one easily—just repeat the opening statement attention step—and repetition serves to drive the point home. Since final argument does not have the same restrictions as opening statement, you can recast the attention step into more argumentative language. Some things cannot be said in opening because they are not evidence, but reasonable inferences from the evidence. If that is the case, you can augment the attention step with those inferences which could not be stated in opening. Restating the attention step as the statement of facts serves another purpose. It implicitly shows that you have proven what you said you were going to prove. For example, the attention step and statement of facts from the Frank Leonard/Rebecca MacGregor murder could be handled in the following manner.

> **Opening Statement Attention Step.** Frank Leonard shot Rebecca MacGregor in the back, and he shot her in the back, and he shot her in the back, and he shot her in the back.
>
> **Final Argument Statement of Facts.** Frank Leonard shot Rebecca MacGregor in the back, and he shot her in the back, and he shot her in the back, and he shot her in the back. As he shot her, he chased her around the living room. With each shot, he got closer and closer. Twice he held the gun within two feet of her back and shot her. Then he held the gun within a foot of her back and shot her. Then, when she fell face forward onto the sofa, he pressed the gun to the flesh of her back and shot her.

The statement of facts can be quite short in a case with eyewitness testimony and few reasonable inferences to draw. In a circumstantial evidence case, the statement of facts must be much longer, as the story can sometimes only be told with reference to the reasonable inferences from the circumstantial evidence. Take the following attention step:

> **Opening Statement Attention Step.** Byron Farrior took a ride with Terry Sammons. He took a little money from Terry Sammons. He took some beer from Terry Sammons. Later that night, Byron Farrior took a sawed-off shotgun, and with that shotgun, he took Terry Sammons' life. Then he took the rest of Terry Sammons' money, and he took Terry Sammons' car and burned it. Then he went home and took a nap.

The fact narration in the opening statement cataloged all the sightings of Farrior and Sammons on the night of the murder and then described the collection of the tangible circumstantial evidence and how the examination of that evidence pointed to Byron Farrior as the killer. What went on between the two was the subject only of reasonable inference, and the prosecutor saved these inferences for the statement of facts in the final argument. The final argument began like this:

> **Final Argument Statement of Facts.** Byron Farrior took a ride with Terry Sammons. He took a little money from Terry Sammons. He took some beer from Terry Sammons. But he wasn't going to take any guff off of Sammons. When Sammons began to get irritated with him, Byron Farrior took a sawed-off shotgun, and with that shotgun, he took Terry Sammons' life. Then he took the rest of Terry Sammons' money, and he took Terry Sammons' car and burned it. Then he went home and took a nap. [The statement of facts then flashed back to the meeting between the two men and went on from this point to a detailed description of the transaction between them based on reasonable inferences drawn from the circumstantial evidence].

3. THE DIVISION

The Division sets forth where the parties agree and where they disagree and identifies the point(s) to adjudicate. The point to adjudicate is the issue to be tried: identity, alibi, insanity, reasonable doubt, or whatever other issue(s) may be in dispute. From this point forward, the entire economy of the final argument should be directed toward carrying the point to adjudicate.

> (1) In order to prove larceny of a horse, we have to prove that the defendant took the victim's property and carried it away, that the property was a horse, that the victim did not consent to the taking, and that the defendant intended to convert the property to his own use and benefit and deprive the owner of the use of the property. The defendant himself admits he took the victim's horse and sold it at the livestock market, but he says that the owner sold it to him. The owner says he did nothing of the kind. Everyone agrees that the defendant took the horse. Everyone agrees that

the defendant sold the horse. The only question is, did the victim consent to the taking by selling the horse to the defendant? Let's look at the evidence and see what it tells us about whether the victim consented . . . .

(2) The offense of DUI involves driving a motor vehicle while under the influence of alcoholic beverages to the extent that the normal faculties are impaired. The defendant, W.C. Fields, admits he was driving and admits he was drinking. The only question we have to resolve is this—was he impaired?

(3) The judge will tell you in his instructions that the elements of murder in the first degree are:

Sharon Marie Renfro is dead.

The death was caused by the criminal agency of Marshal Lee Gore.

The killing was premeditated.

There is no question about Ms. Renfro being dead. We all heard the medical examiner and the forensic anthropologist tell us their conclusions from an examination of Ms. Renfro's skeletonized remains. And there is no question but that the death was caused by the criminal agency of someone. A woman living in Tennessee just doesn't disappear and then several months later reappear in a wooded area in Florida with no clothes and her wrists bound and it not be murder. Sharon Marie Renfro was murdered. There are really only two questions that remain to be answered, and they can be answered easily.

Who killed Sharon Marie Renfro?

Was the killing premeditated.

Now let's look at the evidence that shows us Marshal Lee Gore killed Sharon Marie Renfro, and that he premeditated her murder.

4. THE CONFIRMATION AND REFUTATION

The confirmation is the heart of the argument. In the confirmation you set forth the arguments which should carry the day for your side of the controversy. Here you must make the appeal to logos. It is important that the confirmation set forth what is good about your case, not what is bad about the defense's case. You should mention the defense's evidence only as it tends to support your case. There is a time and a place to rebut the defense; the confirmation is neither the time nor the place. The refutation follows the confirmation, and as the name implies, the refutation is where you answer the defense arguments. You can map out the confirmation in much greater detail than you can the refutation. Why is that? Because opposing counsel has not yet made her final argument. You do not really know what she is going to say. You can anticipate her argument with a greater or lesser degree of certainty, but you can never know what she is going to say until she has said it. For this reason, the refutation is the only part of the final argument that you do not want to write out verbatim before the trial. The refutation portion of your final argument notes should be an outline of anticipated arguments with notes of counter arguments for each. As opposing counsel makes her argument, listen carefully, checking off on your worksheet each argument she makes and crossing through each one she omits. She may make some arguments you did not anticipate. Note them down, with a reply for each.

5. THE CONCLUSION

Aristotle taught that the conclusion is where advocates attempt to:

(1) Inspire the jury with a favorable opinion of the prosecution and an unfavorable opinion of the defense (ethos); or

(2) Amplify the force and points of the prosecution arguments and mitigate the defense arguments (logos); or

(3) Rouse anger toward the defendant or pity toward the victim (pathos); or

(4) Restate in summary their facts and arguments (logos).

A blatant, heavy-handed attempt at objectives (1) or (3) would almost certainly result in a mistrial or, worse yet, a reversal. You should strive for objective (2) or (4) but construct the conclusion so that a byproduct of the conclusion is objective (1) or (3). A properly constructed opening statement attention step appeals to ethos and pathos as a byproduct of the way the facts are put together. If your final argument statement of facts is a fleshed-out version of your attention step, you can often do no better in conclusion than to restate the attention step one more time.

> Ladies and gentlemen, Frank Leonard shot Rebecca MacGregor in the back. And he shot her in the back. Again and again he shot her in the back. Two of those shots came from within two feet of her back. One shot came from within a foot. The last shot came as she lay bleeding to death on her sofa. And it came from a muzzle pressed to the flesh of her back. That's cold blooded, premeditated, first degree murder. That's the verdict that justice demands, and that's the verdict that I ask you to return. Thank you.

E. PUTTING IT ALL TOGETHER

Now let us put the various parts of the speech together and see how the *Rhetorica's* arrangement works as a unified whole in the modern courtroom.

Introduction. Raymond Carlton was supposed to be a protector. He chose to be a predator. He was supposed to defend. He chose to defile. Raymond Carlton wore a badge. That badge was supposed to be a shield against wrongdoers. He used it as a shield for wrongdoing.

Statement of Facts. Raymond Carlton, a deputy sheriff with the Camden County Sheriff's Office, wore his uniform to Kitty Winter's home. In his uniform pocket he carried crack cocaine. He used that crack at Kitty's home and shared it with her. He decided that sharing cocaine with Kitty entitled him to have sex with her. When she disagreed, he beat her up. He forced her into her bedroom and raped her. After her raped her, he offered to share her body with some of his friends. Kitty fled her home naked and afraid. She ran to Sarah Safehaven's home and reported what Carlton had done.

Division. Now Carlton stands charged with sexual battery. The crime of sexual battery has three elements:

(1) Kitty Winter was over twelve years of age or older.

(2) Raymond Carlton committed an act upon Kitty Winter in which his penis penetrated the vagina of Kitty Winter.

(3) The act was committed without the consent of Kitty Winter.

This boils down to proof of three things—age, penetration, and nonconsent. Kitty Winter is 31 years old. Even the defendant will agree that she's over twelve. Raymond Carlton's penis penetrated Kitty's vagina. Even he will agree with that.

The only thing that Carlton disagrees with is nonconsent. He says it was romance, not rape. The only question we have to answer is—did Kitty consent? Was it rape or romance? All the evidence points to rape.

Confirmation. First, we have Kitty Winter's word for it that she didn't consent, and that word alone is enough to prove the case beyond a reasonable doubt. If that was all we had, we'd be justified in convicting Carlton of sexual battery. But that isn't all. Not by a long shot. Fact after fact agrees with Kitty's testimony. Fact after fact shows that it was rape, not romance. Let's look at those facts:

(1) Ted Mixon saw Carlton beating up on Kitty. That might pass for foreplay in some people's book, but it's much more consistent with rape than romance.

(2) Ted Mixon and Bill Helton heard Kitty yelling in the back room. Helton described it as "shrieking." Those weren't screams of joy. They were howls of pain. These were the protests of a victim. It was rape, not romance.

(3) Kitty Winter ran away from her own home. After a session of pleasant sex, people might do any number of things—cuddle, talk, smoke a cigarette, raid the refrigerator, or even roll over and go to sleep. Running away from home is not on the list. It was rape, not romance.

(4) Don't just look at the fact that she ran away. Look how she left. Of all the ways to get out of a house, the bathroom window is the least likely to be used by someone who just had a pleasant evening of sex. It was rape, not romance.

(5) She didn't just jump out the window and run away. She wasn't wearing a stitch of clothes. Run away from home. Through the bathroom window. Naked. And there was snow on the ground.

(6) If someone has been raped, we expect an immediate outcry. Kitty made an immediate report of the rape. Not to the police. She had been raped by the police. She told Ted Mixon, but Mixon didn't help, and Raymond Carlton raped her again. Then she pretended she needed to go to the bathroom. When Carlton let her go, she jumped out the window and ran naked through the snow to Sara Safehaven's house and told her everything.

(7) Sara called rescue, and they took Kitty to the hospital. At the hospital they gave Kitty medical treatment. Nurses take a medical history as a part of the treatment. The doctor has to know what's wrong in order to give the right treatment. Again Kitty told the nurse about the rape.

(8) When Doctor Saunders examined Kitty, he found just what you'd expect to find on a woman who had been raped. Bruising to the groin and thighs. Inflamed vaginal area. Semen in the vagina. Doctor Saunders wrote in his medical notes that his findings were "consistent with that of a person who had been repeatedly raped."

Refutation: Against all this evidence, we have the word of a sworn law enforcement officer saying she consented. Raymond Carlton, the football hero lawman took an oath to tell the truth. How can we doubt his word when such a man as Carlton swears it's the truth? This man who today took an oath to tell the truth was under an oath to enforce the law back in January of last year. He broke that oath when he put that crack cocaine in his pocket. He broke that oath when he took the cocaine out of his pocket and smoked it. He broke that oath when he gave Kitty some of the cocaine. He broke that oath when he beat Kitty up. He broke that oath when he raped her. He broke that oath when he offered Kitty's body to Mixon and Helton. This man has forsworn his oath so many times in so many ways, how can we possibly believe his oath when he says Kitty consented?

Conclusion: Raymond Carlton was supposed to be a protector. He chose to be a predator. He was supposed to defend. He chose to defile. Raymond Carlton wore a badge. That badge was supposed to be a shield against wrongdoers. He used it as a shield for wrongdoing. Don't let him get away with it. The witnesses have spoken. You have heard. The facts are before you. I ask for judgement.

On final argument, the party with the burden of proof (plaintiff or prosecution) customarily makes an opening final argument, followed by opposing counsel's argument, and then the plaintiff makes a closing final argument to reply to the defense argument. The classical arrangement works well for the party with the middle argument. Later we will discuss how to modify the classical arrangement to fit the prosecutor's two arguments.

Although the technology of persuasion has changed since the time of Aristotle, the theory has not. Jury trials actually have a structure like the *Rhetorica's* classical speech. Jury selection serves as the introduction when the advocate seeks to obtain an audience which is attentive, receptive, and well disposed. The prosecution's opening statement performs the function of the statement of the case. The defense attorney's opening statement acts as the division by drawing the issues. The prosecution's case in chief is the confirmation, and the defense case is the refutation. Final arguments are the conclusion. Take away the other technological paraphernalia of the modern courtroom, and modern trial procedure is not so very different from ancient trial procedure.

1. UNIFIED ARRANGEMENT OF OPENING STATEMENT AND FINAL ARGUMENT

Argument is an attempt at persuasion. Everything advocates do in the courtroom should be aimed at persuading the jury to find for their side. Consequently, everything done the courtroom is some form of argument. Advocates feel hamstrung in the opening statement and presentation of evidence because of the rules against arguing. Consider the opening statement, the presentation of the evidence, and the final argument as all part of a unified whole, with each component building on the previous toward the goal of finally persuading the jury to see things your way. From the first word of the opening statement's attention step, you should have a clear vision of where you want to be in the final argument's conclusion. Introduce your case theory early, in the attention step if possible. Next give your fact narration, a detailed statement of the case, as though you were telling a friend about your case. For an exit line, conclude by repeating the attention step. By the time you have concluded the opening statement, you have repeated the story three times. It may not be eloquent or pretty, but repetition is the sincerest form of persuasion.

Next present the evidence, taking care to see to it that the evidence confirms the opening statement and case theory. Never over-promise in opening statement. Never exaggerate in opening statement. If anything, the opening statement should slightly understate your case. As it unfolds even more strongly than you represented, the jury will be even more convinced by your evidence. If it unfolds more weakly than your opening statement, you lose credibility. After both sides rest, you make your final argument. Final arguments are done differently from jurisdiction to jurisdiction. In some situations, the state opens and closes; in others, the defense opens and closes; sometimes the state opens and the defense closes without the state having an opportunity to respond. We will discuss first the arrangement of argument in those situations where the defense has the last word. The opening statement has already given the jury the introduction and statement of the case of the Classical argument, so it might seem good to simply begin with the division:

> Henry Baker is charged with DUI, and the judge is going to tell you that the state has to prove three things beyond a reasonable doubt before you can convict him. The state must prove: (1). Baker was driving an automobile, and (2). He was under the influence of alcohol, and (3). His normal faculties were impaired. Let's look at the first element. Officer Gregson saw Baker driving. Baker admits he was driving. The first element is proved beyond a reasonable doubt. Now for the second element. Baker himself admits he had two beers. He was under the influence of alcohol. The third element is the only question we have to answer, "was he impaired?"

If the case is short and simple, no harm will be done by simply beginning with the division, but it never hurts to have the jury hear the case theory repeated in compelling fashion. If you do nothing else, repeat the attention step's fact capsule. Once that is done, go to the division and set out the issues. Then come the confirmation, refutation, and conclusion. Do not refute in the confirmation. In the confirmation you should mention the defense evidence only as it supports your case theory. The conclusion can be a final repeat of the opening statement attention step. A unified arrangement for both opening statement and final argument is set forth below.

(1) Prosecution Opening
- (a) Attention Step
- (b) Fact Narration
- (c) Exit Line

(2) Defense Opening

(3) Prosecution Case

(4) Defense Case

(5) Rebuttal (if any)

(6) Prosecution Argues
- (a) Introduction
- (b) Statement of Case
- (c) Division
- (d) Confirmation
- (e) Exit Line

(7) Defense Argues

(8) Prosecution Argues
- (f) Introduction
- (g) Refutation
- (h) Conclusion

If the defense gets to open and close, then the arrangement from paragraph 6 on could be modified as follows:

(6) Defense Argues

(7) Prosecution Argues
- (a) Introduction
- (b) Statement of the Case
- (c) Division
- (d) Confirmation
- (e) Refutation
- (f) Conclusion

(8) Defense Argues

2. DELIVERY

Once the arguments have been invented and arranged, they must be delivered both memorably and convincingly. A memorable argument is not necessarily convincing, and a convincing argument is not necessarily memorable. It may take little convincing to win a particular juror over to your side but then that juror must become an advocate for you in jury deliberations. If the juror cannot retain and reiterate your arguments during deliberation, she might not be able to persuade her fellow jurors to see things your way. The solution is to deliver the arguments in striking, memorable fashion.

The *Sylva Rhetoricae*[17] names, defines, and gives examples of more than 400 techniques for amplifying arguments and rendering them memorable, but we will take an extended look at only one—the tricolon. The tricolon is a series of three parallel elements, each of which shares a quality with each of the other elements. The elements can be of the same length, they can alliterate, or they can rhyme. The classic example of the tricolon is Julius Caesar's letter to the Roman Senate announcing his victory over Pharnaces II of Pontus: *"Veni, vidi, vici."* If we were to translate Caesar's message into English, "I came, I saw, I conquered," the elements lose the unity of length and rhyme, but they still alliterate. Aristotle's rhetorical trinity—ethos, logos, and pathos—share length and rhymes, but do not alliterate, as do the *Rhetorica's* three essentials of case theory—brevity, clarity, verity. Let us expand the definition of tricolon to include not only elements which alliterate or rhyme, but also elements which form acrostics. Examples of such argumentative tricolons follow.

> **Acrostic:** The offense of DUI is driving while under the influence of alcoholic beverages to the extent that the normal faculties are impaired. Three things we have to prove, and they spell DUI. Driving. Under the influence. Impairment. Let's look at the evidence and see if we have everything necessary to prove DUI . . .

> **Alphabetic:** This case is as easy as A.B.C. A: The defendant was arrested inside the victim's home. B: The defendant had the victim's belongings in his pocket. C: The defendant confessed.

For some unknown reason groups of three make for the most memorable arguments. Even if the points aren't in the form of tricolons, they carry more weight grouped in threes. Try to make your points in groups of threes and try to make the threes into tricolons. If you only have two points, take one of them and divide it in two. Do not force an artificial unity of alliteration or rhyme. The tricolons must be natural. Take the trilogy of "motive, means, and opportunity." You could force it into a

---

[17] Burton, Gideon O., Sylva Rhetoricae, 2007. Brigham Young University. <https://rhetoric.byu.edu/>.

tricolon of sorts by changing "opportunity" to "moment," but the stilted terminology would rob the tricolon of its force. Do not make your tricolons too ornate or too cute. You want them to advance your argument, not compete with it.

3. VISUAL AIDS

We previously discussed some of the numerous topical forms that arguments can take, but three topics lend themselves very well to audiovisual presentation—compounding, contrast, and comparison. Let us return to the Enoch Drebber case. The prosecutor in that case did nothing other than stand before the jury and orally deliver his arguments. He could have greatly intensified his arguments by using visual aids. The central enthymeme of the defense argument was a variation of the strawman attack discussed above: Ignoring all other evidence of guilt, the defense attorney argued "Sixty percent of the population has Type O blood; therefore anyone in that 60 percent could have committed the rape. With 60 percent of the population as possible suspects, there is reasonable doubt and you cannot convict Enoch Drebber." The prosecutor replied by placing the strawman argument back into the context of all the other available arguments. He should have intensified his argument by presenting his series of enthymemes with the aid of a chart. A comparison chart of the Drebber argument would look like Figure 16–1, a contrast chart like Figure 16–2, and a compounding chart like Figure 16–3. The prosecutor could have opened his final argument with either the compounding chart from Figure 16–3 or the comparison chart from Figure 16–1, and replied to the defense strawman attack with the contrast chart from Figure 16–2 in closing final argument.

We humans gather information through all our senses, not just our sense of hearing. Television replaced radio because we actually prefer to use multiple senses. This preference is due in large part to the fact that we learn better when more than one sense is engaged. Many lawyers, however, seem to be so intoxicated by the sound of their own voices that they seldom think of engaging any sense other than the jurors' sense of hearing. This is a capital mistake. As Ross Perot demonstrated in the presidential debates of 1992, even the crudest of visual aids can be very effective. Thus you can achieve a highly persuasive effect by simply placing your arguments down on posterboard or a flip chart and showing them to the jury.

The comparison, contrast, and compounding charts shown in Figures 16–1, 16–2, and 16–3 do not exhaust the possibilities for the making of arguments by means of visual aids. Suppose in the Enoch Drebber case that the defense presented Red Herring as potentially being the rapist. Suppose further that Herring is a short, skinny, hirsute man with a high-pitched voice who comes from down south, lives nowhere near the victim, and vehemently denies raping the victim. You could make a quite compelling argument by making a chart with three columns, one for the rapist, one for Drebber, and one for Herring. The chart would quite graphically compare Drebber to the rapist while simultaneously contrasting Herring with the rapist. With a modicum of inventiveness you can devise a simple visual aid to make any of the arguments discussed in Section B above.

Figure 16-1: Comparison Chart

The Rapist	Enoch Drebber
1. Big, burly bald man.	1. Big, burly bald man.
2. Raspy voice.	2. Raspy voice.
3. Lives near victim.	3. Lives near victim.
4. From "up north."	4. From "up north."
5. Cut his finger.	5. Cut his finger.
6. Has Type O blood.	6. Has Type O blood.
7. Committed rape.	7. "Won't deny" rape.

Figure 16-2: Contrast Chart

60% of Population	Enoch Drebber
1. Have Type O blood.	1. Has Type O blood.
2. Not big, burly bald men.	2. Big, burly bald man.
3. No raspy voice.	3. Raspy voice.
4. Don't live near victim.	4. Lives near victim.
5. Not from "up north."	5. From "up north."
6. Didn't cut their finger.	6. Cut his finger.
7. Didn't commit rape.	7. "Won't deny" rape.

Figure 16-3: Compounding Chart

Who has Type O blood?	Enoch Drebber
Who is a big, burly bald man?	Enoch Drebber
Who has a raspy voice?	Enoch Drebber
Who lives near the victim?	Enoch Drebber
Who comes from "up north?"	Enoch Drebber
Who cut his finger?	Enoch Drebber
Who "won't deny" the rape?	Enoch Drebber
Who is guilty of rape?	**Enoch Drebber**

Any of these arguments could be put on a flip chart, butcher paper, an overhead projector, or a Powerpoint, Corel Presentations, Adobe Acrobat, or some similar computer presentation program. With a presentation program the most artistically disinclined can make a professional looking presentation. You can also animate the presentation program, introducing one argument at a time and preventing Type A jurors from reading ahead instead of listening to your arguments. If you have a flip chart or butcher paper, lightly tape strips of paper over each point, pulling the strips off one at a time as you make each argument. Even the simplest of cases can be improved by the use of visual aids. Charts, graphs, and diagrams can be used as demonstrative aids during a witness's testimony, and can be used again in final argument to refresh the jury's memory of the testimony and to argue the points supported by that testimony. The very least that you can do with a presentation program is to make a simple animated bullet chart to intensify each point as it is made. This will not only help the jury absorb your arguments, the presentation program will serve as an outline to prompt you to remember the arguments you need to make. If you want to take another small step toward improving your arguments with a presentation program, place your photographic evidence and documentary evidence on presentation program slides, and as you talk about various aspects of the case, display the images to the jury.

4. ARRANGEMENT AND DELIVERY ON A HEAVY CASE LOAD

You might say "I don't have time for all that; I'm too busy," with some justification. You must not, however, simply abdicate your duty to prepare your cases because you have a heavy case load. That heavy docket is populated with simple cases, all of which have a limited number of basic fact patterns. There are only so many ways a person can shoplift, and only so many ways that someone can drive under the influence. After a relatively brief period of time working on such a docket, you will be familiar with all of them. You ought to have a pattern argument for all of them. Just as a seamstress can create an infinitely varied number of dresses from a single pattern, you ought to be able to modify your pattern arguments to fit an infinitely varied set of minor variations in your fact pattern. Do not trust yourself to carry these patterns around in your head. Write them down. If you do not keep your patterns in writing, the afternoon you need one, you will not be able to recall it because you have a splitting headache. In addition to your notebook of pattern arguments, use a final argument worksheet. The worksheet should have an elements checklist and the now familiar three sections of strengths (build), weaknesses (preserve), and rebuttal (destroy). In the strengths section, write the arguments you feel will carry the day for you. In the weaknesses section, write down the weaknesses in your case, and why they do not matter. Under rebuttal, write the anticipated defense arguments, with your proposed answer to those arguments. See Figure 16–4 for an example final argument worksheet. Even if you have done absolutely nothing to prepare for final argument, when you go to court on the morning of trial, put a blank copy of the final argument worksheet in your case file. If nothing else, during the course of the trial you can jot down notes under the appropriate headings as thoughts occur to you.

Figure 16-4: Final Argument Worksheet

Defendant: Marcus Hemming	
Charge: Conspiracy to Traffic in Cannabis	
Element	**Proof**
1. Date	Officer McConnell, videotape
2. Venue	Officer McConnell, videotape
3. Intent	Sam Snitch
4. Agreement	Alvin Accomplice
Strengths	
1. Videotape of drug transaction	
2. Audiotapes of telephone calls	
3. Accomplice's coconspirator declarations	
Weaknesses	**Answers**
1. Sam Snitch, C.I.	"It takes a thief..."
2. Alvin Accomplice, traitor.	Who else for a witness? Hemming hired him.
3. "Small time operators"	Not necessarily.
4. Renunciation.	Didn't do enough to renounce.
Rebuttal	**Answers**
1. Delay in warrant.	Only two weeks.
2. Delay in arrest.	It took a while to find him.
3. "I made a mistake to come here."	You sure did, you committed a crime.

F. IMPROPER ARGUMENTS

In arguing your case before a jury, it is important that your arguments resonate with logos and only incidentally with ethos and pathos. A surefire way to get a mistrial or reversal is to go overboard in your appeal to ethos and pathos or to make an argument based on sophism (false logos). Some jurisdictions are more stringent in forbidding such appeals, and some are more lax.

What follows is a nonexhaustive listing of arguments that have been found improper. Some of these may be permitted in your jurisdiction, but you must be sure that they have met with appellate approval. The safest approach to such arguments is: "When in doubt, leave it out."

1. Burden shifting—Suggesting that the defendant has a duty to come forward with evidence. Paul v. State, 980 So.2d 1282 (4th DCA Fla. 2008) (Insinuating that the defendant needed to prove that the prosecutor's witness was lying in order to be found not guilty).
2. Pitting—Pitting one witness against another. Northard v. State, 675 So.2d 652, 653 (4th DCA Fla. 1996) (prosecutor's argument was impermissible because it asked the jury to determine who was lying as the proper test of determining guilt).
3. Misstating the law—Clewis v. State, 605 So.2d 974 (3d DCA 1992) (Telling the jury that they could find a reasonable doubt only if they believed the defendant).
4. Misstating the facts—Gore v. State, 719 So.2d 1197 (Fla. 1998) (Saying that the defendant had killed three women when he in fact only killed two).
5. Belittling the defense role—Suggesting that the role of the defense lawyer is not worthy of respect. Briggs v. State, 455 So.2d 519, 520 (1st DCA Fla. 1984) ("[A]t least since 1953, prosecutors have been placed on notice that arguments directed to the role of defense attorneys are not proper").
6. Belittling the legal defense—Attacking the propriety of the defense raised. Servis v. State, 855 So.2d 1190, 1192 (5th DCA Fla. 2003) ("And the second tragedy in this case is the defense doing all they can to throw whatever they can against the wall and see what sticks").
7. Appeal to roles—Suggesting that the jury should make a certain finding because of the role of some party, advocate, or witness. Davis v. State, 801 So.2d 141 (4th DCA 2001)

(Telling jury they should believe police officers because they were police officers).

8. Arguing in opening statement—First v. State, 696 So.2d 1357 (2d DCA Fla. 1997) (Calling a defense witness a liar in opening statement).

9. Sending a messages—The purpose of a criminal trial is to determine whether the defendant has been proved guilty beyond a reasonable doubt; not encourage the jury to make a broad ranging statement on current culture. Richardson v. State, 604 So.2d 1107, 1109 (Fla.1992) (Urging jury to show the defendant the same amount of mercy that the defendant showed the victim).

10. Comment on the defense's failure to produce evidence or to call witnesses—Thomas v. State, 726 So.2d 369, 370 (4th DCA Fla. 1999) ("Comments by a prosecutor that a defendant has failed to call a witness are cause for reversal because, at least in part, they may lead the jury to believe that the defendant has the burden of proving his innocence").

11. Comment on the defendant's failure to testify—Rodriguez v. State, 753 So.2d 29, 37 (Fla.2000) ("any comment on, or which is fairly susceptible of being interpreted as referring to, a defendant's failure to testify is error and is strongly discouraged").

12. Comment on the defendant's post-arrest silence. Rimmer v. State, 825 So.2d 304, 322 (Fla. 2002).

13. Reference to facts not in evidence. Maddox v. State, 827 So.2d 380 (3d DCA Fla. 2002) (Suggesting that more evidence could have been presented).

14. Reference in opening statement to facts which do not come into evidence. Rutledge v. State, 374 So.2d 975 (Fla. 1979) (Mention of a tape recording in opening statement which was subsequently ruled inadmissible).

15. Attacks on the defendant's character—Janenson v. Sate, 656 So.2d 586 (3d DCA Fla. 1995) (Calling the defendant a career criminal); Evans v. State, 838 So.2d 1235 (2d DCA Fla. 2003) (Attributing criminal conduct based on race).

16. Attacks on the defense attorney's character—Crew v. State, 136 So.3d 101, 109 (5th DCA Fla. 2014) ("Verbal attacks on the personal integrity of opposing counsel are inconsistent with the prosecutor's role and are unprofessional").

17. References to one's own character—Ruiz v. State, 743 So.2d 1, 5 (Fla.1999) (Arguing that the state only charges the guilty).
18. Statements of personal opinion as to the guilt of the defendant—Cummings v. State 412 So.2d 436 (4th DCA Fla. 1982).
19. Bolstering a witness's character—Buckner v. State, 689 So.2d 1202 (3d DCA Fla. 1997) (Commenting that an officer was "very credible" and that he testified truthfully because he "was putting his job on the line").
20. Irrelevant or unsubstantiated attacks on a witness's character—Brighton v. State, 141 So.3d 579 (4th DCA Fla. 2014) (Suggesting that a defense witness manufactured evidence, without a foundation in the record, is completely improper).
21. Unsubstantiated attacks on a witness's character—First v. State, 696 So.2d 1357 (2d DCA Fla. 1997) (Calling a witness a liar without a firm evidentiary basis for doing so).
22. Arguing the Golden Rule—"Put yourself in the victim's shoes." Williamson v. State, 994 So.2d 1000 (Fla. 2008)
23. Imaginary script—Gonzalez v. State, 136 So.3d 1125, 1153 (Fla. 2014) ("An imaginary script is a subtle form of a golden rule argument in which the prosecutor asks the jury to put the prosecutors own imaginary words in the victims mouth, thereby trying to unduly create, arouse and inflame the sympathy, prejudice and passions of the jury to the detriment of the accused").
24. Flag waving—Ruiz v. State, 743 So.2d 1 (Fla. 1999) (Urging the jury to do their civic duty just as her father had done his duty in Desert Storm).
25. Quoting scripture—Lawrence v. State, 691 So.2d 1068, 1074 n.8 (Fla. 1997) ("Although we recognize that the prosecutor's biblical reference in this case was not reversible error, we again caution prosecutors, as we did in Bonifay [v. State, 680 So.2d 413 (1996)], that arguments invoking religion can easily cross the boundary of proper argument and become prejudicial.")

PRACTICAL EXERCISE

Almost every sentence in the following example final argument is objectionable. Analyze each sentence of the final argument and state the legal grounds for objection. Also state whether each improper argument offends by undue appeal to ethos, pathos, or fractured logic.

> Well, you heard it. On the one hand you heard the testimony of Officer Gregson, who daily puts his life on the line to protect you and your children, who has no axe to grind and nothing to gain. Just one courageous member of that thin blue line that separates us from the barbarians in our society. On the other hand you heard from the defendant's drinking buddy—a beer bellied, beer guzzling, bar hopping convicted felon who's known the defendant all his life.
>
> The question is, who's lying? They can't both be telling the truth. If the defendant is innocent, Officer Gregson is a liar. And we know Officer Gregson has no reason to lie. The defendant's witness lied, and he lied like a cheap clock. We know he lied, because he disagreed with Officer Gregson. Just look at the defendant. Look at who he hired for a lawyer. He's got the best lawyer money can buy. Anybody that would spend that much money on a lawyer has to be guilty. If you ever get into trouble and you're guilty as homemade sin, he's the man you want to hire. Just don't buy a used car from him. But it doesn't matter.
>
> Even though the defense attorney did such a great job of objecting and keeping you from hearing important evidence, we were still able to get in enough evidence to prove the defendant guilty. I've been a prosecutor for thirty years and I've seldom seen a more open and shut case. And the only evidence the defendant could come up with to show that he didn't do it was the testimony of his drunk buddy. If he was so innocent, he'd have more evidence than that. Where are his witnesses? There are none. Why not? Because he's guilty. If he's so innocent, why didn't he take the trouble to get up off his behind, walk those few feet to the witness stand, and tell you himself that he didn't do it? Isn't that the least he could do? And why didn't he do it?
>
> Because he's guilty. Ladies and gentlemen, put yourselves in the victim's shoes. Your home is your most sacred sanctuary. If you can't feel safe anywhere else, you should feel safe at home. To desecrate someone's home is one of the most awful crimes known to man. How would you like to have the defendant defile your home the way he did the victim's home? Invade your privacy. Paw through your things. Take your hard-earned money. Steal your priceless heirlooms. Trash your home. You wouldn't like it, would you? It's time to tell the defendant that you don't like what he did. It's time to tell the defendant that you're not going to put up with what he did.

If we're ever going to stem the rising tide of crime in this country, we're going to have to do it one case at a time—one guilty verdict at a time. And we've got to start right now. Right here and right now. The barbarians are at the gates. Civilization is in flames. You sit in the jury box with a bucket of water.

Are you going to pour it onto the ground with a not guilty verdict? Or are you going to throw it onto the fire with a guilty verdict? Do your part to take back the streets from the thugs and hoodlums of this world. Make your own home a safer place to live. Vote guilty and take one hooligan off the streets today.

CHAPTER 17

HANDLING MOTIONS AND OBJECTIONS

■ ■ ■

If the law is against you, pound the facts; if the facts are against you, pound the law; if the law and the facts are against you, pound the table.—Anonymous

A. PRETRIAL MOTIONS

A defendant with a poor case faces a bleak prospect at trial. Even for a defendant who has a winner, a trial can be an expensive ordeal. If the defendant can achieve a favorable result without going to trial, then so much the better. If a trial cannot be avoided, then the defendant will want to have the best prospect of victory possible. A defendant can seek to improve her prospects at trial by trying to control the forum which will decide the case or by trying to control the evidence upon which the case will be decided. Defendants seek to achieve all of these objectives by the filing of pretrial motions.

1. MOTIONS TO DISMISS

In civil cases, the classic trial avoidance motion is the motion for summary judgement. In civil cases, either side may file such a motion, but no similar provision exists in criminal cases.[1] In criminal cases, the classic trial avoidance motion is the motion to dismiss. The motion to dismiss can be based on any number of grounds—former jeopardy, statute of limitations, unconstitutionality, speedy trial. The grounds for a motion to dismiss can be limited only by the imagination of counsel. Motions to dismiss are the exclusive province of the defense. In most states, if the prosecution wants a case dismissed, all it has to do is enter a *nolle prosequi*.

When trying to influence the forum that will decide the issues, litigants have several options available. They can move for a change of venue. They can challenge the jury panel in hopes of getting another. They can challenge the judge. They can challenge opposing counsel. None of these challenges works very well for the prosecution. When asking for a change of venue, the litigant must allege (and prove) that the citizenry of the venue are so prejudiced that it is impossible for them to be fair and

[1] Except in New Mexico and Florida, where State v. Foulenfont, 119 N.M. 788, 895 P.2d 1329 (N.M.App. 1995), and Fla.R.Crim.P. 3.190(c)(4) provide for a form of pretrial summary judgement at the behest of the defense.

impartial. A prosecutor is an elected public official who draws his votes from the citizenry of the venue. A prosecutor who alleges prejudice on the part of his constituency does not endear himself to that constituency. A defense attorney, not needing to run for office, does not have this concern. The prosecutor faces a similar problem with challenging the composition of the jury panel. The defense attorney's first allegiance is to her client. The prosecutor's is to the system. To challenge the jury panel, the litigant must allege that the system is broken to the extent that it is not doing a proper job of selecting prospective jurors for the panel. To challenge a judge, the litigant must criticize the judge in some way. Judges are human beings, and human beings tend to remember those who wrong them. A judge occupies a position which makes it very easy to avenge a wrong suffered in one case by ruling against the wrongdoer in another. Prosecutors and defense attorneys who regularly practice before the same judge face this problem, but out-of-town defense attorneys need not fear reprisal. Because of all these considerations and more, prosecutors will most often find themselves defending such motions rather than advocating for them.

2. MOTIONS TO DISQUALIFY

Aristotle wrote that "It is not right to pervert the judge by moving him to anger or envy or pity—one might as well warp a carpenter's rule before using it."[2] The rules governing disqualification of trial judges from state to state may vary, but the dynamics should remain constant. The defense must present a logical, legal reason for believing the trial judge to be biased, and this oftentimes consists of an attack on the judge's character—a tactic likely to stir up emotion in the form of anger. Aristotle's dictum about warping the carpenter's rule was never more appropriate than when moving to disqualify the trial judge. One example from history will illustrate the point.

When Theodore Robert Bundy stood charged with the Chi Omega murders in Tallahassee, Florida, the Hon. John A. Rudd presided over his case. Judge Rudd was an excellent judge whose integrity was above reproach. Nevertheless, the defense filed a motion to disqualify Judge Rudd pursuant to Rule 3.230(d), Fla. R.Crim.P.[3] Without hearing, Judge Rudd denied the motion on its face, finding it legally insufficient to state grounds for recusal. Judge Rudd, however, was angered by the slur on his character and went farther than merely ruling on the legal sufficiency of the motion. He undertook to refute the allegations in the motion. A petition for writ of prohibition followed, and the Supreme Court granted it, with the following language:

---

2 On Rhetoric. 1354a.

3 Now Fla.R.Jud.Admin. 2.160.

> [O]ur rules clearly provide, and we have repeatedly held, that a judge who is presented with a motion for his disqualification "shall not pass on the truth of the facts alleged nor adjudicate the question of disqualification."[4]

The Florida rule required the judge to pass solely on the legal sufficiency of the allegations stated in the motion, not their veracity. Once the judge undertook to refute the factual allegations, he placed himself in an adversarial relationship with the defendant and, by that fact alone, had to be disqualified. If the accusations of the motion to disqualify could warp the rule, the judge might be baited into error. It came as no great surprise that, when the Hon. Edward D. Cowart was appointed to take Judge Rudd's place, one of the first motions filed by the defense was a motion to disqualify Judge Cowart. After a full adversarial hearing on the motion, Judge Cowart simply found that the motion was legally insufficient. Judges, not being confronted with such motions on a regular basis, are naturally inclined to react as Judge Rudd did. It became incumbent upon prosecutors in Florida, when such a motion was filed, to educate their trial judges as quickly as possible to the nuances of motions to disqualify. This usually took the form of posting, by return mail with a copy to the judge, a reply memorandum setting out the law.

The problem of warping the carpenter's rule has been addressed in different ways by the various jurisdictions. Utah has a similar provision to Florida,[5] but seeks to keep the rule straight by providing that the actual decision on the legal sufficiency of the motion should be made by another judge.[6] Other states, such as Idaho[7], provide for peremptory disqualification of trial judges. If a judge is subject to peremptory challenge without having to state reasons, situations like that of *Bundy v. Rudd* are completely avoided. Of course, litigants cannot be allowed to exercise repeated peremptory challenges to judges until they get one they like. Peremptory challenges are limited, and replacement judges must be disqualified for cause.[8]

3. MOTIONS IN LIMINE

Before the codification of rules of evidence, anything went in a criminal prosecution, and litigants were obliged to deal with all sorts of "evidence" that would never see the light of day in a modern courtroom—for example, rumor and evidence obtained by torture. At some time it was decided that certain types of evidence were so lacking in trustworthiness or so inflammatory that they should not be heard by the fact finder. The usual

---

4 Bundy v. Rudd, 366 So.2d 440, 441 (Fla. 1978).

5 Utah R.Crim.P. 29(b)(2).

6 Utah R.Crim.P. 29(c)(2) & 29(c)(3)(A).

7 Idaho R.Crim.P. 25(a).

8 Idaho R.Crim.P. 25(a)(4).

manner of excluding this type of evidence is to stand up and object at trial when it is proffered by the opposition. For any number of reasons, it might be advisable to resolve the admissibility of such evidence before the trial begins. It makes for a crisper, more efficient presentation at trial, and it gives the advocate a better idea of the evidence that will actually be placed before the jury. The proper vehicle for resolving such issues pretrial is the motion in limine, which we will discuss in detail later in the chapter.

4. MOTIONS TO SUPPRESS

Although the trial is touted as a search for truth, it is more accurate to think of it as a search for a truth-based favorable verdict. When a favorable verdict does not fit the truth, advocates have a method for making the truth fit a favorable verdict. It is called the motion to suppress. Perfectly valid, highly relevant truth may be excluded from evidence if it was gathered in contravention of constitutional or statutory safeguards. The motion to suppress a confession or other evidence on constitutional grounds is almost exclusively the province of the defense attorney. The prosecution can seldom exclude unfavorable facts from the jury, and that is as it should be. Acquittals which are at odds with real-world facts can be tolerated far better than convictions at odds with real-world facts.

5. FRIVOLOUS MOTIONS

Pretrial motions fall into four broad categories: frivolous, meritorious, cutting edge, and boilerplate. How you argue those motions depends in large part on the category into which they fall. We will first examine frivolous motions. What would account for the filing of frivolous motions? What type of lawyer would file them? The first type is the true believer. She truly believes that the defendant is innocent and the prosecutor is an agent of evil who should be opposed by all available means. As the British philosopher Anthony Flew observed, when we truly believe in a proposition, we tend toward uncritical acceptance of wretched arguments supporting that proposition.[9] True believers, therefore, oftentimes do not recognize the frivolous nature of a motion. The prosecutor's instinctive reaction toward a true believer is one of scorn. Patience will serve better.

The second type of attorney who will file frivolous motions is the bungler. A remarkable number of people graduate from law school and pass the bar who have very little business in a courtroom. What must you do when confronted by a bungler? Help the bungler as much as possible. Guide her away from land mines. Point her in the right direction when she goes astray. Do whatever can be done to keep the bungler from committing malpractice. This might also include allowing the bungler to get away with minor misfeasance which would otherwise not be tolerated. It is especially

[9] How to Think Straight, Prometheus Books, Amherst, NY, 1998. paras. 1.42, 1.43.

galling to have to do this when you are confronted by an obnoxious bungler, but there is no help for it. You must do what you must do to ensure, insofar as possible, that you will achieve a conviction that will withstand post-conviction litigation.

There is a third type of lawyer who files frivolous motions. We will call this third type the cynic, who can be either an obstructionist or a circumventer.[10] The cynic seeks the Pavlov's dog effect. File a barrage of frivolous motions. Argue each motion as though the fate of Western jurisprudence hangs in the balance, and a denial will result in the greatest miscarriage of justice since the trial of Socrates. Slip in a meritorious motion. A judge who has just denied fifteen consecutive vigorously argued frivolous motions is likely to deny the sixteenth meritorious motion by sheer reflex. There are few defense attorneys who have never celebrated an adverse ruling by slapping their client on the back and saying, "We've got reversible error!" Of course, such an assurance is small comfort to a client who expects to have served 90% of her sentence before the appellate court gets around to reversing the conviction, but it will be music to the ears of someone facing a draconian sentence. The antidote to the cynic is patient vigilance. Make sure that you are wide awake when the cynic slips in that meritorious motion.

6. MERITORIOUS MOTIONS

Which brings us to meritorious motions. How should you deal with a meritorious motion? Three possible responses spring to mind: (1) Vigorously oppose it and hope against hope that neither the judge nor the appellate court notices the merit in the motion. (2) Oppose it on the general principle that prosecutors are supposed to oppose defense motions and hope the judge has the wisdom to see the merit in the motion. (3) Concede the merit of the motion. It is suggested that response (3) is the correct response. What if you believe the motion to be meritorious under the law, but you believe the law to be wrong? Should you oppose the motion in hopes that you can achieve a landmark legal decision? No hard-and-fast answer can be given to such an abstract question, but when answering that question in a concrete situation, it is well to also ask a second question. What is the cost/benefit ratio of introducing another issue into a case already beset with issues? Your goal at trial, first and foremost, is to achieve a conviction which will survive appellate attack. The broader public interest goals of changing already-established precedent should take a back seat to the immediate goal of obtaining a sound conviction.

---

[10] See Chapter 3.

7. CUTTING EDGE MOTIONS

Cutting edge motions come as the synthesis of two things, the language of Supreme Court opinions and the creativity of defense counsel. It is impossible to tell what seemingly innocuous statement of the Supreme Court will become the ore from which the next wave of cutting edge motions will be refined, but it may be instructive to study the history of one wave which may have already crested. When the Court decided *Apprendi v. New Jersey*,[11] it stood for the seemingly unremarkable proposition that a sentence could not be enhanced in excess of the statutory maximum unless the enhancement was supported by allegations contained in the charging document and a jury finding that the allegations were supported by fact. Something similar to this concept has been taught in law school for decades as the principle of *allegata et probata*.

Once the Supreme Court made its pronouncement in *Apprendi*, defense counsel began seeking to determine how far it could be stretched. The answer came two years later in a pair of cases, *Harris v. United States*[12] and *Ring v. Arizona*.[13] *Harris* confronted the issue of whether a mandatory minimum for an aggravating factor could be imposed absent a jury finding that the aggravating factor existed. The Supreme Court held that since the aggravating factor did not cause the sentence to exceed the statutory maximum, there was no need for it to be either pled in the charging document or found by a jury.

Ring addressed *Apprendi's* applicability to capital sentencing. The Supreme Court had already held in *Walton v. Arizona*[14] that it was perfectly proper for a judge to make a factual finding of aggravating circumstances after a jury verdict of guilty of capital murder. When the Court decided *Apprendi*, it specifically found that *Walton* was still good law, holding that the jury found the elements of the crime of capital murder, which made the death penalty applicable, and "once a jury has found the defendant guilty of all the elements of an offense which carries as its maximum penalty the sentence of death, it may be left to the judge to decide whether that maximum penalty, rather than a lesser one, ought to be imposed."[15] Despite *Walton's* precedent and despite the language of *Apprendi*, the Supreme Court in *Ring* held that a death penalty could not be imposed without a jury finding for the death penalty.

Since *Apprendi* dealt with sentences beyond the statutory maximum, and since the statutory maximum for capital murder is the death penalty, and since the Supreme Court held that *Walton* was still good law when it

---

11 530 U.S. 466, 120 S.Ct. 2348 (2000).

12 536 U.S. 545, 122 S.Ct. 2406 (2002).

13 536 U.S. 584, 122 S.Ct. 2428.

14 497 U.S. 639, 110 S.Ct. 3047.

15 530 U.S. at 497, 120 S. Ct. at 2366.

decided *Apprendi*, it would seem obvious that *Apprendi* does not apply in capital cases. But lawyers on the cutting edge of the law sought to extend *Apprendi* to capital cases, and they filed their motions accordingly. *Ring* was not a logical decision. *Ring* was an *ethical* decision. Regardless of the logical language of *Apprendi* in recognizing that *Walton* was still viable, it does not seem ethical that a grand theft charge carrying a statutory maximum of five years requires a jury finding of aggravating circumstances as a predicate for increasing the sentence to six years while a capital murder requires no jury finding of aggravating circumstances as a predicate for imposing the death penalty.

8. BOILERPLATE MOTIONS

It is understandable that true believers, bunglers, and cynics would file boilerplate motions, but why would anyone else? There are two perfectly good reasons that an advocate would file such a motion. The first is self-preservation, the second is issue preservation. The first rule of any endeavor is self-preservation. The lawyer wants to escape criticism or censure as much as possible, and filing boilerplate motions gives the appearance of competence. The second motive, issue preservation, is also a real consideration. No one knows when an appellate court might change its mind, and if the lawyer has not preserved the issue, she cannot take appellate advantage of the court's change in direction. What separates advocates from true believers, bunglers, and cynics is the way advocates argue boilerplate motions. Advocates do not argue such motions vociferously. They present the motions, acknowledging the law is against them, and state that they are preserving the record against a future possible change in the law. If some trend in the precedent can be argued as reason for changing the law in the trial court, they vigorously argue the trend, but otherwise they just preserve the record.

Who knows the next well-settled area of the law that will be unsettled by an appellate court revisiting the issues raised in a boilerplate motion? It was the repeated filing of such boilerplate motions that helped lead to the modern rules of liberal discovery in criminal cases. For example, it is black letter law that a motion for statement of particulars can seek only to narrow the allegations contained in the charging document, but in *State of New Jersey versus Bruno Richard Hauptmann*, the defense filed a twelve paragraph demand for bill of particulars requesting disclosure of circumstantial matters that would nowadays be the subject of criminal discovery, including a request for a statement as to whether all the ransom notes were written in the same hand and whether Bruno Richard Hauptmann wrote them.[16] Although most of the requested disclosures were denied, some were granted. Other pre-discovery motions for bills of

[16] State of New Jersey versus Bruno Richard Hauptmann, Record on Appeal, pp. 4558–4566.

particulars were sometimes successful also. In *Peel v. State*[17] a motion for bill of particulars requested, and the trial court ordered, that the state give the defense a list of the names and addresses of the witnesses the state intended to call at trial. Eventually boilerplate motions for statements of particulars which were really shotgun requests for discovery gave way to today's liberal criminal discovery rules.

B. PREPARATION FOR THE MOTION HEARING

When you pull a defense motion out of your in basket, the first thing you should do is remain calm. Although some prosecutors break out into a cold sweat when they see a defense motion filed in one of their cases, you can survive most of them if you know how to respond to them. The second thing to do is read the motion carefully and assess it. Does it reflect real-world fact? Does it reflect the true state of the law? Does it require an evidentiary hearing, or can you handle it solely with argument? The facts stated in the motion will be couched in the terminology most favorable to the defense. Can you recast them in a light more favorable to the prosecution? If so, do it. The "facts" may not be factual. Never take any statement of fact in a motion at face value. Defense counsel looks at the evidence through rose-colored glasses which sometimes cause innocent misinterpretation of the facts. Sometimes the misinterpretation is not innocent. Once you have assessed the truth value of the factual recitation and recast it in terms more favorable to the state, look at the issue presented. Is the issue truthfully stated? Is it fairly stated? Can it be fairly restated so as to favor a finding for the state? If so, restate it. Make the same sort of analysis of the law cited. A remarkable amount of law gets misinterpreted, and lawyers will often rely on authority that holds dead against them. If you have time, you should prepare a reply brief setting forth your interpretation of the law and facts. It will do two things. (1) It will show the judge that you have done your homework. (2) It will cause you to really think about the law and the facts and think about the best way to make your argument. Determine whether the motion requires an evidentiary hearing, who has the burden, and what the burden is. Some motions will require proof by clear and convincing evidence, others will only require a preponderance of the evidence.

C. MOTION HEARINGS

The defense has a "case theory" for exclusion of the evidence based upon its interpretation of the facts. You should have a "case theory" for inclusion based on your interpretation of the facts. The friction between the two positions will give you the point to adjudicate. You do not make an opening statement in a motion hearing, but your brief in opposition to the

[17] 154 So.2d 910 (Fla.2d DCA 1963).

motion can serve as the "opening argument" of the motion hearing. Set out the case theories and the point to adjudicate and then write an argument explaining why you should prevail. Fill out an order of proof, and you are now ready to go hear the motion. If possible, never rely on a single theory of admissibility for any crucial piece of evidence. Backup theories give you defense in depth. Argue the theories in descending order based on your assessment of their persuasiveness. Make your best argument first and then follow with the second best, and then the third best. If possible, always have at least three theories of admissibility for any crucial piece of evidence. "Your honor, the evidence was lawfully seized with a warrant. Even if the warrant was invalid, the seizure was made with the consent of the defendant. Even if the consent was invalid, the evidence would have inevitably been discovered." Even if you do not argue the lesser theories with any vigor, simply putting them on the record gives appellate counsel another argument to make to the appeals court. If the argument is not at least voiced, it probably cannot be raised for the first time on appeal. More than once in your career, you will have a trial judge scoff at your best argument and find for you based on your fallback argument. More than once you will have an appellate court ignore your best reasons and find for you based upon your worst reasons. Judges are sometimes as inscrutable as juries.

D. PRETRIAL MOTIONS: GOING PROACTIVE

You need not be completely on the defensive during the pretrial phase. In addition to the proactive discovery measures discussed in Chapter 9, there are numerous provisions for proactive settlement of issues. One of those provisions is Rule 201 of the Federal Rules of Evidence, relating to judicial notice. This rule has been adopted and adapted by many states.[18] Whereas the Federal Rule and the rules of Arkansas, Utah, Montana, and Wyoming provide that judicial notice is compulsory if it is "requested by a party and [the court is] supplied with the necessary information," the Florida rules require timely written notice. Although written notice and a pretrial hearing may not be required by the state rule, it makes sense as good housekeeping. It seems better to spend a few hours before trial disposing of such matters than to chase a jury out of the courtroom to stare at the walls of the jury room while the issue is decided mid-trial. Such delays will be numerous enough without adding in hearings which could have been held pretrial.

1. SUMMARY EVIDENCE

Federal Rule of Evidence 1006 provides another little used but useful tool. The rule provides for introduction of massive amounts of evidence in

[18] E.g. Ark.R.Evid. 201; West's Fla.Stat.Ann. §§ 90.202 & 20.203; Idaho R.Evid. 201; Mont.R.Evid. 201; Utah R.Evid. 201; Wyo.R.Evid. 201.

the form of summaries, and it too has been adopted by many states.[19] The rule provides that the contents of voluminous writings, recordings, or photographs which cannot conveniently be examined in court may be presented in the form of a chart, summary, or calculation. Once again, only the Florida rule for summary evidence requires timely written notice, but the giving of such notice makes good housekeeping and good sense. Three examples will demonstrate the usefulness of the summary evidence rule.

During the Orlando trial of Theodore Robert Bundy, it was essential to place the time of the victim's death at or near the time that Bundy had been in Lake City. The body had lain in the woods for approximately two months, and it was partially mummified, partially skeletonized. The surest indication of time of death came from maggot activity. A certain number of generations of maggots could be shown to have lived on the body. Maggots do not reproduce below a certain temperature. The medical examiner did a study of temperatures from various weather stations in the area and did a chart showing the daily temperatures between the victim's disappearance and her recovery. The number of days at which the temperature was conducive to maggot activity coincided with the number of generations of maggots found on the body. Conclusion: The victim died shortly after her disappearance and at a time close to when Bundy was in Lake City. It would have been a monumental undertaking to admit all the predicate information necessary to get the chart into evidence. Rule 1006[20] would have saved the day had the Bundy case not predated Florida's adoption of the Federal Rules of Evidence. The prosecution team decided to forego trying to admit the chart, but the defense did such a thorough job of cross-examining the medical examiner that he produced it and testified from it on cross.

Another area where summary evidence can prove useful is in the proving up of motive and of the pecuniary gain aggravating circumstance. Financial difficulties on the part of the defendant oftentimes serve as a motive for crime. Those difficulties could be demonstrated by the introduction of several banker's boxes of mind-numbingly boring financial records; or they could be demonstrated by the testimony of a CPA who has done a financial analysis and who can summarize the defendant's plight.

Murders are oftentimes the byproduct of drug smuggling conspiracies. Drug smuggling conspiracies generate voluminous telephone calls. Criminal intelligence analysts can chart and graph those phone calls to demonstrate the patterns of calls that lead up to and follow individual smuggles, and also the flurries of phone calls that surround crises such as the arrest of a mule.

---

[19] E.g. Ark.R.Evid. 1006; West's Fla.Stat.Ann. § 90.956; Idaho R.Evid. 1006; Mont.R.Evid. 1006; Utah R.Evid. 1006; Wyo.R.Evid. 1006.

[20] West's Fla.Stat.Ann. § 90.956.

2. PROACTIVE USE OF THE MOTION IN LIMINE

Back in the late 1940's, the Air Force conducted a series of tests, known as Project MX981, to determine the effects of extreme acceleration and deceleration on the human body. At a press conference on the project, Colonel John Paul Stapp was asked how they had been able to manage such a dangerous project without someone suffering serious injuries. Stapp attributed their safety record to an engineer on the project named Edward Murphy. Stapp said Murphy had a law that they payed strict attention to. Of course, the modern formulation of that law is "if anything can go wrong, it will." Stapp said that with that law in mind, they carefully considered all possibilities of disaster before doing a test and did their best to provide against them.[21]

Anyone who has ever tried a criminal case knows full well that Murphy's Law reigns supreme in the courtroom. You can deal with this fact of life in one of two ways. You can stomp blindly into the courtroom and blunder into every available pitfall, dealing with each new disaster on a catch-as-catch-can basis, or you can carefully consider all the possibilities of disaster before going to trial and do your best to provide against them. The motion in limine serves as an excellent tool for providing against disaster. Oftentimes you confront opposing counsel who combine an expansive definition of relevance with a resolute determination to sneak in questionable evidence or to wear down the trial judge into admitting the evidence by dint of repeated proffers. Settle such matters pretrial with a motion in limine, and the trial will flow much more smoothly. If you know opposing counsel to be particularly obtuse, the motions in limine will have to address even the most basic issues. If opposing counsel has a realistic grasp of the rules of evidence and an inclination to exercise that grasp, then you can reserve motions in limine for truly controversial issues. The subject matter of such motions is limited only by your imagination, and the more you can settle pretrial, the more smoothly the trial will run.

Motions in limine are not, however, motions to suppress. If the motion addresses a cut-and-dried issue (e.g., Motion to Prevent Impeachment of State's Witness with DUI Conviction), then the ruling will be final. If, however, the motion addresses an issue which depends upon the interpretation of other evidence, (e.g., Motion to Prevent Introduction of Purportedly Exculpatory Other Act Evidence), then a pretrial ruling is only preliminary and subject to change based on how the evidence unfolds at trial. One Florida court expressed this concept in colorful language:

> A trial court's pre-trial ruling on a motion in limine is tentative because the shifting sands of the trial in progress may cause a

[21] Spark, Nick T., A History of Murphy's Law, Periscope Film, 2006. pp. 13–14.

trial judge to rethink an earlier evidentiary ruling based on a maturing understanding of the case.[22]

Other jurisdictions, although they do not voice the rule so eloquently, have a similar view of the finality of a motion in limine.[23] The non-finality of a motion in limine means that at trial you may renew a motion that was denied pretrial. It also means that the pretrial granting of a motion in limine does not conclusively settle the matter, and the defense may also ask for renewed consideration during the trial. Even if failure to renew the motion at trial does not preclude raising the issue on appeal, an attorney would be foolish not to renew the motion at trial—the judge just might change her mind.

E. MAKING OBJECTIONS

John Juror once sat on two homicide trials in the same week. In the first trial the defense attorney, Lawrence Litigator, adopted the strategy of objecting to everything, enthusiastically trying to disrupt the trial as much as possible with numerous objections and marathon arguments. His objections were almost always overruled, and his client was convicted. In the other trial, the defense attorney, Aaron Advocate, rarely objected, but his objections were almost always sustained. The jury acquitted. John came away from his experience thinking that Lawrence was far and away the better lawyer than Aaron. Why? Because Aaron hardly objected at all. Despite the juror's impression, a constant barrage of objections is not necessary to good lawyering. It can even be counterproductive. Good lawyers know when and how to object.

Some defense attorneys deem it their duty to grind the wheels of justice to a screeching halt with a steady stream of objections, no matter how ill-conceived they might be. The lawyers who try this hope for one of five things: (1) The prosecution will become so disheartened that an acceptable plea offer will be forthcoming. (2) The prosecutor will get so bemused and befuddled that he will overlook something and thereby lose the case. (It has happened more than once). (3) The prosecutor will become so enraged that he will do something stupid and cause a mistrial. (This, too, has happened more than once). (4) The judge will become so conditioned to overruling frivolous objections, she will fail to recognize the valid objections and will overrule them, too, thereby building in reversible error. (5) The judge will make an erroneous ruling which is fatal to the State's case. The answer to all these strategies, of course, is patient persistence.

---

[22] McCallister v. State, 779 So.2d 615, 615–616 (Fla.App. 5th DCA 2001).

[23] E.g. Ohler v. United States, 529 U.S. 753, 120 S.Ct. 1851 (2000); Nolen v. State, 278 Ark. 17, 643 S.W.2d 257 (1982); State v. Silva, 898 A.2d 707 (R.I. 2006).

For many reasons, prosecutors cannot pursue these strategies in making objections. Whereas a victim cannot file a post-acquittal motion attacking the competency of a prosecutor who mishandled a barrage of objections, a defendant can and will file such a postconviction motion alleging incompetent assistance of counsel by a defense attorney who mishandled a barrage of objections. Prosecutors cannot appeal acquittals caused by erroneous rulings, but defendants can and will appeal such convictions. What strategy, then, should you use in making objections at trial? Before you make an objection, you should engage in a three-step analysis:

(1) Is it objectionable?

(2) Does it hurt?

(3) Can you ease the pain by objecting?

Lawyers often object because evidence hurts regardless of whether they have valid grounds. Without getting into a deep philosophical discussion of the ethics involved, you must acknowledge that, within the dynamics of the trial, defense attorneys can afford to do this, but prosecutors cannot. There are some defense attorneys who have an almost hypnotic ability to talk judges into making silly rulings. This ability will win acquittals because the judge has ruled the prosecution's best evidence inadmissible on some arcane and ill-conceived ground. Even if you might possess such an ability, do not attempt to use it. Defendants can appeal guilty verdicts. You lead a judge into error, and chances are you or one of your colleagues will get to try that case again. You lead enough judges into error and word will get around among the members of the bench. You will become like the little boy who cried wolf. Judges will not listen to your arguments even when you are right.

The fact that a lawyer is doing something objectionable does not necessarily give you a good reason to spring to your feet and object. The objection must serve a useful purpose. The primary reason to object is to stop the bleeding. Some defense attorneys, in their quest for reversible error, will object to the introduction of evidence that they really want admitted. Lawrence Litigator once tried a homicide case in which the prosecution had a taped statement from the defendant. On the tape, the defendant admitted stabbing the victim, but made a strong plea that it was self-defense. Before introducing the statement, the prosecutor checked with Lawrence and, since he wanted the statement in also, Lawrence agreed that the prosecutor did not need to proffer the statement outside the jury's presence. After proving up Miranda, the prosecutor offered the tape into evidence without properly authenticating it. Lawrence objected that the tape had not been properly authenticated and the judge sustained. The prosecutor thanked the witness and announced that he had no further questions. Lawrence angrily demanded that the prosecutor be required to lay the proper predicate and introduce the statement. The prosecutor declined. Lawrence then laid the predicate on cross-examination and again demanded that the prosecution be required to play the tape. The jury never heard the tape. As the old saying goes, "Be careful what you ask for, you may get it."

The primary reason to make an objection that you know will be overruled is to preserve the record for appeal. You have very little right to appeal; therefore, you have very little reason to make doomed objections. Usually, the only thing you can accomplish by making such an objection is to highlight for the jury that you think the objected-to material is harmful to your case. Sometimes you can become so inflamed by passion that you continue to object even after you have been overruled. Little purpose can be served by persisting in an objection, no matter how well-founded, which the judge is not going to sustain.

Sometimes, however, there can be good reasons for objecting to harmless material. In a long-ago trial of a child molester, the bulk of the state's evidence consisted of hearsay reports of abuse by the child victim pursuant to the child hearsay statute. One of the statements the State intended to offer was made to the initial investigating officer. In opening statement, the defense attorney outlined the statement to the officer and made much of the fact that the statement was not nearly as detailed as later statements made by the child. When the defense attorney made the child's statement to the officer the centerpiece of his opening, the prosecutor anticipated that the defense intended to vigorously cross-examine the officer on the child's statement and deleted the child's statement from the officer's order of testimony. When the officer testified, the defense attorney attempted to bring out the contents of the statement on cross-examination. The prosecutor then objected to the introduction of the statement as beyond the scope of direct examination. The evidence was so harmless that he had initially intended to offer it himself. Why should he object to it? When the objection was sustained, the defense was obliged to call the officer as its only defense witness, thereby being forced to take the officer on direct examination rather than cross and giving the prosecutor the advantage of being able to ask the officer leading questions about the statement on cross-examination.

There can even be times when you would want to make an objection that you know the judge will overrule. Suppose you want to do something during the trial that is of questionable admissibility. You have done your research and are ready to make a good faith offer of the evidence, but you believe the judge will likely be predisposed to rule against you. Before you get to the point of trying to do this thing, the defense attorney gives you a gift. She tries it herself. You rise to your feet, make a half-hearted objection, and get it overruled. Now, for this trial, the judge has set the ground rules.

Having once ruled the evidence admissible, the judge will be hard-pressed to rule against you when you later try the same thing.

At other times, you can use an objection as a discovery tool. Sometimes the defense will do something that totally mystifies you. You ask yourself "What the heck are they up to?" Mystical questions are always objectionable on relevance grounds. Get up to your feet, object, get to the bench and find out what the defense is driving at.

Some things ought to be done properly, and you should insist that opposing counsel adhere to the time-honored formulas for accomplishing certain tasks. One area where this is especially true is in laying Queen Caroline's predicate for impeachment by prior inconsistent statement. As common as this form of impeachment is, it is amazing how few attorneys do it correctly. The requisites of the predicate are there for a purpose, and that purpose is fairness. Each element of the predicate gives the witness notice. She is put on notice as to when she purportedly made the statement, where she made it, to whom she made it, and what she is supposed to have said. Each of these facts draws her attention with greater and greater certainty to the statement. Omission of any element of the predicate could confuse the witness. Insist that the predicate be laid properly. Insisting on a proper predicate for impeachment by prior inconsistent statement constitutes just one example of the use of objections to protect your witnesses. You should be eternally vigilant to interpose proper objections to improper questioning, but your assessment of the witness's capacity to protect herself should govern how vociferously you object. Depending on how you assess your witness's intelligence, maturity, and eloquence, you may decide she can protect herself far better than you can. For example, you might object to questions calling for speculation propounded to a child witness, where you might allow a veteran law enforcement officer to go ahead and speculate for opposing counsel.

Some lawyers make objections for less than laudable motives. Given the paucity of drama in most cases, you should work to make cases interesting for the jury. When you work to do this, then the other side works to spoil the dramatic effect. Nothing can spoil dramatic effect worse than a well-timed objection. In this case, opposing counsel does not care whether the objection is well-founded or whether it will be sustained, she simply wants to break the flow of persuasion with a lengthy sidebar. If opposing counsel infuses the trial with drama in an objectionable way, then certainly object. But it is not proper to make frivolous objections simply to parry a telling blow.

Some lawyers just naturally detest each other, and when they get to court, they work hard to make life miserable for each other. They forget the cardinal rule that you should not fight opposing counsel, you should try your case to the jury. Many times this takes the form of endless, vehemently argued objections over the most inconsequential of issues. Never lose sight of the primary aim, which is to obtain a fair, impartial, just verdict of guilty. Objections which do not further that aim impede it.

1. OBJECTIONS AND THE HOLISTIC TRIAL

For teaching purposes, we subdivide trials into their component parts and study the individual parts of the trial without much regard for what goes before or comes after. As you study each individual part, you sometimes forget that each part is an indispensable segment of the whole trial. You should do voir dire with an eye toward final argument. Your direct examination should be influenced by what was said in opening statements and by the expected defense. It is the same with objections. You might want to decline to make an objection within the context of one trial, but not within the context of another. Before the first witness is called or the first objection is made, you want to have a firm idea of: What you hope to prove. How you hope to prove it. How you will seek to influence the jury to see things your way. What the defense will likely be. How the defense will seek to prove their case and influence the jury to vote against you. Once you have a firm idea of these things, you have armed yourself with the information you need to evaluate whether, when, and how to object. When you have properly done your homework, you can even anticipate prior to trial when you will want to object. Then you do your research, find your case law, and can stand up and say something more convincing than what one young prosecutor said in a hotly contested murder case, "Your honor, that just ain't right!"

You will occasionally confront the situation where you have anticipated the objection, done your research, argued your objection brilliantly, and the judge has, despite all logic and reason, ruled against you. At this point you can curse your abominable luck in having to appear before a judge of such low intellect; you can throw in the towel; or you can work to find some way to put a positive spin on the disaster that has befallen you. Be diligent to find the silver lining to the cloud of that adverse ruling.

2. THE METHODOLOGY OF OBJECTING

Knowing how to object is almost as important as knowing when to object. Ritual adds solemnity to any proceeding. You can give an aura of respectability to the most ridiculous activities when you infuse them with ritual. Court proceedings are and should be solemn, dignified affairs. Time honored ritual calls for objections to be made from the feet, not from the seat. You want to stand on your feet, state your objection clearly and succinctly, making extended arguments outside the hearing of the jury, and receive the ruling stoically. The making of jury arguments in the guise of stating grounds for an objection is objectionable. You should not make a habit of doing it, and you should not tolerate its being done. Later on, we will discuss some situations where this rule should be relaxed.

3. THE MANNER OF OBJECTING

Mere compliance with the formalities of objecting does not an effective objection make. If you are to object effectively, you must keep in mind your audience, and tailor the manner of your objection to send the correct message to your audience. Whenever an objection is made, you have potentially a minimum of five audiences, and which of those audiences is most important often depends on the nature of your objection and what you hope to accomplish by objecting. Your audiences are:

(1) The trial judge. This audience may or may not be sympathetic, and the judge will almost certainly have an entirely different set of aims and objectives than you. The judge is almost always concerned with the sacred cow of "judicial economy," whatever that is. Many judges also have a paranoid fear of reversal. Others just want to get to the golf course at a decent time on Friday afternoon. Sometimes the most dangerous judge is the one whose philosophy is "to heck with the law, I just want to be fair." It is important that you try to discern your judge's agendas and concerns, and tailor your manner of objecting to fit those agendas.

(2) The jurors. Standard jury instructions tell the jurors not to concern themselves with why objections are made or what might have transpired had an objection been ruled on differently.[24] It may be that the jurors do not concern themselves with the jury instruction. The cardinal rule of objecting in front of the jury comes from a deodorant commercial: "Never let them see you sweat." Your objection may be the turning point in the case. A negative ruling may spell disaster for your side. You may be desperate. The jury must never suspect this.

(3) The appellate court: Always lurking in the background, ever present but never seen, is the danger that a group of strangers in a far distant city is going to turn your fabulous victory into a crushing defeat. They may even immortalize your lapses of judgement in the pages and on the database of the West Reporter System. How you do what you do can have a profound effect on what they decide to do about what you have done.

(4) Your fans in the courtroom: The court personnel whom you have befriended, the victim and/or the victim's family, and other persons of like nature all constitute an audience that you

---

[24] See, e.g. Florida Standard Jury Instructions in Criminal Cases 2.1. 2004. Florida Supreme Court. 27 June 2025. <https://www.floridabar.org/rules/florida-standard-jury-instructions/>.

have a natural desire to impress. You should almost never allow your decisions to be dictated by a desire to please this group.

(5) The media: Reality shows rely on a common human trait—when people have television cameras pointed at them, they tend to act in the most unreal fashion imaginable. Do not under any circumstances allow yourself to become intoxicated with media attention. Too many times lawyers perform for the media and not in their client's best interest. Do not try to look good for the media. Do not worry about looking bad in the media if what you are doing will help you win the case. Remember the old saying, "We wouldn't care as much what people thought about us if we only knew how seldom they thought about us."

Some very good attorneys have one glaring weakness. Every motion they file, every objection they make, they act as though they believe that the matter is one of utmost jurisprudential, constitutional, moral, and ethical importance, and an adverse ruling will signal the decline and fall of Western civilization. The judge, consequently, does not know when they are serious. If you fight every objection as though you were Leonidas at Thermopylae, you might win some inconsequential battles, but you could lose the war.

If you must make a technical objection, you should probably do so more in sorrow than in anger. "I'm sorry, your honor, but I must object and insist that counsel lay the proper predicate." If opposing counsel has no clue as to what the proper predicate is, do not engage in gamesmanship. Delineate how the predicate is deficient. Tyro lawyers make endless mistakes, and the fields are white unto harvest for the making of endless objections. Keeping in mind the caveat that some things ought to be done correctly, you should show as much mercy as you can to the newly-hatched lawyer. Considerations above and beyond mere altruism dictate this approach. When trying cases with a fledgling attorney, some judges take great delight in sustaining "no proper predicate" objections without delineating wherein the predicate is insufficient. If opposing counsel does not object, the judge will sometimes object sua sponte, and you can be sure that such an objection will be sustained. This results in a tremendous waste of time and needless embarrassment of counsel. If this happens to you, ask how the predicate is deficient. If neither the judge nor opposing counsel will delineate the correct predicate, undertake to discover it in the same way that Thomas Edison discovered the correct filament for his light bulb—by trial and error. Eventually you will happen upon the correct predicate or the judge will relent and tell you where it is deficient.

After the objection has been sustained and opposing counsel has been educated as to how to do it, if she persists in doing it wrong, you may allow your voice to reflect a slight amount of frustration as you continue to hold her feet to the fire. Some lawyers think that they can wear court and counsel down by obtusely repeating the error again and again. You must not allow yourself to be beaten into submission by opposing counsel's resolute insistence on doing it wrong.

Many rookie prosecutors think that questionable conduct by opposing counsel is a mere fact of life, and that they should let the most scurrilous accusations and innuendos slide off their thick skin like so much water off a duck's back. "After all," they say, "we are all professional aren't we, and everybody realizes that this is just so much meaningless lawyer talk." Can you be sure that the jury does? You can smile professionally through one not guilty verdict after another by ignoring slurs on your character. There used to be an evidentiary rule known as the tacit admission rule. If a suspect was accused of a crime and he did not deny it, the suspect was deemed to have admitted it.[25] Although *Miranda v. Arizona*[26] has largely defanged the tacit admission rule,[27] this sort of argument from silence remains powerful. By not responding to such accusations and innuendos, you tacitly admit them, and juries will render their verdicts accordingly.

You need to object to such baseless libel of yourself and your officers, and it should be done vehemently, even angrily. You should be angry enough to let the jury know in no uncertain terms that you are not guilty, but not so angry as to be unprofessional. Do not do as one prosecutor did after being repeatedly accused of racism. The prosecutor patiently objected on several occasions and was sustained. When defense counsel renewed his accusations in final argument, the prosecutor rose to his feet, objected, stated his grounds, and further added that if defense counsel made another such accusation, he was going to personally punch defense counsel in the nose. Luckily, the judge was as fed up with defense counsel's tactics as was the prosecutor. He sustained the objection without holding the prosecutor in contempt, and the trial continued without further allegations of racism. A display of an appropriate level of anger accompanied by a demeanor suggesting that such accusations are beneath contempt should have been enough.

4. REASON, RATIONALE, AND EXPLANATION

Almost all actions, including judicial rulings, can be understood on the basis of up to three things—reason, rationale, and explanation. Reason is why we do things. Rationale is how we justify the action to ourselves, and explanation is how we justify it to others. If you scratch yourself, your reason, rationale, and explanation for that action may be identical—you itch. More complex activity frequently involves differences among reason,

---

[25] Lovvorn v. State, 192 Tenn. 336, 241 S.W.2d 419 (1951).

[26] 384 U.S. 436, 86 S.Ct. 1602 (1966).

[27] Ledune v. State, 589 S.W.2d936 (Tenn.Cr.App. 1979).

rationale, and explanation. Take the typical bar fight homicide. The defendant's reason for killing is usually quite simple, he was drunk and angry. Being drunk and angry is not a personally satisfying reason for killing someone, so the killer usually rationalizes that the victim had it coming. Although the killer may be satisfied with this rationale, the law is not, therefore the killer offers an explanation—the legal justification of self-defense. Oftentimes this justification is little more than a lame excuse. A jury's reason for finding the defendant not guilty might be that they like the defendant and do not like the victim. Their rationale would most likely be that the victim had it coming, and they might explain their verdict as the product of reasonable doubt. A judge, being a one-person jury, works the same way. We have all seen legal opinions that make no sense. When we read these opinions, we wonder what the author was thinking about. How could sane minds achieve such insane results? If the judge's explanation seems more like an excuse than a justification, then we can safely conclude that somewhere beneath the surface, we can find unstated reasons. The reasons can run the gamut from the sublime to the ridiculous, but they are usually there. What does this have to do with objections? When you argue objections, you must be ever cognizant of the fact that simply giving the judge a legal justification for ruling your way will not ensure a favorable ruling. You must also give the judge a reason for ruling your way. Judicial economy frequently motivates a judge's ruling far more than judicial precedent. If you can persuade the judge that ruling your way will turn a six-week trial into a two-week trial, then a favorable ruling has become more likely. If you can persuade a judge that ruling your way is going to save the taxpayers untold thousands of dollars, then a favorable ruling has become more likely. Many judges have a misguided sense of fairness. They seem to believe that it is far more important to be fair than it is to be legally correct. When opposing counsel begin to appeal to such a judge's sense of fairness to the defendant's rights, you had better have a more persuasive answer than, "Nevertheless, Judge, the law says otherwise," or you are going to get killed. You must find countervailing fairness arguments. Always remember, a judge, believing she has sufficient reason to rule one way, will ignore the legal justification for ruling the other way, and find an excuse to rule for reason over justification.

5. UNDERSTANDING THE RULING

When the judge does rule, you must make sure that you understand the ruling. When you prepare your witnesses to testify, you always tell them that they should ask for clarification of questions that they do not understand. The reason for this is simple: A witness can destroy her credibility by giving ill-conceived answers to half-understood questions. Likewise, you can destroy your case by charging off to perform some ill-conceived act based on your misconception of the judge's ruling. You can wander off into the minefield of mistrial, get yourself held in contempt, or even lose a case outright because you do not understand what the judge meant. Finding out what the judge means by a ruling can be tricky. You do not want to appear to be arguing with the judge or questioning the judge's wisdom. Arguing with the judge over a ruling may cause the court retainers to admire your spunk, but it almost never accomplishes anything other than to supply the judge with a reason to rule against you on the next issue to arise. You must be polite, be concise, and convey the true impression that you are honestly seeking to understand the judge's ruling.

F. MEETING OBJECTIONS

Making objections is easy compared to meeting them. The ideal way to meet an objection is to anticipate it and prepare for it. You can really impress the judge if you meet opposing counsel's objection with a citation to a case decided within the past week. Usually you can anticipate the objections to the more important things you will attempt during the course of the trial. A little preliminary research can go miles toward achieving a favorable ruling. The most important thing about meeting objections is that you not get rattled or disconcerted by the objection or the judge's ruling. Remain calm, keep your eye on the objective, and continue to plod forward to meet the objective.

When you are ruled against, remember, there is more than one way to skin a cat. Oftentimes your objective is not objectionable, merely your method of achieving it. One frustration common to all judges is to sit on the bench and watch a lawyer attempting to use improper means to introduce proper evidence. If a lawyer is trying to do a proper thing improperly and an objection is made, it must be sustained. Other times lawyers voice inappropriate objections to evidence when there is a valid objection available if they could just find it. Some judges will rule on such objections by saying "overruled on those grounds," or "sustained on those grounds." This is a tipoff to counsel that they are attempting to achieve a praiseworthy goal by blameworthy means. The judge is telling you "take another stab at it, there is a way if you can find it." Other times the judge will simply rule without this subtle coaching. If a judge rules against you on one ground, you must begin to think of other ways to achieve the objective, other ways to prove the point. A piece of evidence which is objectionable on one ground may be perfectly admissible on another. At other times a judge may not like the admissibility of a piece of evidence on one ground but love it on another. A document may be a business record, or it may be past recollection recorded, or both. A child's statement about a sexual assault may be child hearsay or a medical history. A victim lying in a puddle of blood proclaiming that "Arthur Livingston just shot me!" may not have made a dying declaration, but it may very well be an excited utterance. Just as each important fact in a trial should be proven from multiple sources, each important piece of evidence should be justifiable on multiple theories of admissibility. In pretrial preparation you should wargame the admission of each important piece of evidence and develop at least three theories of admissibility for each.

You will not win every objection you make. The judge will not rule with you on every issue. You cannot take every adverse ruling as a personal insult. You must always keep your eye on the prime objective of the trial and subordinate all your emotions and feelings to that objective. You must pick your fights wisely and always be prepared to "roll with the punches," achieving your objective by whatever fair means you find available.

PRACTICAL EXERCISE

1. You are prosecuting a first-degree murder which occurred at a bar. At the time of the shooting the defendant's blood alcohol level was 0.28. Evidence of intoxication can negate premeditation in your jurisdiction. Although the seizure of the blood sample from the defendant was perfectly proper, the defense moves to suppress the blood alcohol results. You review the evidence and determine that your chances of getting a verdict of guilty as charged will be greatly increased by the granting of the motion. How should you respond to this motion?

2. Suppose that somehow the local newspaper learns of the motion, and an enterprising reporter gets a copy from the clerk's office. The paper prints a first-page story on the motion and an editorial criticizing the police for incompetence in seizing the blood alcohol sample. The editorial is followed up in subsequent issues by several letters to the editor, all of which are highly uncomplimentary to the police department. Does this factor change your analysis of what you should do? Should it make any difference?

INDEX

References are to Pages